AF668708

RECENT RESEARCH IN PĀṆINIAN STUDIES

Recent Research in Pāṇinian Studies

George Cardona

MOTILAL BANARSIDASS PUBLISHERS
PRIVATE LIMITED • DELHI

First Edition: Delhi, 1999
Second Revised Edition: Delhi, 2004

ISBN: 81-208-1637-4

Also available at:
MOTILAL BANARSIDASS

41 U.A. Bungalow Road, Jawahar Nagar, Delhi 110 007
8 Mahalaxmi Chamber, 22 Bhulabhai Desai Road, Mumbai 400 026
236, 9th Main III Block, Jayanagar, Bangalore 560 011
120 Royapettah High Road, Mylapore, Chennai 600 004
Sanas Plaza, 1302 Baji Rao Road, Pune 411 002
8 Camac Street, Kolkata 700 017
Ashok Rajpath, Patna 800 004
Chowk, Varanasi 221 001

Printed in India
BY JAINENDRA PRAKASH JAIN AT SHRI JAINENDRA PRESS,
A-45 NARAINA, PHASE-I, NEW DELHI 110 028
AND PUBLISHED BY NARENDRA PRAKASH JAIN FOR
MOTILAL BANARSIDASS PUBLISHERS PRIVATE LIMITED,
BUNGALOW ROAD, DELHI 110 007

TABLE OF CONTENTS

PREFACE TO THE SECOND REVISED EDITION

I am happy to learn that *Recent Research in Pāṇinian Studies*, published in 1999, has gone out of print in such a relatively short time. I am also glad that it is possible to have a reprint of this work appear quickly. Due to other work, I have not been able to bring the bibliography fully up to date. However, I can briefly give information on work which was originally listed as forthcoming and has, to my knowledge, now appeared in print.

To begin with, the edition of the first part of the *Sūkti-ratnākara* noted in the addition (p. 371) has been published: शेष-नारायणविरचितः सूक्तिरत्नाकरः ([पातञ्जल] महाभाष्यटीका) प्रथमः भागः — प्रथमद्वितीये आह्निके श्री. वामनशास्त्री भागवत व्याकरणपारंगत इत्येतैः अनेकहस्तलिखिताधारेण संपाद्य विषयसूचि-परिशिष्टादिभिः संयोज्य संपादितः *Sūkti-ratnākara (Commentary on Patañjali's Mahābhāṣya) by Śeṣa Nārāyaṇa*, Fascile I: Āhnikas 1 and 2, Edited on the basis of a number of Mss and furnished with an introduction, synoptic contents and appendix by Vāman Śāstrī Bhāgavat (= ASS 140), Pune, 1999.

The following articles listed as forthcoming in the main bibliography have also appeared: Aklujkar, Ashok Narhar: b: "A response to Dr. Peter Scharf", StII 21 (1997): 1-4, c: Swami Prabhananda and J. L. Shaw (eds.), *Concepts of Knowledge: East and West. Papers from a Seminar held from 4 January to 10 January, 1995, at the Ramakrishna Mission Institute of Culture* (Calcutta: Ramakrishna Mission Institute of Culture, 1999 [2000]), pp. 1-19 (Italian translation, "Il punto di vista epistemologico di Bhartṛhari", in Federico Squarcini (ed.), *Verso l'India, oltre l'India: Scritti e ricerche sulle tradizioni intellettuali sudasiatiche* (Milano: Mimesis, 2002), pp. 207-218), g: "Metarules of Paninian Grammar: Vyadi's *Paribhāsāvṛtti* by Dominik Wujastyk", BSOAS 61(1998):353-355, h: Robert L. Arrington (ed.), *A Companion to the Philosophers* (Malden, MA/ Oxford: Blackwell, 1998), pp. 561-565; Cardona, George: a: Geert Booij, Christian Lehmann, Joachim Mugdan (eds.), *Morphologie/Morphology: Ein internationales Handbuch zur Flexion und Wortbildung/An International Handbook on Inflection and Word-formation* (Berlin/New York: Walter de Gruyter, 2000), 1. Halband/Volume 1, article 5, pp. 41-51, b, c: Sylvain Auroux, E. F. K. Koerner, Hans-Josef Niederehe (eds.), *History of the Language Sciences/ Geschichte der Sprachwissenschaften/Histoire des sciences du langage* (Berlin/New York: Walter de Gruyter, 2000), Volume 1/1. Teilband/Tome 1, V, article 17, pp. 113-124, article 21, pp. 157-166, d-f : "L'analisi linguistica come paradigma della scienza vedica (1. *śikṣā* (fonetica), 2. *vyākaraṇa* (grammatica), 3. *nirukta* (analisi semantica)", in *Storia della scienza* (editor-in-chief Sandro Petruccioli, Roma: Istituto della Enciclopedia Italiana, 2001), vol. 1, pp. 740-56, g: "La tradizione del vyākaraṇa (grammatica) (1. L'*Aṣṭādhyāyī* di Pāṇini, 2. Le grammatiche non pāṇiniane, 3. I rapporti fra il vyākaraṇa e le scuole filosofiche)", in *Storia della scienza* (editor-in-chief Sandro Petruccioli, Roma: Istituto della Enciclopedia Italiana, 2001), vol. 1, pp. 821-31, h: Rajendra I Nanavati (chief editor), पुराण-इतिहास-विमर्शः *Purāṇa-Itihāsa-Vimarśaḥ, Essays in Honour of Prof. S. G. Kantawala* (Delhi/Varanasi: Bharatiya Vidya Prakashan, 1998), pp. 313-335, j: JAOS 118 (1998): 239-244, k: JAOS 119 (1999): 88-125; Deshpande, Madhav Murlidhar: a: Hannes Kniffka (ed.), *Indigeneous Grammar Across Cultures* (Frankfurt: Peter Lang, 2001), pp. 33-51, b: Dick van der Meij (ed.), *India and Beyond: Aspects of Literature, Meaning, Ritual and Thought, Essays in Honour of Frits Staal* (London/New York: Kegan Paul International, 1997), pp. 71-127, c: Histoire, Epistemologie, Langage, tome XX.1 (1998): 5-28; Houben, Jan E. M.: a, a': ABORI 78 (1997 [1998]): 177-198 (postscript: 190-193), b: StII 21 (1997): 71-77, d: RSO 72 (1999): 101-142, e: "*Sūtra* and *bhāṣyasūtra* in Bhartṛhari's Mahābhāṣyadīpikā: on the theory and practice of a scientific genre", in Dick van der Meij (ed.), *India and Beyond: Aspects of Literature, Meaning, Ritual and Thought, Essays in Honour of Frits Staal* (London/New York: Kegan Paul International, 1997), pp. 271-305.

Corrections of typographic errors have been incorporated in the text, and I have added to the list of corrigenda to *Pāṇini, A Survey of Research* and *Pāṇini, his Work and its Traditions, volume I.* I am grateful to Professor Avanindra Kumar for his careful reading of the latter work and his kind review (*Journal of the Indian Council of Philosophical Research* 17 (1999): 196-200), where he pointed out most of the corrigenda listed.

George Cardona
Philadelphia
January 28, 2003

PREFACE TO THE FIRST EDITION

In the preface to the reprint of *Pāṇini, A Survey of Research* (Delhi: Motilal Banarsidass, 1997, p. vi), I said that materials originally intended to appear in an updated second edition of this volume would be published in a separate volume. I now present this work to the scholarly public.

I cover here work done since 1975, including materials which came to my knowledge up to December of 1997. I have also included much of what I discussed in "Pāṇinian studies" (Cardona [1989]), for two chief reasons: the volume in which this was published is not easily available to all scholars, and the quality of editing left much to be desired. I do not have to emphasize that the bibliographic information supplied in the present work is definitely not exhaustive, far from it. Even a cursory look at the pertinent sections of Dandekar (1985, 1993) suffices to show that a very large number of articles and monographs has been produced and that many of these are difficult to obtain. I have, however, read the works to which I refer except for those that are marked with asterisks, and I think that I have covered the major works and the trends these reflect.

In order to allow readers to relate more easily scholarship of earlier times with the recent work I cover in this volume, section headings include parenthetical references to sections in my earlier survey.

As I mentioned in my preface to that book, the principal aim of a survey such as this is to inform readers of work that has been done and of trends in the field. That includes reporting on controversies. When an author is a participant in such arguments, this will naturally be reflected in a survey of the field, as it is in the present work. In some instances, my discussion goes on at considerable length. Even in a survey, I consider this appropriate. It would be improper merely to disagree with other scholars or dismiss their claims without treating the evidence necessary to demonstrate that such disagreement is based on facts and not on mere opinion or bias, all the more so because some very sweeping claims have been made recently on the basis of what I cannot but consider insufficient consideration of evidence. Although I disagree with much of what several major scholars have proposed and although the style of reference requires repeatedly mentioning the names of these scholars, I think that I have met my goal of dealing with points of view and evidence.

Some of the notational conventions observed in this volume differ from those accepted for *Pāṇini, A Survey of Research*. Bold face italics are used here to indicate markers appended to Sanskrit elements, which appear transliterated in italics. In addition, accented Vedic passages are transliterated with accents marked in the way adopted in Cardona (1997a:li-lxiv). With regard to notation, one further point has to be mentioned. In the original survey components of complex terms were separated by hyphens and a circumflex was placed over vowels to indicate the result of sandhi alteration across such divisions; e.g. dhātu-pāṭha, gaṇa-pāṭha, Mahā-bhāṣya, Mitâkṣarā, and Sidchânta-kaumudī instead of dhātupāṭha, gaṇapāṭha, Mahābhāṣya, Mitākṣarā, and Siddhāntakaumudī. I have now abandoned this practice.

When citing the work of other scholars, I have of course, retained their notation and left unchanged their punctuation and spelling. Moreover, to avoid the appearance of excessive fault finding, I have been very sparing in the use of 'sic!'. Consequently, readers will find some things left unemphasized which may be obvious infelicities or outright errors. I ask them to believe that I have scrupulously consulted the sources, which readers also are of course free to do.

I must also mention something concerning the Romanization of Indian names. As is well known, various Roman versions of a single spelling in an Indian script may be found. For example, for कपिलदेव शास्त्री one finds 'Kapila Deva Shastri' (1967a) and 'Kapil Dev Shastri' (1985) on the title pages of works by the same author. I have adopted here the Roman spelling found in the most recently published works. In addition, I have followed the practice adopted by individual scholars concerning how their names are cited. For example, in Coward and K. Kunjunni Raja (1990:593a), K. Kunjunni Raja is listed under 'Raja, K. Kunjunni'. Accordingly, I have listed him under 'Raja'.

I now turn to the pleasant task of giving thanks. First and foremost, I wish to express deep gratitude to my wife Joanne, who for forty years has patiently read and commented on things I have written. With a sharp eye, unerring sense of style, and keen intelligence, she has saved me from many a blunder and added clarity to what I have written.

The present work includes three indexes, as indicated on page 323. In this connection, it is my great pleasure to acknowledge a favor done by

Ms. Katrin Baar of the University of Hamburg. Of her own volition, Ms. Baar compiled an index locorum of primary literature referred to in my original survey and had it sent to me through her teacher, Professor Albrecht Wezler. I have incorporated this, with minor changes, as my third index and wish to express my deep appreciation for such a generous act of cooperation on the part of a fellow scholar.

I am also happy to acknowledge the help of friends and colleagues who have sent me copies of their work over the years. I am especially indebted to Ashok N. Aklujar, Johannes Bronkhorst, Madhav M. Deshpande, Subhash Kak, Hideyo Ogawa, Rama Nath Sharma, Albrecht Wezler and Toru Yagi. Ashok Aklujkar, Madhav Deshpande, Bh. Krishnamurti and Raffaele Torella were extraordinarily generous in sending me materials which I would otherwise not have been able to consult.

It is my special pleasure to thank those friends who read and commented on drafts of this survey: Ashok N. Aklujkar, Madhav M. Deshpande, Hideyo Ogawa, Rama Nath Sharma, and Jon Yamashita. Their willingness to read my work and offer detailed valuable suggestions for its improvement has encouraged me, though their continued generosity and kindness comes as no surprise:

किमत्र चित्रं यत्सन्तः परानुग्रहतत्पराः ।

Philadelphia, May 29, 1998 George Cardona

POSTSCRIPT

The reader for Motilal Banarsidass, Dr. Kanshi Ram, went through the text submitted and noted some typographical errors, for which I thank him. Between the time I submitted the script and September 7th, when I received the press reader's corrections, I was able to consult some works which were not accessible to me earlier. I am grateful to the New York Public Library and Dr. Sunita Vaze of its Oriental Division.

Philadelphia, September 8, 1998 George Cardona

CONVENTIONS AND ABBREVIATIONS

&

BIBLIOGRAPHY

CONVENTIONS AND ABBREVIATIONS

I observe here the conventions observed in my earlier survey (Cardona [1976a:3-4]), with two exceptions. Where authors and editors have given titles first in Devanāgarī or another Indian script and then in English, I retain this order and do not transliterate. Instead of two asterisks, a single asterisk is now used to indicate a work I have not been able to consult. I also follow the usual practice in Romanization except where authors and editors themselves deviate from this; for example, '*Shabdakaustubh*' instead of *Śabdakaustubha* under Bal Shastri (1988a).

The following abbreviations are used in addition to those already listed in my survey (1976a:5-12).

A: Aṣṭādhyāyī.
AJOS: Aligarh Journal of Oriental Studies.
ALPS: Adyar Library Pamphlet Series.
ANIS: Alt- und Neu-Indische Studien.
AS: Asiatische Studien (Études Asiatiques), Zeitschrift der Schweizerischen Gesellschaft für Asienkunde (Revue de la Société suisse d'études asiatiques).
AUSSL: Acta Universitatis Skovdensis, Series Linguistica.
BEHESHP: Bibliothèque de l'École des Hautes Études, Sciences Historiques et Philologiques.
BEI: Bulletin d'Études Indiennes.
BIB: Bibliotheca Indo-Buddhica.
BIG: Bibliothek indogermanischer Grammatiken.
BIL: Brill's Indological Library.
BCNSOGU: Bulletin of the Cultural and Natural Sciences in Osaka Gakuin University.
BIT: Bibliotheca Indo-Tibetica.
BKSSL: Beiträge zur Kenntnis südasiatischer Sprachen und Literaturen.
BSAF: Beiträge zur Südasienforschung, Südasien-Institut, Universität Heidelberg.
CPVS: Chaukhambha Prachyavidya Series.
CRBGM: Chowkhambā Rāṣṭrabhāratī Granthamālā.

CSBGM: The Chaukhamba Surbharati Granthamala.
CSL: Current Studies in Linguistics.
FoL: Folia Linguistica, Societas Linguistica Europea.
GIS: Gonda Indological Studies.
GJGM: Gaṅgānāthajhā-Granthamālā.
GKGM: M. M. Gopināthakavirāja-Granthamālā.
GOS: Groningen Oriental Series.
GUJA: Gauhati University Journal of Arts.
HF: Historische Forschungen. [successor to Zeitschrift für vergleichende Sprachforschung.]
HL: Historiographia Linguistica.
HPGM: Harjivandas Prachyavidya Granthamala.
HSK: Handbücher zur Sprach- und Kommunikationswissenchaft.
HUSFL: The Hiroshima Universities Studies, Faculty of Letters.
IBS: Innsbrucker Beiträge zur Sprachwissenschaft.
IJAR: International Journal of Approximate Reasoning.
IJSL: International Journal of the Sociology of Language.
IT: Indologia Taurinensia. Official organ of the International Association of Sanskrit Studies, Torino.
JASBo.: Journal of the Asiatic Society of Bombay.
JDSRBU: Journal of the Department of Sanskrit, Rabindra Bharati University, Calcutta.
JEAS: Journal of the European Āyurvedic Society.
JPTS: Journal of the Pali Text Society.
JSAOU: Journal of the Sanskrit Academy, Osmania University.
KDSS: Krishnadas Sanskrit Series.
KSVS: Kendriya Sanskrit Vidyapeetha Series.
LES: Linguistica Extranea, Studia.
LIS: Language in Society.
MMŚKŚGM: M. M. Śivakumāraśāstrī-Granthamālā.
ORIS: Oriental Research Institute Series.
OUPL: Osmania University Publications in Linguistics.
PB: प्रज्ञा-भारती Prajñā-Bhāratī, P. J. Jayaswal Research Institute, Patna.
PBGM: Prācyabhāratīgranthamālā.
PSGM: Parimal Saṃskṛta Granthamālā.
PPM: Parāmarśa Prakāśanamālā.

PUIS: Panjab University Indological Series.
PBV: Praci-Bhasha-Vijnan, Indian Journal of Linguistics.
Ṛtam: Journal of the Akhila Bharatiya Sanskrit Parishad, Lucknow.
RVBDGM: Rājasthānaviśvavidyālayabhāratīyadarśanagranthamālā (University of Rajasthan Studies in Indian Philosophy).
SAGM: Sampūrṇānanda-Granthamālā.
ŚĀJGM; Śrī Ātmānand Jain Granthamālā.
Saṃbhāṣā: Nagoya Studies in Indian Culture and Buddhism, Department of Indian Philosophy, University of Nagoya.
ŚBSMSGM: Śrībālamukunda Saṃskṛta Mahāvidyālaya Śaṃśodhana Granthamālā.
SCI: Studies of Classical India.
SGDOS: Sri Garib Dass Oriental Series.
ŚGPŚGM: Śrīguruprasādaśāstri-granthamālā.
SHLS: Studies in the History of the Language Sciences.
SLL: Studies in Language Learning.
SLP: Studies in Linguistics and Philosophy.
ŚPS: Śata-Piṭaka Series, Indo-Asian Literatures.
SV: Saṃskṛta-Vimarśaḥ, राष्ट्रीय-संस्कृतसंस्थानस्य षाण्मासिकी शोध-पत्रिका, Delhi.
SVPGM: संस्कृतविद्यापीठग्रन्थमाला, Delhi: Shri Lal Bahadur Shastri Sanskrita Vidyapitha.
VBJP: Viśva Bharati Journal of Philosophy.
Vidya: Journal of Gujarat University, C: Languages.
VPGM: The Vrajajivan Prachyabharati Granthamala
Zinbun: Annals of the Institute for Research in Humanities, Kyoto University.
ZvS: Zeitschrift für vergleichende Sprachforschung. [formerly: KZ]

BIBLIOGRAPHY

Abhyankar, Kashinath Vasudev

1976 "वैयाकरणैः पदकारा अनुवर्त्या अनुवर्त्यं वा व्याकरणं पदकारैः", Festschrift K. A. Subrahmania Iyer, pp. 313-316.

Abhyankar, Kashinath Vasudev and Jayadeva M. Shukla

1986 *A Dictionary of Sanskrit Grammar* Third edition (= GOS 184) (Vadodara: M. S. University of Baroda).

Abhyankar, Vasudev Shastri

1978 श्रीमत्सायणमाधवाचार्यप्रणीतः सर्वदर्शनसंग्रहः महामहोपाध्याय अभ्यंकरोपाह्व वासुदेवशास्त्रिविरचितया दर्शनाङ्कुराभिधया व्याख्यया समेतः ... तृतीया आवृत्तिः माईणकरोपाह्वगोविन्दसूनुना त्र्यम्बनकेण पुनर्मुद्रणकर्मण्यवलोकिता *Sarvadarśana-saṁgraha of Sāyaṇa-Mādhava, Edited with an Original Commentary in Sanskrit by the late Mahāmahopādhyāya Vasudev Shastri Abhyankar, Third Edition Seen through the Press by T. G. Mainkar* (= GovOS A 1) (Pune: BORI).

Agrawal, S. S. and Subas Pani (Eds.)

1994 *Proceedings of 'Akshara 94' on Information Technology Applications in Language, Script & Speech* (*February 25-26, 1994, New Delhi*) (New Delhi: BPB Publications).

Aithal, K. Parameswara

1991 *Veda-Lakṣaṇa* : *Vedic Ancillary Literature, A Descriptive Bibliography* (= BSAF 143) (Stuttgart: Steiner).

1996 "Pāṇini's Aṣṭādhyāyī and Vedic ritual literature", Festschrift Berger, pp. 1-7.

Akamatsu, Akihiko

1993 "*Pratibhā* and the meaning of the sentence in Bhartṛhari's Vākyapadīya", in: Bhate and Bronkhorst (1993), pp. 37-43.

Aklujkar, Ashok Narhar

1978 "The number of kārikās in Trikāṇḍī book II", ALB 42:142-163.

1981 "Interpreting Vākyapadīya 2.486 historically (part 1)", Festschrift K. Kunjunni Raja, pp. 581-601.

1982 "Interpreting Vākyapadīya 2.486 historically (part 2)", Festschrift de Jong, pp. 1-10.

1983a "The Aṣṭādhyāyī as a case in textual criticism (part 2)", in: Joshi and Laddu (1983), pp. 1-10.

1983b Foreword to K. A. Subramania Iyer (1983:ix-xix).

1988-89 "Prāmāṇya in the philosophy of the grammarians", Festschrift R. V. Joshi, pp. 15-28.

1989a "The number of Pramāṇas according to Bhartṛhari", WZKS 33:151-158.

1989b "Saṃbandha and abhisaṃbhandha", JIP 17:299-307.

1990 "Bhartṛhari", in: Coward, H. G. and K. Kunjunni Raja (1990), pp. 121-174.

1991a "Interpreting Vākyapadīya 2.486 historically (Part 3)", Festschrift S. D. Joshi, pp. 1-47.

1991b "Syntactic gleanings from Bhartṛhari's Trikāṇḍī", in: Hock (1991a), pp. 1-11.

1991c "Bhartṛ-hari's concept of the Veda", in: Deshpande (1991a), pp. 1-18.

1993a "An introduction to the study of Bhartṛ-hari", in: Bhate and Bronkhorst (1993), pp. 7-36.

1993b "Once again on the authorship of the Trikāṇḍī-Vṛtti", in: Bhate and Bronkhorst (1993), pp. 45-57.

1994 "The ṭīkākāra mentioned by Skanda-Maheśvara", Festschrift Bhagwat, pp. 9-25.

1996a "The early history of Sanskrit as a supreme language", in: Houben (1996a), pp. 59-85.

1996b "Some theoretical observations on word order in Sanskrit", Festschrift Thieme, pp. 1- 25.

1997 "Kashmir and Patañjali's Mahābhāṣya", Conference 1997a:407.

forthcoming

a Critical edition of Bhartṛhari's *Trikāṇḍī,* with word index of kārikās and the Vṛtti.

b Rebuttal of Scharf (1994).

c "The epistemological point of view of Bhartṛ-hari". [Appearing in the proceedings of the "Concept of knowledge" seminar organized by the Ramakrishna Mission Institute of Culture, Calcutta, 1995.]

*d *The Philosophy of Bhartṛ-hari's Trikāṇḍī.* [I have seen an abbreviated version.]

*e *Excursions into Pre-Bhartṛhari Thought* (Pune: BORI). [Three lectures in the series Pandit Shripad Shastri Deodhar Memorial Lectures.]

*f "Sociolinguistic history of ancient India: need for a paradigm change" [Listed as forthcoming in Houben (1996a:447).]

g Review of Wujastyk (1993), BSOAS.

h "Bhartṛhari", in: Robert L. Arrington (ed.), *A Companion to the Philosophers, Blackwell's Companions to Philosophy*.

Al-George, Sergiu

1978 "Are Pāṇini's sūtras descriptive or prescriptive sentences?", ABORI 58-59 (Diamond Jubilee Volume):27-36.

1983 "On negative compounds: A parallel between Pāṇini and Aristotle", in: Joshi and Laddu (1983), pp. 137-140.

Ananthanarayana, H. S.

1976 *Four Lectures on Pāṇini's Aṣṭādhyāyī* (Annamalainagar: Annamalai University). [l: A brief account of Indian grammatical tradition (1-21), 2: Pāṇini's technique of description (22-39), 3: Topical treatment in Pāṇini's grammar (40-62), 4: Pāṇini and modern linguistics (63-82). I have changed the notation to accord with the one generally used; e.g. 'Pāṇini' instead of 'Pa:ṇini'.]

*1980 *Ancient Indian Contribution to Linguistic Theory, Method and Analysis* (S. K. Chatterji memorial extension lecture) (Calcutta: University of Calcutta).

1981 *Pratyāhāras in Pāṇini's Aṣṭādhyāyī* (Hyderabad: D. K. Dakshayani).

1986a "Treatment of homonymy in Pāṇini's Aṣṭādhyāyī", in: Krishnamurti, Masica, Sinha (1986), pp. 49-59.

1986b "*Tolkāppiyam* and *Aṣṭādhyāyī* — a comparative study", Festschrift Sinha, pp. 479-490

1991-92 "Bhartṛhari on semantics and pragmatics", Festschrift Katre, pp. 211-219.

Añjanī Kumārī

1990-91 "लेट् लकार : एक विवेचन", KURJ 24-25:330-340. [In Hindi.]

Anonymous

1980 *Mahābhāṣyadīpikā of Bhartṛhari* भर्तृहरिविरचिता महाभाष्यदीपिका

(Bhandarkar Oriental Research Institute Post-Graduate and Research Department Series) (Poona: BORI). [Facsimile edition of the extant manuscript.]

Aravinda Kumar

1997 "नागेशदिशा धात्वर्थविमर्शः", Conference 1997b:175-177. [In Sanskrit.]

Arya, Sudyumna

1985 "कतिपय वार्त्तिककार-प्रोक्त शब्दों का भाषा-वैज्ञानिक अध्ययन", in: Dandekar and Navathe (1985), pp. 26-28. [In Hindi.]

Auroux, Sylvain (Ed.)

1989 *Histoire des idées linguistiques, Tome I* : *La naissance des métalangages en orient et en occident.* (Liège-Bruxelles: Pierre Mardaga). [Chapter V: La tradition indienne. V.2-5 = Pinault (1989a-d), V.6 = Zimmermann (1989).]

Avanindra Kumar

1981 *Archaic Words in Pāṇini's Aṣṭādhyāyī* (Delhi: Parimal Publications). [1. Introduction: history of grammar etc., 2. Physical world in its larger aspects, 3. Territorial and political divisions, 4. Castes, varṇas and social divisions, 5. Food and drinks [sic], 6. Religious books and acts, 7. Animals and belonging to them [sic], 8. Trees, 9. Weights and measures, 10. Miscellaneous.]

1988-89 "Apabhraṃśa: communication of meaning", Festschrift R. V. Joshi, pp. 283-291.

1996 सव्याख्य अष्टाध्यायी-पदानुक्रम-कोश *A Word Index of Pāṇini's Aṣṭādhyāyī* (= PSGM 44) (Delhi: Parimal Publications). [Glosses and paraphrases in Hindi.]

Avasthi, Shiv Shankar

1990 भगवद्भर्तृहरिविरचितं वाक्यपदीयम् तत्कृतया वृत्त्या संवलितम् तच्च हिन्दीविवरणसमलंकृतम् (प्रथमं ब्रह्मकाण्डम्) *Vākyapadīya of Śrī Bhartṛhari along with his own Vṛtti (First: Brahmakāṇḍa), Edited with a Hindi Commentary by Dr. Shiv Shankar Avasthi* (= VBSGM 168) (Varanasi: Chowkhamba Vidyabhawan).

Bal Shastri

1986a "उपपदविभक्तिः", Sāg. 25.1:49-56. [In Sanskrit.]

1986b "उपपदविभक्त्यर्थः", Sāg. 25.2:75-82. [In Sanskrit.]

1987 श्रीमद्भगवत्पतञ्जलिमुनिविरचितं पातञ्जलं महाभाष्यम् ... अध्यायः महामहोपाध्यायश्रीनागोजिभट्टविरचितमहाभाष्यप्रदीपोद्योतोद्भासितेन, महामहोपाध्यायश्रीकैयटोपाध्यायविरचितेन प्रदीपेन विराजितम् आचार्यश्रीगुरुप्रसादशास्त्रिणा व्याकरणाद्याचार्येण महता परिश्रमेण संशोधितं, टिप्पण्या च संयोजितम् *Mahabhashya of Patanjali with the Commentaries Mahabhashya Pradipodyota of Shree Nagoji Bhatta and Mahabhashya-Pradip by Kaiyat, Edited by Acharya Shree Guru Prasad Shastri (Second edition), Revised by Dr. Bal Shastri* (= ŚGPŚGM 1) (Varanasi: Vani Vilas Prakashan). [8 volumes in 7: I.2: adhyāya 1, pādas 2-4, II: adhyāya 2, III: adhyāya 3, IV: adhyāya 4, V: adhyāya 5, VI: adhyāya 6, VII-VIII: adhyāyas 7-8.]

1988a श्रीमद्भगवत्पतञ्जलिमुनिविरचितं पातञ्जलं महाभाष्यम् प्रथमाध्याय प्रथमपाद नवाह्निकरूपं प्रथमखण्डम् श्रीकैयटोपाध्यायप्रणीतेन प्रदीपेन श्रीनागेशभट्टविरचितेन महाभाष्यप्रदीपोद्योतेन श्रीभट्टोजिदीक्षितविरचितेन शब्दकौस्तुभेन च विराजितम् आचार्यश्रीगुरुप्रसादशास्त्रिणा व्याकरणाद्याचार्येण प्रणीतयाभिनवराजलक्ष्मीटीकया च समलङ्कृतम् *Mahabhashya of Patanjali, Vol. I Part I (Nawahnikam) with Bhattoji Deekshita's 'Shabdakaustubh', Nagojibhatta's 'Uddyota' and Kaiyata's 'Pradipa' with the commentary 'Avinavarajlakshmi' by Pt. Guru Prasad Shastri, Edited by Dr. Bal Shastri* (= ŚGPŚGM 1) (Varanasi: Vani Vilas Prakashan).

1988b "सहार्थश्च साहित्यम्", Sāg. 26.3:61-66. [Also 1988c; in Sanskrit.]

1988c "सहार्थश्च साहित्यम्", Saṃskṛta-Vimarśaḥ 16:83-91 [Also 1988b; in Sanskrit.]

1991/92 (Ed.) महामहोपाध्यायनागेशभट्टविरचितः लघुशब्देन्दुशेखरः श्रीविश्वनाथनन्दिभट्ट-विरचितयाऽभिनवचन्द्रिकाटीकया, श्रीवैद्यनाथपायगुण्डेविरचितया चिदस्थिमालाटीकया, श्रीसदाशिवभट्टविरचितेन तिलकेन, श्रीमद्भट्टोदयङ्करपाठकविरचितया ज्योत्स्नाटीकया, श्रीराघवेन्द्राचार्यकृतया विषमपदविवृत्या, कारकप्रकरणे श्रीशिवनारायणशास्त्रिविरचितया विजयाटीकया श्रीगुरुप्रसादशास्त्रिविरचितया वरवर्णिन्या, किञ्च टिप्पण्या च विराजितः *Laghu Shabdendu Shekar of M. M. Nagesh Bhatt with Six Rare Commentaries and Explanatory Note by Acharya Guru Prasad Shastri* 2 volumes (= ŚGPŚGM 2) (Varanasi: Vani Vilas Prakashan). [Reedition of work first published in

1936: Benares: Bhargava Pustakalaya. The Devanāgarī title is given as it appears on the title page of volume 2.]

Bālā, Śaśi

1994 भट्टिकाव्य एवं पाणिनीय व्याकरण का तुलनात्मक अध्ययन (Delhi: Vidyanidhi Prakashan). [Originally a Kurukshetra University doctoral dissertation. In Hindi.]

Balasubrahmanyam, Malladi Dakshinamurti

1975 "A note on Vedic *gamadhye*", Festschrift Vishva Bandhu, pp. 12-16.

1976 "Pāṇini 3.4.10 and the Vedic facts", SVUOJ 19:5-9. [See also 1981c.]

1979 "ase-words in Pāṇini and the Veda", Festschrift Sternbach, pp. 65-74.

1981a *The System of kṛt Accentuation in Pāṇini and the Veda.* (= KSVS 32) (Tirupati: Kendrīya Saṃskṛta Vidyāpīṭham).

1981b "Accent it-s in the kṛt suffixes", Festschrift K. Kunjunni Raja, pp. 543-555.

1981c "Pāṇini 3, 4, 10", PB 1.57-61. [See also 1976.]

1983a "On Pāṇini VI.1.158", Festschrift Jani, pp. 189-198.

1983b "An accentual note on Vedic *voḍhave*", Festschrift Sreekrishna Sarma, pp. 229-240.

1984 "*Subhagaṁkaraṇī* in *AV* 6,139,1", Festschrift Dandekar, pp. 21-27.

1985 "*Arya*: an accentual study", Festschrift Dandekar, pp. 112-127. [= M. D. Balasubrahmanyam (1969a).]

Bandini, Giovanni

1980 *Die Erörterung der Wirksamkeit* : *Bhartṛharis Kriyāsamuddeśa und Helārājas Prakāśa, zum ersten Male aus dem Sanskrit übersetzt, mit einer Einführung und einem Glossar versehen* (= BSAF 61) (Wiesbaden: Steiner).

1982 "Die Erörterung der Person : Bhartṛharis *Puruṣasamuddeśa* und Helārājas *Prakāśa*, zum ersten Male übersetzt und mit einem Kommentar versehen", ZDMG 132:150-173.

Bandyopadhyay, Pratap

1981 "Sanskrit indeclinables (upasargas and nipātas) and their meanings", Festschrift Chatterji, pp. 45-74.

1994 "Some grammatical terms in Pāṇini", Festschrift Chatterjee, pp. 69-72.

Banerjee, Rabi Sankar

1984 *Concept of Asiddhatva in Pāṇini* (*Along with a Connected History of Grammatical Studies in Ancient India*) (Calcutta: Sanskrit Pustak Bhandar).

Banerjee, Satya Ranjan

1992 "Dionysius Thrax and Pāṇini on Parts of Speech", Festschrift Mukherji I, pp. 72-81.

Banerji, Sures Chandra

1996 *Historical Survey of Ancient Indian Grammars* (*Sanskrit, Pali and Prakrit*) (Delhi: Sharada Publishing House).

Bare, James S.

1976 *Phonetics and Phonology in Pāṇini : The System of Features Implicit in the Aṣṭādhyāyī* (= Natural Language Studies 21) (Ann Arbor: Phonetics Laboratory, University of Michigan).

Barthakuria, Apurba Chandra

1997 "Women in the writings of Sanskrit grammarians", Conference 1997a:407-408.

van Bekkum, Wout, Jan Houben, Ineke Sluiter and Kees Versteegh (Eds.)

1997 *The Emergence of Semantics in Four Linguistic Traditions : Hebrew, Sanskrit, Greek, Arabic* (= SHLS 82) (Amsterdam/ Philadelphia: John Benjamins).

Benson, James W.

1990 *Patañjali's Remarks on* aṅga (Delhi: Oxford University Press). [Revised version of doctoral dissertation, Stanford University, 1984.]

Bergdahl, Roland R.

1988 *The Sādhanasamuddeśa (Kā. 1-44) of Bhartṛhari's Vākyapadīya with the Commentary Prakāśa of Helārāja.* [University of Pennsylvania Ph. D. dissertation, unpublished.]

Bhagavat, Vamanashastri Balakrishna

1980 "शब्दः शब्दार्थः, तयोः संबन्धः", in: S. D. Joshi (1980a), pp. 235-237. [In Sanskrit.]

1984 परमलघुमंजूषा (भाषेच्या स्वरूपाची तात्त्विक भूमिका मांडणारा नागेशभट्टलिखित ग्रंथ) भाग पहिला (मूळ व मराठी अनुवाद) (= PPM 4) (Pune: Philosophy Department, University of Poona). [In Marathi.]

1985 पाणिनीय व्याकरण आणि भाषा-तत्त्वज्ञान (Bombay: महाराष्ट्रराज्य साहित्य आणि संस्कृति मंडळ). [In Marathi.]

1988 पाणिनीय व्याकरणाचे अंतरंग (= ŚBSMSGM 3) (Pune: Ṭiḷaka Mahārāṣṭra Vidyāpīṭha). [In Marathi.]

1990 "मुखं व्याकरणम् । ", Festschrift Kavīśvara, pp. 40-44. [In Sanskrit.]

1991 "Viṃśati padāni ... triṃśat ... catvāriṃśat", Festschrift S. D. Joshi, pp. 49-53. [In Sanskrit.]

1993 "श्रीमद्भर्तृहरिः नागेशश्च", in: Bhate and Bronkhorst (1993), pp. 59-65. [In Sanskrit.]

Bhagavat, V. B. and Saroja Bhate

1986 *Mahābhāṣyadīpikā of Bhartṛhari, fascicle III : Āhnika VI, Part I, Critically Edited* (= BORIS 25) (Pune: BORI).

1990 *Mahābhāṣyadīpikā of Bhartṛhari, fascicle VII : Āhnika VI, Part II, Critically Edited* (= BORIS 34) (Pune: BORI).

Bhandare, V. V.

1986 *Sanskrit Speech Habits and Pāṇini* (*with special reference to Sandhi, Samāsa and the roots-chapters of Pāṇini's Aṣṭādhyāyī*) (Delhi: Mala Ahuja for Takshila Hardbounds).

1996 "Structural and semantic aspects of dvandva compounds", ABORI 76 (1995):89-96.

Bharadvaj, Kamla (Kamalā Bhāradvāja)

1996 पतञ्जलिकृत महाभाष्य के श्लोकवार्त्तिक (Delhi: Nag Publishers). [In Hindi.]

Bharadvaj, Sudhi Kant

1994 "Linguistic evaluation of karmapravacanīyas", ABORI 74 (1993):141-151.

Bharati, Akshar, Vineet Chaitanya, and Rajeev Sangal

1995 *Natural Language Processing, A Pāṇinian Perspective* (New Delhi: Prentice-Hall of India).

Bhat, M. S.

1985-86 "Text-critical problems of Haradatta's *Pada Mañjarī*, a commentary on *Kāśikā*", JASBo. 60-61: 62-66.

Bhate, Saroja Vidyadhar

1980a "Treatment of roots *dīdhī* and *vevī* in *Pāṇini*'s grammar", CASS-St. 5: 7-12.

1980b "The character of the middle voice in Pāṇini's grammar", CASS-St. 5: 81-87.

1981 "Pāṇini and Yāska: principles of derivation", ABORI 62:235-241.

1982 "A note on *karmakartari*", CASS-St. 6:173-176.

1983 "The place of P. 1.2.22 and P. 7.2.51 in the Aṣṭādhyāyī", ABORI 63(1982):227-232.

1987a "Grammar and lexicon", ABORI 68:563-570.

1987b "The meaning adhikāras in the taddhita section of the Aṣṭādhyāyī: an analysis", IIJ 30:81-92.

1989 *Pāṇini's Taddhita Rules* (= PCASS B 10) (Pune: University of Poona).

1990 "त्रिमुनिव्याकरणातील संस्कृतभाषे चा विकास", Festschrift Kavīśvara, pp. 73-79. [In Marathi.]

1989-91 "Language and grammar: ancient Indian approach", JASBo. 64-66:18-23.

1991 "Vyañjanā as reflected in the formal structure of language", Festschrift S. D. Joshi, pp. 55-64.

1993a "Bhartṛhari on language and reality", in: Bhate and Bronkhorst (1993), pp. 67-73.

1993b "Computer understanding of Pâṇini's saṃjñâsûtras", in: Rajan and Srinivasan, pp. 105-109.

1994 "पाणिनी आणि राजवाडे", Festschrift Bhagavat, pp. 26-31. [In Marathi.]

1997 "Exegetics of Sanskrit grammar", Conference 1997a:410.

Bhate, Saroja and Johannes Bronkhorst (Eds.)

1993 *Proceedings of the First International Conference on Bhartṛhari, University of Poona, January 6-8, 1992* (= AS 47.1) (Bern: Peter Lang, 1993). [Reprint 1994, 1997: *Bhartṛhari, Philosopher and Grammarian* : *Proceedings of the First International Conference on Bhartṛhari*, (*University of Poona, January 6-8, 1992*) (Delhi: Motilal Barnarsidass).]

Bhate, Saroja and Subhash Kak
1993 "Pāṇini's grammar and computer science", ABORI 72-73 (1991 & 1992):79-94.

Bhate, Saroja and Yashodhara Kar
1993 *Word Index to the Vākyapadīya of Bhartṛhari* (*together with the complete text of the Vākyapadīya*) (Delhi: Eastern Book Linkers).

Bhatia, Kanta Rani
1992 भर्तृहरि का वाक्यपदीय पुण्यराज की दृष्टि में (Delhi: Bharatiya Vidya Prakashan). [In Hindi.]

Bhatt, Vasantkumar Manubhai
1979 "સન્ધ્યક્ષરો - ए, ओ, ऐ અને औ વર્ણો-વિષે મહાભાષ્યમાં પ્રાપ્ત થતી વિચારણા", Svādhyāya 16.4:366-372. [In Gujarati.]
1981 "लिङ्गविशिष्टपरिभाषा पाणिन्यभिप्रेताऽऽसीन्न वा", VS 18.1:1-7. [In Sanskrit.]
1985 "समर्थः पदविधिः । (पा. सू. २।१।१) સૂત્રનું અર્થઘટન", Vidya 25.1-2(1982):117-150. [In Gujarati.]
1987a પુરુષોત્તમદેવની લઘુપરિભાષાવૃત્તિનું વિવેચનાત્મક અધ્યયન અર્થાત્ (પાણિનીય-સંસ્કૃત-વ્યાકરણ શાસ્ત્રમાં પ્રાપ્ત થતી પરિભાષાઓ (metarules) નું વિવેચનાત્મક અધ્યયન) (A Critical Study of Puruṣottamadeva's Laghu-Paribhāṣāvṛtti) (Amdavad: Gujarat University). [Originally a Gujarat University doctoral dissertation. In Gujarati.]
1987b वैयाकरणसिद्धान्तकौमुद्यां सञ्ज्ञाप्रकरणम् (મૂળગ્રન્થ, ગુજરાતી અનુવાદ, વિવરણ અને પ્રસ્તાવના સહિત) (Ahmedabad: Sarasvati Pustak Bhandar). [Commentary in Gujarati.]
1987c वैयाकरणसिद्धान्तकौमुद्याम् कारकप्रकरणम् (ગુજરાતી ભાષાન્તર, વિમર્શ અને 'વિશેષ' સાથે) (Ahmedabad: Sarasvati Pustak Bhandar). [Commentary in Gujarati.]
1988 "पाणिनीयसूत्रयोर्हेतुपदस्यार्थः", Festschrift Charu Deva Shastri, pp. 83-90. [In Sanskrit.]
1990 સંસ્કૃત વાક્યસંરચના (સંસ્કૃત વાક્યવિન્યાસ પદ્ધતિ) (Amdavad: Sarasvati Pustak Bhandar). [In Gujarati.]

Bhatta, V. P.
1990 "Accusative case endings after words standing for 'time' and 'distance'", BDCRI 50:115-124.

Bhattacharya, Adityanath
1988 "करणत्व-विमर्शः", VS 25.2-4 (= डा॰ चारुदेव-शास्त्रि-स्मृतिविशेषाङ्कः):99-115. [In Sanskrit.]

Bhattacharya, Bishnupad
1985 *Bhartṛhari's Vākyapadīya and Linguistic Monism* (Professor K. V. Abhyankar Memorial Lectures [Third Series]) (= BORIS 25) (Pune: BORI).

Bhattacharya, Dipak
1995 "Māmakī and the Altindische Grammatik", Festschrift Shah, pp. 135-136.

Bhattacharya, Gopikamohan
1993 "On paśya mṛgo dhāvati", Festschrift S. D. Joshi, pp. 65-73.

Bhattacharya, Hrishikesh
1984 "व्याकरण-विधित ईश्वरविमर्शः", PB 4:41-43.

Bhattacharya, Kamaleswar
1980 "Nāgārjuna's arguments against motion: their grammatical basis", Festschrift Gaurinath Sastri, pp. 85-95.
1980-81 "The grammatical basis of Nāgārjuna's arguments: some further considerations", Festschrift Sternbach, pp. 35-43.

Bhaṭṭāchārya, Manudeva
1985 श्रीमत्कौण्डभट्टविरचितम् बृहद्वैयाकरणभूषणम् [श्रीमद्भट्टोजिदीक्षितकृत-वैयाकरणमतोन्मज्जन-व्याख्यानम्] 'रूपाली' टिप्पणी-परिशिष्टादिभर्विभूष्य सम्पादितम् *Bṛhadvaiyākaraṇabhūṣaṇam of Śrī Kauṇḍ Bhaṭṭa [A Commentary of Bhaṭṭojidikshita's Vaiyakaraṇa-matonmajjanam] Edited with 'Rūpalī' Notes and Appendix.* (= HPGM 2) (Varanasi: Chaukhamba Amarbharati Prakashan). [Appendixes: A. Bhaṭṭoji's Vaiyākaraṇa-matonmajjana (334-340), B. Alphabetical index of kārikās (341-342), C. Comparison of verses from the Vaiyākaraṇa-matonmajjana and comparable ones from the Vākyapadīya (343-345).]

Bhim Sen Shastri
1979 न्यास-पर्यालोचन जिनेन्द्रबुद्धिकृत काशिकाविवरणपञ्जिका का आलोचनात्मक अध्ययन *A Study of Nyāsa [A Critical Study of Jinendrabuddhi's Nyāsa, the Commentary on Kāśikā]* (Delhi: Bhaimī Prakāśana). [1979 doctoral dissertation, Delhi

University. In Hindi.]

1984 अ-इ-उ-ण्, ऋ-लृ-क् आदि — प्रत्याहार-सूत्रों का निर्माता कौन? (नन्दिकेश्वरकाशिकासहित) (Delhi: Bhaimī Prakāśana). [Appendixes 1-9: the sound lists in the Kātantravyākaraṇa, Cāndravyākaraṇa, Jainendravyākaraṇa, Śākaṭāyanavyākaraṇa, Sarasvatīkaṇṭhābharaṇa, Siddhahemaśabdānuśāsana, Malayagiriśabdānuśāsana, Sārasvatavyākaraṇa, Mugdabodhavyākaraṇa, Saṅkṣiptasāra, and Harināmāmṛtavavyākaraṇa (36-45), text of Nandikeśvarakāśikā (46-48).]

Bhīma Siṁha (see also Vedālaṅkāra)

1988 "क्ङिति चेति सूत्रविमर्शः", Sāg. 26.4:55-68. [In Sanskrit.]

1996 "संरचना-लाघव की दृष्टि से कुछ पाणिनीय सूत्रों पर विचार", Festschrift Shri Niwas Shastri, pp. 225-232. [In Hindi.]

Biswal, Banamali

1995 *The Samāsaśaktinirṇaya of Kauṇḍabhaṭṭa* : *Chapter V of the Vaiyākaraṇabhūṣaṇa, Critically Edited with Introduction and Exhaustive Explanatory Notes* (Allahabad: Padmaja Prakashan). [Revision of Poona University doctoral dissertation, 1991.]

Bronkhorst, Johannes

1980a *Theoretical Aspects of Pāṇini's Grammar* (Leiden: Leiden University). [Doctoral dissertation. I (1-17): The role of meaning in Pāṇini's grammar (see 1980b), III (34-53): Nirukta and Aṣṭādhyāyī: their shared presuppositions (see 1981b), IV (54-74): Asiddha in the Aṣṭādhyāyī: A misunderstanding among the traditional commentators? (see 1980c), VI (99-117): The orthoepic diaskeuasis of the Ṛgveda and the date of Pāṇini (see 1981c).]

1980b "The role of meaning in Pāṇini's grammar", IL 40 (1979): 146-157. [See 1980a.]

1980c "Asiddha in the Aṣṭādhyāyī: a misunderstanding among the traditional commentators?", JIP 8:69-85. [See 1980a.]

1981a "Meaning entries in Pāṇini's Dhātupāṭha", JIP 9:335-357.

1981b "Nirukta and Aṣṭādhyāyī: their shared presuppositions", IIJ 23:1-14. [See 1980a.]

1981c "The orthoepic diaskeuasis of the Ṛgveda and the date of

Pāṇini", IIJ 23:83-95. [See 1980a.]

1982a "Some observations on the padapāṭha of the Ṛgveda", IIJ 24:181-189.

1982b "The variationist Pāṇini and Vedic: a review article", IIJ 24:273-282. [Review-article of Kiparsky (1979).]

1983 "On the history of Pāṇinian grammar in the early centuries following Patañjali", JIP 11:357-412.

1984a "Nirukta, Uṇādi sūtra, and Aṣṭādhyāyī: A review article", IIJ 27:1-15. [Review-article of Madhukar Anant Mehendale, *Nirukta Notes, Series II*.]

1984b Review of Kiparsky (1982), IIJ 27:309-314.

1986 *Tradition and Argument in Classical Indian Linguistics : The Bahiraṅga-paribhāṣā in the Paribhāṣenduśekhara* (= SCI 6) (Dordrecht: Reidel). [Appendixes: I: The original text of the Paribhāṣenduśekhara on paribhāṣā 50 (157-162) (Romanized text), II: A contradiction in the Paribhāṣenduśekhara (163-172), III: On the relative chronology of Nāgeśa's grammatical works (173-176), IV: Changes in Nāgeśa's opinions regarding the bahiraṅgaparibhāṣā and the nājānantaryaparibhāṣā (177-187), V: The Laghuśabdaratna (188-191). Originally a University of Poona doctoral thesis, 1979.]

1987a *Mahābhāṣyadīpikā of Bhartṛhari, Fascicle IV : Āhnika I, Critically Edited* (= BORIS 28) (Pune: BORI).

1987b *Three Problems Pertaining to the Mahābhāṣya* ("Pandit Shripad Shastri Deodhar Memorial Lectures" [Third Series]) (= BORIS 30) (Pune: BORI). [I: The first vārttikas in the Mahābhāṣya (1-13), II: The text history of the Mahābhāṣya(14-42), III: The Mahābhāṣya and the development of Indian philosophy (43-71).]

1987c "Further remarks on Bhartṛhari's Vedic affiliation", in: Festschrift Rau, pp. 215-223.

1987d Review of M. M. Deshpande (1985a), IIJ 30:296-301.

1987e Review of Rau (1985a), Kratylos 32:52-57.

1988 "Études sur Bhartṛhari, 1: L'auteur et la date de la Vṛtti", BEI 6:105-143.

1989 "Studies on Bhartṛhari, 2: Bhartṛhari and Mīmāṁsā", StII 15:101-117. [See also Bronkhorst 1994a.]

1990a "What is *asiddha* ?", ABORI 70 (1989): 309-311.

1990b "Vārttika", WZKS 34:123-146.

1991a "Pāṇini and the nominal sentence", ABORI 71(1990):301-304.

1991b "Studies on Bhartṛhari, 3: Bhartṛhari on sphoṭa and universals", AS 45:5-18. [Appendix: the authorship of the Vṛtti (17-18).]

1991c "Two literary conventions of classical India", AS 45:210-227.

1991d "Pāṇini and the Veda reconsidered", Festschrift S. D. Joshi, pp. 75-121.

1992a "Études sur Bhartṛhari, 4: L'absolu dans le Vākyapadīya et son lien avec le Madhyamaka", AS 46:56-80.

1992b "Pāṇini's view of meaning and its western counterpart', in: Maxim Stamenov (ed.), *Current Advances in Semantic Theory*, (Amsterdam/Philadelphia: John Benjamins), pp. 455-464.

1992c Review of Coward and Kunjunni Raja (1990), AS 47:718-725.

1993 "Studies on Bhartṛhari, 5: Bhartṛhari and Vaiśeṣika", in: Bhate and Bronkhorst (1993), pp. 75-94.

1994a "Bhartṛhari and Mīmāṁsā", Festschrift Mandan Mishra, pp. 371-388. [See also 1989.]

1994b "The author of the Three Centuries (Studies on Bhartṛhari, 6)", Festschrift Bhagwat, pp. 32-41.

1995 "A note on Patañjali and the Buddhists", ABORI 75(1994): 247-254.

1996a "Studies on Bhartṛhari, 7: grammar as the door to liberation", ABORI 76 (1995): 97-106.

1996b "Audumbarāyaṇa revisited", Festschrift Shri Niwas Shastri, pp. 197-201.

1996c "Pāṇini and the Kaṭhas", Festschrift Thieme, pp. 59-65.

Caillat, Colette (Ed.)

1989 *Dialectes dans les littératures indo-aryennes* (*Actes du colloque international organisé par l'UA 1058 sous les auspices du CNRS*) (= PICI 55) (Paris: Institut de Civilisation Indienne).

Cardona, George

1972 Review of Hoffmann (1967), Kratylos 14 [1970 (1972)]: 47-51.

1975a "Paraphrase and sentence analysis: some Indian views", JIP 3: 259- 281.

1975b "A note on the formulation of Pāṇini 6.1.67", AOR Silver Jubilee Volume, pp. 11-20.

1976a *Pāṇini, A Survey of Research* (= Trends in Linguistics State-of-the-Art Reports 6) (The Hague: Mouton). [Indian Edition, 1980: Delhi: Motilal Banarsidass; reprinted 1997.]

1976b "Some features of Pāṇinian derivations", in: H. Parret (ed.), *History of Linguistic Thought and Contemporary Linguistics* (Berlin: de Gruyter), pp. 137-158.

1976c "Subject in Sanskrit", in: M. K. Verma (ed.), *The Notion of Subject in South Asian languages* (= South Asia Studies, University of Wisconsin, Madison, Publications Series 2) (Madison: University of Wisconsin), pp. 1-38.

1976d "On the Pāṇinian view regarding agency and animation", Festschrift K. A. Subrahmania Iyer, pp. 135-145.

1976e "On rules of Pāṇini's grammar said to expatiate on other rules", JOIB 25:241-251.

1977a "A note on morphophonemic and phonetic rules in Sanskrit", MO 10 (Jubilee Volume):1-6.

1977b Review of Joshi-Roodbergen 1973, JOIB 26:328-342.

1977c Review of Laddu (1974), Lg. 53:221-224.

1978a "Relations between causatives and passives in Indo-Iranian", in: Braj B. Kachru (ed.), *Linguistics in the Seventies : Forum Lectures Presented at the 1978 Linguistic Institute* (special volume of SLS, vol. 8, no. 2), pp. 1-42.

1978b "Still again on the history of the Mahābhāṣya", ABORI 58-59 (Diamond Jubilee Volume):79-99.

1978c "पाणिनि आणि पाणिनीय या विषयांवरील अर्वाचीन अध्ययनातील काही प्रवृत्ति" ["Some attitudes in recent work on Pāṇini and

Pāṇinīyas", Marathi translation by K. S. Arjunwadkar], in: R. N. Dandekar and C. G. Kashikar (eds.), प्राचीनभारतीयविद्येचे पुनर्दर्शन [वेदशास्त्रोत्तेजकसभा शताब्दि-स्मारक-ग्रन्थ] [Centenary volume of the Vedaśāstrottejaka Sabhā (Pune)], pp. 59-75.

1979 Review of Scharfe (1977), IIJ 21:117-139.

1980a "On the paribhāṣā *upapadavibhakteḥ kārakavibhaktir balīyasī*", Festschrift Thieme, pp. 27-48.

1980b "On the Āpiśalaśikṣā", Festschrift Gaurinath Sastri, pp. 245-256.

1980c Review of Rau (1977), IIJ 22:53-56.

1981a "On reasoning from anvaya and vyatireka in early Advaita", Festschrift Sanghvi, pp. 79-104.

1981b "On the domain of Pāṇini's metarule 1.3.10: *yathāsaṁkhyam anudeśaḥ samānām*", Festschrift K. Kunjunni Raja, pp. 394-409.

1981c "Grammar and philosophy", in: Peter Gaeffke and Susan Oleksiw (eds.), *Systems of Communication and Interaction in South Asia* [*Summaries of papers from the South Asia Seminar, University of Pennsylvania, 1979-1980*], pp. 3-11.

1982 "Vedic causatives", in: Dharmadhikari (1982), pp. 17-38.

1983a *Linguistic Analysis and Some Indian Traditions* (Pandit Shripad Shastri Deodhar Memorial Lectures [First Series]) (= BORIS 20) (Pune: BORI). [I: Phonetics and phonological rules in grammar (1-36), II: Bases, affixes and meanings (37-116), III: Some questions concerning the sentence and its constituents (117-159).]

1983b "On the formulation of Aṣṭādhyāyī 8.3.4: *anunāsikāt paro 'nusvāraḥ*", Festschrift Sreekrishna Sarma, pp. 199-205.

1984 "On the Mahābhāṣya evidence for a Pāṇinīya Dhātupāṭha without meaning entries", Festschrift Dandekar, pp. 79-84.

1985a "On Yāska's etymology of *daṇḍa*", in: S. S. Janaki (ed.), *MM. Professor Kuppuswami Sastri Birth Centenary Commemoration Volume* (Madras: The Kuppuswami Sastri Research Institute), part 2, pp. 33-42.

1985b Review of M. D. Balasubrahmanyam (1981a), JOIB 34.269-272.

1986a "Phonology and phonetics in ancient Indian works: the case of voiced and voiceless elements", in: Krishnamurti, Masica, Sinha (1986), pp. 60-80.

1986b "Pāṇini and Uṇādisūtra 2.84", ALB 50:46-57.

1987a "Indian grammarians on vowel alternations in Sanskrit", ABORI 68:233-244.

1987b "Some neglected evidence concerning the development of abhinihita sandhi", Festschrift Rau, pp. 59-68.

1987c "On Sanskrit *bhunákti* 'aids, serves, protects'", Festschrift Hoenigswald, pp. 65-72.

1988 *Pāṇini, his Work and its Traditions, Volume I: Background and Introduction* (Delhi: Motilal Banarsidass). [See 1997a.]

1989 "Pāṇinian studies", in: V. N. Jha (1989), pp. 49-84.

1990a "On attitudes towards language in ancient India", Sino-Platonic Papers 15:1-19.

1990b "La linguistica indiana", in: *Storia della linguistica, a cura di Giulio C. Lepschy* (Bologna: il Mulino), Volume I, pp. 51-84. [Italian translation of Cardona (1994).]

1990c "Indo-Aryan", in: Comrie (1990), pp. 21-30.

1990d "Sanskrit", in: Comrie (1990), pp. 31-52.

1990e "A note on "dative agents" in Sanskrit", in: Verma and Mohanan (1990), pp. 141-145.

1991a "On the dialect status of Vedic forms of the types *dakṣ-* / *dhakṣ-*", Festschrift Krishnamurti, pp. 263-273.

1991b "On Pāṇini, Śākalya, Vedic dialects and Vedic exegetical traditions", Festschrift S. D. Joshi, pp. 123-134. [See 1997c.]

1991c "A passage from the Paramalaghumañjūṣā", Festschrift Bhattacharya, pp. 39-44.

1991d "A path yet taken: Some Indian arguments concerning time", JAOS 111:445-464.

1992a "On the development of presents like *bibhéti*", Festschrift Kelkar, pp. 1-13.

1992b "Indian grammatical traditions and historical linguistics", in: Edgar C. Polomé and Werner Winter (eds.), *Reconstructing Languages and Cultures* (= Trends in Linguistics, Studies and Monographs 58) (Berlin, New York: Mouton de

Gruyter), pp. 239-259.

1993a "On comparatives and superlatives formed to finite verbs in Sanskrit", ABORI 72-73 (1991 & 1992): 409-422.

1993b "The bhāṣika accentuation system", StII 18:1-40.

1993c Review of Coward and K. Kunjunni Raja (1990), JAOS 113:137-139.

1994 "Indian Linguistics", in: G. C. Lepschy (ed.), *A History of Linguistics, Vol. I : The Eastern Traditions of Linguistics* (London, New York: Longmann), pp. 25-60. [Original English version of Cardona (1990b).]

1995 "A note on *asti* ...", Festschrift Shah, pp. 137-140.

1996a "Some thoughts on ārṣaprayoga", Festschrift Shri Niwas Shastri, pp. 173-196.

1996b "Amreḍita compounds?", Festschrift Thieme, pp. 67-72.

1997a *Pāṇini : His Work and its Traditions, Part I : General Introduction and Background*, Second edition, revised and enlarged (Delhi: Motilal Banarsidass). [See 1988.]

1997b "Escape rules in Pāṇini: sūtras of the type *anyebhyo'pi dṛśyate*", Conference 1997a:412-413. [See forthcoming i.]

1997c "Vedic traditions and descriptions of grammarians", in: Witzel (ed.), pp. 33-38. [See 1991b.]

1998 "*kiṁ tarhi* in the Mahābhāṣya", Festschrift Watkins, pp. 63-73.

forthcoming

a "Old Indic grammar", in: Geert Booij, Christian Lehmann, and Joachim Mugdan (eds.), *Morphology : A Handbook on Inflection and Word Formation-Morphologie : Ein Handbuch zur Flexion und Wortbildung* (Berlin, New York: de Gruyter), chapter 5.

b "Pāṇini", in: Sylvain Auroux, Konrad Koerner, Hans-Josef Niederehe, and Kees Versteegh (eds.), *Geschichte der Sprachwissenschaften-History of the Language Sciences-Histoire des sciences du langage* (Berlin, New York: de Gruyter), chapter 21.

c "The organization of grammar in Indian linguistics", in: Sylvain Auroux, Konrad Koerner, Hans-Josef Niederehe, and

Kees Versteegh (eds.), *Geschichte der Sprachwissenschaften-History of the Language Sciences-Histoire des sciences du langage* (Berlin, New York: de Gruyter), chapter 25.

d "Śikṣā", in: *Storia della scienza, vol. III: Le scienze extraeuropee*, part II: The sūtras, article 9 (Roma: Istituto della Enciclopedia Italiana).

e "Vyākaraṇa", in: *Storia della scienza, vol. III: Le scienze extraeuropee*, part II: The sūtras, article 11 (Roma: Istituto della Enciclopedia Italiana).

f "Nirukta", in: *Storia della scienza, vol. III: Le scienze extraeuropee*, part II: The sūtras, article 12 (Roma: Istituto della Enciclopedia Italiana).

g "Vyākaraṇa", in: *Storia della scienza, vol. III: Le scienze extraeuropee*, part V: The sciences in the classical period and later, article 31 (Roma: Istituto della Enciclopedia Italiana).

h "Ideal and performance in Sanskrit", Festschrift S. G. Kantawala.

i "Pāṇinian sūtras of the type अन्येभ्योऽपि दृश्यते", Festschrift Jambūvijaya.

j "A new edition of Vyāḍi's *Paribhāṣāvṛtti*", JAOS 118.2 (1998). [Review-article of Wujastyk (1993).]

k "Approaching the Vākyapadīya", JAOS. [Review-article of Houben (1995a).]

Caturvedī, Jagadīśa

1980 पदार्थ-विभाग-परिशीलनम् (Varanasi: Kishor Vidya Niketan). [In Sanskrit.]

Chakraborty, Parboty (Pārvatī Cakravartī)

1994 "पाणिनेर्व्याकरणस्य स्वरूपपर्यालोचनम्", in: Keshab Chandra Dash (1994), pp. 188-195. [In Sanskrit.]

Chaturvedi, Mithilesh

1975 "On some formations involving luk-elision", Festschrift Vishva Bandhu, pp. 42-49.

*1976 *A Study of the Vṛttisamuddeśa of Vākyapadīya.* [University of Delhi Ph.D. dissertation, under publication.]

Chokshi, Kamaleshwar Kumar

1997 "अष्टाध्याय्याः आन्तरिकं सङ्ग्रथनम् अष्टविद्याशब्दसिद्धिश्च", Conference 1997b:178. [In Sanskrit.]

Comrie, Bernard (Ed.)

1990 *The Major Languages of South Asia, the Middle East and Africa* (London: Routledge).

Conference

1997a *Xth World Sanskrit Conference, International Association of Sanskrit Studies, January 3-9, 1997, Taralabalu Kendra, Bangalore* : *English Abstracts* (New Delhi: Rashtriya Sanskrit Sansthan).

1997b *Xth World Sanskrit Conference, International Association of Sanskrit Studies, January 3-9, 1997, Taralabalu Kendra, Bangalore* : *Sanskrit Abstracts* (New Delhi: Rashtriya Sanskrit Sansthan).

Coward, Harold G. "*Kumārila's* theory of word meaning in relation to the

1994 *sphoṭa* theory of *Bhartṛhari*", Festschrift Mandana Mishra, pp. 215-219.

Coward, Harold G. and K. Kunjunni Raja (Eds.)

1990 *Encyclopedia of Indian Philosophies, V* : *The Philosophy of the Grammarians* (Princeton: Princeton University Press). [Indian edition: Delhi: Motilal Banarsidass.]

Dāhāla, Lokamaṇi

1989/90 व्याकरणशास्त्रेतिहासः (Varanasi/Delhi: Bhāratīya Vidyā Prakāśana). [In Sanskrit.]

Dahiya, Yajanveer (see also Yajan Veer)

1995 *Pāṇini as a Linguist* : *Ideas and Patterns* (Delhi: Eastern Book Linkers). [Sanskrit preface (xi-xlviii), appendix: accented Aṣṭādhyāyī (238-298).]

Dandekar, Ramachandra Narayana

1985 *Vedic Bibliography, Fourth Volume* (= GovOS B 13) (Poona: BORI). [Section VII. Vedāṅgas: 23: Sikṣā, Prātiśākhya (173-180); 25: Vyākaraṇa: Pāṇini (200-240); 26: Nirukta: Nighaṇṭu: Yāska (240-249).]

1993 *Vedic Bibliography, Fifth Volume* (= GovOS B 17) (Poona: BORI). [Section VII. Vedāṅgas: 23: Sikṣā, Prātiśākhya

(137-143); 25: Vyākaraṇa: Pāṇini (158-200); 26: Nirukta: Nighaṇṭu: Yāska (200-206).]

Dandekar, R. N. and P. D. Navathe (Eds.)

1985 *Proceedings of the Fifth World Sanskrit Conference, Varanasi, India : October 21-26, 1981* (New Delhi: Rashtriya Sanskrit Sansthan).

Das, Karunasindhu

1984 "On the concept of elision as a phenomenon in Pāṇini's grammar", JDSRBU 1:24-30. [See 1985.]

1985 "On the concept of elision as a phenomenon in Pāṇini's grammar", in: Dandekar and Navathe (1985), pp. 131-137. [See 1984.]

1986 *Paribhāṣās in the Pāṇinian System of Grammar* (Calcutta: Sanskrit Book Depot). [Based on a doctoral dissertation submitted to Calcutta University in 1977.]

1990 *A Pāṇinian Approach to Philosophy of Language : Kauṇḍabhaṭṭa's Vaiyākaraṇabhūṣaṇasāra, Critically Edited and Translated into English* (Calcutta: Sanskrit Pustak Bhandar).

1994a (Ed.) *Semantic-syntactic Relations : A Philosophical approach: Abhirāma's Kārakaṭippaṇī of the Saṁkṣiptasāra School, Critically Edited* (Calcutta: Sanskrit Pustak Bhandar).

1994b "Apropos of case-relationship in general and genitive in particular — a Pāṇinian view-point", in: Keshab Chandra Dash (1994), pp. 146-153.

Das, Rahul Peter

1990 "Miscellanea de operibus āyurvedicis", JEAS 1:47-68. [49-53: 4. Caraka's compounds.]

1992 "Miscellanea de operibus āyurvedicis (II)", JEAS 2:6-35. [27-29: 35. On *vātika-*, *paittika-*, *ślaiṣmika-*, *sānnipātika-*.]

Dascal, Marcelo, Dietfried Gerdarhus, Kuno Lorenz and Georg Meggle (Eds.)

1992 *Sprachphilosophie/Philosophy of Language/La philosophie du langage : Ein internationales Handbuch zeitgenössischer Forschung/ An International Handbook of Contemporary Research/Manuel international des recherches contemporaines* Vol. I (= HSK 7.1) (Berlin, New York: de Gruyter).

Dasgupta, Surendranatha

1991 *The Mahābhāṣya of Patañjali with Annotations* (*Āhnika I-IV*) (Edited by Sibajiban Bhattacharyya) (Delhi: Indian Council of Philosophical Research).

Dash, Achyutananda

1990 "The semantic representation of accusative case-endings", Festschrift Sankalia, pp. 105-112.

1991 "The syntactic role of adhi- in the Pāṇinian kāraka-system", Festschrift S. D. Joshi, pp. 135-160.

1992 "Kāraka-theory for knowledge representation", Saṃbhāṣā 13:43-63.

Dash, Achyutananda and Brendon S. Gillon

1990 "On formalizing Pāṇini's *kāraka* for sentence derivation", BDCRI 50:173-181.

Dash, Keshab Chandra

1994 *Indian Semantics, A Computational Model* (Delhi: Agam Kala Prakashan).

Dash, Narendra Kumar

1988 "स्फोटतत्त्वसमीक्षा", Charu Deva Shastri, pp. 133-137. [In Sanskrit.]

1991 *Puruṣottamadeva as Grammarian* (Delhi: Agam Kala Prakashan).

1993 *A Survey on Sanskrit Grammar in Tibetan Language* (Delhi: Agam Kala Prakashan).

Dash, Prafulla Chandra

1980 "Candra and the 'asaṁjñaka vyākaraṇa'", CASS-St. 5:187-197.

1986 *A Comparative Study of the Pāṇinian and Cāndra Systems of Grammar* (*Kṛdanta Portion*) (New Delhi: Ramanand Vidya Bhawan).

Dash, Radhamadhab

1993 "Idioms on agriculture as available in the Kāśikā", JOIB 42:115-121.

Dass, Ayodhya Chandra
1988 "Pāṇini and accent", KURJ 22:173-179.

Datta, Pradyot Kumar
1994 *Pāṇini and Prātiśākhya : A Comparative Study in Etymological and Grammatical Approach* पाणिनिप्रातिशाख्ययो-स्तुलनात्मकमालोचनम् (Calcutta: Sanskrit Pustak Bhandar). [ii-xxx: English introduction, 1-5: प्राक्कथनम् 'Pāṇini and Prātiśākhya' (in Sanskrit), 6-9: পাণিনি ও প্রাতিশাখ্যের সম্বন্ধ (Bengali version); the remainder in Sanskrit. Originally a Ph.D. thesis, University of Calcutta, 1989.]

Davesar, Indu
1985 पाणिनीयसूत्रपाठ और जैनेन्द्रसूत्रपाठ का तुलनात्मक अध्ययन (विशेषतः संज्ञा,परिभाषा एवं अनुबन्ध के सन्दर्भ में) (Meerut: Anu Books). [In Hindi.]

Deshpande, Madhav Murlidhar
1975a *Critical studies in Indian grammarians, I : The Theory of Homogeneity* [*Sāvarṇya*] (= The Michigan Studies in South and Southeast Asian Languages and Linguistics, 2) (Ann Arbor: University of Michigan, Center for South and Southeast Asian Studies).
1975b "The scope of homogeneous representation in Pāṇini", AOR Silver Jubilee Volume: 271-291.
1975c "Phonetics of V in Pāṇini", ABORI 56:45-65.
1975d "Phonetics of short A in Sanskrit", IIJ 17:195-209.
1975e "A note on *tṛcá*", IIJ 17:249-250.
1976a "New materials on the Kautsa-vyākaraṇa", JOIB 26:131-144.
1976b "On the Ṛk-Prātiśākhya 13.5-6", IL 37:171-181.
1978a "Pāṇinian grammarians on dialectal variations in Sanskrit", ALB 42:61-114.
1978b "Sentence-cognition in Nyāya epistemology", IIJ 20:195-216.
1979a *Sociolinguistic Attitudes in India : An Historical Reconstruction* (= LES 5) (Ann Arbor: Karoma).
1979b "History, change and permanence: a classical Indian perspective", in: Gopal Krishna (ed.), *Contributions to South Asian Studies, I : History, Religion and Politics*

(New Delhi: Oxford University Press), pp. 1-28.

1979c "Candragomin's syntactic rules: some misconceptions", IL 40:133-145.

1980a *Evolution of Syntactic Theory in Sanskrit Grammar : Syntax of the Sanskrit Infinitive -tumUN* (= LES 10) (Ann Arbor: Karoma).

1980b "Recent studies in Patañjali's Vyākaraṇa-Mahābhāṣya", OLZ 75:309-321. [Review-article of Joshi-Roodbergen (1974).]

1981a "Sanskrit gerund constructions: syntactic disputations", IIJ 23:167-185.

1981b "Pāṇini and Paṇinīyas on dialectal variation in Sanskrit", Kuppuswami Shastri Research Institute, Golden Jubilee Volume, pp. 49-73.

1981c "Revisiting Pa:Nini 7.3.73", IL 42:58-64.

1982 "Pāṇini and the Vedic evidence: a peep into the past", in: Dharmadhikari (1982), pp. 52-65.

1983a "Linguistic presuppositions of Pāṇini 8.3.26-27", in: Joshi and Laddu (1983), pp. 23-42.

1983b "Pāṇini as a frontier grammarian", in: *Papers from the 19th Regional Meeting, Chicago Linguistic Society*, pp. 110-116.

1984 Review of Kiparsky (1979), Lg. 60:161-164.

1985a *Ellipsis and Syntactic Overlapping: Current Issues in Pāṇinian Syntactic Theory* (*The Pandit Shripad Sastri Deodhar Memorial Lectures* [*Second series*]) (= BORIS 24(Pune: BORI) [I: Ellipsis and syntactic overlapping in Pāṇini: a review of current ideas (1-32), II: Natural ellipsis and prescribed word-deletion in Sanskrit grammar (33-60), III: From Pāṇini to his successors: theoretical and historical change (61-89).]

1985b "Historical change and the theology of eternal Sanskrit", ZvS 98:112-149. [See also 1993a.]

1985c "Sanskrit grammarians: differing perspectives in cultural geography", Festschrift Tripathi, pp. 57-68.

1986a "Sanskrit grammarians on diglossia", in: Krishnamurti, Masica, Sinha (1986), pp. 312-321.

1986b "Some facets of Pāṇinian morphology", ALB 50:478-489.

1987a "From uttarapadalopa to madhyamapadalopa: implications for theoretical change", ABORI 67(1986):251-257.

1987b "Pāṇini's syntax of Sanskrit gerund constructions: an alternative view", Festschrift Rocher, pp. 242-266.

1987c "Pāṇinian syntax and the changing notion of sentence", ABORI 68:55-98. [See also 1991e.]

1987d "Strategies of Sanskrit grammarians in defense of Vedic religion", AJOS 4:75-86.

1988 "Pāṇini and the northwest dialect", in: *Languages and Culture* : *Studies in Honor of Edgar C. Polomé* (Ed. Mohamed Ali Jazayery and Werner Winter) (Berlin: Mouton-de Gruyter), pp. 111-121.

1989a "Vedic syntax: a select bibliography", in: V. N. Jha (1989), pp. 29-48.

1989b Review of Katre (1987), Lg. 65:646-648.

1990a "Semantics of *kārakas* in Pāṇini: an exploration of philosophical and linguistic issues", in: Matilal and Bilimoria (1990), pp. 33-57.

1990b "Some features of the sampradāna kāraka in Pāṇini", in: Varma and Mohanan (1990), pp. 147-159.

1990c "Ellipsis in modern linguistics and Pāṇini", ABORI 70 (1989):103-124.

1991a (Ed.) *Panels of the VIIth World Sanskrit Conference, Vol. V* : *Pāṇini and the Veda* (Leiden: Brill).

1991b "Prototypes in Pāṇinian syntax", JAOS 111:465-480.

1991c "Ditransitive passive in Pāṇini", IIJ 34:19-35.

1991d "Pāṇini 7.2.15 (yasya vibhāṣā): a reconsideration", Festschrift S. D. Joshi, pp. 161-176.

1991e "Pāṇinian syntax and the changing notion of sentence", in: Hock (1991a), pp. 31-43. [See also 1987b.]

1991f "Pāṇinian reflections on Vedic infinitives: On the meaning of *tumartha*", in: Hock (1991a), pp. 45-53.

1991g "Pāṇinian reflections on Vedic infinitives: on infinitives with *-tosUN* and *-KasUN*", in: Deshpande (1991a,) pp. 19-31.

1991h "Diglossia in the writings of Sanskrit grammarians", in:

Southwest Journal of Linguistics, Studies in Diglossia, volume 10, pp. 23-40.

1992a *The Meaning of Nouns, Semantic Theory in Classical and Medieval India, Nāmārthanirṇaya of Kauṇḍabhaṭṭa Translated and Annotated* (= SCI 13) (Dordrecht: Kluwer). [Revised version of Deshpande (1972b).]

1992b "Ditransitive constructions in Patañjali's Mahābhāṣya", Festschrift Janaki, pp. 41-50.

1992c "Sociolinguistic parameters of Pāṇini's Saṃskrit", Festschrift Ghatage, pp. 111-130.

1992d "Bhartṛhari", in: Dascal et al. (1992), pp. 269-278.

1992e "Pāṇini in the context of modernity", Festschrift Kelkar, pp. 15-27.

1992f "Justification for verb-root suppletion in Sanskrit", HF 105:18-49.

1993a *Sanskrit and Prakrit: Sociolinguistic Issues* (= MLBD Series in Linguistics 6) (Delhi: Motilal Banarsidass). [17-32: "*Loka*: The linguistic world of Patañjali"; 53-74: "Historical change and the theology of eternal (*nitya*) Sanskrit" (see also 1985b); 75-82: "Sanskrit grammarians: differing perspectives in cultural geography".]

1993b "The changing grammar of salvation", ABORI 72-73 (1991 & 1992):275-294.

1993c "The changing notion of śiṣṭa from Patañjali to Bhartṛhari", in: Bhate and Bronkhorst (1993), pp. 95-115.

1994a "Grammars and grammar-switching in Vedic recitational variations", ALB 60:41-63.

1994b प्राचीन भारतीय ध्वनिशास्त्र — काही वैशिष्ट्ये, Festschrift Bhagwat, pp. 57-69. [In Marathi.]

1994-95 "Pāṇini and the distinctive features", BDRI 54-55:87-97.

1995a संस्कृत आणि प्राकृत भाषा — व्यवहार, नियमन, आणि शास्त्रचर्चा (Pune: Shubhda Sarasvat Publications). [3: पाणिनीच्या 'भाषे'च्या सामाजिक सीमारेषा (71-97), 4: पतंजलीच्या महाभाष्यातील भाषाव्यवहार (99-123), 7: लौकिक व्यवहारातील संस्कृतभाषा (183-217). In Marathi.]

1995b "Ancient Indian phonetics", in: Koerner and Asher (1995), section IV (Antiquity-India), pp. 72-77.

1995c "The notion of distinctive features in Sanskrit phonetics", Festschrift Shah, pp. 125-134.
1996a "Contextualizing the eternal language: features of priestly Sanskrit", in: Houben (1996a), pp. 401-436.
1996b "The Vedic traditions and origins of grammatical thought in ancient India", in: *Langue, style et structure dans le monde indien : Centenaire de Louis Renou* (Actes du Colloque international [Paris, 25-27 janvier 1996]) (édité par Nalini Balbir et Georges-Jean Pinault avec la collaboration de Jean Fezas) (= BEHESHP 334) (Paris: Champion), pp. 145-170.
1997a "Who inspired Pāṇini?", JAOS 117:444-465.
1997b *Śaunakīyā Caturādhyāyikā : A Prātiśākhya of the Śaunakīya Atharvaveda, with the Commentaries Caturādhyāyībhāṣya, Bhārgava-Bhāskara-Vṛtti and Pañcasandhi, Critically Edited, Translated and Annotated* (= HOS 52) (Cambridge: Department of Sanskrit and Indian Studies, Harvard University).
1997c "*Kārakas* : direct and indirect relationships", Conference 1997a:415-416.
1997d "Pāṇini and the distinctive features", Festschrift Shevoroshkin, pp. 72-87.
forthcoming
a "The Vedic context of Pāṇini's grammar", in: *Indigenous Traditions* (Ed. H. Kniffka) (Berlin: Mouton-de Gruyter).
b "Building blocks or useful fictions: changing view of morphology in ancient Indian thought", Festschrift Frits Staal.
c "Evolution of the notion of authority (*prāmāṇya*) in the Pāṇinian tradition", in: *Histoire, épistémologie, langage* (Paris: Société d'Histoire et d'Épistémologie des Sciences du Langage).

Deshpande, Madhav M. and Hans Henrich Hock
1991 "A bibliography of writings on Sanskrit syntax", in: Hock (1991a), pp. 219-244.

Devasthali, Govind Vinayak
1980 "Pāṇini's kāraka-theory", in: S. D. Joshi (1980a), pp. 47-56.

1983 "Apropos of *vibhāṣā*", in: Joshi and Laddu (1983), pp. 157-165.

1984 "*Pāṇini* and Vedic — a critique", ABORI 64 (1983):137-148.

1985 "*Paribhāṣā* (introduction and general survey)", Festschrift Dandekar, pp. 1-13. [= Devasthali (1969).]

Devasthali, G. V. and G. B. Palsule

1989 *Mahābhāṣyadīpikā of Bhartṛhari, Fascicle VI : Āhnika IV, Critically Edited* (= BORIS 32) (Pune: BORI).

Dharmadhikari, Trivikram Narayan (Ed.)

1982 तिलक-महाराष्ट्र-विद्यापीठ-शाखाभूत वैदिक-संशोधनन-मण्डलेन प्रकाशितः सुवर्णमहोत्सत-ग्रन्थः *Golden Jubilee Volume, Vaidika Saṁśodhana Maṇḍala* (Pune: Vaidika Saṁśodhana Maṇḍala).

Dharmendra Kumar

1996 काशिकावार्त्तिकव्याख्या (Delhi: Triveni Prakashan). [In Hindi.]

Dighe, Shanti S.

1997 संहितायाम् । *A Book on Pāṇinīya Rules of Sandhi* (Vadodara: Shanti S. Dighe).

Dīkṣita, Mārtaṇḍaśāstrī

1980 "पश्य मृगो धावति, पचति भवति इत्येतयोः शाब्दबोधविचारः", in: S. D. Joshi (1980), pp. 229-230. [In Sanskrit.]

Dīkṣita, Puṣpā

1997 "लकाराणां पुनर्व्यवस्थापनम्", Conference 1997b:187-189. [In Sanskrit.]

Dīxita, Girijeśa Kumāra (Ed.)

1987 श्रीनागेशभट्टविरचितः परिभाषेन्दुशेखरः श्रीशेषशर्मसूरिविरचितया सर्वमङ्गलाख्य-व्याख्यया समलङ्कृतः *Paribhāṣenduśekharaḥ of Śrī Nāgeśa Bhaṭṭa with the Commentary Sarvamaṅgalā by Śrī Śeṣaśarma Sūri* (= SBS 36) (Varanasi: Sampurnanand Sanskrit University). [Originally a Vidyāvāridhi thesis.]

Dubey, Satya Prakash (Ed.)

1995 आचार्यविश्वेश्वरसूरिविरचितः व्याकरणसिद्धान्तसुधानिधिः प्रथमो भागः आद्याध्यायत्रयात्मकः *Vyākaraṇa Siddhāntasudhānidhi of Ācārya Viśveśvara Sūri, Part I* (*Chapters I to III*) (Jodhpur: Rajasthan Patrika).

Dvivedi, H. P.

1978 *Studies in Pāṇini : Technical Terms of the Aṣṭādhyāyī* (Delhi: Inter-India Publications). [Revised version of Patna University doctoral thesis entitled *Some Aspects of the Technical Terms of the Aṣṭādhyāyī.*]

Dwivedi, Janaki Prasad

1987 संस्कृत के बौद्ध वैयाकरण *Buddhist Grammarians, Commentators and Tibetan Translators of Sanskrit Grammar*(= BIT XIII) (Sarnath, Varanasi: Central Institute of Higher Tibetan Studies). [In Hindi. Chapter 2: संस्कृतव्याकरणों के बौद्ध व्याख्याकार (135-292): 2.5: काशिकावृत्तिकार जयादित्य और वामन (167-171), 2.6: काशिकाकार आचार्य वामन (172-189), 2.8: भागवृत्तिकार आचार्य विमलमति (194-202), 2.9: न्यासकार बोधिसत्त्वदेशीय आचार्य जिनेन्द्रबुद्धि (203-217), 2.16: रूपावताररचयिता आचार्य धर्मकीर्ति (245-258), 2.17: भाषावृत्तिकार आचार्य पुरुषोत्तमदेव (259-272), 2.19: दुर्घटवृत्तिकार आचार्य शरणदेव (275-283).]

Dwivedi, R. C.

1992 "Bhartṛhari and Kashmir Śaivism", Festschrift Mukherji I, pp. 240-246. [See also (1993).]

1993 "Bhartṛhari and Kashmir Śaivism", ABORI 72-73 (1991 & 1992): 95-107. [See also (1992).]

Dwivedī, Śrī Brahma Dutta

1985 म॰म॰ श्रीकौण्डभट्टकृत-वैयाकरणभूषणसारः (दर्पण-हिन्दीभाष्योपेतः) *Vaiyākaraṇabhūṣaṇasāra by M. M. Kauṇḍa Bhaṭṭa* (*with 'Darpaṇa' & Hindi commentary*). (= CPVS 17) (Varanasi: Chaukhambha Orientalia).

Falk, Harry

1993 *Schrift im alten Indien : Ein Forschungsbericht mit Anmerkungen* (= ScriptOralia 56) (Tübingen: Gunter Narr Verlag).

Festschrift Agrawal

1981 *Professor Jagannath Agrawal Felicitation Volume* (Ed.: S. Bhaskaran Nair) (= VIJ 19.1-2).

Festschrift Berger

1996 *Nānāvidhaikatā : Festschrift für Hermann Berger* (Ed.: Dieter B. Kapp) (= BKSSL 4) (Wiesbaden: Harrassowitz).

Festschrift Bhagwat

1994 वाचस्पत्यम् (पं. वामनशास्त्री भागवत अभिनंदन ग्रंथ) *Vācaspatyam* (*Pt. Vamanshastri Bhagwat Felicitation Volume*) (Eds.: Saroja Bhate, Madhav Deshpande) (Pune: Vaidika Samshodhana Mandala).

Festschrift Bhattacharya

1991 *Prajñājyoti* : *Prof. Dr. Gopikamohan Bhattacharya Commemoration Volume* (Eds.: Debabrata Sen Sharma and Manabendu Banerjee) (Kurukshetra: Nirmal Book Agency).

Festschrift Caillat

1987-88 *Professor Colette Caillat Felicitation* Volume (= IT 14).

Festschrift Charu Deva Shastri

1988 डा° चारुदेव-शास्त्रि-स्मृति-विशेषाङ्कः (= VS 25.2-4).

Festschrift Chatterjee

1994 *Cultura Indica, Tributes to an Indologist* : *Professor Dr. Asoke Chatterjee Sastri* (Editor-in-chief: Biswanath Banerjee, editors: Mrinal Kanti Gangopadhyay, Dipak Ghosh, Ratna Basu) (Delhi: Sharada Publishing House).

Festschift Chatterji

1981 *Suniti Kumar Chatterji Commemoration Volume* (General ed.: Bhakti P. Mallik) (Burdwan: The University of Burdwan).

Festschrift Dandekar

1984 *Amṛtadhārā* : *Professor R. N. Dandekar Felicitation Volume* (Ed.: S. D. Joshi) (Delhi: Ajanta Publications).

1985 *Glimpses of Veda and Vyākaraṇa, Reflections on Some Less Familiar Topics* : *Professor R. N. Dandekar Felicitation Volume* (Ed.: G. V. Devasthali) (Bombay: Popular Prakashan). [Identical to Festschrift R. N. Dandekar (1969).]

Festschrift Gaurinath Sastri

1980 *A Corpus of Indian Studies* : *Essays in Honour of Professor Gaurinath Sastri* (Board of editors: A. L. Basham, Ramaranjan Mukherji, Bimal Krishna Matilal, K. Kunjunni Raja, R. V. Joshi, A. L. Thakur, Gopikamohan Bhattacharya, Manabendu Banerjee) (Calcutta: Sanskrit Pustak Bhandar).

Festschrift Ghatage

1992 *Vidyā-vratin* : *Professor A. M. Ghatage Felicitation Volume* (Ed.: V. N. Jha) (= SGDOS 160) (Delhi: Sri Satguru Publications).

Festschrift Hoenigswald

1987 *Festschrift for Henry M. Hoenigswald Presented on the Occasion of his Seventieth Birthday* (Eds.: George Cardona and Norman H. Zide) (Tübingen: Gunter Narr Verlag).

Festschrift Hoffmann

1985 *Festgabe für Karl Hoffmann, Teil I* (= MSS 44).

Festschrift Ingalls

1980 *Sanskrit and Indian Studies* : *Essays in Honour of Daniel H. H. Ingalls* (Eds.: M. Nagatomi, B. K. Matilal, J. M. Masson, E. C. Dimock Jr.) (Dordrecht: Reidel).

1985 *Indological Studies Dedicated to Daniel H. H. Ingalls* (Ed.: E. Bender) (= JAOS 105.3).

Festschrift Janaki

1992 *Dr. S. S. Janaki Felicitation Volume* (Editorial committee: K. K. Raja, S. S. Janaki, R. N. Sampath, G. Mishra, V. Kameswari) (= JOR 66-72 [1968-92]) (Madras: The Kuppuswami Sastri Research Institute).

Festschrift Jani

1983 *Aruṇa-Bhāratī* : *Professor A. N. Jani Felicitation Volume* (*Essays in Contemporary Indological Research*) (Eds.: B. Datta, U. C. Sharma, Nitin J. Vyas) (Baroda: Professor A. N. Jani Felicitation Volume Committee).

Festschrift de Jong

1982 *Indological and Buddhist Studies* : *Volume in Honour of Professor J. W. de Jong on his Sixtieth Birthday* (Eds.: L. A. Hercus, F. B. J. Kuiper, T. Rajapatirana, E. R. Skrzypczak) (Canberra: Faculty of Asian Studies).

Festschrift R. V. Joshi

1988-89 *Studies in Indology* : *Professor Rasik Vihari Joshi Felicitation Volume* (Eds.: A. Kumar, Jean le Mée, M. M. Agrawal, S. P. Narang, V. Upadhyay) (Delhi: Shree Publishing House).

Festschrift S. D. Joshi

1991 *Pāṇinian Studies* : *Professor S. D. Joshi Felicitation Volume* (Eds.: Madhav M. Deshpande and Saroja Bhate) (= Center for South and Southeast Asian Studies, University of Michigan, Number 37) (Ann Arbor: The University of Michigan Center for South and Southeast Asian Studies).

Festschrift Kamlesh Kumari Kulashrestha

1992 संस्कृत-संगीत-वैजयन्ती श्रीमती कमलेश कुमारी कुलश्रेष्ठ स्मृत्यभिनन्दन ग्रन्थ *Studies in Sanskrit and Musicology* : *Smt. Kamlesh Kumari Kulshreshtha Commemoration Volume* (Eds.: Sushma Kulashreshtha and Satya Pal Narang) (Delhi: Eastern Book Linkers).

Festschrift Katre

1991-92 *S. M. Katre Felicitation Volume* (= BDCRI 51-52).

Festschrift Kavīśvara

1990 प्रसन्न पारिजात ब्रह्मश्री दत्तमहाराज कवीश्वर गौरव ग्रंथ (Ed.: D. B. Kerura) (Pune: ब्रह्मश्री दत्तमहाराज कवीश्वर गौरव समिति).

Festschrift Kelkar

1992 *Language and Text* : *Studies in Honour of Ashok R. Kelkar* (Eds.: R. N. Srivastava, Suresh Kumar, K. K. Goswami, R. V. Dhongde) (Delhi: Kalinga Publications).

Festschrift Krishnamurti

1991 *Studies in Dravidian and General Linguistics* : *A Festschrift for Bh. Krishnamurti* (Eds.: B. Lakshmi Bai and B. Ramakrishna Reddy) (= OUPL 6) (Hyderabad: Centre of Advanced Study in Linguistics, Osmania University).

Festschrift K. Kunjunni Raja

1981 *Dr. K. Kunjunni Raja Felicitation Volume* (Editorial board: Radha Burnier, K. Kunjunni Raja, A. G. Krishna Warrier, A. A. Ramanathan) (= ALB 44-45 [1980-1981]).

Festschrift Lienhard

1995 *Sauhṛdyamaṅgalam* : *Studies in Honour of Siegfried Lienhard on his 70th Birthday* (Eds.: Mirja Juntunen, William L. Smith, Carl Suneson) (Stockholm: The Association of Oriental Studies).

Festschrift Mandan Mishra
1994 *Studies in Mīmāṁsā* : *Dr. Mandan Mishra Felicitation Volume* (Ed.: R. C. Dwivedi) (Delhi: Motilal Banarsidass).

Festschrift Mukherji
1992 *Corpus of Indological Studies* : *Professor Ramaranjan Mukherji Felicitation Volume* (Editor-in-chief: Anantalal Thakur) 2 volumes (continuous pagination) (Delhi: Sharada Publishing House).

Festschrift Oberhammer
1994 *Orbis Indicus Gerhardo Oberhammer lustrum XIII. exigenti ab amicis discipulisque oblatus* (Eds.: R. A. C. Mesquita and Ch. H. Werba) (= WZKS 38)

Festschrift Rao
1987 *Studies in Indian Culture* (*Sāhitya Śiromaṇi Professor S. Ramachandra Rao Felicitation Volume*) (Bangalore: Professor S. Ramachandra Rao Felicitation Committee).

Festschrift Rau
1987 *Festschrift Wilhelm Rau zur Vollendung des 65. Lebhensjahres dargebracht von Schülern, Freunden und Kollegen* (Eds.: Heidrun Brückner, Dieter George, Claus Vogel, Albrecht Wezler) (= StII 13/14).

Festschrift Rocher
1987 *Festschrift for Ludo Rocher* (= ALB 51).

Festschrift Sanghvi
1981 *Studies in Indian Philosophy* : *A Memorial Volume in Honour of Pandit Sukhlalji Sanghvi* (Eds.: Dalsukh Malvania and Nagin J. Shah) (= L. D. Series 84) (Ahmedabad: L. D. Institute of Indology).

Festschrift Sankalia
1990 *Professor H. D. Sankalia Memorial Volume* (= BDCRI 49).

Festschrift Shah
1995 शिल्पसंवित् *Consciousness Manifest*: *Studies in Jaina Art and Iconography and Allied Subjects in Honour of Dr. U. P. Shah* (Chief ed.: R. T. Vyas) (Vadodara: Abhinav Publications [Oriental Institute]).

Festschrift Shevoroshkin

1997 *Indo-European, Nostratic, and Beyond : Festschrift for Vitalij V. Shevoroshkin* (Eds.: Irén Hegedüs, Peter A. Michalove and Alexis Manester Ramer) (= Journal of Indo-European Studies Monograph 22) (Washington, D.C.: Institute for the Study of Man).

Festschrift Shri Niwas Shastri

1996 श्रीज्ञानामृतम् *Śrījñānāmṛtam : A Memorial Volume in Honour of Prof. Shri Niwas Shastri* प्रो° श्रीनिवास शास्त्री स्मृतिग्रन्थः (Chief ed.: Vijaya Rani, managing editor: V. K. Goyal) (Delhi: Parimal Publications).

Festschrift Sinha

1986 श्री गोपाल चन्द्र सिंह — स्मृत्यङ्क *Shri Gopal Chandra Sinha Commemoration Volume* (Eds.: J. P. Sinha, A. K. Kalia) (= Ṛtam 16-18 [1984-1986]) (Lucknow: Akhila Bharatiy Sanskrit Parishad).

Festschrift Sreekrishna Sarma

1983 *Surabhi : Sreekrishna Sarma Felicitation Volume* (Editorial board: K. S. Ramamurthi, K. S. R. Datta, G. G. V. R. Ramanujacharyulu, S. R. Matha, M. Srimannarayana Murti) (Tirupati: Prof. E. R. Sreekrishna Sarma Felicitation Committee).

Festschrift Sternbach

1979 *Dr. Ludwick Sternbach Felicitation Volume, Part One* (= IT 7).

1980-81 *Dr. Ludwick Sternbach Memorial Volume* (= IT 8-9).

Festschrift K. A. Subrahmania Iyer

1976 *Prof. K. A. S. Iyer Felicitation Volume* (Editor-in-chief: J. P. Sinha) (= Ṛtam 2-6, June 1970-January 1975) (Lucknow: Akhila Bharatiy Sanskrit Parishad).

Festschrift Thieme

1980 *Festschrift Paul Thieme zur Vollendung des 75. Lebensjahres dargebracht von Schülern und Freunden* (Eds.: Georg Budruss, Albrecht Wezler) (= StII 5/6).

1996 *Veda-Vyākaraṇa-Vyākhyāna : Festschrift Paul Thieme zum 90. Geburtstag am 18. März 1995 dargebracht von Schülern,*

Freunden und Kollegen (Eds.: Hanns-Peter Schmidt, Albrecht Wezler) (= StII 20).

Festschrift Tripathi

1985 *Professor Ram Suresh Tripathi Commemoration Volume* (Ed.: U. C. Sharma, associate editors: S. R. Sarma, G. C. Sarma) (= AJOS 2.1-2).

Festschrift Vishva Bandhu

1975 *Acharya Dr. Vishva Bandhu Commemoration Volume, Part II* (Ed.: K. V. Sharma) (= VIJ 13.1-2).

Festschrift Watkins

1998 *Mír Curad : Studies in Honor of Calvert Waktins* (Eds.: Jay Jasanoff, H. Craig Melchert, Lisi Olivier) (= IBS 92) (Innsbruck: Institut für Sprachwissenschaft der Universität Innsbruck).

Filliozat, Pierre-Sylvain

1975 "On the analysis of Sanskrit compounds and derivatives", AOR Silver Jubilee Volume: 81-95.

1975-86 (Tr.) *Le Mahābhāṣya de Patañjali avec le Pradīpa de Kaiyaṭa et l'Uddyota de Nāgeśa.* (= PIFI 54,1-4). (Pondichéry: Institut Français d'Indologie). [54, 1 (1975): adhyāya 1, pāda 1, āhnika 1-4; 54, 2 (1976): adhyāya 1, pāda 1, āhnika 5-7; 54, 3 (1976): adhyāya 1, pāda 1, āhnika 8-9; 54, 4 (1980): adhyāya 1, pāda 2; 54, 5 (1986): adhyāya 1, pāda 3.]

1978 "Śivarāmendra Sarasvatī's interpretation of "sthānivad ādeśaḥ" Pāṇini 1.1.56", ABORI 58-59 (Diamond Jubilee Volume):619-626.

1983 "The Pāṇinian concept of *karmakartṛ*", in: Joshi and Laddu (1983), pp. 11-16.

1984 "On the semantic use of the word *sphoṭa*", Festschrift Dandekar, pp. 133-140.

1988 *Grammaire sanskrite pāṇinéenne* (Collection Connaissance des Langues) (Paris: Bocard).

1991 *An Introduction to Commentaries on Patañjali's Mahābhāṣya* ("Professor K. V. Abhyankar Memorial Lectures" [Fourth Series]) (= BORIS 35) (Pune: BORI). [I: Patañjali and his commentators (1-32), II: Patañjali's definition of śabda (33-85).]

1992a *Le Sanskrit* (= «Que sais-je?» 1416) (Paris: Presses Universitaires de France). [Pp. 37-43: Les structures pâninéennes.]

1992b "Le *sphoṭa*", Les Cahiers de Philosophie 14:155-169.

1993 "Ellipsis, lopa and anuvṛtti", ABORI 72-73 (1991 & 1992):675-87.

Forthomme, Dominique

1993 *Le Dhātukāvya de Nārāyaṇabhaṭṭa, un poème didactique sanskrit : Étude, texte, traduction, notes et indices* (= Publications du Département d'Indologie 80) (Pondichéry: Institut Français de Pondichéry, École Française d'Extrême-Orient).

Ganeri, Jonardan

1995 "Vyāḍi and the realist theory of meaning", JIP 23:403-428.

Gaurinath Śāstrī

1981 *A Study in the Dialectics of Sphoṭa* (Delhi: Motilal Banarsidass).

1984 म° म° हाराणचन्द्रभट्टाचार्यविरचिता कालसिद्धान्तदर्शिनी

(Ed.) *Kālasiddhāntadarśinī of M. M. Hārāṇacandra Bhaṭṭācārya* (= SBGM 120) (Varanasi: Sampurnanand Sanskrit University).

1991 *The Philosophy of Bhartṛhari* (Delhi, Varanasi: Bharatiya Vidya Prakashan).

Gayāvāla, Lal Shankar

1997 "पाणिनिकात्यायनपतञ्जलिनाऽपठिताः केचन अन्ये द्विकर्मकधातवः तेषां प्रयोगाश्च (Some double accusative verbs untraced by Pāṇini Kātyāyana Patañjali and their usage)", Conference 1997b:177-178. [In Sanskrit.]

Ghatage, Amrit Madhav

1983 "Systematics of Pāṇini's Aṣṭādhyāyī", in: Joshi and Laddu (1983), pp. 17-21.

1984 "Uktārthānām aprayogaḥ", Festschrift Dandekar, pp. 141-151.

1990 "Patañjali on P. VIII.1.1", Festschrift Kavīśvara, pp. 29-31.

1991-92 "Pāṇini-VIII-1-7", Festschrift Katre, pp. 125-126.

Ghosh, Manomohan

1986 *Pāṇinīya Śikṣā or The Śikṣā Vedāṅga Ascribed to Pāṇini (being the most ancient work on Indo-Aryan Phonetics) Critically Edited in all its Five Recensions with an Introduction, Translation and Notes together with its two Commentaries*). (Delhi-Madras: Asian Humanities Press). [Reprint of Ghosh (1938).]

Gillon, Brendan S.

1993 "Bhartṛhari's solution to the problem of *asamartha* compounds", in: Bhate and Bronkhorst (1993), pp. 117-133.

1995 "The autonomy of word formation: evidence from classical Sanskrit", IL 56:15-52.

Giri, Goswami Prahlad

1987 श्रीपाणिनिमुनिविरचिता पाणिनीयशिक्षा पं° श्रीरुद्रप्रसाद अवस्थीकृत-स्वरवैदिकपंक्तिविवरण-सटिप्पण-'प्रदीप'संस्कृतटीकासमेत-'प्रह्लाद'-हिन्दीव्याख्यासहिता हिन्दीव्याख्याकारः सम्पादकश्च गोस्वामी प्रह्लाद गिरिः *Pāṇinīyaśikṣā of Pāṇini, Edited with 'Pradip' Sanskrit Commentary, Svaravaidic Panktivivarana, Notes of Pt. Rudraprasad Avasthi and 'Prahlad' Hindi Commentary* (= HSS 59) (Varanasi: Chowkhamba Sanskrit Series Office).

Glauch, Sonja, Robert Plath, and Sabine Ziegler (Eds.)

1992 *Karl Hoffmann : Aufsätze zur Indoiranistik, Band 3* (Wiesbaden: Dr. Ludwig Reichert Verlag).

Gogoi-Chutia, Laksahira

1988 "A note on the concept of lakṣaṇā in the vyākaraṇa literature", GUJA 34:203-210.

Gokhale, Pratibha P.

1976 "Various ways of naming a verbal root in the *Aṣṭādhyāyī*", CASS-St. 3:101-111.

Gune, Jayashree Achyut

1978 *The meaning of tenses and moods : The Text of Kauṇḍabhaṭṭa's Lakārārtha-nirṇaya, with Introduction, and Explanatory Notes* (Pune: Deccan College Postgraduate and Research Institute). [Originally a University of Pennsylvania doctoral dissertation, 1974.]

1980 "The meaning of *Liṅ* according to the Nyāya and the

Vyākaraṇa schools", in: S. D. Joshi (1980a), pp. 155-168.

Hall, Robert A., Jr. (Ed.)

1987 *Leonard Bloomfield : Essays on his Life and Work* (= SHLS 47) (Amsterdam/ Philadelphia: John Benjamins). [With the collaboration of Konrad Koerner.]

Hattori, Masaaki

1993 "Kamalaśīla's interpretation of some verses of the Vākyakāṇḍa of Bhartṛhari's Vākyapadīya", in: Bhate and Bronkhorst (1993), pp. 135-140.

Hejib, Alaka and Aravind Sharma

1981 "A note on Pāṇini 6.1.87", Festschrift K. Kunjunni Raja, pp. 635-638.

Herzberger, Hans G. and Radhika Herzberger

1981a "Bhartṛhari's paradox", Festschrift Sanghvi, pp. 279-299. [See 1981b.]

1981b "Bhartṛhari's paradox", JIP 9:1-17. [See 1981a.]

Herzberger, Radhika

1986 *Bhartṛhari and the Buddhists, An Essay in the Development of Fifth and Sixth Century Indian Thought* (= SCI 8) (Dordrecht: Reidel).

Hill, Stephen R. and Peter G. Harrison

1991 *Dhātu-Pāṭha : The Roots of Language : The Foundations of the Indo-European Verbal System* (London: Duckworth).

Hock, Hans Henrich

1985 "Sanskrit double-object constructions: will the real object please stand up?", PVB 12:50-70.

1989 "Research on Sanskrit syntax: a progress report", in: V. N. Jha (1989), pp. 90-107.

1990 "Oblique subjects in Sanskrit?", in: Verma and Mohanan (1990), pp. 119-139.

1991a (Ed.) *Studies in Sanskrit Syntax : A Volume in Honor of the Centennial of Speijer's Sanskrit Syntax (1886-1986)* (Delhi: Motilal Banarsidass).

1991b "Possessive agents in Sanskrit?", in: Hock (1991a), pp. 55-69.

1991c "Causees, passive agents, or instruments? Instrumental

NPs with causatives in early and later Vedic prose", in: Hock (1991a), pp. 71-93.

Hock, Hans Henrich and Rajeshwari Pandharipande

1976 "The sociolinguistic position of Sanskrit in pre-Muslim India", in: Braj Kachru (ed.), *Dimensions of Bilingualism : Theory and Case Studies* (= SLL 1.2), pp. 105-138. [See also 1978.]

1978 "Sanskrit in the pre-Islamic sociolinguistic context of South Asia", in: Braj Kachru, and S. N. Sridhar (eds.), *Aspects of Sociolinguistics in South Asia* (= IJSL 16), pp. 1-25. [Abbreviated version of 1976.]

Hoffmann, Karl

1967 *Der Injunktiv im Veda* (Heidelberg: Winter).

1980 "Das Verbaladjektiv von *hvṛ* bei Pāṇini", Festschrift Thieme, pp. 87-98. [Reprinted: Glauch et al. (1992:749-760).]

Honda, Yoshichika

1993 "Bhartṛhari's definition of *kriyā*", in: Bhate and Bronkhorst (1993), pp. 141-154.

Houben, Jan E. M.

1989-90 "The sequencelessness of the signifier in Bhartṛhari's theory", IT 15-16:119-129.

1992 "Bhartṛhari's *samaya* / Helārāja's *saṃketa*: a contribution to the reconstruction of the grammarians' discussion with the Vaiśeṣikas on the relation between 'śabda' and 'artha'", JIP 20:219-242.

1992-93 "Bhartṛhari's perspectivism (3): On the structure of the third kāṇḍa of the Vākyapadīya", Sambodhi 18:1-32.

1993 "Who are Bhartṛhari's *padadarśins*? On the development of Bhartṛhari's philosophy of language", in: Bhate and Bronkhorst (1993), pp. 155-169.

1995a *The Saṃbandha-samuddeśa (Chapter on Relation) and Bhartṛhari's Philosophy of Language : A Study of Bhartṛhari's Saṃbandha-samuddeśa in the Context of the Vākyapadīya with a Translation of Helārāja's Commentary Prakīrṇa-Prakāśa* (= GIS II) (Groningen: Egbert Forsten). [Revised version of Utrecht University doctoral thesis, 1992.]

1995b "Bhartṛhari's perspectivism (2): Bhartṛhari on the primary unit of language", in: Klaus D. Dutz, Kjell-Åke Forsgren (eds.), *History and Rationality : The Skövde Papers in the Historiography of Linguistics* (= AUSSL 1) (Münster: Nodus Publikationen), pp. 29-62.

1995c "Bhartṛhari's solution to the liar and some other paradoxes", JIP 23:381-401.

1995d "Bhartṛhari's familiarity with Jainism", ABORI 75(1994):1-24.

1995e "Early Indian authors and linguistic change (Postscript to: Bhartṛhari's familiarity with Jainism)", ABORI 75:255-256.

1996a (Ed.) *Ideology and Status of Sanskrit : Contributions to the History of the Sanskrit Language* (= BIL 13) (Leiden, New York, Köln: E. J. Brill).

1996b "Socio-linguistic attitudes reflected in the work of Bhartṛhari and later grammarians", in: Houben (1996a), pp. 157-193.

1997 "The Sanskrit tradition", in: van Bekkum et al., pp. 49-145. [Section 6 (84-98): Grammar and semantics in the early Pāṇinian tradition.]

forthcoming

a "Bhartṛhari's Vākyapadīya and the ancient Vṛtti (1): the Vṛtti and Vṛṣabhadeva's Paddhati on Vākyapadīya 1.46a *ātmabhedaṁ / ātmabhedas ...* ", ABORI.

a' "Postscript: A note on Pt. Raghunātha Śarmā's interpretation of VP 1.46 and Vṛtti", ABORI. [Addendum to forthcoming a.]

b "Bhartṛhari's Vākyapadīya and the ancient Vṛtti (2): the Vedic background of the author of the Vākyapadīya-Vṛtti."

c "Philosophy and philology East and West: need and basis for a global approach." [Paper read at the International seminar on the past, present and future of Indology, Pune University, 13-16 January 1997, to be published in the proceedings of this seminar by the Sahitya Akademi, Delhi.]

d "The theoretical position of Bhartṛhari and the respectable grammarian."

*e "*Sūtra* and *bhāṣyasūtra* in Bhartṛhari's Mahābhāṣyadīpikā",

Festschrift Frits Staal.

Hueckstedt, Robert E.

1995 *Nearness and Respective Correlation : A History of the Interpretations of Aṣṭādhyāyī 6.1.77 : iko yaṇ aci* (Wiesbaden: Harrassowitz).

Ingalls, Daniel H. H.

1991 "A note on Pāṇini 3.1.26, vārttika 8", Festschrift S. D. Joshi, pp. 201-208.

Jagannatha, S.

1997 "भावलक्षणा सप्तमी", Conference 1997b:179. [In Sanskrit.]

Jain, Vrashabh Prasad

1984 त्रिमुनि व्याकरणम् (Aliganj [Eta]: Mahavir Prakashan). [In Sanskrit.]

*1986 *The Theory of Case: A Comparative Study of Fillmore's Case Grammar and Pāṇini's Kāraka System.* [Agra University Ph. D. dissertation, unpublished. Mentioned in Jain (1997):131.]

1989-90 "The concept of case/*kāraka*: a comparative statement", IT 15-16:131-143.

1997 "Towards the verb grammar", Saṃbhāṣā 18:125-131.

Jambūvijaya

1966-88 तार्किकशिरोमणिजिनशासनवादिप्रभावकाचार्यप्रवरश्रीमल्लवादिक्षमाश्रमणप्रणीतं द्वादशारं नयचक्रम् आचार्य श्रीसिंहसूरिगणिवादिक्षमाश्रमणविरचितया न्यायागमानुसारिण्या वृत्त्या समलंकृतम् ... टिप्पणादिभिः परिष्कृतः सम्पादकः ... मुनि जम्बूविजयः *Dvādaśāraṃ Nayacakram of Ācārya Śrī Mallavādi Kṣamāśramaṇa with the Commentary Nyāyāgamānusāriṇī of Śrī Siṃhasūri Gaṇi Vādi Kṣamāśramaṇa ... Edited with Critical Notes by Muni Jambūvijayajī* (= ŚĀJGM 92, 94, 95) 3 volumes (Bhavnagar: Sri Jain Atmanand Sabha). [Vol. 1 (1966): aras 1-4, vol. 2 (1976): aras 5-8, vol. 3 (1988): aras 9-12.]

1983-87 (Ed.) कलिकालसर्वज्ञ आचार्यभगवत् श्री हेमचन्द्रसूरि विरचितम् द्व्याश्रय महाकाव्यम् श्री अभयतिलकगणिविरचितया टीकया समेतम् *Dvyāśraya Mahākāvyaṁ by Acharya Hemachandrasuri with a Commentary by Shri Abhayatilaka Gani* 2 volumes (I [cantos 1-10]: Manfarā [Kutch]: Shri Manfarā Jain Swetambar Moortipoojaka Sangh,

II (cantos 11-20): Sanchore [Rajasthan]: Shri Sanchore Swetambar Moortipoojak Jain Sangh).

Jani, Jaydev A.

1991 "Pāṇinian impact on Bhojavyākaraṇa of Mahopādhyāya Vinayasāgara", Festschrift Bhattacharya, pp. 51-55.

Jayaswal, Sitala Prasada

1995 वैयाकरणसिद्धान्तलघुमञ्जूषायाः स्फोटान्तभागीयरत्नप्रभाटीकायाः समालोचनात्मकमध्ययनम् (Delhi: Parimal Publications). [Originally a Sampurnanand Sanskrit University doctoral dissertation. In Sanskrit.]

Jha, Baidya Natha

1990 *A Glimpse of the History of Sanskrit Grammar* (Varanasi: Kishor Vidya Niketan).

Jha, Girish K.

1992 "'*akaḥ savarṇe dīrghaḥ*' — revisited (Pāṇini 6.1.101)", VIJ 30:45-50.

1996 "Palatal law and Pāṇini", JOIB 45:149-156.

1997 "Nāgeśa on *varṇasphoṭa*", Conference 1997a:421-422.

Jhā, Satīśa Candra

1985 कात्यायनवार्तिकानां भाषाशास्त्रीयमध्ययनम् (*A Linguistic Study of the Vārtikas of Kātyāyana*) (Muzaffarpur: Bihar Manisha) [In Sanskrit.]

Jha, Shankarji

1995 *Sanskrit Grammar, Linguistic and Philosophical Analysis* (Chandigarh: Arun Publishing House).

1997 "Analysis of 'time' in the light of the grammatic philosophy of Sanskrit", Conference 1997a:422-423.

Jhā, Śivakānta

1994 पाणिनीयव्याकरणे स्त्रीप्रत्ययानामध्ययनम् (Jaipur: Hansa Prakashan). [In Sanskrit.]

Jha, Sukheshwar

1997 "Reappraisal of Bhaṭṭoji with special reference to his Siddhāntakaumudī", Conference 1997a:423-424.

Jha, Vashishtha N.

1980 "Naiyāyikas' concept of *pada* and *vākya*", in: S. D. Joshi (1980), pp. 85-94.

1986 *Studies in Language, Logic, and Epistemology* (Delhi: Pratibha Prakashan). [Chapter 5 (54-69): "On ekārthībhāva and vyapekṣā"; see also 1991.]

1989 (Ed.) *New Horizons of Research in Indology* (*Silver Jubilee Volume*) (= PCASS E 10) (Pune: University of Poona). [Silver jubilee volume of the Centre of Advanced Study in Sanskrit, Pune.]

1991 "On ekārthībhāva and vyapekṣā", Festschrift S. D. Joshi, pp. 209-229. [See also 1986.]

1992 *A Linguistic Analysis of the Ṛgveda-Padapāṭha* (= Pre-Pāṇinian Grammatical Traditions [Part-II]) (= SGDOS 192) (Delhi: Sri Satguru Publications). [Revised version of 1974 University of Poona Ph.D. thesis. Section I.6 (56-61): 'Pāṇini and Śākalya'.]

Jitasingh "Khokharaḥ"

1988 "पाणिनेः अष्टाध्याय्यामुपवर्णिता आचार्याः", VS 25.2-4 (= डा° चारुदेव-शास्त्रि-स्मृति-विशेषाङ्कः):129-132. [In Sanskrit.]

Joshi, Dayashankar Mohanlal

1981 "Sentence and transformation in Pāṇini", Festschrift Chatterji, pp. 116-121.

Joshi, Madhav Ganesh, Nipanikar (Ed.)

1992 स्वरयुक्ता अष्टाध्यायी (Āḷaṁdī: the author). [1-65: accented text of the Aṣṭādhyāyī, 66-126: unaccented text of sūtras alphabetically arranged. Introduction (unnumbered pages) in English and Sanskrit by S. D. Joshi.]

Joshi, Sivaram Dattatreya

1976a "Sanskrit grammar", in: *Rāmakrishna Gopal Bhandarkar as an Indologist : A Symposium* (ed. R. N. Dandekar) (Poona: BORI), pp. 113-142.

1976b "Pāṇini's rules: 1.4.49, 1.4.50 and 1.4.51", CASS-St. 3:59-71.

1978 "The ordering of rules in Pāṇini's grammar", ABORI 58-59 (Diamond Jubilee Volume): 667-674.

1980a (Ed.) *Proceedings of the Winter Institute on Ancient Indian Theories on Sentence-Meaning* (*held in March 1979*) (= PCASS E 6) (Pune: University of Poona).

1980b "Kauṇḍa Bhaṭṭa on sphoṭa", Festschrift Gaurinath Sastri, pp.

221-235.

1980c "The contribution of R. G. Bhandarkar to the study of Sanskrit grammar", Festschrift Ingalls, pp. 33-60.

1981 "Kauṇḍa Bhaṭṭa on the meaning of compounds", Festschrift K. Kunjunni Raja, pp. 369-389.

1982a "The functions of *asiddhatva* and *sthānivadbhāva* in Pāṇini's *Aṣṭādhyāyī*", CASS-St. 6:153-168.

1982b "The reflexive constructions in Pāṇini", CASS-St. 6:199-217.

1982c "Pāṇini's rules: 2.2.11 and 2.4.2", in: Dharmadhikari (1982), pp. 123-128.

1982d "Presidential address, Indian linguistics section", PAIOC 30 (Visva Bharati, Santiniketan) (Pune: BORI), pp. 91-111.

1983 "Pāṇini's rule 1.3.67", Festschrift Sreekrishna Sarma, pp. 63-74.

1984 "The role of boundaries in the Aṣṭādhyāyī", Festschrift Dandekar, pp. 181-186.

1985 "Sentence-structure according to Pāṇini", Festschrift Dandekar, pp. 14-26. [= S. D. Joshi (1969c).]

1989a "The rejection of P.1.1.58: a confirmation of the exclusively positive aspect of sthānivadbhāva", ABORI 69(1988): 217-228.

1989b "Patañjali's views on *Apaśabdas*", in: Caillat (1989), pp. 267-274.

1990a "Koṇḍa (or Kauṇḍa) Bhaṭṭa", in: Coward and K. Kunjunni Raja (1990), pp. 255-308.

1990b "पाणिनेः अष्टाध्यायी", Festschrift Kavīśvara, pp. 32-35. [In Sanskrit.]

1993 "Kauṇḍa Bhaṭṭa on the Meaning of Sanskrit Verbs (1)", Saṃbhāṣā 14:1-40. [Part 1 of S. D. Joshi (1960).]

1995 "Kauṇḍa Bhaṭṭa on the Meaning of Sanskrit Verbs (2)", Saṃbhāṣā 16:1-66. [Part 2 of S. D. Joshi (1960).]

1997 "Kauṇḍa Bhaṭṭa on the Meaning of Sanskrit Verbs (3)", Saṃbhāṣā 18:1-34. [Final part of S. D. Joshi (1960).]

Joshi, S. D. and Saroja Bhate

1983 "The role of the particle *ca* in the interpretation of the Aṣṭādhyāyī", in: Joshi and Laddu (1983), pp. 167-227.

1984 *The Fundamentals of Anuvṛtti* (= PCASS B 9) (Pune: University of Poona).

Joshi, S. D. and Paul Kiparsky

1979 "Siddha and asiddha in Pāṇinian phonology", in: D. Dinnsen (ed.), *Current Approaches to Phonological Theory* (Bloomington: Indiana University Press), pp. 223-250.

Joshi, S. D. and S. D. Laddu (Eds.)

1983 *Proceedings of the International Seminar on Studies in the Aṣṭādhyāyī of Pāṇini (held in July 1981)* (= PCASS E 9) (Pune: University of Poona).

Joshi, S. D. and J.A.F. Roodbergen

1973 *Patañjali's Vyākaraṇa-mahābhāṣya : Tatpuruṣāhnika (P. 2.2.2-2.2.23), Text, Translation and Notes* (= PCASS C 7) (Pune: University of Poona).

1974 *Patañjali's Vyākaraṇa-mahābhāṣya: Bahuvrīhidvandvāhnika (P. 2.2.23-2.2.38), Text, Translation and Notes* (= PCASS C 9) (Pune: University of Poona).

1975 *Patañjali's Vyākaraṇa-mahābhāṣya : Kārakāhnika (P. 1.4.23 -1.4.55), Text, Translation and Notes* (= PCASS C 10) (Pune: University of Poona).

1976 *Patañjali's Vyākaraṇa-mahābhāṣya : Anabhihitāhnika (P. 2.3.1-2.3.7), Text, Translation and Notes* (= PCASS C 11) (Pune: University of Poona).

1980 *Patañjali's Vyākaraṇa-mahābhāṣya : Vibhaktyāhnika* (P. *2.3.18-2.3.45), Text, Translation and Notes* (= PCASS C 12) (Pune: University of Poona).

1981 *Patañjali's Vyākaraṇa-mahābhāṣya : Prātipadikārtha-śeṣāhnika (P. 2.3.46-2.3.71), Text, Translation and Notes* (= PCASS C 14) (Pune: University of Poona).

1983 "The structure of the Aṣṭādhyāyī in historical perspective", in: Joshi and Laddu (1983), pp. 59-95.

1985 "On Pāṇini 1.1.56", Festschrift Ingalls, pp. 469-477.

1986 *Patañjali's Vyākaraṇa-mahābhāṣya : Paspaśāhnika : Introduction, Text, Translation and Notes* (= PCASS C 15) (Pune: University of Poona).

1987 “On siddha, asiddha, and sthānivat”, ABORI 68:541-549.

1989 *Patañjali's Vyākaraṇa-Mahābhāṣya : Sthānivadbhāvāhnika, Part 1, Edited with Translation and Notes* (Pune: BORI).

1991 *The Aṣṭādhyāyī of Pāṇini with Translation and Explanatory Notes, Volume I (1.1.1-1.1.75)* (Delhi: Sahitya Akademi).

1991-92 “Evidence in the *Kāśikāvṛtti* for an authentic Pāṇinian tradition independent of Patañjali”, Festschrift Katre, pp. 131-135.

1992 “On ekaśeṣa”, Festschrift Ghatage, pp. 101-110.

1993a *The Aṣṭādhyāyī of Pāṇini with Translation and Explanatory Notes, Volume II (1.2.1-1.2.73)* (Delhi: Sahitya Akademi).

1993b “The *siddha*-principle as presupposed by some *Pāṇinisūtras*”, ABORI 72-73 (1991 & 1992):47-58.

1994a *The Aṣṭādhyāyī of Pāṇini with Translation and Explanatory Notes, Volume III (1.3.1-1.3.93)* (Delhi: Sahitya Akademi).

1994b “On Pāṇini's 1.4.23 kārake”, Festschrift Chatterjee, pp. 82-90.

1995 *The Aṣṭādhyāyī of Pāṇini with Translation and Explanatory Notes, Volume IV (1.4.1-1.4.110)* (Delhi: Sahitya Akademi).

Joshi, Venkatesh Laxman (Venkateshshastri)

1980a “Pāṇini and Pāṇinīyas on saṁhitā”, in: Koparkar and Thite (1980), pp. 20-26. [See V. L. Joshi (1965, 1969).]

1980b “Pāṇini and Pāṇinīyas on parasavarṇa”, in: Koparkar and Thite (1980), pp. 27-28.

1980c “अनुस्वारस्य परसवर्णविषये पाणिनिः पाणिनीयाश्च”, in: Koparkar and Thite (1980), pp. 29-33. [In Sanskrit.]

1980d ““Parā vāk” and Sanskrit grammarians”, in: Koparkar and Thite (1980), pp. 34-35.

1980e “नागेशभट्टैः स्वीकृता “परा वाक्””, in: Koparkar and Thite (1980), pp. 36-39. [In Sanskrit.]

1980f “The significance of the word “bhāṣā” in the Aṣṭādhyāyī”, in: Koparkar and Thite (1980), pp. 40-48.

1980g “Some historical observations in the descriptive grammar of Pāṇini”, in: Koparkar and Thite (1980), pp. 49-59.

1980h "The ten predecessors mentioned in the Aṣṭādhyāyī", in: Koparkar and Thite (1980), pp. 60-65.

1980i "Reduplicated forms treated as basic roots (dhātu) in the Aṣṭādhyāyī", in: Koparkar and Thite (1980), pp. 66-69.

1980j "'Even Homer nods' (The fault of '*anyonyāśraya*' in the Aṣṭādhyāyī and a new suggestion to avoid it)", in: Koparkar and Thite (1980), pp. 70-78.

1980k "An introduction to the last age in Pāṇini's school", in: Koparkar and Thite (1980), pp. 79-90.

1980l "Some words from the Bhāṣāvṛtti of Puruṣottama Deva, translated by Professor L. Renou", in: Koparkar and Thite (1980), pp. 91-94.

1980m "A short note on the root niñj", in: Koparkar and Thite (1980), pp. 99-101.

1980n "The word saṅghatitha and Pāṇini", in: Koparkar and Thite (1980), pp. 102-106. [In Sanskrit with English summary (102).]

1980o "Authorship of the Laghu Śabdaratna", in: Koparkar and Thite (1980), pp. 107-161.

Junnarkar, P. J.

1977-88 *An introduction to Pāṇini* 4 volumes (1977, 1980, 1983, 1988) (Vadodara: Shanti Dighe).

Kahrs, Eivind

1992a "Exploring the *Saddanīti*", JPTS 1992:1-212.

1992b "What is a *tadbhava* word?", IIJ 35:225-249.

Kak, Subhash

1987 "The Pāṇinian approach to natural language processing", IJAR 1987.1:117-130.

Kansara, N. M.

1989 "The Vaidika vyākaraṇa of Bhojadeva", JOIB 38:309-313.

Kapil Dev Shastri

1975 नागेशभट्ट-कृत वैयाकरणसिद्धान्तपरमलघुमञ्जूषा (मूल ग्रन्थ, अनुवाद एवं समीक्षात्मकव्याख्या) (Kurukshetra: Kurukshetra University).

1985 नागेशभट्टप्रणीता वैयाकरणसिद्धान्तमञ्जूषा *Nāgeśa Bhaṭṭa's Vaiyākaraṇasiddhāntamañjūṣā* (Kurukshetra: Vishal Publications). [Appendixes: I: Vaiyākaraṇa-siddhāntamañjūṣā *versus* Vaiyākaraṇa-bhūṣaṇa (273-352), II: Vaiyākaraṇasiddhāntamañjūṣā *versus* Vaiyākaraṇasiddhānta-laghumañjūṣā (353-499).]

Kapoor, Kapil

1991-92 "Pāṇini vyākaraṇa: questions of theory and order", Festschrift Katre, pp. 137-145.

1997 "What is the function of grammar? Patañjali, Buddhists and Kumārila Bhaṭṭa", Conference 1997a:426-427.

Kar, Dinabandhu

*1980 *Semantic Basis of the Aṣṭādhyāyī.* [University of Poona Ph. D. dissertation, referred to in Dinabandhu Kar (1991:238 note 1).]

1991 "Parts of speech in Pāṇini", Festschrift S. D. Joshi, pp. 231-238.

Kar, Yashodhara

1994 "The role of the ekasaṁjñādhikāra", Festschrift Bhagwat, pp. 76-87.

1997 "A note on *karaṇa* and linguistics", Conference 1997a:428.

Katre, Sumitra Mangesh

1981 *A Glossary of Grammatical Elements and Operations in the Aṣṭādhyāyī* (Mysore: Central Institute of Indian Languages).

1987 *Aṣṭādhyāyī of Pāṇini* (Austin: University of Texas Press). [Indian edition, 1989: Delhi: Motilal Banarsidass. The reprint corrects typographical errors.]

1988-89 "The governing rules saṁ-hitā-yām (6.1.22; 3.114; 8.2.108) in Pāṇini", Festschrift R. V. Joshi, pp. 1- 4. [Punctuation as shown.]

1989 "Pāṇini and Indo-Aryan", in: V. N. Jha (1989), pp. 85-89.

Kelly, John D.

1993 "Meaning and the limits of analysis: Bhartṛhari and the Buddhists, and post-structuralism", in Bhate and Bronkhorst (1993), pp. 171-194.

1994 "Bhartṛhari's gentle erudition: śakti, apoddhāra, saṃgraha and the task of a grammarian", Festschrift Bhagwat, pp. 88-106.

Khanduri, Satyanarayan Shastri
1987 पद-वाक्य-प्रमाणज्ञस्य श्रीभर्तृहरेः वाक्यपदीयम् [ब्रह्मकाण्डम्] श्रीवामदेवाचार्यस्य संस्कृत-हिन्दी-'प्रतिभया'व्याख्यया समन्वितम् सम्पादकः आचार्य पं॰ सत्यनारायणशास्त्री खण्डूड़ी *Vākyapadīyam [Brahmakāṇḍam] of Bhartri Hari the Great Scholar of Pada, Vākya and Pramāṇa, with 'Pratibhā' Sanskrit-Hindi Commentaries by Shri Vamdev Acharya, Edited by Acharya Pt. Satyanarayan Shastri Khanduri* (= KDSS 97) (Varanasi: Krishnadas Academy).

Khare, G. H.
1984 "Why are there two ह-s in the *Māheśvara-sūtras*?", ABORI 64(1983): 255-257.

Kiparsky, Paul
1979 *Pāṇini as a Variationist* (= CSL 7) (Cambridge, Pune: MIT and Poona University Press, in collaboration with the Centre of Advanced Study in Sanskrit, University of Poona). [Also published as PCASS B 6. S. D. Joshi is listed as editor of the volume.]
1982 *Some Theoretical Problems in Pāṇini's Grammar* (Professor K. V. Abhyankar Memorial Lectures [Second Series]) (= BORIS 16) (Pune: BORI). [I: Case, control, and ellipsis (1-54), II: The Vedic and Pāṇinian accent systems (55-76), III: The ordering of rules in Pāṇini's grammar (77-121).]
1987 "What is siddha?", ABORI 68: 295-303.
1991a "On Pāṇinian studies: a reply to Cardona", JIP 19: 331-367.
1991b "Economy and the construction of the śivasūtras", Festschrift S. D. Joshi, pp. 239-261.
1995 "Pāṇinian linguistics", in: Koerner and Asher (1995), section IV (Antiquity-India), pp. 59-65.

Klein, Jared S.
1985 *Toward a Discourse Grammar of the Rigveda, Volume I : Coordinate Conjunction, Part 1 : Introduction, ca, utá* (Heidelberg: Winter).

Koerner, E. F. K. and Ronald E. Asher (Eds.)
1995 *Concise History of the Language Sciences from the Sumerians to the Cognitivists* (Oxford: Pergamon).

Koparkar, D. G. and G. U. Thite (Eds.)
1980 *Problems in Sanskrit Grammar by* (*late*) *Pt. Venkateshshastri Joshi* (Pune: Dastane Ramchandra and Co.).

Krishnamacharya, K. A.
1985 "केषाञ्चिच्छब्दानां प्रयोगविषये पाणिनिपतञ्जल्योः मतभेदः", in: Dandekar and Navathe (1985), pp. 216-218. [In Sanskrit.]

Krishnamacharyulu, K. V. R. (see also Ramakrisnamacharyulu, K. V.)
1994 "Pāṇinian linguisitics and computational linguistics", in: Keshab Chandra Dash (1994), pp. 122-135.

Krishnamurti, Bh., Colin P. Masica and Anajani K. Sinha (Eds.)
1986 *South Asian Languages* : *Structure, Convergence and Diglossia* (= MLDB Series in Linguistics III) (Delhi: Motilal Banarsidass).

Kshirsagar, V. K.
*1991 *Pāṇini — Explained and Defended* (Bombay: Shri Sudhir Damle). [Appendix A: A list of technical terms, Appendix B: A list of suffixes, Appendix C: A list of augments and substitutes. Information supplied by Ashok Aklujkar.]

Kudo, Noriyuki
1994 "Why is "**jñāyate ghaṭaḥ svayam eva*" not accepted? — karmakartari constructions discussed by Navyavaiyākaraṇas", Festschrift Bhagwat, pp. 107-121.
1996 "A study on Sanskrit syntax (1): *Śabdakaustubha* on P. 1.4.23", Saṃbhāṣā 17:27-64.
1997 "A study on Sanskrit syntax (2): *Śabdakaustubha* on P. 1.4.24 [*Apādāna* (1)]", Saṃbhāṣā 18:143-181.

Kulkarni, Nirmala R.
1995 *A Grammatical Analysis of the Taittirīya-Padapāṭha* (Pre-Pāṇinian Grammatical Traditions [Part-II]) (= SGDOS 192) (Delhi: Sri Satguru Publications).

Kumar, Aravinda: See Aravinda Kumar.

Kumar, Avanindra: See Avanindra Kumar.

Kumar, Dharmendra: See Dharmendra Kumar.

Kumārī, Añjanī: See Añjanī Kumārī.

Kunjunni Raja, K: see Raja, K. Kunjunni

Laddu, Sureshachandra Dnyaneshwar

1974 *Evolution of the Sanskrit Language from Pāṇini to Patañjali : Primary Formations* (*Pāṇini* 3.1.91 — 3.2.83) (Poona: University of Poona).

1980a "A lexical analysis of 'vākya' as used by Kātyāyana and Patañjali", CASS-St. 5:199-207.

1980b "The concept of *vākya* according to Kātyāyana and Patañjali", in: S. D. Joshi (1980a), pp. 223-228.

1982 "A reconsideration of the history of the *Mahābhāṣya*", CASS-St. 6:187-197. [See 1985b.]

1983 "Pāṇini's *nipātana* and the factor of accent", in: Joshi and Laddu (1983), pp. 229-232.

*1984/86 "Contribution towards the date of the grammarian Patañjali", Ṛtam 16-18:193-195.

1985a "The laukika and yājñika accentuation with the munitraya of Sanskrit grammar", Festschrift Dandekar, pp. 93-111. [= Laddu (1969a).]

1985b "A reconsideration of the history of the Mahābhāṣya", in: Dandekar and Navathe (1985), pp. 218-220. [Continuation: 1982.]

1986 "Contribution towards the date of the grammarian Patañjali", Festschrift Sinha, pp. 193-195.

1987 "How early were the handbooks on derivation (*prakriyā*) in Sanskrit grammar?", ABORI 68:593-601.

1990 "An interpolation in Kātyāyana's vārttikapāṭha", ABORI 70 (1989):312-316.

Laddu, S. D. and Kamal Lochan Kar

1983 *A Select Bibliography on the Development of Sanskrit Language Compiled by Prof. S. D. Laddu and Kamal Lochan Kar, Edited by S. P. Sharma.* [No publisher is named.]

Lalithambal, K. S.

1995 *Dharmakīrti's Rūpāvatāra : A Critical Study* (= BIB 153) (Delhi: Sri Satguru Publications).

Le Mée, Jean

1988-89 "Pāṇinīyas and engineers", Festschrift R. V. Joshi, pp.

113-121.

Limaye, Vishnu Prabhakar

1976 "Pāṇini in Dārila in *Kauśikasūtra*", Festschrift K. A. Subrahmania Iyer, pp. 335-352.

1978 "*Ākumāraṁ yaśaḥ Pāṇineḥ* corrupt for *ākumāri yaśaḥ Pāṇineḥ*?", ABORI 58-59 (Diamond Jubilee Volume):727-732.

Limaye, V. P., G. B. Palsule, and V. B. Bhagavat

1985 *Mahābhāṣyadīpikā of Bhartṛhari, Fascicle II : Āhnika 5, Critically Edited* (= BORIS 23) (Pune: BORI).

Lindtner, Chr.

1993 "Linking up Bhartṛhari and the Bauddhas", in: Bhate and Bronkhorst (1993), pp. 195-213.

Mahadeva Sastri and Panditaratnam K. Rangacharya (Eds.)

1984 *Mādhavīyadhātuvṛtti of Sri Sāyaṇācārya* श्री सायणाचार्यविरचिता माधवीयधातुवृत्तिः Volume I, second edition (= ORIS 145) (Mysore: Oriental Research Institute). [Through *dīkṣ**a*** of the bhvādigaṇa (I.600).]

Mahavir

1978 *Pāṇini as Grammarian* (*with special reference to compound formations*) (Delhi: Bharatiya Vidya Prakashan). [Originally a Ph. D. thesis, Kurukshetra University, 1971.]

1984 *Samartha Theory of Pāṇini and Sentence Derivation* (Delhi: Munshiram Manoharlal).

1997 "Linguistic models of generative syntax in Pāṇini: a new discovery", Conference 1997a:433-434.

Makkai, Adam and William M. Christie, Jr.

1981 "Whose intellectual ancestor was Pāṇini — really?", Festschrift Chatterji, pp. 134-144.

Manyank, Manjul

1991 "Pāṇini's acquaintance with the Atharvaveda", in: Deshpande (1991a), pp. 32-45.

Matilal, Bimal Krishna

1983 "Some comments of Patañjali under 1.2.64", in: Joshi and Laddu (1983), pp. 119-126.

1985 *Logic, Language and Reality : An Introduction to Indian*

Philosophical Studies (Delhi: Motilal Banarsidass). [Chapter 5 (372-430): "Interaction of grammar and philosophy".]

1988 "Śābdabodha and the problem of knowledge-representation in Sanskrit", JIP 16:107-122.

1990a *The Word and the World : India's Contribution to the Study of Language* (Delhi: Oxford University Press).

1990b "On Bhartṛhari's linguistic insight", in: Matilal and Bilimoria (1990), pp. 3-13.

1991 "Bhavānanda on 'What is a kāraka?'", Festschrift S. D. Joshi, pp. 263-282.

1992 "The sphoṭa doctrine of the Indian grammarians", in: Dascal et al. (1992), pp. 609-620.

Matilal, Bimal Krishna and Purusottama Bilimoria (Eds.)

1990 *Sanskrit and Related Studies : Contemporary Researches and Reflections* (= SGDOS 84) (Delhi: Sri Satguru Publications).

Mazumdar, Pradip Kumar

1977 *The Philosophy of Language in the Light of Pāṇinian and Mīmāṁsā Schools of Indian Philosophy* (Calcutta: Sanskrit Pustak Bhandar). [Originally a Jadav University Ph. D. thesis entitled *Some Aspects of the Philosophy of Sanskrit Grammar*.]

Medharthy, Anandaprakash

1993 वार्त्तिक-प्रकाशः (काशिकास्थ-वार्त्तिकानां व्याख्या *Vārttika-Prakāśaḥ* [*Explanation of Kāśikā-Vārttikās*] (= KSS 246) (Varanasi: Chaukhambha Sanskrit Sansthan). [In Sanskrit.]

Meenakshi, K.

1984 "Grammatical method in Aṣṭādhyāyī and Tokpappiyam", IJDL 13:1-16.

1991a "The genitive in Pāṇini and in epic Sanskrit", in: Hock (1991a), pp. 145-152.

1991b "Vedic infinitives and Pāṇini", in: Deshpande (1991a), pp. 46-54.

Mehendale, Madhukar Anant

1983 "On Pāṇini 1.3.41", ABORI 63(1982):225-226.

1986 "On the Bṛhaddevatā 2.102-103", IIJ 29:117-120.

Mishra, Hari Mohan

1975-76 "A reappraisal of Pāṇini", IT 3-4.317-320.

1986 *A Critique of Pāṇini's Grammar* (Patna: Anupam Publications).

Mishra, Jayamanta

1994 "Pāṇini's approach to chandas", Festschrift Chatterjee, pp. 91-92.

Mishra, Madhusudan

1966 *A Critical Study of the Vārttikas of Kātyāyana* (Delhi: Eastern Book Linkers). [Originally a University of Poona doctoral dissertation.]

Mishra, Mandan, Rudra Deva Tripathi and Brahma Mitra Awasthi (Eds.)

1984 अनुसन्धान-प्रकाशन-विभागीया त्रैमासिकी शोध-पत्रिका शोध-प्रभा [षष्ठविश्वसंस्कृतसम्मेलनविशेषाङ्कः] *Shodha-Prabha, A Quarterly Research-Journal of the Department of Research and Publication (A Special-Issue) on Sixth World-Sanskrit-Conference* (Delhi: Shri Lal Bahadur Shastri Kendriya Sanskrit Vidyapeetha).

Mishra, Rajnish Kumar

1996 *Buddhist Theory of Meaning and Literary Analysis : An Example Study* [Master of Philosophy thesis, Jawaharlal Nehru University, unpublished; chapter 1 (7-83): Philosophy of language and competing Indian theories of meaning.]

Miśra, Ādyāprasāda (Ed.)

1988 कौण्डभट्टविरचितो वैयाकरणभूषणसारः 'सावित्री'-हिन्दी-व्याख्योपेतः *Vaiyākaraṇabhūṣaṇasāra of Kauṇḍabhaṭṭa with 'Sāvitrī' Hindi Commentary* (= GJGM 11) (Varanasi: Sampurnanand Sanskrit University).

Miśra, Devaswarupa

1978 महाभाष्यनिगूढाकूतयः *Mahābhāṣyanigūḍhākūtayaḥ* (= SBS 22) (Varanasi: Sampurnanand Sanskrit University). [In Sanskrit.]

Miśra, Gopabandhu

1997 "कृत्-तद्धितप्रयोगे उद्देश्यद्वयस्य समीक्षणम्", Conference 1997b:191. [In Sanskrit.]

Miśra (Mishra), Harsha Nath

1974 चान्द्रव्याकरणवृत्तेः समालोचनात्मकमध्ययनम् *A Critical Study of*

Chandra Vyakaran Vritti (= SVGM 22) (Delhi: Lal Bahadur Shastri Sanskrita Vidyapitha). [Delhi University Ph. D. dissertation. In Sanskrit.]

Miśra, Muralīdhara

1977-80 रामचन्द्राचार्यप्रणीता प्रक्रियाकौमुदी श्रीकृष्णविरचितया प्रकाशव्याख्यया पं° मुरलीधरमिश्रकृतया रश्मिटिप्पण्या च संवलिता *Prakriyākaumudī by Rāmacandrācārya with Prakāśa by Śrīkrişṇa, Edited with his 'Raśmi' by Pt. Muralīdhara Miśra* 3 volumes (= SBGN 111- 112) (Varanasi: Sampurnanand Sanskrit University). [I-II: 1977, III: 1980. For volume I, the series number appears as 112 on the dustjacket and 111 on the title pages; for the other volumes the series number appears as 112.]

Miśra, Prabhākara (Ed.)

1982 श्रीकौण्डभट्टविरचितो वैयाकरणभूषणसारः प्रभाकरीहिन्दी तथा संस्कृतटीकासहितः (Varanasi: Arabinda Miśra and Makaranda Miśra).

Miśra, Rāmamanohara

1983 भूषणसार-परमलघुमञ्जूषयोः सिद्धान्तानां समीक्षा *Bhūṣaṇasāra-paramalaghumañjūṣayoḥ siddhāntānāṃ samīkṣā* (= SBS 32) (Varanasi: Sampurnanand Sanskrit University). [In Sanskrit.]

Miśra, Rāmanārāyaṇa

1991 स्फोटमीमांसा *Sfotamīmāṁsā* (= Laghu-Granthamālā 47) (Varanasi: Sampurnanand Sanskrit University). ['Sfotamīmāṁsā' is the Romanization which appears on the English title page.]

Miśra, Śivakumāra

1992 "वर्ण-समाम्नाय के वर्ण-क्रम की व्यवस्था", Festschrift Kamlesh Kumari Kulshreshtha, pp. 80-85. [In Hindi.]

Miśra, Vidhātā

1988-89 "धात्वर्थपरामर्शः", Festschrift R. V. Joshi, pp. 317 - 321. [In Sanskrit.]

Misra, Vidya Niwas (Ed.)

1987 कौण्डभट्टप्रणीतं वैयाकरणभूषणम् भाग-१ *Kauṇḍabhaṭṭa's Vaiyākaraṇabhūṣaṇam (A Treatise on Philosophy of Grammar), Vol. I* (Delhi, Varanasi: Bharatiya Vidya Prakashan). [Complete text (1-254) with notes (255-412) and index of kārikās (413-414.]

Miśra, Viśvanātha

1993 "निपातार्थ-विचारः", VS 30.4:57-63. [In Sanskrit.]

1996 "वाचमर्थोऽनुधावति", Festschrift Shri Niwas Shastri, pp. 202-204. [In Sanskrit.]

Mukherji, Gurusankar

1992 "Some linguistic problems: sarūpāṇām ekaśeṣa ekavibhaktau", Festschrift Mukherji II, pp. 360-368.

Mukhopadhyaya, P. K.

1994 "Indian theories of śābdabodha and knowledge representation in AI", in: Keshab Chandra Dash (1994), pp. 9-51.

Murti, M. Srimannarayana: see Srimannarayana Murti, M.

Murti, P. Srirama

1992 "Pratibhā, sphoṭa and dhvani", Festschrift Kelkar, pp. 51-56.

Naradeva Śāstrī

1987 पाणिनीय-शब्दार्थसम्बन्ध-सिद्धान्तः (Delhi: Pipaṭhiṣu-Prācyavidyā-Pratiṣṭhānam). [In Sanskrit.]

1988 "पाणिनीयवाक्यस्वरूपसमीक्षा", Festschrift Charu Deva Shastri, pp. 53-72. [In Sanskrit.]

Narang, Satya Pal

1988-89 "A dialect of Sialkot in Pāṇini", Festschrift R. V. Joshi, pp. 197-210.

Narasimhacharya, M. S.

1973-83 *Commentaires sur le Mahābhāṣya de Patañjali et le Pradīpa de Kaiyaṭa* : *Mahābhāṣyapradīpavyākhyānāni* (= PIFI 51, 1-10.) (Pondichéry: Institut Français d'Indologie). [I (1973): adhyāya 1, pāda 1, āhnikas 1-4; II (1975): adhyāya 1, pāda 1, āhnikas 5-7; III (1976): adhyāya 1, pāda 1, āhnikas 8-9; IV (1977): adhyāya 1, pādas 2-4; V (1978): adhyāya 2; VI (1979): adhyāya 3; VII (1980): adhyāya 4; VIII (1981): adhyāya 5; IX (1982): adhyāya 6; X (1983): adhyāya 7-8. The commentaries are: Rāmacandra Sarasvatī's Laghu-vivaraṇa, Īśvarānanda's Vivaraṇa, Annambhaṭṭa's Uddyotana, Śivarāmendra Sarasvatī's Ratnaprakāśa, the Nārāyaṇīya by Nārāyaṇa, student of Dharmarāja, and Nārāyaṇīya by Nārāyaṇa, son of Devaśarman. A chart in vol.

X (ix) shows which parts contain which commentaries. Volume X contains a long introduction on the commentaries (xi-xciii) by Narasimhacharya: Introduction aux commentaires du Mahābhāṣya et du Pradīpa.]

1986 *Commentaires sur le Mahābhāṣya de Patañjali et le Pradīpa de Kaiyaṭa : Mahābhāṣyapradīpaprakāśa par Pravartakopādhyāya* (= PIFI 73) (Pondichéry: Institut Français d'Indologie). [From beginning to the end of the second adhyāya.]

Narayan, Meenambal

1991 *Nāgeśa and the Mahābhāṣya* (= SGDOS 110) (Delhi: Sri Satguru Publications).

Nene, Gopāla Śāstrī

1987 महामहोपाध्यायभट्टनागेशकृतो लघुशब्देन्दुशेखरः महामहोपाध्यायपण्डित-प्रवरश्रीभैरवमिश्रविरचितया चन्द्रकलया टीकया समेतः ... 'पेण्डसे' इत्युपनामकेन विष्णुतनूजेन नरहरिशर्मणा बृहद्भूमिकया टिप्पण्यादिभिश्च संपूरितो जगन्नाथशास्त्रिनिर्मितटिप्पणीसहितश्च संशोधितः ... पं° गोपालशास्त्री नेने महोदयेन संशोधितः परिष्कृतश्च *Laghuśabdenduśekhara by Nāgojibhaṭṭa with a Commentary Chandrakalā by Bhairava Miśra, Edited by Narahari Śāstrī Peṇḍse, Re-edited by Gopāla Śāstrī Nene* (= KSS 5) 2 volumes (Varanasi: Chaukhambha Sanskrit Sansthan). [I: through avyayībhāva section, II: to end.]

Nipanikar, Madhav Ganesh Joshi: see Joshi, Madhav Ganesh, Nipanikar.

van Nooten, Barend

1983 "Vivakṣā-, or intention to speak, as a linguistic principle", in: Joshi and Laddu (1983), pp. 43-52.

Oberlies, Thomas

1989 *Studie zum Cāndravyākaraṇa : Eine kritische Bearbeitung von Candra IV.5.52-148 und V.2* (= ANIS 38) (Stuttgart: Steiner). [Revised version of 1986 doctoral dissertation, University of Tübingen. In Oberlies (1996:316), this is referred to as Studien zum Cāndravyākaraṇa I.]

1992 "Verschiedene neu-entdeckte Texte des Cāndravyākaraṇa und ihre Verfasser (Studien zum Cāndravyākaraṇa II)", StII 16/17:161-184.

1996 "Das zeitliche und ideengeschichtliche Verhältnis der Cāndra-Vṛtti zu anderen V(ai)yākaraṇas (Studien zum Cāndravyākaraṇa III)", Festschrift Thieme, pp. 265-317.

Oetke, Claus

1986 Review of Bandini (1980), ZDMG 136:150-165.

1997 "On the so-called Bhartṛhari-paradox", Conference 1997a:250-251.

Ogawa, Hideyo

1987 "The use of the particle *eva* in the Aṣṭādhyāyī", JIBS 16.35:1009-1006 (12-15).

1988 "Mahābhāṣya ad P 1.3.1 (1)", HUSFL 47:52-74. [In Japanese with English summary (73-74).]

1989 "Mahābhāṣya ad P 1.3.1 (2)", HUSFL 48:62-81. [In Japanese with English summary (81).]

1990 *Action and Language — A Study of Sanskrit Semantics* : *The Meanings of Verbal Roots* (HUSFL 49 Special Issue No. 3). [In Japanese with English summary (117-119).]

1992 "Mahābhāṣya ad P 1.3.1 (3)", HUSFL 51:40-58. [In Japanese with English summary (58).]

1993 "Mahābhāṣya ad P 1.3.1 (4)", HUSFL 53:21-41. [In Japanese with English summary (40-41).]

1994 "Mahābhāṣya ad P 1.3.1 (5)", HUSFL 54:41-61. [In Japanese with English summary (60-61).]

Palsule, Gajanana Balakrishna

1982 "Two Vedic rules of Pāṇini: 8.3.47 and 8.3.10", in: Dharmadhikari (1982), pp. 185-188.

1984 "*Devānāṁ-priyaḥ*: has it any Vedic antecedents?", Festschrift Dandekar, pp. 313-317.

1985a *Mahābhāṣyadīpikā of Bhartṛhari, Fascicle I* : *Āhnika III, Critically Edited* (= BORIS 22) (Pune: BORI).

1985b "Patañjali's interpretation of *RV* 10.71.2", Festschrift Dandekar, pp. 27-29. [= Palsule (1969b).]

1987 "Tādarthye caturthī vis-à-vis Pāṇini's treatment of kārakas and the dative", ABORI 68:653-659.

1988 *Mahābhāṣyadīpikā of Bhartṛhari, Fascicle V* : *Āhnika II, Critically Edited* (= BORIS 31) (Pune: BORI).

1991a "A glimpse into a pre-Pāṇinian view about vikaraṇas", Festschrift S. D. Joshi, pp. 283-288.

1991b "Pāṇini and the Vedic verbal system with special reference to the modal forms", in: Deshpande (1991a), pp. 55-64.

1991-92 "Did Pāṇini have a private concept of the guṇa phenomenon?", Festschrift Katre, pp. 161-165.

1993a "Points of agreement and difference between the Vākyapadīya and the Mahābhāṣya-dīpikā in the matter of sphoṭa", in: Bhate and Bronkhorst (1993), pp. 215-220.

1993b "Problems of text reconstruction in the Mahābhāṣya-Dīpikā", ABORI 72-73 (1971 & 1972):395-408.

1994 "*Sphoṭa* in Bhartṛhari's linguistic philosophy", Festschrift Bhagwat, pp. 128-131.

Palsule, G. B. and V. B. Bhagavat

1991 *Mahābhāṣyadīpikā of Bhartṛhari, Fascicle VIII : Āhnika VII, Critically Edited* (= BORIS 37) (Pune: BORI).

Panda, Ganesh Prasad

1997 "The concept of time in Indian grammatical tradition (1)", Saṃbhāṣā 18:97-124. [Preface, chapter I (Introduction) and bibliography of a revised version of University of Poona doctoral dissertation, 1992. The remaining parts are to appear in the same journal.]

Panda, R. C.

1982 "Thoughts on Patañjali's definition of śabda", CASS-St. 6:131-138.

Pande, Gopal Dutt (Ed.)

1987 पाणिनि-विरचिता अष्टाध्यायी (पदच्छेद-वृत्ति-वार्तिक-टिप्पणी-सहिता) परिष्कर्त्ता म°म° पण्डितराज डॉ° श्रीगोपालशास्त्री 'दर्शनकेशरी' ... सम्पाकः प्रो° गोपालदत्तपाण्डेयः *Aṣṭādhyāyī of Pāṇini (with Preface, Containing Separation of Words, Mode of Explanation, Supplementary Rules and Foot-notes), Elaborated by M. M. Panditraj Dr. Gopal Shastri, Edited by Prof. Gopal Dutt Pande* third edition (= CSGM 19) (Varanasi: Chaukhamba Surbharati Prakashan). [Pp. 103-105: Pāṇinīyaśikṣā following Yudhiṣṭhira Mīmāṁsaka (1967/8).]

Pandey, Amar Nath

1986 वररुचिप्रणीतः वाररुचसङ्ग्रहः श्रीनारायणकृतया दीपप्रभाख्यया समुपेतः *Vārarucasaṅgraha of Vararuchi with the Commentary "Dīpaprabhā" of Nārāyaṇa, Edited with Introduction and Annotations* (= KSS 237) (Varanasi: Chaukhambha Sanskrit Sansthan).

1992 "Bhaṭṭoji Dīkṣita and the terms योग and प्रयोग in the context of vibhakti", Festschrift Mukherji II, pp. 506-513.

1997 "A note on the sūtra '*samānakartṛkayoḥ pūrvakāle*'", Conference 1997a:438-439.

Pāṇḍeya, Kamalāprasāda

1992-93 "माहेश्वर सूत्रों में हकार के द्विरुपदेश के नौ प्रयोजन", ŚPP 22-23:177-181. [In Hindi.]

Pandeya, Ramajna

1986 व्याकरणदर्शनपीठिका Second edition (= SBAM 12) (Varanasi: Sampurnanand Sanskrit University). [In Sanskrit.]

Pandeya, Ramji

1990 "प्रतिभोत्पत्तिप्रक्रिया", SV 18:58-64. [In Sanskrit.]

Pāṇḍeya, Śrīkānta

1990 व्याकरणशास्त्रदृष्ट्या सम्बन्धस्वरूपपर्यालोचनम् (Delhi: Vidyanidhi). [In Sanskrit.] [Originally a Sampurnanand Sanskrit University dissertation, 1984.]

Pandeya, Upendra

1990 "वर्णमातृका वर्णसमाम्नायश्च", Sāg. 28.1:47-51. [In Sanskrit.]

Pandit, M. D.

1985 "Pāṇini: a statistical picture of Sanskrit sounds-I", Festschrift Dandekar, pp. 128-138. [Identical to Pandit (1969).]

1989 *A Concordance of Vedic Compounds Interpreted by Veda (Volume 1)* (= PCASS B 10) (Pune: University of Poona).

1990 *Zero in Pāṇini* (= PCASS B12) (Pune: University of Poona).

1992 "svatantraḥ kartā (Pāṇini 1.4.54)", Festschrift Ghatage, pp. 131-139.

Pandya, Bhagavati Prasad

1988-89 "शाब्दबोधः", Festschrift R. V. Joshi, pp. 305-315. [In

Sanskrit.]

Pataskar, Bhagyalata

1991 "An ordering principle (*anavakāśa*) in Indian grammatical tradition", Saṃbhāṣā 12:1-8.

Patel, Niharika Kanubhai

1997 "The *vivṛtopadeśa* of *akāra* in the māheśvarasūtra '*aiuṇ*'" Conference 1997a:439.

Patel, Vijayānanda

1997 "गतिकारकोपपदानां कृद्भिः सह समासवचनं प्राक् सुबुत्पत्तेः इति परिभाषायाः विमर्शः", Conference 1997b:189-190. [In Sanskrit.]

Pathak, Purushottam Prasad

1995 नागेशमते परिभाषाणां विवेचनम् *Nāgeshamate Paribhāṣāṇām Vivechanam* (Delhi: Eastern Book Linkers). [In Sanskrit.]

Pāṭhaka, Savitā

1997 महाभाष्यदीपिका-विमर्शः (Delhi: Nag Publishers). [Originally a Delhi University doctoral dissertation. In Hindi.]

Pāṭhaka, Śrīśaṁkaradeva (Ed.)

1990 अष्टाध्यायीसूत्रपाठः वार्त्तिकगणपाठसहितः अनुवृत्तिनिर्देशसमन्वितश्च (Panipat: Anītā Ārṣa Prakāśana).

Patnaik, Tandra

1988 "Language, thought and communication: an appraisal of Bhartṛhari's theory of language", IPQ 15:349-368.

1989 "Some reflections on Bhartṛhari's notion of sentence meaning", VBJP 24-25:118-129.

1991 "A note on Bhartṛhari's theory of Sphoṭa", Prajñā 11: 59-65.

1994 *Śabda : A Study of Bhartṛhari's Philosophy of Language* (New Delhi: D. K. Printworld).

Pawate, I. S.

1987 *The Structure of the Aṣṭādhyāyī* (Delhi: Amar Prakashan). [Reprint of Pawate (1935).]

Peri Sarveswara Sharma

1981a "Correctness of the vocative singular form *subhru*", Festschrift K. Kunjunni Raja, pp. 410-414.

1981b See Rau (1981).

1985a "What kind of compound is the word pratyakṣa", ALB

49:14-29.

1985b "Haradatta's Padamañjarī: an analysis", Festschrift Tripathi, pp. 75-94.

1985-87 "Some problems raised with regard to the concluding verses of the Vākyapadīya of Bhartṛhari", BhV 45/7:1-12.

1987a "What is *apoddhāra* in Bhartṛhari's Vākyapadīya?", AJOS 4:105-118.

1987b "Eight topics which form the subject-matter of the Vākyapadīya", Festschrift Rau, pp.219-233.

1993 See Rau (1993a).

Peri Suryanarayana Shastri (Peri Sūryanārāyaṇaśāstrī)

1983 "धात्वर्थमुख्यविशेष्यकशाब्दबोधः", Festschrift Sreekrishna Sarma (Sanskrit section), pp. 9-21.

1987 नागेशभावप्रकाशः (नागेशकृत लघुमञ्जूषायां धात्वर्थनिपातार्थयोः व्याख्या) (Cittur: Vijaya Press). [I have cited the title as it appears on the cover. The inside title page has नागेशभावप्रकाशसहितायां लघुमञ्जूषायां धात्वर्थ निपातार्थविचारौ.]

1988 नागेशभावप्रकाशः (नागेशकृत लघुमञ्जूषायां सुबर्थवादे प्रथम द्वितीयार्थविचारौ) (Cittur: Vijaya Press).

Pinault, Georges-Jean

1989a "Travaux à partir du corps védique", in: Auroux (1989), pp. 303-330.

1989b "Pāṇini et l'enseignement grammatical", in: Auroux (1989), pp. 331-353.

1989c "Procédés pāṇinéens", in: Auroux (1989), pp. 354-370.

1989d "Le système de Pāṇini", in: Auroux (1989), pp. 371-400.

Potter, Karl H.

1990 "Bibliography on Grammar (*vyākaraṇa*)", in: Coward and K. Kunjunni Raja (1990), pp. 433-548.

Prabhā Kumārī

*1990 जैनाचार्यों का संस्कृत व्याकरण को योगदान (Delhi: Nirmāṇa Prakāśana). [In Hindi.]

Radicchi, Anna

1985 "Notes on *Cāndravyākaraṇa*", in: Dandekar and Navathe (1985), pp. 282-286.

1985-88 *La teoria pāṇiniana dei Samāsa secondo l'interpretazione delle scuole grammaticali indiane dal quinto all'ottavo secolo d. C.* 2 volumes (= Materiali dell'Istituto di Glottologia Università di Cagliari, anno accademico 1982-1983, 1983-1984) (Firenze: Edizione Librarie Italiane Estere).

1991 "On gaṇapāṭhas and the gaṇapāṭha ascribed to Pāṇini", in: Deshpande (1991a), pp. 65-73.

1993 "Vivakṣā in the Vākyapadīya", in: Bhate and Bronkhorst (1993), pp. 221-233.

Raghavan, V.

1976 "The dates of Helārāja and Kaiyaṭa", Festschrift K. A. Subrahmania Iyer, pp. 105-109.

Raghu Vira

1981 *Vedic Studies: A Collection of the Research Papers of Prof. Dr. Raghu Vira* (= ŚPS 272) (Delhi: Mrs. Sharada Rani). [16-18: "The author of the Śiva-sūtras" (reprint of Raghu Vira [1930]); 19-36: "Discovery of the lost phonetic sūtras of Pāṇini" (reprint of Raghu Vira [1931]); 346-369: "Āpiśali-śikṣā" (reprint of Raghu Vira [1934]).]

Raghunātha Śarmā

1976 भर्तृहरिप्रणीतं वाक्यपदीयम् (ब्रह्मकाण्डम्) हरिवृषभकृतया स्वोपज्ञवृत्त्या ... श्रीरघुनाथशर्मणा विरचितया अम्बाकर्त्रीव्याख्यया च सहितम् *Vākyapadīyam Part I (Brahma-Kāṇḍam) with the Commentary Svopajñavṛtti by Harivṛṣabha and Ambākartrī by Pt. Raghunātha Śarmā* (= SBGM 91) (Varanasi: Sampurnanand Sanskrit University). [Reissue of Raghunātha Śarmā (1963) with new pagination; reissued again, 1988.]

1977 भर्तृहरिप्रणीतं वाक्यपदीयम् [तृतीयकाण्डम्] (वृत्तिसमुद्देशात्मकम्) हेलाराजविरचितया प्रकाशव्याख्यया श्रीरघुनाथशर्मणा विरचितया अम्बाकर्त्रीव्याख्यया समलङ्कृतम् *Vākyapadīyam [part III] (Padakāṇḍa) (Vṛttisamuddeśa) with the Commentary 'Prakāśa' by Helārāja and Ambākartrī by Pt. Raghunātha Śarmā* (= SBGM 91) (Varanasi: Sampurnanand Sanskrit University).

1979 वाक्यपदीयम् [तृतीयं काण्डम्, द्वितीयो भागः] (भूयोद्रव्य-गुण-दिक्-साधन-क्रिया-काल-पुरुष- संख्या-उपग्रह-लिङ्गसमुद्देशात्मकम्) हेलाराजविरचितया

प्रकाशव्याख्यया प॰ रघुनाथशर्मणा विरचितया अम्बाकर्त्रीव्याख्यया समलङ्कृतम् *Vākyapadīyam [Part III, vol. II] (Bhūyodravya-Guṇa-Dik-Sādhana-Kriyā-Kāla-Puruṣa-Saṅkhyā-Upagraha and Liṅga Sumuddeśa) with the Commentary 'Prakāśa' by Helārāja and Ambākartrī by Pt. Raghunātha Śarmā* (= SBGM 91) (Varanasi: Sampurnanand Sanskrit University).

1980a वाक्यपदीयपाठभेदनिर्णयः [प्रथमो भागः] लेखकः सम्पादकश्च प॰ रघुनाथशर्मा *Vākyapadīyapāṭhabhedanirṇaya [Part I], Written and Edited by Pt. Raghunātha Śarmā* (= SBGM 116) (Varanasi: Sampurnanand Sanskrit University). [Brahmakāṇḍa and Vakyakāṇḍa.]

1980b भर्तृहरिप्रणीतं वाक्यपदीयम् [द्वितीयो भागः] (वाक्यकाण्डम्) पुण्यराजकृतया टीकया श्रीरघुनाथशर्मप्रणीतया अम्बाकर्त्रीव्याख्यया च सहितम् *Vākyapadīyam [Part II] (Vākyakāṇḍam) by Bhartṛhari with the Commentary of Puṇyarāja and Ambākartrī by Pt. Raghunātha Śarmā* (= SBGM 91) (Varanasi: Sampurnanand Sanskrit University). [Reissue of Raghunātha Śarmā (1968) with new pagination.]

1991 वाक्यपदीयपाठभेदनिर्णयः [द्वितीयो भागः] प्रणेता सम्पादकश्च 'पद्मश्रीः' पण्डितरघुनाथशर्मा सहायकसम्पादकः डॉ॰ नरेन्द्रनाथ पाण्डेयः *Vākyapadīyapāṭhabhedanirṇaya [Part Two], Written and Edited by 'Padmaśrī' Pt. Raghunātha Śarmā, Assistant Editor Dr. Narendra Nātha Pāṇḍeya* (= SBGM 116) (Varanasi: Sampurnanand Sanskrit University). [Jātisamuddeśa.]

Raja, K. Kunjunni

1976 "Pāṇini's concept of a sentence", ALB 40:165-170. [Reprinted: K. Kunjunni Raja (1982: 178-184).]

1979 (Ed.) *Ārṣaprayogasādhutvanirūpaṇam* (= ALPS 43) (Adyar: The Adyar Library and Research Centre). [Reprint from ALB 42.]

1982 *Rājasudhā : Collected Papers of Dr. K. Kunjunni Raja* (Madras: The Dr. Kunjunni Raja Ṣaṣṭyabdapūrti Celebrations Committee).

1983 "भर्तृहरिर्दिङ्नागश्च", Festschrift Sreekrishna Sarma (Sanskrit section), pp. 35-40.

1987 "yarvāṇastarvāṇaḥ", ABORI 68:537-539.
1990a "Ṭīkā on Patañjali's Mahābhāṣya", in: Coward and K. Kunjunni Raja (1990), pp. 172-174.
1990b "Paramalaghumañjūṣā", in: Coward and K. Kunjunni Raja (1990), pp. 324-340.
1990c "Sphoṭavāda", in: Coward and K. Kunjunni Raja (1990), pp. 342-349.
1991 "On the interpretation of vā padāntasya (8.4.57)", Festschrift S. D. Joshi, pp. 289-291. [Thus titled, although the usual number of the sūtra is 8.4.59.]

Rajan, M. A. S. and S. H. Srinivasan (Eds.)
1993 संवित् *Sanskrit and Computer-based Linguistics : Proceedings of the Seminar on 'Knowledge Representation in Sanskrit and Allied Semantic Theories', Bangalore March 6-7, 1993* (Melkote: Academy of Sanskrit Research).

Rājarājavarmā, A. R. (A. R. Rajaraja Varma)
1990 लघुपाणिनीयम् अ. रा. राजराजवर्मणा प्रणीतम् (*Sanskrit*) *Laghupāṇinīyam Grammar* Second edition (Thiruvananthapuram: University of Kerala). [Preface by M. Harihara Sastry (v-ix). In Sanskrit, with English prefaces to first and second editions. The English title page says this is a reprint of 1911 publication, but the prefaces to the second edition (xiii-xiv, xv-xvi) are dated 20th November and 5th September 1913.]

Rama, Goparaju (Goparāju Rāmā)
1995 धातुप्रत्ययालोकः धात्वर्थचन्द्रिका च (Allahabad: Rajan Prakashan). [In Sanskrit with English introduction.]

Ramachandrudu, P. Sri and V. Sundara Sarma (Eds.)
1981 श्रीहरदत्तमिश्रविरचिता पदमञ्जरी (वामनजयादित्यविरचितायाः काशिकाया व्याख्या) *Padamañjarī by Śrī Haradattamiśra : A Commentary on Kāśikā of Vāmana and Jayāditya* 2 volumes (= SAS 25, 26) (Hyderabad: Sanskrit Academy, Osmania University). [I: adhyāyas 1-4, II: adhyāyas 5-8.]
1985 पाणिनीयाष्टाध्यायीसूत्र-वृत्तिः काशिका तृतीयो भागः (सूची) द्वितीयः सम्पुटः *Kāśikā (A Commentary on Pāṇini's Grammar) by Vāmana and Jayāditya, Part III (Indices), Vol. II* (= SAS 32)

(Hyderabad: Sanskrit Academy, Osmania University).

1985-86 बोधिसत्त्वदेशीयाचार्य श्रीजिनेन्द्रबुद्धिपाद-विरचिता न्यासापराख्या काशिकाविवरणपञ्जिका *Nyāsa (Kāśikāvivaraṇapañjikā), A Commentary on Kāśikā of Jayāditya and Vāmana by Bodhisattvadeseeyacharya Sri Jinendra Buddhi Pada* 2 volumes (= SAS 33, 35) (Hyderabad: Sanskrit Academy, Osmania University). [I: adhyāyas 1-4, II: adhyāyas 5-8.]

1987 महामहोपाध्यायनागेशभट्टविरचितः परिभाषेन्दुशेखरः भागवतुल हरिशास्त्रिणा विरचितेन वाक्यार्थचन्द्रिकाख्यव्याख्यानेन समलङ्कृतः *Paribhāṣenduśekhara by Mahāmahopādhyāya Nāgeśa Bhaṭṭa with the Commentary Vākyārthacandrikā by Bhāgavatula Hariśāstry* (= SAS 36) (Hyderabad: Sanskrit Academy, Osmania University). [On the Sanskrit title page, the editors' names appear in full as पुल्लेल श्रीरामचन्द्रः and विठदेवुनि सुन्दरशर्मा.]

Ramakrishnamacharya

1985 "अथादेशाः वाचकाश्चेत् पदस्फोटः ततः स्फुटः (वै°सि°का° ६४)", in: Dandekar and Navathe (1985), pp. 291-295. [In Sanskrit.]

Ramakrisnamacharyulu, K. V. (see also Krishnamacharyalu, K. V. R.)

1993 "Pāṇinian linguistics & computational linguistics", in: Rajan and Srinivasan, pp. 52-62.

Ramamurti, Rajam

1983 "What happens when foreign grammatical terms are used to describe an indigenous language? A South Dravidian situation", IJDL 12:335-344.

Ramseier, Yves

1993 "Bibliography on Bhartṛhari", in: Bhate and Bronkhorst (1993), pp. 235-267.

1994 "Bhartṛhari et la nescience", AS 48:1363-1368.

Rangacaryulu, S. T. K. S.

1989 "पाणिनीये वृत्तिस्वरूपम्", Sāg. 27.3:97-100. [In Sanskrit.]

Rau, Wilhelm

1977a *Bhartṛharis Vākyapadīya : Die Mūlakārikās nach den Handschriften herausgegeben und mit einem Pāda-Index versehen* (= AKML XLII, 4) (Wiesbaden: Steiner).

1977b "Zwei neue Vākyapadīya-Handschriften", StII 3:114-123.

1980 "Bhartṛhari und der Veda", Festschrift Thieme, pp. 167-180.

1981 *Vākyapadīyaprameyasaṃgraha : ein anonymes Scholion zum zweiten Kāṇḍa des Vākyapadīya zusammen mit Peri Sarveswara Sharma nach der einzigen bekannten Handschrift herausgegeben* (= AMGG Jahrgang 1978, Nr. 2) (München: Fink).

1984 "Three further *kārikā*-mansucripts of the Vākyapadīya", Festschrift Dandekar, pp. 343-349.

1985a *Die vedischen Zitate im Vyākaraṇa-Mahābhāṣya* (= AAWLM Jahrgang 1985, Nr. 4) (Stuttgart: Steiner).

1985b "Einige textkritisch bemerkenswerte Zitata in Patañjalis Vyākaraṇa-Mahābhāṣya", Festschrift Hoffmann, pp. 161-170.

1985c "Ein bisher unzugängliches Trivandrum-MS des Vākyapadīya", StII 10:3-7.

1988 *Bhartṛharis Vākyapadīya : Vollständiger Wortindex zu den* mūlakārikās (= AAWLM Jahrgang 1988, Nr. 11) (Stuttgart: Steiner). [172-175: bibliographical supplement.]

1991 *Bhartṛharis Vākyapadīya II : Text der Palmblatt-Handschrift Trivandrum S.N. 532 (= A)* (= AAWLM Jahrgang 1991, Nr. 7) (Stuttgart: Steiner).

1993a *Die vedischen Zitate in der Kāśikā Vṛtti nach Vorarbeiten Dr. S. Sharma Peris zusammengestellt* (= AAWLM Jahrgang 1993 Nr. 5) (Stuttgart: Steiner).

1993b "A new manuscript of the Vākyapadīya-mūlakārikās", StII 18:213-216.

1996 "Die vedischen Zitate in der Candra-Vṛtti", Festschrift Thieme, pp. 327-338.

Ray, Keshav Kumar

1988 "सम्प्रदानत्वविमर्शः", SV 16:34-44. [In Sanskrit.]

Rishi, R. M.

*1975 *The Nipātana-sūtras in the Aṣṭādhyāyī (with Special Reference to the Primary Nominal Derivations)*. [University of Poona Ph.D. dissertation, unpublished. Referred to in Laddu (1983:229 note 1).]

Rocher, Rosane
1975 "India", in: *Current Trends in Linguistics, Volume 13 : Historiography of Linguistics* (Ed.: Thomas A. Sebeok, assoc. eds.: Hans Aarslef, Robert Austerlitz, Dell Hymes, Edward Stankiewicz) (The Hague, Paris: Mouton), pp. 3-67.

Rogers, David E.
1987 "The influence of Pāṇini on Leonard Bloomfield", in: Hall (1987), pp. 89-138.

Roodbergen, J. A. F.
1990 "Three introductory compositions", ABORI 70(1989):242-247.
1991 "Time for a little something", Festschrift S. D. Joshi, pp. 293-321.

Ruegg, David Seyfort
1978 "Mathematical and linguistic models in Indian thought: the case of zero and śūnyatā", WZKS 22:171-181.
1994 "*Pramāṇabhūta*, **pramāṇa(bhūta)-puruṣa*, *pratyakṣa-dharman* and *sākṣātkṛtadharman* as epithets of the *ṛṣi*, *ācārya* and *tathāgata* in grammatical, epistemological and Madhyamaka texts", BSOAS 57:303-320.

Saini, Ranjit Singh
1985 श्रीशरणदेवविरचिता दुर्घटवृत्तिः ... त. गणपतिशास्त्रिणा शोधिता लघुटिप्पण्या च संयोजिता डा° रणजीतसिंह सैनी विरचितया प्रस्तावनया पदानुक्रमणिकया च संयुक्ता *The Durghaṭavṛtti of Śaraṇadeva, Edited with Notes by T. Gaṇapati Śāstrī, with Introduction and Index by Dr. R. S. Saini* (Delhi, Varanasi: Bharatiya Vidya Prakashan). [See T. Gaṇapati Śāstrī (1909).]
1989 (Ed.) पद्मनाभदत्तप्रणीतम् सुपद्मव्याकरणम् *The Supadma-vyākaraṇa of Padmanābhadatta* (Delhi, Varanasi: Bharatiya Vidya Prakashan).
1995 (Ed.) वादीन्द्रचक्रचूडामणिमहापण्डितक्रमदीश्वरप्रणीतम् संक्षिप्तसारव्याकरणम् महाराजाधिराजश्रीमज्जुमरनन्दीकृता रसवती-वृत्तिः तथा औत्थासनिक-पण्डितगोयीचन्द्रकृता विवरणी-टीका समेतम् (प्रथमो भागः) *Saṁkṣiptasāra Vyākaraṇa of Vādīndracakracūḍāmaṇi-mahāpaṇḍita Kramadīśvara with Rasavatī-Vṛtti by Mahārājādhirāja*

Jumaranandī and Vivaraṇī-ṭīkā by Autthāsanika Pt. Goyīcandra (*Vol. 1*) (Delhi, Varanasi: Bharatiya Vidya Prakashan).

Sankara Rama Sastri, C. (Ed.)

1994 *Aṣṭādhyāyī-sūtra-pāṭha of Pāṇini with Vārtikas, Gaṇas, Dhātupāṭha, Pāṇinīya Śikṣā and Paribhāṣāpāṭha* ॥ अष्टाध्यायीसूत्रपाठः ॥ वार्तिक-गणपाठ-धातुपाठ-पाणिनीयशिक्षा-परिभाषापाठसहितः (Delhi: Sharada Publishing House). [Reprint of 1937 edition with an introduction by Ratna Basu.]

Sankaranarayana, S.

1992 "Janikartuḥ prakṛtiḥ (Aṣṭādhyāyī 1.4.30)", ALB 56:128-169.

Sarangi, Alekha Chandra

1976 "An enquiry into Pāṇini's placement of the tācchīlika suffixes within the present suffixes section", CASS-St. 3:121-129.

1985 *Development of Sanskrit from Pāṇini to Patañjali* (Delhi: Bharatiya Vidya Prakashan). [Originally a University of Poona doctoral thesis.]

1995 *Gleanings in the Sanskrit Grammatical Tradition* (Delhi: Eastern Book Linkers).

Sarma, C. R. S.

1995 "Kartaa and animacy", IL 56:135-139.

Sarma, Isvara

1994 सिद्धान्तकौमुदी वैदिकी-प्रक्रिया - एक समीक्षात्मक अध्ययन (Delhi: Parimal Publications). [In Hindi.]

Śarmā, Kṛṣṇakānta

1984 "शब्दपूर्वयोग", in: Mandan Mishra et al. (eds.), pp. 75-79. [In Hindi.]

Śarmā, Śrīkṛṣṇa: See Śrīkṛṣṇaśarmā.

Śarmā, Sureśacandra: See Sharma, Suresh Chandra.

Śāstrī, Naradeva: See Naradeva Śāstrī.

Sastry, B. R. and V. Sundara Sarma (Eds.)

1976 श्रीवामनजयादित्यविरचिता पाणिनीयाष्टाध्यायीसूत्रवृत्तिः काशिका तृतीयो भागः (सूची) प्रथमः सम्पुटः *Kāśikā* (*A Commentary on Pāṇini's Grammar*) *by Vāmana and Jayāditya, Part III* (*Indices*), *Vol.*

I (= SAS 23) (Hyderabad: Sanskrit Academy, Osmania University).

Śaṭhakopatātācārya, N. R.

1988 "द्वितीयाकर्मत्वविचारः", Sāg. 27.1:51-54. [In Sanskrit.]

Satya Vrat Shastri

1992 "Pāṇini's regard for usage", Festschrift Kamlesh Kumari Kulshreshtha, pp. 61-65.

Scharf, Peter M.

1992 "The term '*ākṛti*' and the concept of class property in the Mahābhāṣya", WZKS 36:31-48.

1993 "Assessing Śabara's arguments for the conclusion that a generic term denotes just a class property", JIP 21:1-10.

1994 Review of Hock (ed.) (1991a), JAOS 114:485-487.

1995a "Early Indian grammarians on the limits linguistic convention places upon a speaker's intention", JAOS 115:66-76.

1995b "Does Pāṇini prohibit prohibitive compounds? An analysis of negation in the term *anupasarge*", WZKS 39:15-24.

1996 *The Denotation of Generic Terms in Ancient Indian Philosophy*: *Grammar, Nyāya and Mīmāṃsā* (= TAPS 86.3) (Philadelphia: American Philosophical Society). [Revised version of University of Pennsylvania doctoral dissertation, 1990.]

1997 "Recognizing speech between sound and meaning", Conference 1997a:448-449.

Scharfe, Hartmut

1977 *Grammatical literature* (*A history of Indian literature, part II, fascicle 2*) (Wiesbaden: Harrassowitz).

1981 "Overinterpretation versus redundancy", Festschrift K. Kunjunni Raja, pp. 352-357.

1983 "Secondary noun formation in Pāṇini's grammar — what was the great option?", in: Joshi and Laddu (1983), pp. 53-57.

1989 "Something old and something new: two traditional approaches to Pāṇini", JAOS 109:653-658. [Review-article of Katre (1987) and Cardona (1988).]

1996 "Bartholomae's Law revisited or how the Ṛgveda is

dialectally divided," Festschrift Thieme, pp. 351-377.

Sharma, Amita (Amitā Śarmā)

1984 "पाणिनि व्याकरण - पदसंस्कार अथवा वाक्यसंस्कार", in: Mandan Mishra et al. (eds.), pp. 67-74. [In Hindi.]

1995 पुरुषोत्तमदेवविरचित ज्ञापकसमुच्चय (मूल, हिन्दीटीकासहित) (Delhi: Nag Publishers). [Text with Hindi commentary.]

Sharma, Chandradatta (Candradatta Śarmā) (Ed.)

1989 भट्टयज्ञेश्वरप्रणीता गणरत्नावली पाणिनिमुनेर्गणपाठस्य दुर्लभा महत्त्वपूर्णा व्याख्या (शब्द-सूच्या समलंकृता) (Calcutta: Śrīmatī Sāvitrīdevī Bāgaḍiyā Trust).

Sharma, Dadhiram (Ed.)

1988 श्रीमन्महर्षिपतञ्जलिविनिर्मितं व्याकरणमहाभाष्यम् श्रीमदुपाध्यायकैयटप्रणीतेन भाष्यप्रदीपेन श्रीमन्नागेशभट्टविरचित-भाष्यप्रदीपोद्द्योतोद्भासितेन समुल्लसितेन सप्तमाऽष्टमाध्याय-व्याख्यानभूतम् अङ्गाधिकार-प्रकीर्णविधि-रूपम् षष्ठं खण्डम् *Vyākaraṇamahābhāṣya of Patañjali with the Commentary Bhāṣyapradīpa of Kaiyaṭa Upādhyāya and the Supercommentary Bhāṣyapradīpoddyota of Nāgeśa Bhaṭṭa, Volume VI Aṅgādhikāra-prakīrṇa Vidhirūpam (As depicted in Chapters VII & VIII of Ashtadhyayi)* (= VPGM 23) (Delhi: Chaukhamba Sanskrit Pratisthan).

Sharma, Ladukeshvar Shatapathi (Laḍukeśvara Śatapathī Śarmā)

1985 "अनुस्वार-विमर्शः", in: Dandekar and Navathe (1985), pp. 331-335. [In Sanskrit.]

Sharma, Mukunda Madhava

1994 "A note on the architectonics of the Aṣṭādhyāyī of Pāṇini", Festschrift Chatterjee, pp. 107-112.

Sharma, Premlal

1988 "अव्ययानि तेषां स्वराश्च", Festschrift Charu Deva Shastri, pp. 163-167. [In Sanskrit.]

Sharma, Radheshyam

1984-85 "कर्म कारक : एक परिशीलन", KURJ 18-19:224-229. [In Hindi.]

Sharma, Rajendra Prasad (Rājendra Prasāda Śarmā)

1993 बौद्धार्थबाह्यार्थपर्यालोचनम् (= RVBDGM 1) (Jaipur: Rajasthan University). [In Sanskrit.]

1997 "अष्टाध्याय्यां बाध्यबाधकभावस्वीकारस्य बाध्यता", Conference 1997b:194-195. [In Sanskrit.]

Sharma, Ram Karan

1989 "Pāṇini on linguistic description", JAOS 109.635-637.

1992 "The role of the "invisible" in Pāṇinian description: a summary", Festschrift Mukherji II, pp. 442-443.

1995 "Primary derivatives with temporal connotations", Festschrift Lienhard, pp. 305-310.

Sharma, Rama Nath

1975 "Referential indices in *Pāṇini*", IIJ 17:31-39.

1976a. पाणिनिव्याकरण में प्रजनक प्रविधियां (Agra: Central Hindi Institute). [Three lectures: 1: अष्टाध्यायी और उसका स्वरूप (4-16) [1.1: अधिकार और अनुवृत्ति (5-8), 1.2: व्याकरणिक इकाई और प्रक्रिया (8-16)], 2: जेनेरटिव प्रक्रिया, क्रमवीक्षण और ट्रैफिक सिद्धांत (16-40), 3: अभिसंबंध और अर्थनिर्णय (40-48). In Hindi.]

1976b "Word derivation in *Pāṇini*", FoL 9:215-228.

1982 Review of Kiparsky (1979), LIS 12:349-415.

1987 *The Aṣṭādhyāyī of Pāṇini, Volume I : Introduction to the Aṣṭādhyāyī as a Grammatical Device* (Delhi: Munshiram Manoharlal).

1990 *The Aṣṭādhyāyī of Pāṇini, Volume II : English Translation of Adhyāya One with Sanskrit Text, Transliteration, Word-Boundary, Anuvṛtti, Vṛtti, Explanatory Notes, Derivational History of Examples, and Indices* (Delhi: Munshiram Manoharlal).

1992 "Pāṇini and reference to variable antecedents", Festschrift Kelkar, pp. 29-42.

1995 *The Aṣṭādhyāyī of Pāṇini, Volume III : English Translation of Adhyāyas Two and Three with Sanskrit Text, Transliteration, Word-Boundary, Anuvṛtti, Vṛtti, Explanatory Notes, Derivational History of Examples, and Indices* (Delhi: Munshiram Manoharlal).

Sharma, Shrikrishna

1993 आचार्य आपिशलि की कृतियों का समीक्षात्मक अध्ययन (Kurukshetra, Delhi: Nirmal Book Agency). [Appendix 1: आपिशल-मतत-संग्रह (160-167), Appendix 2: आपिशली (sic!) शिक्षा (168-174). In Hindi.]

Sharma, Subodh
1990 "व्याकरणदर्शने विवर्तः परिणामो वा", SV 18:28-34. [In Sanskrit.]
Sharma, Suresh Chandra
1994 रूपमालाविमर्शः (श्रीमत्परमहंसपरिव्राजकाचार्यविमलसरस्वतीविरचितायाः रूपमालायाः विवेचनात्मकमध्ययनम्) (Delhi: Nag Publishers). [Originally a Gaṅgānatha Jhā Kendrīya-Saṁskṛta-Vidyāpīṭha doctoral dissertation. In Sanskrit.]
Sharma, Umashankar
1994 संस्कृतव्याकरण में कारकतत्त्वानुशीलन पाणिनितन्त्र संदर्भ में (= CSBG 11) (Varanasi: Chowkhamba Surabharati Prakashan). [In Hindi.]
Sharma, Virendra
1977 वाक्यपदीय-सम्बन्धसमुद्देश हेलाराजीय व्याख्या के प्रकाश में एक विवेचनात्मक अध्ययन *Vākyapadīya Sambandha-Samuddeśa : A Critical Study with Special Reference to the Commentary of Helārāja* (= PUIS 9) (Hoshiarpur: Vishveshvaranand Vishva Bandhu Institute of Sanskrit and Indological Studies, Panjab University). [In Hindi.]
Shastri, Acharcya Madhusudan
1983 पण्डितराजजगन्नाथविरचितं मनोरमा-कुचमर्दनम् विमर्शमयी 'बालक्रीडा' हिन्दी-व्याख्योपेतम् *Manoramā-kuchamardana of Panditarāj Jagannāth, Edited with Balakrida Hindi Commentary* (= KDSS 34) (Varanasi: Krishnadas Academy).
Shastri, Charu Deva
1982 शब्दापशब्दविवेकः (Delhi: Nag Publishers). [In Sanskrit.]
1990 *Pāṇini : Re-interpreted* (Delhi: Motilal Banarsidass).
Shastri, Naradeva: See Naradeva Śāstrī.
Shastri, Ram Sharan
1976 पाणिनीयव्याकरणशास्त्रे वैशेषिकतत्त्वमीमांसा *A Critique of the Vaiśeṣika Tattvas in the Pāṇinian System of Grammar* (Delhi: the author). [In Sanskrit.]
Shukla, Jayadev M.
1975 પાણિનીય સંસ્કૃત વ્યાકરણશાસ્ત્રપરંપરાનો ઇતિહાસ *History of the Pāṇinian System of Sanskrit Grammar* (Ahmedabad: Gujarat University). [In Gujarati.]
1983 "The *ṇatva*-rules in the Aṣṭādhyāyī (VIII.4.1-39)", in:

Joshi and Laddu (1983), pp. 109-118.
1984 महावैयाकरणभर्तृहरिविरचितं वाक्यपदीयं गुर्जरभाषानुवादटिप्पणसहितम् *Bhartṛhari's Vākyapadīya with Gujarati translation and notes* (= L. D. Series 98) (Ahmedabad: L. D. Institute of Indology).

Siderits, Mark
1985 "Word meaning, sentence meaning and *apoha*", JIP 13:133-151.
1991 *Indian Philosophy of Language : Studies in Selected Issues* (= SLP 46) (Dordrecht: Kluwer).

Siṁhala, Ūṣā
1989 दुर्घटवृत्तिः एक परिशीलन (Delhi: Parimal Publications). [In Hindi.]

Singh, Jag Deva
1979 "Technical terms in Pāṇini", IJDL 8.1:7-16.
1981 "Phonological change in Pāṇini: his theoretical assumptions", IJDL 10.1:58-81.
1985-86 "Pāṇini's theory of substitution and derivation of verbal forms", IT 13:137-163.
1988 "Pāṇini's treatment of kāraka: a probe into his analytic procedure (part one: apādāna)", IJDL 17.1:79-106.
1991 *Pāṇini : His Description of Sanskrit. An Analytical Study of the Aṣṭādhyāyī* (Delhi: Munshiram Manoharlal).
1991-92 "Pāṇini on eka-śeṣa", Festschrift Katre, pp. 379-385.

Sitaramanjaneyulu, K.
1988 "शब्दब्रह्म", JSAOU 10:31-37. [In Sanskrit.]

Śivanārāyaṇa Śāstrī
1991 महाभाष्य-प्रदीप-प्रकाश (प्रथम तथा द्वितीय आह्निक) (= PSGM 32) (Delhi: Parimal Publications). [In Hindi.]

Smith, Henry
1992 "Brevity in Pāṇini", JIP 20:133-147.

Speijer, J. S.
1886 *Sanskrit syntax* (Leiden: Brill). [Reprinted 1968, Kyoto: The Rinsen-Shoten Bookstore.]

Sreekrishna Sarma, E. R.
1981 "Sphoṭa and Śaṃkara", Festschrift K. Kunjunni Raja, pp.

223-228.
1986 "Bhartṛhari as an Advaitin", ALB 50: 579-585.

Śrīkṛṣṇaśarmā
1991 व्याकरण-साहित्य-दर्शनशास्त्रानुसारिणी वृत्तिमीमांसा (Jodhpur: Rājasthānīya-Granthāgāraḥ). [In Sanskrit.]

Srimannarayana Murti, M.
1981a "Time according to Bhartṛhari", Festschrift Agrawal, pp. 140-146.
1981b "Bhartṛhari on svaṃ rūpaṃ śabdasyāśabdasṃjñā", Festschrift K. Kunjunni Raja, pp. 602-613.
1982 "Divisions of time according to Indian grammarians", ALB 46:12-24.
1986 "Different views regarding the signification of the primary suffix *tvā*", ALB 50:561-578.
1988 "Contextual referent and relation of identity", ALB 52: 61-82.
1991 "H-sound in the pratyāhāra-sūtra-s of Pāṇini", ALB 55: 1-14.
1993 "On the nomenclature 'Saṁskṛta'", ALB 57:58-71.
1997 "*Vāgyoga* of the grammarians", Conference 1997a:436.

Śrīnārāyaṇa Miśra
1981 श्रीमन्नागेशभट्टविरचितः परिभाषेन्दुशेखरः परिभाषप्रकाशाख्यहिन्दीव्याख्या-विभूषितः *Paribhāṣenduśekhara by Śrī Nāgeśa Bhaṭṭa with the Hindi Commentary Paribhāṣāprakāśa by Śrīnārāyaṇa Miśra* (= CPVS 15) (Varanasi: Chaukhambha Orientalia).
1985 श्रीशरणदेवकृता श्रीसर्वरक्षितप्रतिसंस्कृता दुर्घटवृत्तिः ... श्रीनारायणमिश्रेण कृतया विवृत्या परिशिष्टादिना च समेता *The Durghaṭavṛtti by Śaraṇadeva Revised by Śrī Sarvarakṣita with the Vivṛti and Appendices by Śrīnārāyaṇa Miśra* (= Ratnabharati Series 12) (Varanasi: Ratna Publications).
1996 श्रीमद्विद्वद्वरवामन-जयादित्यविरचिता पाणिनीयसूत्रवृत्तिः काशिका सटिप्पण-'प्रकाश'-हिन्दीव्याख्योपेता *Pāṇinīyavyākaraṇasūtravṛtti Kāśikā of Pt. Vāmana and Jayāditya, Edited with the 'Prakāśa' Hindi Commentary and Introduction* (= KSS 37) 2 volumes Seventh edition (Varanasi: Chaukhambha Sanskrit Sansthan).

Śrīvaiṣṇava, Ayodhyādāsa
1997 "मतभेदपुरस्सरं समासस्य लक्षणं भेदाश्च", Conference 1997b:197-198. [In Sanskrit.]

Staal, Fritz
1995 "Indian theories of meaning", in: Koerner and Asher (1995), section IV (Antiquity-India), pp. 66-71. [Section 2: The Grammatical tradition (66b-68a), section 3.2: Bhartṛhari (69b-70a).]

Subrahmanyam, K.
1989 "The divergent views on sphoṭa theory", VIP 27:52-57.

Subrahmanyam, P. S.
1975 "Deep structure and surface structure in Pāṇini", IL 36:346-366.
1976 "Kārakas and case markers", in: *Dravidian Case System* (Eds. S. Agesthialingom and K. Kushalappa Gowda) (Annamalainagar: Annamalai University), pp. 201-220.
1983 "Pāṇini's use of semantics", in: Joshi and Laddu (1983), pp. 127-136.
1985 "Pāṇini and semantically deviant sentences", IL 46.1-2:1-8.
1988 "Pāṇini's derivation of the imperative mood", IL 49:54-65.
1992 *Pāṇini's Aṣṭādhyāyī* (Smt. Radha S. Katre Memorial Lectures, third series) (Pune: Linguistic Society of India). [I: The derivational process in Aṣṭādhyāyī (7-21), II: Syntax in Aṣṭādhyāyī (22-28), III: Pāṇini's derivation of the imperative mood (29-40). Appendix (41-42): references to Pāṇinian sūtras, with translations. I have normalized the Romanization, with *ā* instead of *a:*.]

Subramania Iyer, K. A.
1977 *The Vākyapadīya of Bhartṛhari, Kāṇḍa II : English Translation with Exegetical Notes* (Delhi: Motilal Banarsidass).
1981 "Bhartṛhari on the sentence", Festschrift K. Kunjunni Raja, pp. 15-49.
1982 *The Vākyapadīya : Some Problems* (Professor K. V. Abhyankar Memorial Lectures [First series]) (= BORIS 14) Pune: BORI). [I: Some aspects of Bhartṛhari's *śabdādvaita*

(1-11), II: Bhartṛhari on *sphoṭa* (12-50), III: The *Vākyapadīya* and the *pramāṇas* (51-69).]

1983 श्रीभर्तृहरिविरचितं सवृत्तिवाक्यपदीयद्वितीयकाण्डम् पुण्यराजकृतटीकोपेतम् *The Vākyapadīya of Bhartṛhari* (*An Ancient Treatise on the Philosophy of Sanskrit Grammar*), *Containing the Ṭīkā of Puṇyarāja and the Ancient Vṛtti : Kāṇḍa II*, *Edited by K. A. Subramania Iyer with a Foreword by Ashok Aklujkar* (Delhi: Motilal Banarsidass).

Sujit, K. N., K. Suryanarayan, and G. V. Singh

1994 "An intelligent computer-aided instruction system for Paninian grammar", in: Agrawal and Pani, pp. 385-393.

Śukla, Kālikā Prasāda (Ed.)

1977 नागेशभट्टविरचिता वैयाकरणसिद्धान्तमञ्जूषा *Vaiyākaraṇasiddhānta mañjūṣā by Nāgeśa Bhaṭṭa* (= MMŚKŚG 3.) (Varanasi: Sampurnanand Sanskrit University).

1991 श्रीमन्नागेशभट्टविरचितः परिभाषेन्दुशेखरः पण्डितश्रीयागेश्वरशास्त्रिविरचितया 'हैमवती'टीकया संवलितः *Paribhāṣenduśekharaḥ of Śrī Nāgeśa Bhaṭṭa with the Commentary 'Haimavatī' by Śrī Yāgeśvara Śāstrī* (= MMŚKŚGM 1) Second edition (Varanasi: Sampurnanand Sanskrit University). [First edition, 1975.]

Śukla, Rāmakiśora

1992 व्याकरणशास्त्रे लौकिकन्यायानामुपयोगः *Vyākaraṇaśāstre Laukikanyāyānām Upayogaḥ* (= SBS 44) (Varanasi: Sampurnanand Sanskrit University). [In Sanskrit.]

Śukla, Sūryanārāyaṇa and Rāmagovinda Śukla

1984 महावैयाकरणश्रीभर्तृहरिविरचितं वाक्यपदीयम् (ब्रह्मकाण्डम्) ... श्रीसूर्यनारायणशुक्लेन स्वप्रणीतेन भावप्रदीपाख्यव्याख्यानेन टिप्पणेन च समलंकृतम् तत्पुत्रेण ... श्रीरामगोविन्दशुक्लेन हिन्दीव्याख्यया विशिष्टया भूमिकया च समलंकृत्य सम्पादितम् परिशिष्टलेखकः पण्डितरुद्रप्रसादोऽवस्थी *Vākyapadīya : A Treatise on the Philosophy of Sanskrit Grammar* (*Brahma-kāṇḍa*) *by Bhartṛhari, with the Bhāvapradīpa Sanskrit Commentary and Notes by ... Pt. Śrī Sūryanārāyaṇa Śukla ..., Edited with Hindi Commentary etc., by ... Rāmagovinda Śukla*; *author of the Pariśiṣṭa*: *Pt. Śrī Rudraprasāda Avasthī* Fifth edition (= KSS 124) (Varanasi: Chaukhambha Sanskrit Sansthan). [Hindi introduction:

1-20, index of topics: 1-4, supplementary notes by Pt. Rudraprasāda Avasthī: 161-172, verse index: 173-175.]

Sukumar, Revathy
1997 "On the meaning of the potential suffix (*Liṅ*) according to the schools of Vyākaraṇa, Mīmāṃsā and Nyāya", Conference 1997a:452-453.

Suryanarayan, K.
*1992 *The Philosophical Contents in Patañjali's Mahābhāṣya.* [Unpublished Ph.D. dissertation, University of Poona.]

Suryanarayan, K. and G. V. Singh
1994 "Morphology in Paninian grammar", in: Agrawal and Pani, pp. 417-422.

Thieme, Paul
1982-83 "Meaning and form of the 'grammar' of Pāṇini", StII 8-9:3-34. [Excursus (23-34): The meaning of *vyākaraṇa-* n. and of the verb *vyā + kṛ*. The use of *vi + gṛh* in the Mahābhāṣya.]
*1983 "Misverstandener Pāṇini", ZDMG Suppl. 5:280-288.
1985a "Nennformen aus Anrede und Anruf im Sanskrit", Festschrift Hoffmann, pp. 239-258.
1985b "The first verse of the triṣaptīyam (AV, Ś 1.1 AV, P 1.6) and the beginnings of Sanskrit linguistics", Festschrift Ingalls, pp. 559-565.

Thompson, Stephen
1989-90 "Does Pāṇini's *kāraka* system provide a basis for a universal grammar?", IT 15-16:371-385. [Subtitle: "Illustrated by reference to the Nāsadīya Sūkta and Upaniṣads".]
1994 "The concept of *pratyaya* : a general introduction to the translation of the *pratyaya pāda* of Patañjali's *Mahābhāṣya* (composed c. 150 B.C.) on Pāṇini III.1 (*āhnikas 1 to 6*) under the guidance of Pandit Bhāgavat Sāstrī", Festschrift Bhagwat, pp. 132-138.

Tiwari, Harinarayana
1988 "णत्वविधाने पाणिनिः", Sāg. 26.3:45-54. [In Sanskrit.]
1989 "'मित्'विषये भगवान् पाणिनिः", Sāg. 27.2:51-62. [In Sanskrit.]

Tiwary, Kapil Muni
1984 *Pāṇini's Description of Nominal Compounds* (Patna:

Janaki Prakashan). [Publication of K. M. Tiwary (1968).]
1987 "*tulyāsyaprayatnaṃ savarṇam* Aṣṭādhyāyī (1.1.9)", Festschrift Hoenigswald, pp. 393-398.

Torella, Raffaele
1987 "Examples of the Influence of Sanskrit Grammar on Indian Philosophy", EW 37:151-164.

Tripāṭhī, Bhāgīratha Prasāda 'Vāgīśa Śāstrī'
1980 धात्वर्थविज्ञानम् Dhātvarthavijñānam (= SBS28.) (Varanasi: Sampurnanand Sanskrit University). [In Sanskrit.]

Tripathi, Chandrabhana
1985 "भाषाविज्ञाने स्फोटवादः वैयाकरणसिद्धान्तः", in: Dandekar and Navathe (1985), pp. 386-388. [In Sanskrit.]

Tripathi, Dipti
1986 "Apabhraṃśa in Sanskrit grammar: an appraisal of Bhartṛhari's view", AJOS 3:81-92.

Tripathi, Jaya Shankar Lal
1985 श्रीनागेशभट्ट-विरचिता परमलघुमञ्जूषा 'भावप्रकाशिका' 'बालबोधिनी' संस्कृत-हिन्दी-व्याख्योपेता *Parama-laghu-mañjūṣā of Śrī Nāgeśa Bhaṭṭa, Edited with Bhāvaprakāśikā and Bālabodhinī Sanskrit-Hindi Commentaries* (= KDSS 50.) (Varanasi: Krishnadas Academy).

Tripathi, Jaya Shankar Lal and Sudhakar Malaviya
1984-94 श्रीमद्वामन-जयादित्य- विरचिता पाणिनीयाष्टाध्यायीसूत्रवृत्तिः काशिका श्रीमद्जिनेन्द्रबुद्धिविरचितया न्यासापरपर्यायकाशिकाविवरणपञ्जिकाख्यया विद्वद्वरश्रीहरदत्तमिश्रविरचित-'पदमञ्जरी'-समाख्यया च व्याख्यया सहिता डा° जयशङ्करलालत्रिपाठि-विरचितया 'भावबोधिनी' हिन्दीव्याख्यया च विभूषिता ... *Kāśikā (A Commentary on Pāṇini's Grammar) of Vāmana and Jayāditya with Nyāsa or Kāśikā-vivaraṇapañjikā of Jinendrabuddhi and Padamañjarī of Haradatta Miśra with Bhāvabodhinī Hindi Exposition by Dr. Jaya Shankar Lal Tripāṭhī ... Critically Edited by Dr. Jaya Shankar Lal Tripathi and Dr. Sudhakar Malaviya* (= PBGM 18). 9 volumes (Varanasi: Tara Printing Works).

Tripathi, Kripa Ram
1991 *Arrangement of Rules in Pāṇini's Aṣṭādhyāyī* (Delhi: Parimal Publications).

Tripāṭhī, Nārāyaṇadatta and Rāmanārāyaṇa Datta Śāstrī Pāṇḍeya (Eds.)
saṁ. 2052 श्रीमद्विद्वद्वरवरदराजाचार्यप्रणीता लघुसिद्धान्तकौमुदी 23rd edition (Gorakhpur: Gītā Press). [235-240: लिङ्गपरिचयः, 241-266: Śivasūtras and index of sūtras, 267-269: vārttika index, 270-274: index of verbs cited in gaṇas of the dhātupāṭha section, 275-278: index of verbs not cited in the dhātupāṭha section but used in illustrations, 279-282: gaṇapāṭha selections, 282: paribhāṣās cited.]

Tripathi, Radhavallabh and Achyutanand Dash (Eds.)
1993 *Indian Traditions in Linguistics : Proceedings of UGC National Seminar* भाषाशास्त्र की भारतीय परम्परा (Delhi: Pratibha Prakashan).

Tripāṭhī, Rājanātha
1988 व्याकरणे नागेशकृतिषु तन्त्रस्य प्रभावः *Vyākaraṇe Nāgeśabhaṭṭakṛtiṣu Tantrasya Prabhāvaḥ* (= SBS 37) (Varanasi: Sampurnanand Sanskrit University). [In Sanskrit.]

Tripāṭhī, Rāmadeva
1977 भाषाविज्ञान की भारतीय परम्परा और पाणिनि (Patna: Bihār-Rāṣṭrabhāṣā-Pariṣad). [In Hindi.]

Tripāṭhī, Rāmaprasāda
1987 सिद्धान्तचिन्तामणिः *Siddhāntacintāmaṇiḥ* (= SAGM 15) (Varanasi: Sampurnanand Sanskrit University). [In Sanskrit.]

1989 (Ed.) महर्षियाज्ञवल्क्यादिविरचितः शिक्षासंग्रहः *Śikṣāsaṁgrahaḥ of Yājñavalkya and others* (= GKRGM 3) (Varanasi: Sampurnanand Sanskrit University).

1990 श्रीमन्नागेशभट्टविरचिता वैयाकरणसिद्धान्त-लघुमञ्जूषा [प्रथमो भागः] श्रीदुर्बलाचार्यकृतया 'कुञ्जिका'व्याख्यया श्रीबालम्भट्टकृतया 'कला'व्याख्यया आचार्यश्रीरामप्रसादत्रिपाठिकृतया 'सरला'हिन्दीव्याख्यया च विभूषिता सम्पादकः आचार्यश्रीरामप्रसादत्रिपाठी *Vaiyākaraṇasiddhāntalaghumañjūṣā of Śrī Nāgeśabhaṭṭa [Part One] with three Commentaries: 'Kuñjikā' by Śrī Durbalācārya, 'Kalā' by Śrī Bālambhaṭṭa and 'Saralā' (Hindi Commentary) by Śrī Rāmaprasāda Tripāṭhī* (= GJGM 12) (Varanasi: Sampurnanand Sanskrit University).

Tripāṭhī, Sudarśanācārya
1973-74 लघुकाशिका *Laghukāśikā* 2 volumes (= SBGM 100) (Varanasi: Varanaseya Sanskrit Vishvavidyalaya). [I: adhyāyas 1-4, II: adhyāyas 5-8.]

Tripathi, Tirth Raj (Tīrtharājaḥ Tripāṭhī)
1981 श्रीहरदत्ताचार्यप्रणीतायाः पदमञ्जर्याः पर्यालोचनम् *Haradatta's Padamañjarī — A Critical Study* (New Delhi: Bhavana Prakashan). [Originally a Delhi University doctoral dissertation. Appendix (239-257): Verses cited from the Vākyapadīya. English introduction (xvii-xxi) summarizing the work; the rest in Sanskrit.]

Unebe, Toshiya
1994 "Bhartṛhari on *yogyatā*, the natural competency of word to meaning", Festschrift Bhagwat, pp. 139-149.

Upadhyaya, Baldeva
1985 विमर्शचिन्तामणिः [नानाशास्त्रीयतथ्यानां तर्कयुक्त्या समीक्षणम्] *Vimarsha Chintāmaṇiḥ (A Book of Criticism on Indian Philosophical and Literary Subjects)* (Varanasi: Śāradā Saṁsthānam). [In Sanskrit.]
1985a "महाभाष्यं भोजपुरी च", in: Upadhyaya (1985), pp: 104-106.
1985b "महाभाष्ये देवदत्तस्य जीवनवृत्तम्", in: Upadhyaya (1985), pp: 107-121.
1985c "वाक्यपदीयस्य देशकाल-व्याख्याविमर्शः", in: Upadhyaya (1985), pp: 122-133. [= Preface to Raghunātha Śarmā (1968).]

Vaiṣṇava, Toyanidhi
1997 "'चत्वारि पदजातानि' व्याकरणशास्त्रीयं विवेचनम्", Conference 1997b:191-192. [In Sanskrit.]

Varma, A. R. Rajaraja: see Rājarājavarmā, A. R.

Veda Prakāśa
1979 पतञ्जलि-कृतं व्याकरण-महाभाष्यम् [प्रथम-द्वितीयाह्निक-मात्रम्] महामहोपाध्यायेन माधव-शास्त्रिणा भाण्डारिणा निर्मितया 'स्फोटविमर्शिनी'-संस्कृत-व्याख्यया सहितम् 'महाभाष्यप्रकाशना'-हिन्दीव्याख्याकारः, समीक्षात्मक-भूमिका-लेखकः सम्पाकदकश्च प्रा° वेदप्रकाशः विद्यावाचस्पतिः *Patañjali's Vyākaraṇa-Mahābhāṣya (1st & 2nd Āhnikas only) with Mm. Mādhava Śāstrī Bhāṇḍārī's Sphoṭa-vimarśinī Sanskrit Commentary, Edited & Added with Critical Edition, Notes & Hindi*

Rendering Mahābhāṣya-Prakāśanā by Prof. Veda Prakāśa (Delhi: Meherchandra Lacchmandas).

Vedalankar, Raghuvira

1977 काशिका का समालोचनात्मक अध्ययन [*A Critical Study of the Kāśikā*] (= N. P. Series 15) (Delhi: Nag Publishers). [Appendixes: Differences between readings of sūtras in the Bhāṣya and the Kāśikā based on rule splitting (350), Word differences in sūtras in the Bhāṣya and Kāśikā (350-351), Vārttikas incorporated as sūtras (351-352), Sūtras with additions made in vārttikas (353-356), Different readings indicated by the Kāśikā authors (356-357), Different readings indicated by other grammarians (357-358), Vārttikas given in the Kāśikā (359-387), Vārttikas given in the Kāśikā but not found in the Bhāṣya (388-390), Vārttikas with different readings in the Bhāṣya and Kāśikā (391-393), Iṣṭis given in the Kāśikā (394-398), Phiṭsūtras given in the Kāśikā (399), Uṇādisūtras given in the Kāśikā (399-401), Paribhāṣās given in the Kāśikā (401-403). In Hindi.]

Vedālaṅkāra, Bhīmasiṁha (see also Bhīma Siṁha)

1984 "A critique on Pāṇini's sūtra *na dhātulopa ārdhadhātuke* (1.1.4)", ABORI 64 (1983):241-248.

1987 पातञ्जल महाभाष्य में प्रत्याख्यात सूत्र : एक समीक्षात्मक अध्ययन (Kurukshetra: Nirmal Book Agency). [Originally a Kurukshetra University doctoral thesis. In Hindi.]

1988a पातञ्जलमहाभाष्य में अपूर्व कल्पनाएं (Delhi: Parimal Publications). [In Hindi.]

1988b "अलुक्समासप्रकरणे द्वयोर्वार्तिकयोर्विवेचनम्", VS 25.2-4 (= डा॰ चारुदेव-शास्त्रि-स्मृति-विशेषाङ्कः):175-180. [In Sanskrit.]

Venkatacharya, T.

1980 *The Sāhityakaṇṭakoddhāra, Edited with an Introduction and Notes.* (Delhi: Motilal Banarsidass).

1982 Review of Deshpande (1980a), IIJ 24:132-135.

Venkitasubramonia Iyer, S.

1983a "On variants in the Aṣṭādhyāyī", in: Joshi and Laddu (1983), pp. 141-155.

1983b "Variants in Pāṇinisūtras affecting accent", Festschrift

Sreekrishna Sarma, pp. 11-16. [See 1985]

1985 "Variants in Pāṇinisūtras affecting accent", in: Dandekar and Navathe (1985), pp. 427-432. [See 1983b]

Vergiani, Vincenzo

1993 "The negative asamarthasamāsas in the Pāṇinian tradition", RSO 67:65-81.

Verma, Manindra K. and K. P. Mohanan (Eds.)

1990 *Experiencer Subjects in South Asian Languages* (Palo Alto: The Center for the Study of Language and Information, Stanford University).

Vidyālaṅkāra, Vīrendrakumāra

1988 "संस्कृतव्याकरणे पदविभागः", Festschrift Charu Deva Shastri, pp. 185-189.

1992-93 "संस्कृत-व्याकरणे कालस्वरूप-विमर्शः", VS 29.4:57-62, 30.1:1-5. [In Sanskrit.]

Vijayapāla

1983 अष्टाध्यायीशुक्लयजुर्वेदप्रातिशाख्ययोः मत-विमर्शः (Bahālagaḍha: Rām Lāl Kapūr Trust). [Originally a Sampurnananda Sanskrit University doctoral dissertation. In Sanskrit.]

Visalakshy, P.

1981 "The influence of *Cāndra* and *Kātantra* grammars on *Kāśikāvṛtti*", Festschrift Agrawal, pp. 45-49.

1989 *Development of Sanskrit Language* (*During the Period between the Mahābhāṣya and Kāśikā*) (Trivandrum: Pradeep Publishers). [Appendixes: I.1: The variant readings of sūtras between Mahābhāṣya and Kāśikā based on the yogavibhāga (232-233), I.2: Variant readings of the sūtras between Mahābhāṣya and Kāśikā based on the wordings of the sūtras (234-235), I.3: The vārtikas of Mahābhāṣya given as sūtras in Kāśikā (236), I.4: The vārtikas of Mahābhāṣya incorporated in the sūtras of Kāśikā (237-239), I.5: The variant readings of the sūtras pointed out by Kāśikā (240-241), I.6: The variant readings of the sūtras pointed out by the commentaries of Mahābhāṣya and Kāśikā (242-243), II: The differences between the vārtikas of Mahābhāṣya and Kāśikā (244-248), III.1: Indebtedness of Kāśikā sūtras to

Kātantra sūtras (249), III.2: Indebtedness of Kāśikā sūtras to Cāndra sūtras (250-251), III.3: Indebtedness of Kāśikā vārtikas to the vṛtti and sūtras of Cāndra (252-255).]

Viśana Lāla Gauḍa 'Vyomaśekhara' [Vishan Lal Gaur]

1985 पाणिनीय अष्टाध्यायी के रचना-सिद्धान्त (Gaziabad: Lokāloka Prakāśana). [Originally a 1973 doctoral dissertation; to judge from his sources as listed in the bibliography (243-248), it has not been updated. In Hindi.]

Viṭṭhala, Pāṇḍuraṅga

1988 "महावैयाकरणो भर्तृहरिः", Festschrift Charu Deva Shastri, pp. 143-154. [In Sanskrit.]

1990 "वैयाकरणानां शब्दार्थसम्बन्धसमीक्षा", VS 27.2:25-32. [In Sanskrit.]

Vora, P. R.

1983 "Some noteworthy words of Pāṇinian system", Festschrift Jani, pp. 199-206.

Wayman, Alex

1985 "The gait (*gati*) and the path (*mārga*) — reflexions on the horizontal", Festschrift Ingalls, pp. 579-588.

Werba, Chlodwig H.

1997 *Verba Indoarica, Die primären und sekundären Wurzeln der Sanskrit-Sprache. Pars I : Radices Primariae.* (Wien: Verlag der österreichischen Akademie der Wissenschaften).

Wezler, Albrecht

1975 *Bestimmung und Angabe der Funktion von Sekundär-Suffixen durch Pāṇini* (Wiesbaden: Steiner).

1976 "Some observations on the grammatical terminology of Pāṇini (Marginalia to Pāṇini's Aṣṭādhyāyī II)", in: *German Scholars on India : Contributions to Indian Studies* (edited by the Cultural Department of the Embassy of the Federal Republic of Germany, New Delhi), volume II, pp. 361-379.

1977 'Zum Problem der "negativen Appositionen" bei Pāṇini [Marginalien zu Pāṇinis Aṣṭādhyāyī III]", StII 3:35-70.

1980 "Studien zu Patañjalis Mahābhāṣya I: Der Term svārtha und Paribhāṣā CXIII", Festschrift Thieme, pp. 279-309.

1982 "Paralipomena zum Sarvasarvātmakatvavāda (I):

Mahābhāṣya zu Pāṇ. 4.3.155 und seine einheimischen Erklärer", WZKM 26:149-166.

1986a "Zum Verständnis des Bhāṣya zu Pāṇini 3.3.18 (Studien zu Patañjalis Mahābhāṣya II)", WZKSA 30:91-108.

1986b "Cattle, field and barley: a note on Mahābhāṣya I 337.24-27 (Studies in Patañjali's Mahābhāṣya III)", ALB 50:431-477.

1986c "A note on Mahābhāṣya II 366.26: guṇasaṁdrāvo dravyam: Studies on Mallavādin's Dvādaśāranayacakra II", in: *Buddhism and its Relation to other Religions : Essays in Honour of Dr. Shozen Kumai on his Seventieth Birthday*, pp. 1-33.

1992 "How far did Pāṇini's fame really extend in Patañjali's view? (Studies in Patañjali's Mahābhāṣya IV)", Festschrift Mukherji II, pp. 468-478.

1994a "Once again on Patañjali's definition of a word (Studies in Patañjali's Mahābhāṣya V)", Festschrift Oberhammer, pp. 173-189.

1994b "*Credo, quia occidentale* : a note on Sanskrit *varṇa* and its misinterpretation in literature on Mīmāṃsā and Vyākaraṇa", Festschrift Mandana Mishra, pp. 221-241.

Whitney, William Dwight

1885 *The Roots, Verb-forms and Primary Derivatives of the Sanskrit Language. A Supplement to his Sanskrit Grammar* (= BIG Band II. Anhang II) (Leipzig: Breitkopf and Härtel). [Reprinted 1945 (= AOS 30) (New Haven: American Oriental Socitey).]

Witzel, Michael

1986 "On the archetype of Patañjali's Mahābhāṣya", IIJ 29:249-259.

1989 "Tracing the Vedic dialects", in: Caillat (1989), pp. 97-265.

1990 "Notes on Vedic dialects (1)", Zinbun 1990:31-70.

1997 (Ed.) *Inside the Texts, Beyond the Texts : New Approaches to the Study of the Vedas* (= HOS Opera Minora 2) (Cambridge: Department of Sanskrit and Indian Studies, Harvard University).

Wujastyk, Dominik
1982 "Bloomfield and the Sanskrit origin of the terms 'exocentric' and 'endocentric'", HL 9:179-184.
1983 "Do paribhāṣās wrongly immunize Pāṇini's theory against criticism?", in: Joshi and Laddu (1983), pp. 97-103.
1993 *Metarules of Pāṇinian Grammar* : *The Vyāḍi Paribhāṣāvṛtti, Critically Edited with Translation and Commentary* 2 volumes (= GOS V) (Groningen: Egbert Forsten). [I: Introduction, text with critical apparatus, indices; II: Text and commentary. Originally an Oxford University doctoral thesis. I have given the title as it appears on the title pages; on the covers it appears as *Metarules of Pāṇinian Grammar* : *Vyāḍi's Paribhāṣāvṛtti*.]
1994 "A handlist of the vyākaraṇa manuscripts in the Chandra Shum Shere Collection preserved in the Bodleian Library", Festschrift Bhagwat, pp. 159-209.
1996 Review of Hill and Harrison (1991), BSOAS 59:391-392.

Yagi, Toru
1981 "Pāṇini-sūtra 6.4.3 'nāmi'", JIBS 30:482-485.
1984 *Le Mahābhāṣya ad Pāṇini 6.4.1-19* (= PICI 50.) Paris: Institut de Civilisation Indienne.
1986 "Le *Mahābhāṣya* ad Pāṇini 6.4.22-57: un essai de traduction (I)", BCNSOGU 14:43-70. [See 1988, 1989a, b, 1991, 1994.]
1988 "Le *Mahābhāṣya* ad Pāṇini 6.4.22-57: un essai de traduction (III)", BCNSOGU 17:15-31. [See 1986, 1989a, b, 1991, 1994.]
1987-88 "Le débat du *Mahābhāṣya* ad Pāṇini 6.4.22", Festschrift Caillat, pp. 433-441.
1989a "Le *Mahābhāṣya* ad Pāṇini 6.4.22-57: un essai de traduction (II)", in: Indo-Shisōshi Kenkyū (Studies in the History of Indian Thought) 6 (= Special Issue Dedicated to Professor Masaaki Hattori on the Occasion of his Retirement from Kyoto University), pp. 181-189. [See 1986, 1988, 1989b, 1991, 1994.]
1989b "Le *Mahābhāṣya* ad Pāṇini 6.4.22-57: un essai de

traduction (IV)", BCNSOGU 20:1-19. [See 1986, 1988, 1989a, 1991, 1994).]

1991 "Le *Mahābhāṣya* ad Pāṇini 6.4.22-57: un essai de traduction (V)", BCNSOGU 23-24:31-51. [See 1986, 1988, 1989a, b, 1994.]

1992 "The *asiddha/asiddhavat* reconsidered", WZKS 36:49-58.

1994 "Le *Mahābhāṣya* ad Pāṇini 6.4.22-57: un essai de traduction (VI)", BCNSOGU 28:1-16. [See 1986, 1988, 1989a, b, 1991.]

1995 "On vārttika 1 on Pāṇini's *Aṣṭādhyāyī* 6.4.24", JEAS 4:88-108.

Yajan Veer (see also Dahiya)

1985 "A tale of three terms (*vā*, *vibhāṣā* and *anyatarasyām*)", in: Dandekar and Navathe (1985), pp. 433-440.

Yudhiṣṭhira Mīmāṃsaka

1972 महाभाष्यम् पतञ्जलिमुनि-विरचितम् हिन्दी-व्याख्या-सहितम् द्वितीयो भागः (१।२-४) (Delhi: Śrī Pyārelāl Drākṣādevī Trust). [Text with Hindi translation and notes of Mahābhāṣya 1.2-4.]

1974 महाभाष्यम् पतञ्जलिमुनि-विरचितम् हिन्दी-व्याख्या-सहितम् तृतीयो भागः (द्वितीयोऽध्यायः) (Delhi: Śrī Pyārelāl Drākṣādevī Trust). [Text with Hindi translation and notes of Mahābhāṣya 2.]

1979 महाभाष्यम् पतञ्जलिमुनि-विरचितम् हिन्दी-व्याख्या-सहितम् प्रथमो भागः (प्रथमाध्ययायस्य प्रथमः पादः) (Delhi: Śrī Pyārelāl Drākṣādevī Trust). [Text with Hindi translation and notes of Mahābhāṣya 1.1.]

1984 संस्कृत व्याकरण-शास्त्र का इतिहास 3 volumes (Bahālagaḍha: Rām Lāl Kapūr Trust, saṁvat 2041). [I: fourth edition, II: third edition, III: second edition. In Hindi. Major Appendixes in volume III: 3 (46-58): Readings noted by Nāgeśa on the basis of the Bhāṣya, 4 (59-61): Readings noted by Anantarāma on the basis of the Bhāṣya, 5 (62-81): Pāṇinīyaśikṣā, 6 (82-92): Verses from the Jāmbavatīvijaya, 12 (190-299): Index of names of persons and places alluded to in the work.]

Zimmermann, Francis

1989 "Les théories de la signification", in: Auroux (1989), pp. 401-416.

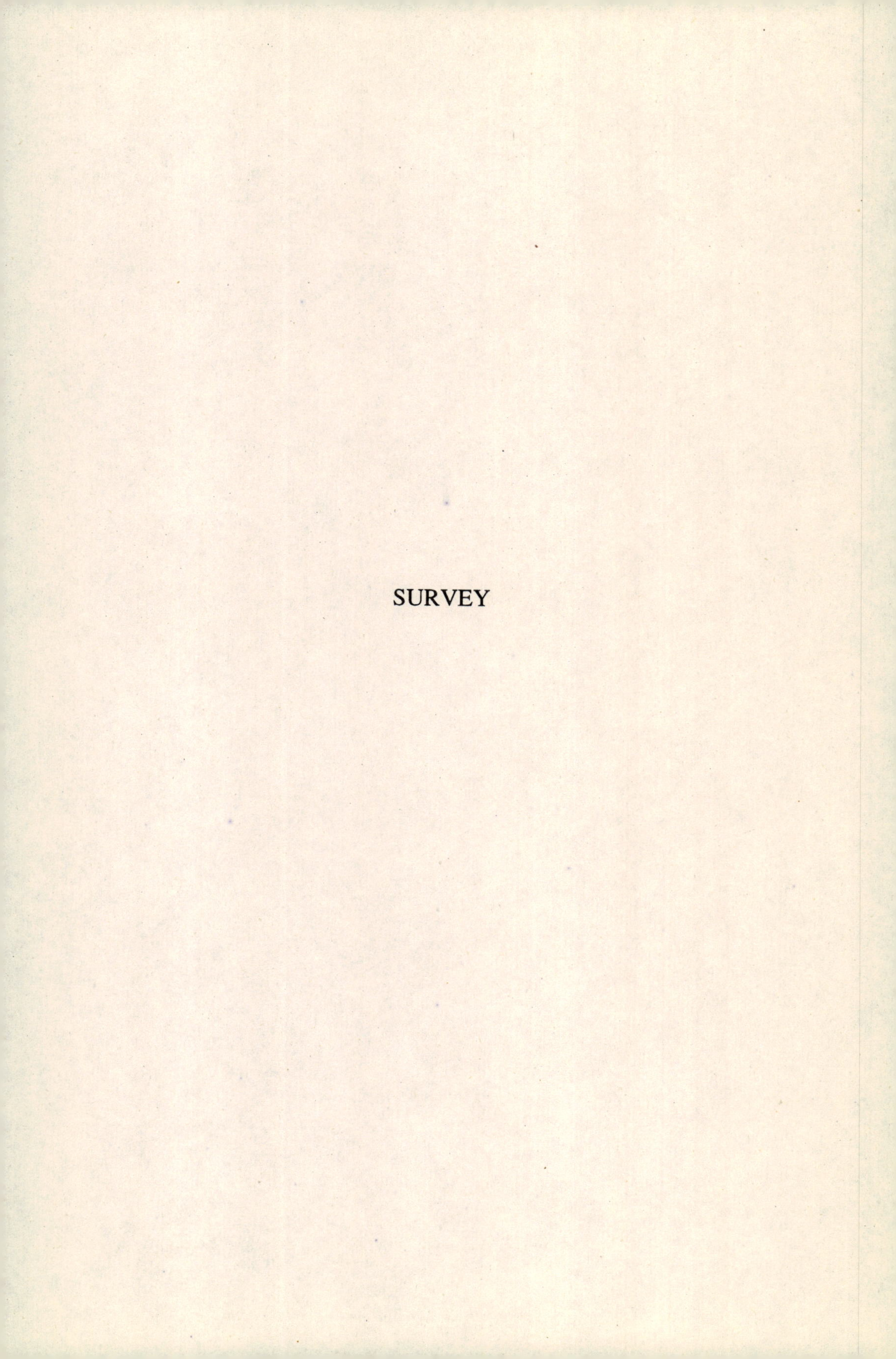

SURVEY

1. HISTORIES OF SANSKRIT GRAMMAR, SURVEYS OF RESEARCH, BIBLIOGRAPHIES

1.1. HISTORIES OF SANSKRIT GRAMMAR (II.1)

Yudhiṣṭhira Mīmāṁsaka (1984) is an expanded version of the author's excellent history of Sanskrit grammar (1973). The third volume includes a set of corrections and additions (1984:III:124-135) and several appendixes, including one (1984:III:106-123) in which Yudhiṣṭhira Mīmāṁsaka has translated into Hindi the references made in my earlier survey to his own history. Lokamaṇi Dāhāla (1989/90) presents succinctly the main facts about the history of Sanskrit grammar. Another general survey of Pāṇinian grammar was composed by Jayadev M. Shukla (1975).

In a work published two decades ago, Scharfe (1977) attempted to cover the overall history of Sanskrit grammar and related areas, including not only Pāṇinian works but also prātiśākhyas, Buddhist and Jaina grammars, śikṣās, grammars of Dravidian languages, 'other systems of grammar' such as the descriptions in the Saṅkṣiptasāra, grammars of Middle Indo-Aryan dialects, the Pārasīprakāśa, and grammars of New Indo-Aryan languages, all in the space of approximately 125 pages; see Cardona (1979) for my opinion of this contribution. The most recent work I know to treat the history of Sanskrit grammar in English is by B. N. Jha (1990).[1] Jha has consulted most of the earlier histories of Sanskrit grammar, which he subjects to some criticism. Thus, concerning Satyakāma Varmā (1971a), he states (1990:iii)

> The author Dr. Satyakāma Varmā has partially succeeded in writing his work named "Sanskrit Vyācaraṇa kā Udbhava aura Vikāsa". He has blindly accepted and supported the views of the western authors and their fòllowers, most of the important views of our scholars have been set aside and therefore his work can not be said to be completely reliable.

Jha (1990:iii) considers that Yudhiṣṭhira Mīmāṁsaka's work of 1973 'is appreciable', and he goes on to say (1990:iii-iv), 'and I am grateful to him for his contribution to the society, to the nation and to the world.' Just before this, however, Jha is considerably more critical (1990:iii):

> The respected Mīmāṁsaka has fully studied texts and his popular book "Sanskrita Vyākaraṇa kā Itihāsa" is an Authentic book on its subject. But after going through his work it is found that his work lacks in Chronology written in an unsystematic way. He has not adopted the proper way of writing the History. The hotch-potch in his work is seen here and there which creates tension to the reader.

I consider, however, that Jha's own work hardly justifies such criticism of others. It is certainly not as informative or richly documented as Yudhiṣṭhira Mīmāṁsaka's. Nor is it well written. Moreover, Jha's reasoning leaves much to be desired. For example, at the beginning of a treatment of 'Vaidika Grammar' (1990:167), Jha lists 'Śukla Yajuḥ Prātiśākhya written by Śaunaka', as though this were Śaunaka's work instead of Kātyāyana's, and 'Atharva-Prātiśākhya written by Śaunaka', as though the Śaunakīyā Caturādhyāyikā were the only prātiśākhya associated with the Atharvaveda and Sūrya Kānta (1939) had not edited another such work. Jha discusses the age of Bhartṛhari (1990:229-235) and concludes, 'The age of the respected Bhartṛhari is fixed up 350 B. C. as per findings of mine.' He does not, however, mention the important work of Jambūvijaya. In support of the claim that Pāṇini composed uṇādisūtras, Jha says (1990:146),

> In Pāṇini's work "Aṣṭādhyāyī" we find a sūtra "Uṇādayo bahulam" 3/3/1. Which evinces that he also wrote some Uṇādi formulae to complete his five fold grammatical work. According to the views of supporters of Pāṇini's grammar there are two different branches of Uṇādisūtras. Those are Pañcapādī (five footed) and Daśapādī (ten footed). Both are equally honoured in grammarian's community, which of them was hinted by Pāṇini is explained here.

Concerning ākṛtigaṇas, that is type listings such that a representative sample of an open set is given as opposed to an exhaustive listing of all members of a closed group, Jha says (1990:391), 'Ākṛtigaṇa: The gaṇa (group) which does not act as per requirement of a particular word of a particular group. This means that those rules which are applicable to different groups of words are called Ākṛtigaṇa.' As can be seen from the citation concerning the uṇādisūtras, Jha rather amusingly translates *pāda* as 'feet'. He does this again when he deals — in a section headed '**Names of Aṣṭādhyāyī feet**' — with certain groups of sūtras and says (1990:108), 'Pāṇini's grammar has been classified into different feet.'

A brief survey of major ideas, methods and controversies in grammar and related śāstras appears in Cardona (1990b, 1994; see also forthcoming a-e, g). The second chapter of Janaki Prasad Dwivedi (1987) contains sections devoted to major commentaries and their authors, including the Kāśikāvṛtti and its commentator Jinendrabuddhi, the Bhāgavṛtti, the Rūpāvatāra, the Bhāṣāvṛtti, and Śaraṇadeva's Durghaṭavṛtti.

Bronkhorst (1983) has contributed a major study on the history of Pāṇinian grammar in the post-Patañjali period. The first part of Bronkhorst's article (1983:357-365) considers evidence showing that some anonymous grammarians who came after Kātyāyana and Patañjali but before Candragomin altered Pāṇini's work in efforts to perfect it. He begins with a discussion of what is said in vārttika 15 to 3.1.87, from which he arrives at the following conclusion (Bronkhorst [1983:357]):

> We must conclude that *yuj* and *sṛj* were added to the fourth gaṇa of the Dhātupāṭha after Patañjali. The fact that the two roots occur brotherly together in the fourth gaṇa (IV.68 and 69) also shows that they were added under the influence of the vārttika and Bhāṣya discussed above.

In addition, Bronkhorst argues (1983:358-361) that Candragomin could not have been the grammarian who inserted *yuj* and *sṛj* in the fourth gaṇa of the Pāṇinian dhātupāṭha, from which he concludes (1983:361):

> In the time preceding Candra grammarians of the Pāṇinian tradition were working to perfect Pāṇini's grammar. These grammarians knew Kātyāyana's vārttikas and Patañjali's *Mahābhāṣya* but rather than studying these works in their own right, they continued the work begun by these two authors. Where Kātyāyana and Patañjali noted that Pāṇini's grammar failed to generate *yujyate* (*brahmacārī yogam*) and *sṛjyate* (*mālām*), our anonymous grammarians made such changes in the Dhātupāṭha so that Pāṇini's grammar was able to generate these forms. It seems further that they did not follow Kātyāyana and Patañjali slavishly, for the changes introduced in the Dhātupāṭha do not account for *asarji* (*mālām*), also mentioned in the *Mahābhāṣya*. With respect to this last point, however, we must be careful: we do not know if our grammarians had not made changes in other parts of the grammar to account for *asarji*.

Bronkhorst goes on (1983:361-364) to consider what is said in the Sarvadarśanasaṅgaha and the Mādhavīyadhātuvṛtti about the term *yoga* and the base *yuj* of the fourth gaṇa. He states (1983:362-363):

> No mention is made of other Dhātupāṭhas which are without the entry *yujA samādhau*. But clearly it did not escape Sāyaṇa's attention that this entry made the vārttika quoted partially superfluous. It is true that the difficulty is explained away. But it is

> impossible to believe that Sāyaṇa — who so often makes mention of the differences between the versions of the Dhātupāṭha — has not considered the possibility that the entry *yujA samādhau* was an addition to the Dhātupāṭha. Indeed, the statement in the *Sarvadarśanasaṃgaha* which is under discussion, may ultimately be the expression of a suspicion, or even of a privately held belief, of Sāyaṇa the author of the *Mādhavīyā Dhātuvṛtti.*

Bronkhorst ends his first section (1983:364-365) by noting one additional change that was effected in the Pāṇinīya dhātupāṭha at a time before Candragomin.

The second section of Bronkhorst's study (1983:365-373) deals with changes in the Pāṇinīya sūtrapāṭha and gaṇapāṭha as known in the Kāśikā. Concerning the sūtrapāṭha, Bronkhorst says (1983:367):

> We conclude that the sūtras were changed by grammarians who were rather well acquainted with Patañjali's *Mahābhāṣya.* They attempted to incorporate what they considered of value in the *Mahābhāṣya* into the *Aṣṭādhyāyī.* At the same time they felt free to disagree with Patañjali. They further preferred a clear, explicit formulation of sūtras to obscure hints.

As to whether these changes in the sūtras were made before or after Candragomin, Bronkhorst admits (1983:367) that the question is hard to answer, but he goes on to consider evidence that he thinks allows a definite conclusion and says (1983:369), 'We conclude that the changes in some of the sūtras of the *Aṣṭādhyāyī* were made before Candra, and were known to him.' In addition, Bronkhorst takes up evidence (1983:369-371) to show that the Kāśikā '... may contain far more deviations from the text known to Patañjali than Kielhorn suspected.' Immediately after this statement, the author says (1983:371), 'It can be argued that Bhartṛhari's *Mahābhāṣyasīpikā* on Patañjali's *Mahābhāṣya* contains an indication that Bhartṛhari was aware that earlier grammarians in the Pāṇinian tradition at times felt free to change the wording of sūtras of the *Aṣṭādhyāyī*.' He then goes on to consider two passages from the Mahābhāṣyasīpikā. Although Bronkhorst admits (1983:372), 'It goes without saying that much is unclear in these two passages from Bhartṛhari's commentary', after further discussion he feels justified in concluding (1983:373), 'It follows that Kuṇi must have lived and worked after Patañjali and before Bhartṛhari.'

The third major section of Bronkhorst's article (1983:373-379) deals with changes made in the Pāṇinīya gaṇapāṭha. In his fourth section

(1983:379-382) Bronkhorst takes up a question that had already bothered Kielhorn: why the Kāśikāvṛtti does not explicitly mention Candragomin's grammar. Bronkhorst's solution is that the authors of the Kāśikā and Candragomin used post-Patañjali works independently. He says (1983:380):

> Since we have come to the conclusion that Candra and the authors of the *Kāśikā* had their knowledge of the sūtras of the *Aṣṭādhyāyī* from a common source (§2.3, above), it does not seem adventurous to assume that this common source consisted of the sūtras of the *Aṣṭādhyāyī* plus one or more commentaries on them. Both Candra and the *Kāśikā* made use of these works and, for this reason, show points of similarity even with respect to features which are not found in the *Mahābhāṣya*. We do not now have to suppose that the authors of the *Kāśikā* made use of, or even knew, Candra's grammar.

Bronkhorst's fifth section (1983:382-383) considers some evidence from the Kāśikā to show (1983:383), '... that the *Kāśikā* has preserved traces from the earlier period in which Patañjali was not always considered authoritative and scholars felt free to improve upon Pāṇini's grammar by making changes in it.' Bronkhorst goes on in the next section (1983:383-391) to deal with some material from the Vyāḍīyaparibhāṣāvṛtti, concluding (1983:391):

> If the above considerations are correct, Vyāḍi's *Paribhāṣāvṛtti* represents one of the very interesting documents of the history of Pāṇinian grammar. It may well be the only surviving text from the unknown period in which Patañjali's *Mahābhāṣya* was not yet taken as the final authority, a period, none the less, in which changes — we don't know how many or how great — were introduced in the *Aṣṭādhyāyī* and all that accompanies it.

The section ends with a reference to Wujastyk's work (1993), then still in manuscript. In his penultimate section (1983:391-398), Bronkhorst takes up the famous concluding verses of the second kāṇḍa of the Vākyapadīya, which regard the period of history to which his study is dedicated. In a brief summary section (1983:398-399), Bronkhorst emphasizes that his study shows '... that the opinion according to which the Pāṇinian system stopped developing with Patañjali, needs rethinking.' The article ends with two appendixes, one on Jayāditya and Vāmana (1983:399-402), the other (1983:402-404) on Śabara and Patañjali.

Bronkhorst's study is rich in both materials and ideas, and it is impossible here to discuss in detail more than a small part of the evidence he adduces in support of his conclusions. In view of the importance of Bronkhorst's article, however, I think it appropriate to consider with care one of the major pieces of evidence upon which he relies: what is said in vārttika 15 on **A** 3.1.87 and the Bhāṣya thereto. The rule in question (**A** 3.1.87: *karmavat karmaṇā tulyakriyaḥ*) is an atideśasūtra which provides that operations associated with a kāraka classed as karman apply when a kāraka spoken of as agent (*kartṛ*) is involved, if the participant in question behaves with respect to the action in the same manner as a karman. This accounts for usages like

(a) *odanaḥ pacyate* 'The rice is cooking.'

(b) *odano' pāci* 'The rice has cooked.'

Now, examples like

(c) *odanaḥ pacyate devadattena* 'Rice is being cooked by Devadatta',

(d) *odano' pāci devadattena* 'Some rice has been cooked by Devadatta'

involve rice as a direct participant in cooking, classed as karman with respect to this act, and affixes are introduced on condition that such a kāraka is to be signified: *pacyate* contains the ātmanepada ending *te* preceded by the vikaraṇa *yak* and *apāci* contains the suffix ***ciṇ***.[2] To account for (a) and (b), Pāṇini assigns the rice in question to the agent (*kartṛ*) category and, by **A** 3.1.87, lets operations associated with a karman apply here also: (a) has *pac-ya-te* as does (c), and both (b) and (d) have *apāci*. In the language of Patañjali's time and place, the following were also possible:

(e) *sṛjyate mālām* '... is respectfully making a garland.'

(f) *asarji mālām* '... has respectfully made a garland.'

(g) *yujyate brahmacārī yogam* 'The brahmacārin attains yoga.'

In 3.1.87 vt. 15 (*sṛjijujyoḥ śyaṁs tu*), Kātyāyana says that the operations extended by **A** 3.1.87 should apply where the bases *sṛj* and *yuj* are involved, but that instead of ***yak***, the vikaraṇa ***śyan*** is to occur. Patañjali[3] both gives the examples (e)-(g) and elaborates on what the vārttika states: one understands *bahulam* and *sakarmakayoḥ* to recur from the preceding vārttika (3.1.87. vt. 14: *duhipacyor bahulaṁ sakarmakayoḥ*), so that an agent is variously (*bahulam*) treated as an object with respect to *sṛj* and *yuj*, if these take an object (*sakarmakayoḥ*). Patañjali also notes that the agent associated with *sṛj* is one endowed with respect (*śraddhopapanne kartari*). In addition, Patañjali distinguishes between what is provided for with *sṛj* and *yuj*. He notes that with respect to *sṛj* the provision is made that an agent is treated as though it were an object in order to allow ***ciṇ*** and ātmanepada affixes; with respect to *yuj*, the provision is made so that the suffix ***yak*** which would be in order for a normal object-agent (*nyāyye karmakartari*) not occur . That is, in both cases, since the verbs as used in (e)-(g) have objects (*sakarmaka*), they do not qualify for the extension stated in **A** 3.1.87. However, *sṛj* and *yuj* differ in that (g) concerns an agent which is previously an object (*karmakartṛ*), so that providing for ***śyan*** blocks ***yak***, which would be appropriate where such an object-agent is concerned. Kaiyaṭa and others others,[4] put it as follows. One starts with a situation where the brahmacārin of (g) is the same person of whom one says

(h) *yogo brahmacāriṇaṁ yunakti* 'Yoga connects (that is, reaches) the brahmacārin.'

Now, since Patañjali does indeed speak here of a karmakartṛ, whatever else one might say about the interpretation of (g), one thing cannot be denied: the verb *yuj* involved here must be one that is like *pac* of (a)-(d), a base that can take an object to begin with. In sum, this has to be ***yujìr*** 'join, connect, yoke' of the seventh gaṇa (*yunakti, yuṅkte*). To be sure, this cannot be ***yuja*** of the fourth gaṇa, which is exemplified by usages like

(i) *sukhaduḥkhe same kṛtvā lābhālābhau jayājayau | tato yuddhāya yujyasva naivaṁ pāpam avāpsyasi* 'Equate happiness and misery, gain and loss, victory and defeat, then strive (gird yourself) for battle; thus you will not incur sin' (Gītā 2.38)

(j) *buddhiyukto jahātīha ubhe sukṛtaduṣkṛte | tasmād yogāya yujyasva* ... 'One who is mentally disciplined (with equanimity) leaves behind here good and bad deeds; therefore strive for yoga ...' (Gītā 2.50)

On the other hand, it is difficult to see how what Kātyāyana says in 3.1.87 vt. 15 and Patañjali says in the Mahābhāṣya on this necessarily leads to the conclusion which Bronkhorst reaches. It is noteworthy that Bronkhorst does not consider the entire Bhāṣya passage in question (see my note 3) and that his reasoning is, I think, lax. In order not to misrepresent him, let me cite in full what he says about this passage (1983:357):

> Vt. 15 to P. 3.1.87 reads: *sṛjiyujyoḥ śyaṃstu*. Patañjali explains (Mbh. II, p. 69.l.15-16): *sṛjiyujyoḥ sakarmakayoḥ kartā bahulaṃ karmavad bhavatīti vaktavyam / śyaṃstu bhavati* / "It must be stated that the agent of [the roots] *sṛj* and *yuj*, when they have an object (*karman*), is often like the object. But [the *vikaraṇa*] is [not *yaK*, but] *ŚyaN*."

The effect of the agent's being like the object is that, instead of active endings, the verb will take passive endings, i.e., *yaK* (P. 3.1.67), Ātmanepada (P. 1.3.13), *CiṆ* (P. 3.1.66). The present vārttika prescribes *ŚyaN* instead of *yaK*, which results in a different accent (P. 6.1.197), but Atmanepada and *CiṆ* remain. The examples in the Bhāṣya illustrating this vārttika are *sṛjyate mālām* and *asarji mālām* for *sṛj*; *yujyate brahmacārīyogam* for *yuj* (Mbh. II, p. 69, l. 16-18).

It is clear that the first and last of these three examples would be accounted for by an occurrence of *yuj* and *srj* in the fourth gaṇa (*divādi*) of the Dhātupāṭha. The present stem of the roots of this gaṇa takes the *vikaraṇa ŚyaN* (P. 3.1.69). An anudātta vowel added as marker would bring about Ātmanepada endings, by P. 1.3.12. It is, however, equally clear that the vārttika and the Bhāṣya discussed above show that *yuj* and *sṛj* were not found in the fourth gaṇa of the Dhātupāṭha at that time.

As I hope to have made clear, however, Patañjali's example (g) and what he says about it do not support the claim Bronkhorst makes. The example is not immediately accounted for on the basis of the fourth gaṇa base *yuj**a***, which does not lend itself to a karmakartṛ. Nor does what Patañjali says require one to conclude that the dhātupāṭha known to him did not contain this base, any more than this example can serve to show this dhātupāṭha did contain this base. In brief, I consider that the major claim upon which Bronkhorst bases so much of his later argumentation itself rests on an insufficient understanding of what is said in the text of the Mahābhāṣya to which Bronkhorst appeals.[5]

1.2. SURVEYS OF RESEARCH (II.2)

Major work done in the area of Pāṇinian studies between 1975 and the mid-1980's is discussed in Cardona (1989). In addition, a fully updated survey of work in this area is to be carried out by Ms. Małgorzata Wielińska of the University of Hamburg.[6]

1.3. BIBLIOGRAPHIES (II.3)

The fourth and fifth volumes of Dandekar's *Vedic Bibliography* (1985, 1993) contain a large number of entries — some with annotations — for work on Pāṇini and related areas, including references to summaries of papers delivered at meetings of the All India Oriental Conference, which were not accessible to me. An extensive recent bibliography on Sanskrit grammar has been compiled by Potter (1990). Although the procedure adopted for listing authors of original works is subject to objection (see Cardona [1993c]) this is a useful and informative bibliography. The select bibliography compiled by Laddu and Kar (1983) is useful but of uneven quality; many of the entries lack important information such as publishers and exact paginations of articles. Ramseier (1993) is a very good bibliography covering editions of both the Vākyapadīya and the Mahābhāṣyadīpikā as well as secondary literature on Bhartṛhari. Through the kindness of the author, I have had access to an updated version of this bibliography in a computer file. Also valuable is Aithal (1991). For, although this work is not specifically devoted to grammar (*vyākaraṇa*), it covers manuscript materials and editions of works such as prātiśākhyas and has an extensive section (pp. 412-426 [**857-859**]) on the Pāṇinīya-śikṣā. Similarly, while they do not concern themselves primarily with Pāṇinian grammar, the bibliographic articles of M. M. Deshpande (1989a) and H. H. Hock (1989), as well as their joint article (1991), include studies that touch on this area. Finally, Wujastyk (1994) merits mention as a useful contribution informing scholars of what is available in a collection of manuscripts of grammatical works.

2. PĀṆINI, KĀTYĀYANA AND PATAÑJALI

2.1. PĀṆINI: THE AṢṬĀDHYĀYĪ

2.1.1. *Editions, translations, indexes and lexicons of the Aṣṭādhyāyī*

2.1.1.1. *Editions and translations of the sūtrapāṭha* (III.1.2.1)

The recent edition of Pāṇini's grammar by Śrīśaṁkaradeva Pāṭhaka (1990) includes vārttikas and indicates anuvṛtti — features found in some earlier editions, such as the one by Gopal Dutt Pande (1987) — and also includes the gaṇapāṭha pertinent to sūtras, at the bottom of the page. Madhav Ganesh Joshi (1992) and Yajanveer Dahiya (1995) give the Aṣṭādhyāyī sūtra-pāṭha with the accentuation observed by paṇḍitas when they recite the text.[7] Cardona (1997a:607-731) has an appendix in which the sūtrapāṭha is given — in both Devanāgarī and Roman scripts — as it may have been received by Kātyāyana, along with indications of modifications suggested by Kātyāyana and Patañjali and incorporated by some later Pāṇinīyas.[8] It is also worth noting that C. Sankara Rama Sastri's edition has recently been reprinted (1994) with an introduction by Ratna Basu.

The most recent complete translation of the Aṣṭādhyāyī into English is that of S. M. Katre (1987). Rama Nath Sharma's translation (1990, 1995) is an excellent piece of work, especially useful for the detailed derivations given. Volume IV (adhyāyas 4-5) is in press, and a fifth volume in two parts (adhyāyas 6-8) is in progress.

S. D. Joshi and J. A. F. Roodbergen (1991, 1993a, 1994a, 1995) have undertaken a joint translation of the Aṣṭādhyāyī.[9] In their preface to the first volume, Joshi and Roodbergen make the following interesting statement: 'We have also come to the conclusion that to some extent, the *Kāśikāvṛtti* has preserved an authentic Pāṇinian tradition, independent of and different from the one followed by and established by Patañjali and his grammatical sources.' This one-page introduction does not contain evidence to back up the conclusion, but some arguments in support of this position are presented in Joshi and Roodbergen (1991-92). The authors begin their presentation noting (1991-92:131a):

... Patañjali is often at a loss how to construe Pāṇini's intention. Especially in the matter of *anuvṛtti* and *nivṛtti* of rules, and in that of applying conflict-solving procedures he cannot serve as the final authority which replaces independent judgement. Moreover, we can identify traces of an authentic Pāṇinian tradition different from and independent of Patañjali. These traces have, to some extent, been preserved by the *Kāśikāvṛtti* (*KV*). We will consider three instances.'

The examples they discuss concern **A** 1.1.36: *antaraṁ bahiryogopa-saṁvyānayoḥ*, **A** 1.1.62: *pratyayalope pratyayalakṣaṇam* in connection with **A** 1.1.56: *sthānivad ādeśo' nalvidhau*, and **A** 1.1.69: *aṇudit savarṇasya cāpratyayaḥ*. Joshi and Roodbergen deal with arguments presented in the Mahābhāṣya and examples from the Kāśikā, all in the short space of less than ten columns. I cannot avoid noting that some of their claims and arguments are weak. Concerning the first sūtra dealt with, they cite the example *antare/antarāḥ gṛhāḥ*, about which they say (1991-92:131a), 'The example is not found in the *Mbh.*' Subsequently (1991-92:131b), they quote the two counter-examples given in the Kāśikā — *anayor grāmayor antare tāpasaḥ prativasati, tasminnantare śītāny udakāni* — and go on to say:

These counter-examples are not found in the *MBh.* The question is, how can the sg. loc. *antare* serve as a counter-example for what, according to the *KV*, should be a pl. nom.? The only satisfactory answer is that the source or sources quoted by the *KV* takes or take P. 1.1.36 to be a general rule, not restricted to the use of *antara* in the pl. nom. In that case, the counter-examples make sense, because here *antare*, which shows nominal inflection, is used instead of *antarasmin.*

That the Mahābhāṣya does not give the example *antare/antarāḥ gṛhāḥ* in its discussion of **A** 1.1.36 does not prove much. The Bhāṣya discussion begins with two vārttikas of Kātyāyana concerning whether the sūtra needs to include *upasaṁvyāna*. One could, then, equally well consider that for Kātyāyana and Patañjali the use of *antare* and *antarāḥ* as alternants referring to something located outside simply did not call for any discussion, so that examples for this usage are not brought up. As for the Kāśikā's counterexamples, it is surprising that Joshi and Roodbergen overlook something the Kāśikā itself says. Immediately after giving the counter-examples, the Kāśikā goes on to say: *madhyapradeśavacano' ntaraśabdaḥ*| *gaṇasūtrasya cedaṁ pratyudāharaṇam* 'The term *antara* (here) signifies a mid place; and this counter-example is relative to the gaṇasūtra.' That is, the Kāśikā accepts *antaraṁ bahiryogopasaṁvyānayoḥ* as a gaṇasūtra under **A** 1.1.27 *sarvādīni sarvanāmāni.* Both this gaṇasūtra and **A** 1.1.36 concern *antara* used with reference to something that is outside something else or is a garment one wraps around oneself. By the former, *antara-* is classed as a pronominal regardless of the endings with which it may occur. **A** 1.1.36 provides that *antara* is optionally a pronominal with respect to the replacement of the nominative plural ending *jas* by *śi.* It is certain, moreover, that at least a gaṇasūtra identical to **A** 1.1.34: *pūrva-parāvaradakṣiṇottarāparādharāṇi vyavasthāyām asaṁjñāyām* was part of the gaṇapāṭha to **A** 1.1.27 as known to Kātyāyana and Patañjali, since the former explicitly refers to this in his vārttika on **A** 1.1.34 (*avarādīnāṁ ca punaḥ sūtrapāṭhe grahaṇānarthakyaṁ gaṇe paṭhitatvāt*). It is, therefore, at least plausible that the other gaṇasūtras known to the Kāśikākāra were part of the gaṇapāṭha known to Kātyāyana and Patañjali. There is, then, no warrant for the conclusion Joshi and Roodbergen reach.

Concerning **A** 1.1.69, Joshi and Roodbergen consider why the rule should state *apratyayaḥ* and remark (1991-92:134b-135a):

> The *KV* clarifies this by providing the correct counter-examples. Two rules are quoted, P. 3.2.160 [sic!], which introduces the single phoneme *kṛt*-suffix *u*, and P. 4.3.9, which introduces the single phoneme *taddhita*-suffix *a*, both without *anubandha*. Consequently, these two suffixes can be included in *aṆ*, and therefore represent their *savarṇa* varieties. But this is not desired. To prevent the over-application of P. 1.1.69 in these cases, the exception *apratyayaḥ* has been stated. We note that these counter-examples are not found in Patañjali's *bhāṣya* on P. 1.1.69 nor in his commentators.

To my understanding, the last statement is meant to imply — if not to state outright — that the Kāśikā has taken its examples from a source outside the tradition of the Bhāṣya. The Kāśikā cites **A** 3.2.168: *sanāśaṁsabhikṣa uḥ* and **A** 4.3.9: *a sāmpratike*. It is to be noted that the Mahābhāṣya discussion on **A** 1.1.69 begins (Kielhorn [1880-85:I.177.18]) by referring to the selfsame sūtras to show why the rule says *apratyayaḥ* : *apratyaya iti kimartham | sanāśaṁsabhikṣa uḥ | a sāmpratika iti.*

In sum, I consider that Joshi and Roodbergen have not made a compelling case for their thesis.

A comparable attitude toward the Mahābhāṣya in considering the Aṣṭādhyāyī is evinced in another article by S. D. Joshi (1982c), in which he takes up two Pāṇinian sūtras to illustrate a general point.[10] Joshi begins his presentation as follows (1982c:123):

> We always follow the examples given in the *Mahābhāṣya* and in the later commentaries in interpreting the rules of Pāṇini. Some of these examples appear to be arbitrarily invented. Such examples which are not attested in literature and which suffer from pedantry cannot serve as a guide to what has been said by the speaker or written by the author of the Sanskrit language.

In the same vein he goes on to say (1982c:123), 'The traditional examples which are not attested in literature and which do not appear at once natural should be looked upon as doubtful ones.' In his discussion of **A** 2.2.11 (*pūraṇaguṇasuhitārthasadavyayatavyasamānādhikaraṇena* [*na* 10, *ṣaṣṭhī* 8]), Joshi considers (1982c:125) the examples *caurasya dviṣan* 'enemy of the thief' and *vṛṣalasya dviṣan* 'enemy of the vṛṣala', which Patañjali cites as requiring the rule to include *-sat-*. A form of *dviṣat-*, with the suffix ***śatṛ***, should not form a compound with a semantically and syntactically related pada that terminates in a sixth-triplet ending, which would otherwise be allowed by the general rule **A** 2.2.8 (*ṣaṣṭhī*). Hence, **A** 2.2.11 includes derivates with affixes called *sat* among those for which compounding with a related genitive term is disallowed. Joshi refutes Patañjali's reasoning as follows (1982c:125):

> But strictly speaking these cannot be the examples for *sat*. The reason is that the technical designation *sat* cannot apply to *ŚatṚ* added to *dviṣ-*. The word *tau* in P. 3.2.127 which defines the term *sat* refers to the suffixes *ŚatṚ* and *ŚānaC* which are substitutes for *lAṬ*. And P. 3.3.14 indicates that the name *sat* is also given to the suffixes *ŚatṚ* and *ŚānaC* when they replace *lṚṬ*. Thus the name *sat* stands for the present and the future participle endings only which serve the marker of the present and future tenses. Since *ŚatṚ* in *dviṣan* is not *sat* how could P. 2.2.11 prohibit compounding in *caurasya dviṣan* ? Consequently, *caurasya dviṣan* cannot be the real example for *sat*.

Now, I have no quarrel with Joshi's saying that under *his* interpretation **A** 3.2.127 (*tau sat*) assigns the name *sat* only to the affixes ***śatṛ*** and ***śānac*** which replace ***laṭ***. As he presents his argument, however, he assumes that this is the only possible interpretation and — at least by silence — that Patañjali too would subscribe to this, hence be involved in faulty reasoning so far as concerns his examples for **A** 2.2.11. This is not the case. **A** 3.2.127 vt. 1 (*tau sad iti vacanam asaṁsargārtham*) argues that the sūtra states *tau* in order to dissociate the affixes to which the name *sat* is assigned from the specific properties it would otherwise have. That is, the name applies to ***śatṛ*** and ***śānac*** whether or not they replace ***laṭ***, ***lṛṭ***. Thus, for Kātyāyana and Patañjali there is no faulty reasoning involved if *sat* in **A** 3.2.127 has for a purpose to disallow compounding of a genitive with a form of *dviṣat*.

Joshi neverthless brings up an important issue. I think, however, that the issue is more subtle than would appear from the manner in which he presents it. We have of course to seek early attestations wherever possible for the data for which rules of the Aṣṭādhyāyī are supposed to account. Yet surely we should not place too much emphasis on Vedic materials exclusively. For Pāṇini describes what is patently a spoken language, with idiomatic usages and turns of phrase that might not be normal for most of the registers adopted in Vedic texts, which in any case represent only a part of the possible data for pre-Pāṇinian usage. Of course later, post-Pāṇinian Sansrkit texts are subject to the same proviso, with the additional issue that for most of the authors in question Sanskrit is not an idiom of common usage.[11] Moreover, it is somewhat presumptuous for a modern scholar — albeit a native speaker of an Indo-Aryan language, hence with more appreciation for Indo-Aryan idiom than a European or other non-Indian — to make such value judgements as Joshi has made. I think a bit more humility, with full attention to all the details of arguments presented by Pāṇinīyas and to the attested materials is in order, without being quick to label something 'arbitrarily invented' or say that such and such examples 'do not appear natural'.

I think it appropriate to note here also the reissue of A. R. Rājarājavarmā's work (1990). In this superb recasting of Pāṇini's work, the author deals with all the topics covered in the Aṣṭādhyāyī, citing sūtras, explaining them in lucid Sanskrit, and giving examples. This is, in effect, a latter-day Siddhāntakaumudī of a very high order.

2.1.1.2. *Editions of the dhātupāṭha and the gaṇapāṭha* (III.1.2.2)

Volume III.1 of the Osmania edition of the Kāśikā with indexes (B. R. Sastry and V. Sundara Sarma [1976]) contains a dhātu-pāṭha text (1976:53-79), preceded (1976:51-52) by a description of markers used with verb bases and their purposes, as well as an index of verb bases (1976:80-145).

An edition of the gaṇapāṭha along with an index of gaṇas appears in volume III.1 (pp. 338-396) of the Osmania edition of the Kāśikā with indexes (B. R. Sastry and V. Sundara Sarma [1976]). Chandradatta Sharma (1989) has edited a previously unpublished commentary on the gaṇas by Bhaṭṭa Yajñeśvara.[12]

2.1.1.3. *Lexicons and indexes* (III.1.2.3)

Abhyankar's dictionary has been revised and enlarged with the collaboration of Jayadev M. Shukla (Abhyankar-Shukla [1986]). The most recent work of this kind, by Avanindra Kumar (1996), is more than the title immediately indicates. Not only is each word of the Aṣṭādhyāyī given, in the form found in the text, together with references to the sūtras; in addition, each entry is accompanied by what is in effect a Hindi translation of the sūtra in which the term occurs. This is an extremely useful, carefully done work of quality.[13] Also still quite useful is Katre (1981).

2.1.2. *Concerning the original text of the Aṣṭādhyāyī*

2.1.2.1. *Evidence of pre-Pāṇinian grammarians* (III.1.3.1)

M. M. Deshpande (1978a:64-75) once more deals briefly with the scholars, such as Āpiśali, to whom Pāṇini refers. In particular, he points to misunderstandings on the part of some modern scholars concerning the intent of these references. Deshpande rightly emphasizes that Pāṇini's references have to do with differences in usage noted by such grammarians.[14] Jitasingh (1988) again takes up very briefly the teachers to whom Pāṇini refers in the Aṣṭādhyāyī.

2.1.2.2. *Extant works which have been attributed to pre-Pāṇinians*

2.1.2.2a. *Āpiśali* (III.1.3.2a)

Raghu Vira's edition (1934) has now been reprinted (1981). In a recent work Shrikrishna Sharma (1993) covers evidence concerning

Āpiśali's name and background and surveys what is known of his grammar (1993:49-102) and the Āpiśala-śikṣā (1993:103-157), an edition of which is also included.

2.1.2.3. *Interpolations in and modifications of the Aṣṭādhyāyī sūtrapāṭha* (III.1.3.3)

There has been a longstanding interest in the textual history of the Aṣṭādhyāyī, including the question of possible interpolations; see Cardona (1976a:153-160). One indication of this continued interest is the fact that I. S. Pawate's work of 1935 has recently been reprinted (1987).

Ghatage (1983) takes up the general issue of how the Aṣṭādhyāyī reflects not only Pāṇini's having incorporated the work of predecessors but also of his own work having been revised by later scholars. Ghatage concentrates on one instance (**A** 6.2.42) with short discussions of related rules, and concludes as follows (1983:21):

> If these observations have any validity, it is clear that the systematics of Pāṇini's grammar is not only due to consolidation of the works of earlier grammarians but is also the effect of a reworking of his text by later scholars. They formulated additional principles and observed further linguistic material and reworked on the text in the light of these principles so carefully as not to leave any trace of the original position. This had the further effect that the newer text could not be understood without the assumptions of these new principles and then it was an easy and convincing argument that they were intended by Pāṇini himself. This very tendency has given rise to the later non-Pāṇinian systems of Sanskrit grammar.

Aklujkar (1983a) has discussed different ways in which an original text could have been modified. For example, he suggests (1983a:3) that *śnasor* in **A** 6.4.111: *śnasor allopaḥ* is the result of corruption: श्न- for श्ना-. Aklujkar goes on to discuss more subtle ways in which one can account for apparent anomalies. Building on the work of scholars like Kielhorn, Cardona (1997a:577-606 [**854-881**]) deals with the criteria for determining modifications in the sūtrapāṭha which can be ascertained from vārttikas and the Mahābhāṣya. For example, it is argued that **A** 1.2.53 was part of the text of sūtras received by Kātyāyana and Patañjali although it has to be considered theoretically an addition to the original text, and that subsequent sūtras (see Cardona [1976a: III.1.3.3f with note 72 and note 192]) were added later. Cardona (1983b) has also argued that the original formulation of **A** 8.3.4 was *ananunāsikāt paro'nunāsikaḥ* and that the text underwent change — through haplology — in oral transmission.

In an important study, S. D. Joshi and J. A. F. Roodbergen (1983) propose to demonstrate that the sections of rules dealing with taddhita affixation and compound formation constitute later additions, so that Pāṇini's original grammar dealt only with the formation of padas in utterances, not also with derivates which take such padas as a basis for deriving compounds and nominal bases with taddhita affixes.[15] They state the object of their concern as follows (1983:59 [section **1.0**]):

> The question is whether it can be argued on the basis of internal evidence that the *taddhita-* and *samāsa-*sections in the *Aṣṭādhyāyī* stem from an author different from the one who worked out the *kāraka-*system and phrased the original text of the *Aṣṭādhyāyī*, and have been added to this text later on. The internal evidence will be provided by inconsistencies of various nature which we notice in different parts of the *Aṣṭādhyāyī*.

In the penultimate section of their paper, they say (1983:92 [section **7**]), 'The question was whether evidence can be shown for the hypothesis that the *taddhita-* and *samāsa-*sections stem from an author different from the one who framed the original *Aṣṭādhyāyī* (see fn. 35) and have been added later on.' This section ends with the following statement (1983:93):

> Therefore, when we come across such major inconsistencies which allow no good solution within the system on the basis of the present text of the *Aṣṭādhyāyī*, we are justified in assuming a different and later source. Our claim in the present article is that we have found a number of such major inconsistencies, and that they can be traced to a single cause, namely, the addition, at a later date, of the *taddhita-* and *samāsa-*sections. This is our hypothesis which involves major surgery in the present text of the *Aṣṭādhyāyī*.

Since, as shown, their claim is that the sūtras which introduce kṛt affixes are part of the original Aṣṭādhyāyī but rules that provide for compounds and introduce taddhita affixes are later additions, Joshi and Roodbergen appropriately start with what is presumably their chief argument, directly concerning the whole sets of rules dealing with elements at issue. They begin by saying (1983:60 [section **1.2**]):

> We know that *kṛt-*suffixes are introduced in the general syntactic sense *kartṛ* (P. 3.4.67). To indicate special syntactic meanings special *kāraka-*designations are used,

like *karaṇa* and *adhikaraṇa* (P. 3.3.117), *karman* (P. 3.4.70), *saṁpradāna* (P. 3.4.73), *apādāna* (P. 3.4.74). In the *taddhita*-section these designations are not used. Here the meaning in which the suffix is prescribed is generally stated by means of a phrase which, apart from indicating a grammatical meaning, specifies a categorical lexical meaning, e.g. *tad adhīte tad veda* (P. 4.2.59), *tasmai hitam* (P 5.1.5), *tena kṛtam* (P. 5.1.37).

Joshi and Roodbergen go on (1983:60-61):

In the *samāsa*-section, to indicate the meaning in which a cp. is to be derived, two types of meanings are used, namely, a general lexical meaning for the cp. as a whole, and a specified *samartha*-relation which holds between the cp.-constituents. Examples of the first type of meaning are *kṣepe* (P. 2.1.26, 42, 47, 64), *adhikārthavacane* (P. 2.1.33), *saṁjñāyām* (P. 2.1.50), *jātiparipraśne* (P. 2.1.63), *anyapadārthe* (P. 2.2.24), *antarāle* (P. 2.2.26), *cārthe* (P. 2.2.29). Examples of the second type are *dvitīyā* (P. 2.1.24), *tṛtīyā* (P. 2.1.30), *caturthī* (P. 2.1.36), *pañcamī* (P. 2.1.37), *saptamī* (P. 2.1.40) and *ṣaṣṭhī* (P. 2.2.8). In this section the use of *kāraka*-designations is very rare. The only examples are P. 2.2.14-16. Here these designations are used to specify the grammatical function of a cp.-constituent which is about to enter into a cp. with a *kṛd*-derivative, and with which the cp.-formation is disallowed. Therefore we may say that in this section, to indicate the second type of meaning, *kāraka*-names are avoided, whereas *vibhakti*-names are used. Pāṇini does not say *karma śritātīta*, etc. (see P. 2.1.24) or *apādānaṁ bhayena* (see P. 2.1.37), but uses the terms *dvitīyā* and *pañcamī* respectively. In the section dealing with *kṛt*-formation, however, the use of *kāraka*-designations is common, whereas that of *vibhakti*-designations is avoided. The point made here is that as regards the phrasing of the rules in the *kṛt*-section on the one hand and in the *taddhita*- and *samāsa*-sections on the other hand there is no evidence to maintain that they necessarily stem from one and the same author.

The conclusion is worded circumspectly here, but what the same authors say later — as cited above — leaves no doubt about their intention. They mean that the compound and taddhita affixation rules are indeed to be considered later additions to the original Aṣṭādhyāyī. Moreover, as is clear from the passages cited, the very wording used by Joshi and Roodbergen can leave no doubt in a reader that they consider crucial to their argument the difference in use of terms: kāraka category names like *karman* as opposed to terms like *dvitīyā*, which refer to sets of endings and padas with these endings. Thus, it is of interest to them that **A** 2.1.24 is *dvitīyā śritātītapatitagatātyastaprāptāpannaiḥ* and not *2.1.24a: *karma* *śritātītapatitagatātyastaprāptāpannaiḥ*.

Joshi and Roodbergen say that the difference in phrasing in the section of kṛt affixation rules and the taddhita and compound sections supports the position that 'there is no evidence to maintain that they necessarily stem from one and the same author.' They thereby seem to imply that *2.1.24a would be a well formed rule acceptable in the original Aṣṭādhyāyī, although they are vague and leave this question unresolved. Consider now the following. A compound *grāmagata-* 'gone to a village' derives in Pāṇini's system from a string *grāma-am*$_2$ *gata-s*$_1$, one pada of which contains a second-triplet ending (an accusative ending). From this string, one can derive a final string *grāmaṁ gataḥ*. Alternatively, the padas can be combined to form a compound (*samāsa*), which is a derived nominal base (*prātipadika*), so that the endings contained in it are deleted (**A** 2.4.72: *supo dhātu-prātipadikayoḥ*): *grāma-am*$_2$*-gata-s*$_1$ → *grāmagata-*. In addition, any form such as *grāmagataḥ* alternates with a string such as *grāmaṁ gataḥ*, so that the composition is optional. Since Pāṇini derives compounds on the basis of strings of syntactically and semantically related padas, moreover, it is appropriate that he state the rule for forming the compound *grāmagata* using *dvitīyā,* which refers to a term with an ending of the second triplet. Such an ending is introduced, by **A** 2.3.2: *karmaṇi dvitīyā*, on condition that a karman is to be signified. Thus, the difference in terminology which Joshi and Roodbergen see as an indication of interpolation fits perfectly with the system of a single grammarian, Pāṇini. Moreover, it is not the case that *2.1.24a would be a well formed rule equivalent to **A** 2.1.24. For as a pada *grāma-am* refers to a karman, so also does a pada such as *grāma-s*$_1$, as in *devadattena grāmo gataḥ.* A compound form *grāmagatas* in *devadatto grāmagataḥ* 'Devadatta has gone to the village' alternates with a pair of related padas, as in *devadatto grāmaṁ gataḥ* 'Devadatta has gone to the village', but **devadattena grāmagataḥ* does not alternate with *devadattena grāmo gataḥ.* A rule *2.1.24a would, however, allow for such an alternation. It is understandable, then, that Pāṇini also could not formulate composition rules like **A** 2.1.24 using kāraka class names such as *karman*.

Rules like **A** 4.2.59: *tad adhīte tad veda* also fit neatly into the derivational system of a single grammarian, Pāṇini. Derivates with taddhita affixes, such as *vaiyākaraṇa-* 'grammarian' are derived as alternates to strings of related padas: *vaiyākaraṇaḥ* = *vyākaraṇam adhīte, vyākaraṇaṁ veda*. The meaning of part of a string *vyākaraṇa-am adhi-s i-ta* is attributed to a constituent of a derivate *vyākaraṇa-a*, namely to the taddhita affix *aṇ*. This affix, moreover, is introduced after the pada *vyākaraṇa-am* to form a derived nominal base *vyākaraṇa-am-a*, the nominal ending of which is then deleted: *vyākaraṇa-am-a-* → *vyākaraṇa-a-* → *vaiyākaraṇa-*. Now, **A** 4.2.59 is part of a set of rules governed by a major heading — **A** 4.1.82: *samarthānāṁ prathamād vā* — whereby affixes are introduced optionally after the first of syntactically and semantically related padas referred to in subsequent rules. These rules, such as **A** 4.2.59, in effect give strings that are equivalent to derivates with the affixes provided for. It is not incongruent, then, that a single grammarian formulate such a rule in the way shown: *tad adhīte tad veda*, using a pronominal form *tad* as a variable for a pada containing a second-triplet ending. And again, it would not do to have a rule *4.2.59a: *karmādhīte karma veda*. The ending *am* signifies a karman in a pada like *utpāta-am*, whence is derived *utpātam*, as in *utpātaṁ veda* '... knows a portent.' In addition, a first-triplet form *utpāta-s* also can signify a karman, as in the passive sentence *utpāto vidyate* 'A portent is known.' But *autpāta-* 'one who knows portents' should be an alternate to a string with *utpātam* and an agentive form such as *veda*. Again, it is understandable that Pāṇini did not formulate a taddhita affixation rule such as **A** 4.2.59 using a kāraka name.

Cardona (1989:50-52) criticized the arguments cited above from Joshi and Roodbergen's article. Kiparsky (1991a) reacted with a polemic against Cardona's critique of Joshi and Roodbergen. He begins his argument against Cardona saying (Kiparsky [1991a:332]), 'Cardona gets off to a poor start by declaring that "the principal reason for adopting this position is the authors' perception of inconsistency in terminology" (p. 50). In fact, Joshi and Roodbergen are hardly at all concerned with terminology.' Kiparsky goes on (1991a:332) to enumerate the rubrics under which Joshi and Roodbergen present their evidence, to complain that Cardona did not deal with enough of this, and then (1991a:333) to say:

> Instead, the bulk of Cardona's discussion consists of an elaborate refutation of an absurd argument of his own invention. Namely, he points out that the mere fact that the *kṛt* section uses *kārakas* while the compound and *taddhita* sections use *vibhaktis* does not show that they stem from a different hand. Quite true, it doesn't — but J &

R never claimed that it does. Their purpose in bringing up this difference between the *kṛt* section and the compound and *taddhita* sections is a different one. It is simply to forestall a potential objection that might be raised to their thesis; as they put it: "... as far as grammatical treatment is concerned, there is no evidence to maintain that the *taddhita*- and *samāsa*-sections necessarily stem from the same author who worked out the *kāraka*-system". Their point is that these facts are *consistent* with separate authorship. That they are also consistent with single authorship was of course presupposed by Joshi and Roodbergen, and did not need to be demonstrated all over again by Cardona. J & R's case *for* separate authorship is based on quite different evidence, namely the evidence listed above and detailed on pp. 61-93 of their article.

Kiparsky evidently did not read with sufficient attention section **1.2** (1983:60-61) of Joshi and Roodbergen's article. To begin with, his citation "... as far as grammatical treatment is concerned ..." is from Joshi and Roodbergen's section **1.3**. Cardona concentrated on what Joshi and Roodbergen said in their section **1.2** for good and sufficient reasons. The aim of the entire article is to demonstrate that the sections of sūtras providing for taddhita affixes and compounds are later additions to an original Aṣṭādhyāyī. Despite the circumspection of statements made earlier, what Joshi and Roodbergen say in section **7** — cited above — can leave no doubt about the authors' aim, as I pointed out (see Cardona [1989:74-75, notes 3, 5]). In addition, it is in section **1.2** that Joshi and Roodbergen present their principal arguments for this thesis. Most of the sections that follow do not deal with taddhita affixation and composition rules as a whole. Indeed, some of the evidence treated is either tangential to these or not related at all. As for Kiparsky's claim that Joshi and Roodbergen 'are hardly at all concerned with terminology', this is shown to be untrue by what these authors say in sections **1.2** and **2.3.1** of their paper, where one encounters the following statements:

We know that *kṛt*-suffixes are introduced in the general syntactic sense *kartṛ* (P. 3.4.67). To indicate special syntactic meanings special *kāraka*-designations are used, like *karaṇa* and *adhikaraṇa* (P. 3.3.117), *karman* (P 3.4.70), *saṁpradāna* (P. 3.4.73), *apādāna* (P. 3.4.74). In the *taddhita*-section these designations are not used. (Joshi-Roodbergen [1983:60])

Therefore we may say that in this section, to indicate the second type of meaning, *kāraka*-names are avoided, whereas *vibhakti*-names are used. Pāṇini does not say *karma śritātīta*, etc. (see 2.1.24) or *apādānaṁ bhayena* (see P. 2.1.37), but uses the terms *dvitīyā* and *pañcamī* respectively. (Joshi-Roodbergen [1983:60-61])

Finally, it may be argued that P 3.2.97-98 have been added later on, because, apart from making use of the *anubandha Ḍ* which commonly belongs to the *taddhita*-section, these rules show another peculiarity. They do not mention the *upapada* with the help of function-names like *adhikaraṇe janer ḍaḥ* and *apādāne' jātau*, but with the help of *vibhakti*-names like *saptamyām* and *pañcamyām* respectively. The latter is the practice of the *taddhita*- and *samāsa*-sections. (Joshi-Roodbergen [1983:67-68])

To be sure, Joshi and Roodbergen are ultimately claiming that the sets of rules they consider interpolations reflect a different methodology. However, their major clue to the possible difference in authorship between these and kṛt affixation rules is precisely the difference in terminology. Finally, it is striking that Joshi and Roodbergen should exert such effort to show inconsistencies only to support the thesis that these facts are consistent with separate authorship but do not rule out single authorship. Nor does their article as published indicate that what Joshi and Roodbergen say in their sections **1.2** and **1.3** is intended in the manner claimed by Kiparsky. It is true that Joshi and Roodbergen begin their section **2.0** (1983:61-62) by noting that they will see whether inconsistencies are to be found in sections of the extant Aṣṭādhyāyī not confined to taddhita affixation and compound formation and say, 'Such inconsistences, if noted, could provide a positive evidence to maintain that the rules concerned have been added to a pre-existent body of rules of which they did not form a part.' Yet, in a subsequent section (**3.3.1**, 1983:74-75) — including some of the evidence which Kiparsky says they view as demonstrating separate authorship — Joshi and Roodbergen end with a statement remarkably like those with which they end sections **1.2** and **1.3**, namely (1983:75): 'Considering what was stated above, it appears that there is sufficient evidence in respect of the way in which meaning is indicated, to maintain that the *taddhita*-section and the *kṛt*-section need not necessarily stem from one and the same author.'

In accordance with what Joshi and Roodbergen say, I conclude that beginning their article by setting forth what they consider evidence to show that the sections on taddhita affixation and compounding show 'no evidence to maintain that they necessarily stem from one and the same author' serves as a stratagem, allowing them to make an apparently temperate claim about taddhita and compounding rules while presenting the only evidence that concerns all these rules in general, hoping then to let additional evidence — the nature of which is not so all encompassing — support this claim, so that they might end with a strong assertion. In my opinion, however, there can be no doubt at all that Joshi and Roodbergen mean the differences they see between the taddhita affixation and compounding rules on the one hand and kṛt affixation rules on the other to be a true index of difference in authorship. Only under this assumption is it possible to explain how Joshi and Roodbergen say subsequently— in their section **2.3.1** — that one can argue that **A** 3.2.97-98 are later additions because they use *saptamyām* and *pañcamyām*, which 'is the practice of the *taddhita*- and *samāsa*-sections.' This assumes that the sections on compounding and taddhita affixation rules have been demonstrated to be additions, so that kṛt affixation rules which follow the procedures observed in these sections also may be treated as interpolations.

For the above reasons, I consider Kiparsky's defense of Joshi and Roodbergen (1983) without merit. In my earlier discussion of Joshi and Roodbergen's article, I concentrated on what to me appeared to be the main argument in support of their thesis, and mentioned only in passing and as illustrating their approach another piece of evidence they adduce. This allowed me to keep within a reasonable space limit and to avoid mentioning some aspects of argumentation which I found embarrassing to the authors, especially to S. D. Joshi, whom I regard as a very learned scholar even when I disagree with him radically. Nor do I propose here to go through every piece of evidence they adduce. To do so would require another monograph. Nevertheless, given the polemic which Kiparsky has written on their behalf, I consider it appropriate to consider here more of what Joshi and Roodbergen claim.

The strongest sort of evidence indicating that part of a received text represents an addition to the original text is demonstrable contradiction between the two layers. In their section **2.4** (1983:68-70) entitled **Internal contradiction**, Joshi and Roodbergen present two pieces of evidence they consider to involve such contradiction. In section **2.4.1** (1983:68-69) they deal with the sūtras **A** 1.2.53-57, which have commonly been considered interpolations. See most recently Cardona (1997a:590-606 [**861-881**]). Joshi and Roodbergen add nothing new to the discussion except for some speculation. Indeed, they are content with considering a standard example, *pañcālāḥ* 'the Pañcāla country', and saying (1983:68):

> This extended meaning ('name of a people' → 'name of a country inhabited by that people') lies outside the realm of grammar. Therefore no grammatical rule teaching this meaning should be phrased. It suffices that we know it from usage.

In connection with this, consider a term like *śaiba-* 'place where the Śibi live'. Clearly, *śaiba-* and *śibi-* are not homophonous. There is no question of saying that *śibi-* somehow has an extended meaning. It is appropriate, then, to account for *śaiba-* as a derivate, with an affix that conditions the replacement of *i* by *ai* and to which the meaning 'abode' (*nivāsa*) is attributed: *śibi-ām* → *śibi-ām-a-* → *śibi-a-* → *śaibi-a-* → *śaiba-*. Pāṇini does this, by means of **A** 4.2.69: *tasya nivāsaḥ*. It is also patent that *pāñcāla-* 'descendent of Pañcāla' differs from *pañcāla-*, and here too the former is accounted for as a derivate with an affix *aṇ*. Now, **A** 4.2.69 would allow the same affix to occur after *pañcāla-ām* in a derivate of the type *śaiba-*, referring to the place where certain people live. The term used with reference to a particular kind of place, namely a janapada, however, is not *pāñcāla-* but *pañcāla-* in the masculine plural (nom. *pañcālāḥ*). Given the contrast *śiba-* : *śaiba-*, it is formally justifiable to say that one also has a parallel pair *pañcāla-*$_1$: *pañcāla-*$_2$, albeit with homophonous terms. Of course, someone else could argue that *pañcāla-*$_2$ is not a separate entity, that it is merely *pañcāla-*$_1$ with an extended meaning, as Joshi and Roodbergen put it. The fact remains that there is indeed formal justification for the Pāṇinian procedure.

In their section **2.4.1**, Joshi and Roodbergen go on (1983:69) to make two points concerning **A** 1.2.53-57:

> In the first place, the rules P. 1.2.53-57 form part of a larger sequence which begins with P. 1.2.49. Here the rules P. 1.2.49-55 specifically deal with *taddhita*-formations. In the second place, the sequence P. 1.2.53-57 need not be regarded as a criticism of Pāṇini. On the contrary, it may be viewed as a defence of Pāṇinian procedure, namely, against a procedure or procedures adopted in the *taddhita*-section. It may well be that a grammarian at a fairly late (post-Kātyāyana) date recorded his protest in the form of these rules against what he saw as an incursion into the realm of lexical meaning by grammar. This conjecture, it may be pointed out, has an important corollary. If it is accepted, at least a part of the *taddhita*-section, namely the rules teaching *lup*-deletion, must be considered as a fairly early (pre-Kātyāyana) addition to an original body of rules. But this, again, raises a question regarding the status of

the *taddhita*-section as a whole: did it or didn't form part of the original body of rules?

This is not cogent argumentation. By bringing in rules preceding **A** 1.2.53-57, Joshi and Roodbergen appear to try to obscure an important distinction: **A** 1.2.49-52 cannot be considered to conflict with Pāṇinian procedures as seen in the taddhita section of rules. **A** 1.2.53-55 do conflict with what is done elsewhere in the grammar. Moreover, **A** 1.2.53 has to do with the extension of gender and number properties to a derivate formed by replacing an affix with the zero designated *lup*, but **A** 1.2.54-55 have to do with the replacement of affixes by this zero. It is equally plausible to assume that a pre-Kātyāyana grammarian proposed that the extension of gender and number properties did not have to be provided for, all the while retaining the derivation of items by replacement with *lup*, and that some grammarian(s) postdating Patañjali but antedating Bhartṛhari further proposed that the derivations with such deletions were not necessary. Joshi and Roodbergen's speculation is certainly not a telling argument against the status of taddhita affixation rules.

What Joshi and Roodbergen say in section **2.4.2** (1983:69-70) is even less cogent. In fact, it is unacceptable by virtue of misrepresenting what Pāṇini provides for. They argue as follows. The anubandha *k* added to kṛt affixes serves to preclude guṇa and vṛddhi substitution (**A** 1.1.5: *kṅiti ca*) in bases. On the other hand, *k* as an anubandha in a taddhita affix serves to show that the affix conditions vṛddhi replacement for the first vowel of its base (**A** 7.2.118: *kiti ca*). They conclude their brief discussion saying:

> The contradiction consists in this that one and the same *anubandha* has two opposite functions, namely, to prevent *vṛddhi* and to cause *vṛddhi*. In fact, this is the only *anubandha* known for that, although it is clear that *anubandha*s may have different functions. The fact that the *anubandha K* is systematically used in two different positions in the two opposite functions does not impair the contradiction, which regards the designation *kit* as such.

It would indeed be an indictment if there were a contradiction. But there is no such contradiction. **A** 1.1.5 is part of a set of rules having to do with replacement by guṇa and vṛddhi vowels where the substituends are not specified. According to **A** 1.1.3: *iko guṇavṛddhī* guṇa and vṛddhi vowels under such circumstances — and provided also that they are referred to by the terms *guṇa* and *vṛddhi* — substitute for vowels denoted by ***ik***, that is, *i u ṛ ḷ* and vowels homogeneous with these. **A** 1.1.5 provides that *guṇa* and *vṛddhi* substitutions thus circumscribed do not apply if the affix that would condition the replacement is marked with *g k ṅ* (see Cardona [1997a:xiii-xiv]). Now, **A** 7.2.118 follows sūtras which specify the substituends for vṛddhi substitution. According to **A** 7.2.115: *aco ñṇiti* (*vṛddhiḥ* [114]), a vṛddhi vowel replaces the final sound of a vowel-final stem if the affix for that base is marked with *ñ* or *ṇ*. By the following sūtra (**A** 7.2.116: *ata upadhāyāḥ*), vṛddhi replacement applies to a penultimate short *a*-vowel of a stem followed by an affix so marked. **A** 7.2.117: *taddhiteṣv acām ādeḥ* then further provides that vṛddhi replacement applies to the first vowel of a stem before a taddhita affix so marked. And **A** 7.2.118 finally lets this substitution apply to the first vowel of a stem followed by a taddhita affix marked with *k*. Clearly, the substituend is explicitly stated: the first vowel of a stem. Accordingly, **A** 1.1.5 does not come into play with **A** 7.2.118. Moreover, it is patent that the Pāṇinīya tradition is correct in considering that **A** 1.1.5 applies only with respect to guṇa and vṛddhi replacement as governed by **A** 1.1.3. If it did not, the rule could come into play to preclude vṛddhi substitution in *kam-i-* 'desire' (affix ***ṇiṅ***: **A** 3.1.10: *kamer ṇiṅ*), thus disallowing *kām-i-* (*kāmayate*), and guṇa substitution — by **A** 6.4.146: *or guṇaḥ* — for the *-u* of a stem such as *ligu-* in *ligu-āyana-* (affix *pha**k***: **A** 4.1.99: *naḍādibhyaḥ phak*): *ligu-āyana-* → *ligo-āyana-* → *laigo-āyana-* → *laigavāyana-* 'descendent of Ligu'. Hence, the marking of taddhita affixes with *k* to show that they condition vṛddhi substitution involves no contradiction with what is provided by **A** 1.1.5.

Joshi and Roodbergen's section **2.4** is obviously intended to demonstrate that the taddhita affixation rules included in the received text of the Aṣṭādhyāyī entail contradiction within the grammar. The only evidence adduced is that given in their sections **2.4.1** and **2.4.2**. As shown, this fails to substantiate their claim.

A contrast between rules introducing kṛt and taddhita affixes is dealt with in Joshi and Roodbergen's section **3.6** (**Discrepancy regarding the use of** *gaṇas* [1983:77-79]). The authors are forced to end their first and longer subsection (**3.6.1**, 1983:77-79) in a lame manner (1983:78):

> Granted that, in view of the numerical difference in the word-material to be handled by the two sections, the discrepancy between the *taddhita*-section and the *kṛt*-section as regards the use of *gaṇas* follows rather naturally. But the fact remains that the

kṛt-section uses only two *gaṇas* in P. 3.1.134 and P. 3.2.60.

In an attempt to strengthen their claim, Joshi and Roodbergen immediately go on (1983:78-79) to question the status of the two kṛt affixation rules just mentioned:

> These rules also, however, are suspect. The first rule should be *nandādigrahādi-pacādibhyo* .... The second rule does not satisfactorily explain the derived words *tādṛśa*, etc. In the meaning of *tādṛśa*, etc. the sense of the verbal base is not clearly visible. That is to say, act of seeing is not denoted by the words *tādṛśa* and similarly derived others. Therefore from discrepancy regarding the use of *gaṇas*, the conclusion could be drawn which favours the assumption of a multiple authorship for both sections.

Joshi and Roodbergen thus consider that the formulation of **A** 3.1.134: *nandigrahipacādibhyo lyuṇinyacaḥ* is improper because the gaṇas beginning with *nandi*, *grah*, and *pac* should be referred to distinctly as *nandyādi, grahādi*, and *pacādi*. Although the authors do not refer to any other sūtra in support of their claim, Pāṇini does in fact have such usage, as in **A** 5.2.100: *lomādipāmādipicchādibhyaḥ śanelacaḥ.* On the other hand, it is a fact that members of a dvandva can be construed individually with a final term of a larger compound into which the dvandva is incorporated; for example, **A** 2.3.46: *prātipadikārthaliṅgaparimāṇavacanamātre prathamā,* where *-mātre* is construed serially with *prātipadikārtha*, *liṅga*, *parimāṇa*, and *vacana*; **A** 4.1.26: *saṁkhyāvyayāder ṅīp*, where *-ādi-* is construed serially with *saṁkhyā* and *avyaya*. Instead of simply asserting that **A** 3.1.134 'should be ...' without any justification for their assertion, Joshi and Roodbergen should have at least attempted to justify their claim.

What they say concerning **A** 3.2.60: *tyadādiṣu dṛśo'nālocane kañ ca* (*kvin* 58) is puzzling. It is hard to see how Joshi and Roodbergen could be arguing that the sūtra as formulated fails to account for derivates like *tādṛśa-*, *tādṛś-* 'such, similar to that'. For Pāṇini explicitly specifies that *dṛś* construed with members of the set beginning with *tyad* takes the affixes ***kañ***, ***kvin*** if the verb is used in a sense other than 'perceive' (*anālocane*). That is, the sūtra lets the affixation apply if *dṛś* has the sense 'appear, seem'. Accordingly, the only manner in which I can appreciate what Joshi and Roodbergen claim when they say, 'The second rule does not satisfactorily explain ...' is to understand that they do not like the derivation of *tādṛśa-* and so on with a base *dṛś* because this base means 'see' and this meaning does not appear in these derivates. That is, they are imposing their analysis of the Sanskrit terms on Pāṇini and thereby claiming that the rule cannot be appropriately reconciled with his procedures. This does not speak favorably for their claim regarding gaṇas.

Another section in which Joshi and Roodbergen deal directly with taddhita affixation in general is **3.3** (**Discrepancies regarding the way meaning is indicated** [1983:74-75]). Here they claim the following (1983:75):

> Strictly grammatically speaking, meaning in the *taddhita*-section could have been indicated by means of abstract patterns like *tasya idam* (prescribing a genitive relationship), *tad asmin* (prescribing a locative relationship) or *tat karoti* (prescribing an action meaning involving an accusative relationship) only. In this way, the rest, that is, lexical meaning which is known from usage anyway, could have been kept outside the realm of grammar. This is in conformance with the ideas which led to the formulation of the sequence P. 1.2.53-57 (see under 2.3.1).
>
> It is in conformance also with the way in which conventional lexical meaning is indicated in the *kṛt*-section. For this purpose, simply the term *saṁjñāyām* is used. Here grammatical meanings are indicated by means of terms like *kartṛ*, *karman*, used in the sg. loc. Specific lexical meanings are only available in the *nipātana* rules.
>
> Considering what was stated above, it appears that there is sufficient evidence in respect of the way in which meaning is indicated, to maintain that the *taddhita*-section and the *kṛt*-section need not necessarily stem from one and the same author.

If I understand Joshi and Roodbergen correctly, a sūtra such as **A** 5.2.94: *tad asyāsty asminniti matup* along with related rules that conform to this structure and mention no lexical meaning would have been sufficient to describe adequately derivates of the type *gomat-* 'rich in cattle'. Now consider the following. One of the rules related to **A** 5.2.94 is **A** 5.2.124: *vāco gminiḥ*, whereby *gmini* follows a pada of the type N-gen. or N-loc. if the nominal base that is the value of N is specifically *vāc* 'speech, word'. This sūtra accounts for a derivate *vāggmin-* 'eloquent'. There are also the terms *vācāla-*, *vācāṭa-* 'verbose'. These two can obviously be analyzed as containing a nominal stem *vāc* : *vāc-āla-*, *vāc-āṭa-*. And **A** 5.2.125: *ālajāṭacau bahubhāṣiṇi* does indeed introduce the affixes *āla**c*** and *āṭa**c***. The same rule specifies that the affixes are introduced if the derivate in question refers to someone who speaks a lot (*bahubhāṣiṇi*). **A** 5.2.125 is an exception to **A** 5.2.124, itself an exception to **A** 5.2.94. According to what Joshi and Roodbergen say, 'strictly grammatically speaking', **A** 5.2.94 and **A** 5.2.124 would have sufficed to describe matters adequately. Presumably, *vācāla-*, *vācāṭa-* 'verbose' would be relegated to the lexicon and not dealt with in the grammar proper. This means that **A** 5.2.124 would now also allow *vāggmin-* in any lexical meaning, including 'verbose'. Moreover, the grammarian in question would now describe through affixation a derivate *vāg-gmin-* (← *vāc-gmin-*) but not describe in a comparable manner the terms *vāc-āla-*, *vāc-āṭa-*, which are obviously also analyzable and relatable to the *vāg-gmin-*. Examples of this sort can be multiplied. The upshot is that a grammar of the sort Joshi and Roodbergen envision — such that only rules of the type **A** 5.2.124, 5.2.94 would be allowed in the taddhita section — would be inadequate for describing the language. Fortunately, the Aṣṭādhyāyī as received is not guilty of this deficiency.

Taddhita affixation is also the topic of Joshi and Roodbergen's section **3.2**, which bears the heading **Discrepancy regarding the way in which words are analysed into stems and suffixes** and consists of only one part, although this is labelled separately (**3.2.1** [1983:73-74]). The authors begin saying, 'Some *taddhita*-rules come near to the rules stating *uṇādi*-suffixes in the way they isolate stems and suffixes. That is to say, in the word analysed the stem-suffix relation is not really recognizable.' They go on to give examples, then conclude by saying, 'These are not really suffixes but words. The *kṛt*-section does not provide similar wild products of word-analysis.' The final example given (1983:74) is 'P. 5.2.37 (*dvayasaC*, *daghnaC* and *mātraC*).' Consider the following. According to the rule Joshi and Roodbergen refer to (**A** 5.2.37: *pramāṇe dvayasaj-daghnañmātracaḥ* [*tad asya* 36]), the suffixes *dvayas**a**c*, *daghna**c*** and *mātra**c*** optionally follow a pada of the type x-nom. such that x is a nominal used in denoting a measure, to form a derivate referring to something whose measure is that denoted by x. For example, *ūrudvayasa-*, *ūrudaghna-*, *urumātra-* refer to something that comes as high as one's thigh. The next sūtra (**A** 5.2.38: *puruṣahastibhyām aṇ ca*) introduces under the same conditions not only the suffixes already provided for but also *a**ṇ***, provided x of x-nom. is *puruṣa-* 'man' or *hastin-* 'elephant'. This accounts for *pauruṣa-*, *puruṣadvayasa-*, *puruṣadaghna-*, *puruṣamātra-*, all referring to something that has the height of a man. Obviously, *pauruṣa-* does not contain any putative suffix that can be identified with a separate independent word. If, then, the terms *-dvayasa-*, *-daghna-*, *-mātra-* of derivates equivalent to *pauruṣa-* also ceased to be used as independent words, one is perfectly justified in treating these as affixes, with the same status as the affix *a*. Historically, of course, these are doubtless to be considered originally independent words. The historical development in question is well known — the Romance suffix of adverbs like French *heureusement* 'happily', Italian *veramente* 'truly', Spanish *verdaderamente* 'truly' is a famous example — and scholars have long since considered the Sanskrit suffixes to be instances of this development. The other examples considered in Joshi and Roodbergen's section **3.2.1** are comparable. To say, as the authors do, that recognizing an affix in such derivates involves a wild word analysis reflects more on their personal preference than on the Pāṇinian derivational system.

Nor is this the only place in their article where Joshi and Roodbergen make assertions merely on the basis of their personal preferences. I have already spoken of what they say in their section **3.6.1**.[16] Consider now what they say in their section **2.2** (1983:63-67) entitled **Break of logical order due to the Introduction of unrelated topics**. Subsection **2.2.1** (1983:63-64) begins as follows:

> The sequence is P. 1.2.45-1.3.1. Word-derivation in the *Aṣṭādhyāyī* is based on two concepts designated by the terms *prātipadika* and *dhātu*. We therefore expect that after the definition of *prātipadika* that of *dhātu* follows immediately. This, however, is not the case. *Prātipadika* is defined in P. 1.2.45-46, but the definition of *dhātu* follows only in P. 1.3.1. The intermediate rules deal with rather disparate material that can be enumerated as follows. :
>
> (1) P. 1.2.47-48 deal with substitution, and should have been put in the *aṅgādhikāra* (P. 6.4.1 ff.) which is the usual place for rules dealing with substitution.
>
> (2) For P. 1.2.49-57 see under 1.4.3.
>
> (3) P. 1.2.58-63 deal with non-grammatical number.
>
> (4) P. 1.2.64-73 deal with *ekaśeṣa*.

In addition, Joshi and Roodbergen suggest (1983:64) that **A** 1.2.46: *kṛttaddhitasamāsāś ca* could be read as two rules: *kṛt*, *taddhitasamāsāś ca*. They then go on to say (1983:64):

> In the third place, in connection with (3) and (4) the following inconsistencies are noted. The sequence P. 1.2.58-63 prescribes number in connection with *jātis* 'generic terms', like *vrīhi* 'rice' and *brāhmaṇa* 'brahmin', and a few specifically mentioned

words. But P. 1.2.53 says that non-grammatical-number need not be taught in grammar, because it is decided by usage. See also under 2.3.1. Moreover, if at all Pāṇini had wanted to phrase rules about number in connection with specific words, the proper place would have been in the sequel of P. 1.4.22.

As can be seen, Joshi and Roodbergen simply assume that **A** 1.2.47-48 should have been put in the section headed by **A** 6.4.1: *aṅgasya*. They say no more, but there is more to say. Consider *bahumālāya* (dat. sg.) 'one who has many garlands' and *bahumālebhyaḥ* (dat.-abl. pl.). These are forms of a compound in which the second term is originally *mālā*- 'garland'. According to the Pāṇinian procedure, **A** 1.2.47: *gostriyor upasarjanasya* applies to replace the *-ā* of the nominal base. In the complex ((*bahumāla*-)*e*), then, the ending *-e* is replaced by *-ya* (**A** 7.1.12: *ṅer yaḥ*), which conditions the replacement of stem-final *-a* by the long vowel *-ā* (**A** 7.3.102: *supi ca*): *bahumāla-e* → *bahumāla-ya* → *bahumālāya*. In ((*bahumāla*-)*bhyas*), the ending conditions the replacement of stem-final *-a* by *-e* (**A** 7.3.103: *bahuvacane jhaly et*). If, as Joshi and Roodbergen suggest should be done, *gostriyor upsarjanasya* is placed in aṅga section, then one starts with ((*bahumālā*-)*e*) and has the final vowel of *bahumālā*- replaced by *-a* not merely because the nominal base in question is an upasarjana in a compound but also because it is a stem, so that the ending conditions this replacement. Then the derivation proceeds as above: *bahumālā-e* → *bahumāla-e* → *bahumāla-ya* → *bahumālāya*. To be sure, the appropriate form is accounted for. However, there is a systematic price to pay under the alternative. Stems with a feminine suffix *-ā* regularly condition augmenting (**A** 7.3.113: *yāḍ āpaḥ*) in a group of endings, including *-ṅe*, as in *mālā-e* → *mālā-yāe* → *mālāyai*. Similarly, endings such as *-bhyas* regularly do not condition shortening in preceding stems with a feminine affix *-ā*, as in *mālābhyaḥ*. Shortening of a final *-ā* is thus more appropriately treated as a function of the structural status of the derivate: *-mālā*- is part of a compound. The structural difference in question is brought out if, following the Pāṇinian procedure, short-vowel replacement is not made to be conditioned by an ending.

What Joshi and Roodbergen say concerning (3) is also not very precise. Aṣṭādhyāyī **A** 1.2.53: *tad aśiṣyaṁ saṁjñāpramāṇatvāt* does not say without qualification 'that grammatical number need not be taught, because it is decided by usage.' This sūtra is related to **A** 1.2.51-52 (*lupi yuktavad* *vyaktivacane, viśeṣaṇānāṁ cājāteḥ*) and these rules can, with equal or greater justification, be understood as extending gender and number properties to a particular set of derivates in which a taddhita affix has been deleted. Nor, as I have noted above, does what Joshi and Roodbergen say in their section **2.4.1** — not 2.3.1 or 1.4.3 — cast any illumination on the issue of **A** 1.2.53-57 being post-Pāṇinian additions.

What Joshi and Roodbergen have to say in other subsections of **2.2** is equally subject to query. **2.2.3** (1983:65-67) begins:

> The break occurs between the sequences P. 1.4.23-55 and P. 2.3.1 ff. The first sequence forms the *kāraka*-section. The section logically expected to come immediately after this sequence is the *vibhakti*-section. However, the treatment of the *vibhaktis* is delayed until P. 2.3.1. What comes in between are sequences dealing with unrelated topics which are best enumerated as follows ...

Joshi and Roodbergen then list six groups of rules, ending with rules of composition (**A** 2.1.1-2.2.38), which is one of the two they consider truly 'order-disturbing.' As is well known, Aṣṭādhyāyī rules in the fourth pāda of the first adhyāya and the first two pādas of the second adhyāya, all headed by **A** 1.4.1: *ā kaḍārād ekā saṁjñā*, consititute a coherent set of rules, in that classes provided for by rules of this group are disjunct and, in cases where rules can conflict, what is provided for in a later rule takes precedence (**A** 1.4.2: *vipratiṣedhe paraṁ kāryam*). From this perspective, the sūtras introducing vibhaktis cannot immediately follow **A** 1.4.23-55 and compounding rules are appropriately included in the section headed by **A** 1.4.1. Although they must be aware of this, Joshi and Roodbergen mention none of it in their section **2.2.3**.

In the same vein, consider what is said in section **2.2.5** (1983:66):

> The disturbing sequence is P. 5.3.3-14. The rules stated here deal with substitution in connection with pronominal stems. However, changes in pronominal stems really belong to *aṅgādhikāra*, compare P. 7.2.86-113. The question is why the sequence under discussion has been put in the *taddhita*-section.

This is all Joshi and Roodbergen say here, although a moment's thought serves to show a very good reason for the distribution of sūtras. **A** 5.3.1: *prāg diśo vibhaktiḥ* heads a set of rules that concern taddhita affixes classed as *vibhakti.* The affixes in question are introduced after *bahu* and pronominals except for those of the subgroup beginning with *dvi* but including *kim* of this subgroup (**A** 5.3.2: *kiṁsarvanāmabahubhyo* *'dvyādibhyaḥ*). The replacements for *idam*, *etad*, and *sarva* by **A** 5.3.3-6 — not 5.3.3-14 — apply before these vibhaktis alone, not before nominal endings in general. The set of rules concerning pronominal replacements in the seventh adhyāya concerns pronominal stems followed by other vibhaktis.

What Joshi and Roodbergen say in their section **2.2.6** (1983:66) is open to a comparable objection. The entire section is as follows:

> The disturbing sequence is P. 5.3.60-65. The rule stated here deals with the substitution for some nominal stems before comparative and superlative suffixes, *īyasUN* and *iṣṭhaN*. However, the substitution for nominal stems really belongs to the *aṅgādhikāra*, compare P. 6.4.156-160. The question is: Why has the sequence under discussion been introduced in the *taddhita*-section?

As one might expect, Pāṇini has a reason for what he does. Having stated (**A** 5.3.58: *ajādī guṇavacanād eva*) that the vowel-initial (*ajādī*) affixes ***iṣṭhan*** and ***īyasun*** occur only with guṇavacana terms, he then states replacements that apply before these vowel-initial affixes. **A** 6.4.156-163 state replacements that apply to stems followed by ***iṣṭhan***, ***īyasun*** and ***imanic*** as well as to parts of these affixes.[17]

It is undeniable, I think, that, in the interest of promoting their main thesis that taddhita and composition rules are later additions to an earlier core grammar, Joshi and Roodbergen are so intent on seeing interpolations and discrepancies that they fail to consider even fairly obvious answers to queries they pose. Indeed, in some instances they appear driven to see discrepancies even where they themselves have to admit a lack of evidence. The following illustrate this. Their section **2.2.2** in its entirety ([1983:64-65]) is as follows:

> The sequence is P. 1.2.73-75. It deals with the term *vṛddha*. The application of this term is restricted to the *taddhita*-formation. We note that the sequence mentioned occurs at the end of a *pāda*, which is at the same time the end of the general *saṁjñā*-section. There is no evidence to conclude that this sequence has been added later on to a pre-existent body of rules. However, if additions are made, they are likely to be made at the end of a section. Therefore the present sequence may be kept in mind as possible evidence.

The entire section **2.2.10** ([1983:67]) is:

> The disturbing sequence is P. 8.3.45-54. It deals with the substitution of *ṣ*. These rules are confined to *samāsa*-formation. We note that the sequence mentioned occurs

> at the end of the *ṣatva*-section. There is no evidence to say that this sequence has been added later on to a pre-existing body of rules. However, if additions are made, they are likely to be made at the end of the section.

And in section **2.2.8** Joshi and Roodbergen say (1983:66), 'As regards the sequence P. 6.1.219-222, we have really no evidence to speak of a break here, because this sequence occurs at the end of a *pāda*.' Yet they end the section with, 'Still, it may be kept in mind as possible evidence, when the picture of the distribution of the *taddhita*-rules in the *Aṣṭādhyāyī* becomes clearer.'

More disturbingly, in their quest for inconsistencies and interpolations, Joshi and Roodbergen show a willingness to misrepresent what a source says. In section **5.4** (1983:89-91), they consider **A** 8.2.2: *nalopaḥ supsvara-saṁjñātugvidhiṣu kṛti*, about which they say (1983:89):

> The difficulty is how to connect the word *kṛti*. Just going by the way the rule has been phrased we would expect *kṛti* to represent a condition in connection with the cp. ending in *-vidhiṣu*, that is, in connection with each of the types of rules specified. But *kṛti* can be meaningfully connected with the constituent *tUK* only. Thus, *-tugvidhiṣu kṛti* is taken to mean 'when a rule applies which deals with (the augment) *tUK* conditioned by a following *kṛt* (-suffix)'. It goes without saying that to convey this meaning the rule should read *nalopaḥ supsvarasaṁjñākṛtitugvidhiṣu*. The impression is that in the present phrasing of the rule the word *kṛti* is rather curiously appended. This impression is further strengthened, when we read what Patañjali says in his *bhāṣya* on *Vt.* III on P. 8.2.7, which deals with the word *tUK* in P. 8.2.2. He says *kṛtīti vakṣyāmi* 'I am going to state the word *kṛti*.' That is to say, he informs us that he will add the word *kṛti* in P. 8.2.2 which originally did not contain that word. What is Patañjali's purpose in doing so?

The construction in question, however, is not unique. Thus, **A** 5.4.74: *ṛkpūrabdhūḥpathām ānakṣe* provides for an affix *a* to be added as a final part of a compound ending with *ṛc* 'verse', *pur* 'city', *ap* 'water', *dhur* (see below) and *pathin* 'way, path'. In addition to the genitive plural *ṛkpūrabdhūḥpathām*, the rule contains a locative singular *anakṣe* 'except with reference to an axle, cart'. This can obviously be connected only with *dhur*, not with any other term of the genitive plural, since only *dhur* ('piece for holding an axle to a wheel, part of a cart pole, where the yoke rests') among the constituents of this genitive denotes something that can be connected with an axle or a cart. **A** 6.4.62: *sicsīyuṭtāsiṣu bhāvakarmaṇor* *upadeśe' jjhanagrahadṛśāṁ vā ciṇvad iṭ ca* as usually interpreted contains the genitive plural *ajjhanagrahadṛśām* and the locative *upadeśe*, which can be construed properly only with the first member of the compound. Consider also **A** 6.1.68: *halṅyābbhyo dīrghāt sutisy apṛktaṁ hal* (*lopaḥ* 66). The ablative *dīrghāt* can be construed only with part of the compound *halṅyābbhyaḥ*, namely *-ṅyāp-*, referring to ***ṅī*** and ***āp***, which have original long vowels. Note, moreover, that the syntax seen in **A** 8.2.2 is not unique to Pāṇini. For example, Kātyāyana's third vārttika on **A** 1.2.44 is: *pryojanaṁ dviguprāptāpannālampūrvopasargāḥ ktārthe.* As Patañjali makes clear in his Bhāṣya on this (Kielhorn [1880-85:I.216.16]: *upasargāḥ ktārthe*), *ktārthe* is construed only with one part of the preceding compound. To be sure, **A** 5.4.74 concerns compounds — rules regarding which Joshi and Roodbergen wish to consider interpolations — and in **A** 6.4.62 one could possibly consider *upadeśej-* part of a compound. Nevertheless, Joshi and Roodbergen might at least have mentioned comparable usages and not have treated **A** 8.2.2 as though it contained a syntactic anomaly unique in the Aṣṭādhyāyī.

Even less acceptable is Joshi and Roodbergen's citation of part of the Mahābhāṣya on **A** 8.2.2 and their confident assertion that Patañjali 'informs us that he will add the word *kṛti* in P. 8.2.2 which originally did not contain that word.' They have taken the Bhāṣya's comments on vārttika 3 to **A** 8.2.2 — not to **A** 8.2.7 — out of context and not represented accurately what Patañjali says. This discussion concerns the reason for the sūtra stating *-tug-*. The discussion begins (Kielhorn [1880-85:III.387.13]) *tugvidhau kim udāharaṇam* 'What is an example for a provision concerning ***tuk***?' The examples *vṛtrahabhyām* (instr.-dat.-abl. du.), *vṛtrahabhiḥ* (instr. pl.) are then given. These are forms of the compound *vṛtrahan-* 'one who has slain Vṛtra', to derive which the kṛt affix ***kvip*** is introduced after *han* (**A** 3.2.87: *brahmabhrūṇavṛtreṣu kvip*) and dropped (**A** 6.1.67: *ver apṛktasya*). The *-n* of *-han-* is deleted by **A** 8.2.7 (*nalopaḥ prātipadikāntasya*), leaving *vṛtraha-bhyām*, *vṛtrahabhis*. *-han* originally was followed by ***kvip***, which is marked with *k*, so that the *-a* of *vṛtraha-* could be eligible for taking the final augment ***tuk*** (**A** 6.1.71: *hrasvasya piti kṛti tuk*). Since, however, according to **A** 8.2.2 deletion of *-n* by **A** 8.2.7 is suspended with respect to augmenting by **A** 6.1.71, the rule **A** 8.2.7 does not supply an item eligible for this augmenting. After citing the two derivates that illustrate the need for including *-tug-*, the Bhāṣya introduces

Kātyāyana's vārttika 3 (*tugvidhau coktam*), which refers one to a statement made elsewhere: 1.1.39 vt. 5: *nalopo vṛtrahabhiḥ*. This vārttika is one of a series of statements in which reasons are given that are supposed to require operating with a metarule according to which something that is provided for by rule is not the cause for doing away with a relation which determined its application in the first place (1.1.39 vt. 3: ... *saṁnipātalakṣaṇo vidhir animittaṁ tadvighātasya*). The form *vṛtrahabhiḥ* is given to illustrate: dropping the *-n* of *vṛtrahan-* is conditioned by the collocation of *vṛtrahan-* and *-bhis*, before which *vṛtrahan-* is a pada; the absence of *-n* results in *-a* followed by *-bhis*, and the very absence of *-n* which brings this about should not destroy the collocation *-a-bhis* by allowing the final augment *-t* to give **vṛtrahat-bhis*. Patañjali, however, remarks (Kielhorn [1880-85:I.97.21-22]: *etad api nāsti prayojanam* I *asiddho nalopaḥ* I *tasyāsiddhatvān na bhaviṣyati*) that this is not a compelling reason for adopting the metarule in question, since *-n*-deletion is suspended — either by **A** 8.2.2 or by virtue of the paribhāṣā *asiddhaṁ bahiraṅgam antaraṅge*. In the Bhāṣya on **A** 1.1.39, then, suspension is invoked in order to avoid admitting that forms like *vṛtrahabhiḥ* show the need for a separate metarule *saṁnipātalakṣaṇo vidhir animittaṁ tadvighātasya*. The Bhāṣya on **A** 8.2.2, however, proceeds differently. After introducing Kātyāyana's allusion to his vt. 5 on **A** 1.1.39 and noting what is said therein, Patañjali then says (Kielhorn [1880-85:III.387.16-17]): *idaṁ tarhi prayojanam* : *kṛtīti vakṣyāmi* I *iha mā bhūt* : *brahmahacchatram bhrūṇahacchāyā* 'Then this is the reason: I [Pāṇini] will state *kṛti* so that (the suspension of the rule dropping word-final *-n*) not apply here: *brahmahacchatram bhrūṇahacchāyā*.' Patañjali thus has another participant remark that Pāṇini includes *-tug-* in **A** 8.2.2 because in the same sūtra he will go on to say *kṛti*. That is, since he will state *kṛti*, he has also to state the operation that applies before a kṛt affix. The Bhāṣya on **A** 8.2.2 ends by rejecting stating (III.387.17-18: *naiṣa saṁnipātalakṣaṇaḥ*) that the deletion of *-n* in deriving *brahmahacchatram* 'the umbrella of one who has slain a Brāhmaṇa', *bhrūṇahacchāyā* 'the shadow of one who has slain a fetus' is not dependent on the collocation of *-han-* with *-chatra-*. Instead, this depends merely on *brahmahan-*, *bhrūṇahan-* being padas by virtue of originally having a nominal ending: *-han-* ← *-han-as*.

It is just about certain that when Patañjali says *idaṁ tarhi prayojanam*

: *kṛtīti vakṣyāmi | iha mā bhūt : brahmahacchatram bhrūṇahacchāyā* he is not stating that he himself will say something to add a term to an original sūtra. To be sure, Kātyāyana and Patañjali frequently suggest reformulations of Pāṇinian sūtras. However, statements of the type *idaṁ tarhi prayojanam ... iti vakṣyāmīti* are frequent, and they never involve reformulations of Pāṇinian rules suggested by Patañjali. By my count, this formula occurs twenty times — including repetitions in a discussion of a single sūtra — as follows:

1.1.34 (I.93.1-2): *idaṁ tarhi prayojanam : vyavasthāyām asaṁjñāyām iti vakṣyāmīti*

1.1.34 (I.93.6): *idaṁ tarhi prayojanam : jasi vibhāṣāṁ vakṣyāmīti*

1.1.56 (I.134.6): *idaṁ tarhi prayojanam : analvidhāv iti pratiṣedhaṁ vakṣyāmīti*

1.1.68 (I.176.9): *idaṁ tarhi prayojanam : aśabdasaṁjñeti vakṣyāmīti*

1.2.27 (I.204.16-17): *idaṁ tarhi prayojanam : eca ig ghrasvādeśa iti vakṣyāmīti*

1.2.69 (I.250.6-7): *idaṁ tarhi prayojanam : ekavac cāsyānyatarasyām iti vakṣyāmīti*

1.2.72 (I.251.18-19): *idaṁ tarhi prayojanam : parasya śeṣaṁ vakṣyāmīti*

1.2.73 (I.252.20-21): *idaṁ tarhi prayojanam : ataruṇeṣv iti vakṣyāmīti*

1.3.67 (I.292.2): *idaṁ tarhi prayojanam : anādhyāna iti vakṣyāmīti*

2.4.12 (I.477.2-3): *idaṁ tarhi prayojanam : sa napuṁsakam iti vakṣyāmīti*

3.2.126 (II.128.19): *idaṁ tarhi prayojanam : acayoga iti vakṣyāmīti*

3.3.136 (II.162.1): *idaṁ tarhi prayojanam : anahorātrāṇām iti vakṣyāmīti*

3.3.136 (II.162.6): *idaṁ tarhi prayojanam : bhaviṣyatīti vakṣyāmīti*

3.3.145 (II.164.4-5): *idaṁ tarhi prayojanam : upapadasaṁjñāṁ vakṣyāmīti*

3.4.4 (II.170.17-18): *idaṁ tarhi prayojanam : yathāvidhīti vakṣyāmīti*

3.4.5 (II.170.22-23): *idaṁ tarhi prayojanam : sāmānyavacanasyeti vakṣyāmīti*

4.3.98 (II.314.12): *idaṁ tarhi prayojanam : vāsudevaśabdasya pūrvanipātaṁ vakṣyāmīti*

5.1.3 (II.338.19): *idaṁ tarhi prayojanam : saṁjñāyām iti vakṣyāmīti*

5.1.113 (II.363.1): *idaṁ tarhi prayojanam : caura iti vakṣyāmīti*

7.1.95-96 (III.275.18-19): *idaṁ tarhi prayojanam* : *vibhāṣā vakṣyāmīti*. *vibhāṣā tṛtīyādiṣv acīti*

The citations in question involve references to Pāṇinian sūtras, parts of sūtras, or procedures provided for in sūtras, with one exception: the Bhāṣya on 3.2.126. This concerns a vārttika. Reference is made to what Kātyāyana says in vt. 2 on **A** 3.1.26: *kartuś ca lakṣaṇayoḥ paryāyeṇācayoge*. The Bhāṣya's statement *idaṁ tarhi prayojanam* : *kṛtīti vakṣyāmi* made in the commentary on **A** 8.2.2 is like the other statements given above. The only difference is that here one has *vakṣyāmi* instead of *vakṣyāmīti*. I do not have an explanation for the fact that all the editions known to me have this reading. On the other hand, despite this difference, I think it obvious that the argumentation is of the same kind. Accordingly, I have no hesitation at all in concluding that *idaṁ tarhi prayojanam* : *kṛtīti vakṣyāmi* must indeed refer to *kṛti* which is included in the Pāṇinian sūtra known to Patañjali, and that the claim made by Joshi and Roodbergen on the basis of a partial citation of the passage lacks justification.

It is noteworthy that Joshi and Roodbergen also get little in return. After a discussion of how *vṛtrahacchattra*- and *vṛtrahabhyām* are derived (1983:89-90), they end their section **5.4** as follows (1983:91):

> To achieve the *asiddhatva* of *nalopa* in connection with *tUK* followed by a *kṛt*-suffix only, Patañjali has added *kṛti* to P. 8.2.2. But now the question is, if *kṛti* did not form part of the original rules, what would be Pāṇini's solution of the problem? The conjecture is that in the original text of the *Aṣṭādhyāyī* the *tUK* stated in P. 6.1.71 belonged to the *aṅgādhikāra*, or in any case to the *siddha*-section, whereas the *tUK* mentioned in P. 6.1.73-75 belonged to the *asiddha*-section, after the prescribing (sic!) *nalopa*. In this arrangement the *nalopa* is *siddha* as far as the application of the purely phonological *tUK* (P. 6.1.73-75) is concerned. Also, the *nalopa* is automatically *asiddha* as far as the application of *kṛti tuk* is concerned. Therefore the addition of the word *kṛti* is not required in P. 8.2.2, and the problem discussed above simply did not arise for Pāṇini as the author of the original text of the *Aṣṭādhyāyī*.

In sum, according to the received text of the Aṣṭādhyāyī, the sūtras **A** 6.1.71-76 (*hrasvasya piti kṛti tuk, saṁhitāyām, che ca, āṅmāṅoś ca, dīrghāt, padāntād vā*) form a coherent set of rules concerning the addition of the final augment ***tuk***, both as conditioned by a kṛt affix and in purely phonological contexts. Having formulated this set of rules, which cannot be placed in the section headed by **A** 6.4.1: *aṅgasya*, Pāṇini then stated **A**

8.2.2 in the manner known to Kātyāyana and Patañjali: *nalopaḥ supsvarasaṁjñātugvidhiṣu kṛti*. In the original Aṣṭādhyāyī as Joshi and Roodbergen would have it, on the other hand, the rules in question are split up, one to be placed in the section preceding **A** 8.2.1: *pūrvatrāsiddham*, the rest in the Tripādī. The sole justification for this is Joshi and Roodbergen's contention that **A** 8.2.2 is poorly formulated and that Patañjali introduced *kṛti* into an original rule that lacked this term. As shown, neither of these claims is justified.

Returning to the principal thesis set forth by Joshi and Roodbergen at the beginning of their article, let me finally consider their section **2.3** (1983:67-68), entitled **Inconsistency in the use of** *anubandhas*. In section **2.3.1** (1983:67-68), the authors deal with the marker *ḍ*, noting that it is used with 15 taddhita affixes and on three occasions in connection with affixes that are not taddhitas. One of these affixes is ***ḍā***, which according to **A** 2.4.85: *luṭaḥ prathamasya ḍāraurasaḥ* replaces ***tip*** and *ta* that derive from the L-affix ***luṭ*** in accounting for so-called periphrastic future forms; e.g. *kartā* '... will do, will make', *adhyetā* '... will study, will learn'. The possible problem associated with this marker is well known[18] and summarized by Joshi and Roodbergen: 'Here, strictly speaking, the *Ḍ* cannot serve to drop the *ṭi*-portion of the preceding stem, because the latter is not *bha*. Even then, since the *Ḍ* has no other function, we assume that the *ṭi*-portion of the preceding verbal stem is deleted.' They go on to remark (1983:67-68):

> In this respect we further note the following incongruities. In the first place, the rule P. 2.4.85 should come in the section which deals with substitutes for finite verb endings (P. 3.4.77-112), at least, if the periphrastic future is not regarded strictly as a purely nominal formation. In the second place, *Ḍ* is not commonly used as an *anubandha* for non-*taddhita*-suffixes.
>
> We note that the rule 2.4.85 itself is somewhat suspect. It has been put at the end of a *pāda*. It has no connection with the preceding rules. The question may also be asked whether the periphrastic future was known to Pāṇini. But the answer here obviously requires the discussion of a number of other rules, and, therefore, must be postponed to a later occasion.
>
> Finally, it may be argued that P. 3.2.97-98 have been added later on, because, apart from making use of the *anubandha Ḍ* which commonly belongs to the *taddhita*-section, these rules show another peculiarity. They do not mention the *upapada* with the help

of function-names like *adhikaraṇe janer ḍaḥ* and *apādāne' jātau*, but with the help of *vibhakti*-names like *saptamyām* and *pañcamyām* respectively. The latter is the practice of the *taddhita*- and *samāsa*-sections.

It is indeed striking that **A** 3.2.97: *saptamyāṁ janer ḍaḥ* and **A** 3.2.98: *pañcamyām ajātau* use terms referring to triplets of nominal endings and not terms designating kārakas to signify which endings are introduced. Thus, for example, **A** 3.2.1: *karmaṇy aṇ* has *karmaṇi* and **A** 3.2.15: *adhikaraṇe śeteḥ* (*ac* 9) has *adhikaraṇe*. One need not, however, immediately jump to the conclusion which Joshi and Roodbergen invite one to reach, namely that **A** 3.2.97-98 are later additions to an original corpus of rules.

Let us briefly consider some features of the rules mentioned. **A** 3.2.1 is a well known sūtra, whereby the kṛt affix ***aṇ*** follows a verb to signify an agent (**A** 3.4.67: *kartari kṛt*) of the action denoted by that verb, if this is construed with a co-occurring term signifying an object (*karmaṇi*) of the act in question. Thus, if *kṛ* is construed with a term *kumbha*- 'pot' that is used to designate an object of making, the verb takes the affix ***aṇ*** to signify the agent of making. The nominal *kumbha*-, now syntactically connected to a derivate with a kṛt affix, thereby is followed by a sixth-triplet ending to signify an object (**A** 2.3.65: *kartṛkarmaṇoḥ kṛti*): *kumbha-ām kār-a-* (- *kṛ-a*). The related terms obligatorily combine to form a compound (**A** 2.2.19: *upapadam atiṅ*), within which endings are deleted. In this way, Pāṇini accounts for a derivate *kumbhakāra*- 'pot maker', forms of which do not alternate with syntactic strings such as **kumbhānāṁ kāraḥ*. Conversely, *kumbhānāṁ kartā* 'maker of pots', which has the derivate *kar-tṛ*- — with the agent affix ***tṛc*** (**A** 3.2.133: *ṇvultṛcau*) — does not alternate with a compound form **kumbhakartā*, since derivates of the type *kartṛ*- do not regularly enter into composition (**A** 2.2.16: *kartari ca* [*tṛjakābhyām* 15, *ṣaṣṭhī* 8, *na* 10]). Similarly, **A** 3.2.15 introduces ***ac*** after *śī* 'lie, sleep' construed with a term signifying a locus (*adhikaraṇa*) relative to this act. For example, *śī* takes this affix if it is syntactically connected with *kha-i*, which has the seventh-triplet ending ***ṅi*** signifying a locus (**A** 2.3.36: *saptamy adhikaraṇe ca*). The related derivates obligatorily combine to form a compound *khaśaya*- 'one who lies in heaven'. Now, let us consider the possibility of stating *3.2.97a: *adhikaraṇe janer ḍaḥ* and *3.2.98a: *apādāne' jātau*. These would introduce ***ḍa*** after *jan* 'be born' construed with any nominal term signifying a locus (*adhikaraṇe*) and a term signifying an apādāna, provided the nominal in question does not refer to a class characterized by a generic property (*ajātau*). Both **A** 3.2.97 and *3.2.97a would properly account for derivates such as *saroja-* 'born in a lake (i.e. a lily)'; similarly, both **A** 3.2.98 and *3.2.98a would account for a derivate like *duḥkhaja-* 'born of misery'. *3.2.97a and *3.2.98 would, however, allow derivates like *tatraja-* and *tatoja-*, which are not provided for by **A** 3.2.97-98. This is as follows. An adhikaraṇa can be designated by a term containing a seventh-triplet ending. In addition, if such a term contains a nominal base of the set consisting of *bahu* 'many' and *kim* (interrogative) as well as other pronominals except those in the subgroup beginning with *dvi* 'two', then it is optionally followed by the taddhita affix ***tral*** (**A** 5.3.10: *saptamyās tral*). For example, *tad-i* optionally takes the suffix ***tral*** : *tad-i-tra* (→ ... *tatra*), thus accounting for the fact that forms like *tasmin* (loc. sg. masc.-nt.) and *tatra* alternate. The derivate *tatra-* itself is a nominal base, hence is followed by an ending to form a pada. The ending in question is a first-triplet ending, introduced only on condition that the meaning of the base as well as a number and gender are to be signified; e.g. *tatra-s*, with the nominative singular ending ***su***. Since the derivate is a member of the avyaya class, moreover, the ending following it is deleted. Similarly, *tatas* is derived by introducing ***tasil*** after a term with a fifth-triplet ending, thus accounting for the alternation between *tatas* and nominal forms like *tasmāt* (abl. sg. masc.-nt.). Now, *tatra* signifies an adhikaraṇa, and this term can be construed with *jan*, as in *tatra jātaḥ* 'born there'. And *tatas* of *tato jātaḥ* 'arisen from that' signifies an apādāna, in this case an original element from which something arises (**A** 1.4.30: *janikartuḥ prakṛtiḥ*). By **A** 3.2.98, *jan* construed with *tad-as* could take the suffix ***ḍa***, so as to give a derivate *tajja-* 'which has arisen from that'. Such a derivate is actually attested in fairly early Sanskrit: Chāndogyopaniṣad 3.14.1: *sarvaṁ khalv idaṁ brahma tajjalān iti śānta upāsīta*, where *tajja-* of *tajjalān* 'arisen from it (brahman), absorbed into it, breathing through it' occurs; Śaṅkara quite rightly paraphrases *tajja-* with *tasmād brahmaṇo jātam*. In addition, **A** 3.2.4: *supi sthaḥ* (*kaḥ* 3) introduces ***ka*** after *sthā* construed with a term that ends in any nominal ending (*supi*). This sūtra thus allows not only for derivates like *tatstha-* but also *tatrastha-*, both meaning 'situated in that'. The latter is not attested in early Vedic, but it is certainly attested later. In fact, Patañjali uses it three times; for example, in the Bhāṣya on 1.3.9 vt. 9, where it is said that a marker is perceived as situtated in the element to which it is attached (Kielhorn [1880-85:I.265.20]: *tatrastho hy asāv upalabhyate*). Nor is this restricted to śāstra literature. For example, *tatrasthāḥ* is used in Rāmāyaṇa 6.20.22 (*te tu dharmātmanā dṛṣṭā rākṣasendreṇa rākṣasāḥ* | *vibhīṣaṇena tatrasthā nigṛhītā yadṛcchayā*) with reference to Rāvaṇa's spies, who were seen by Vibhīṣaṇa as they observed him with Rāma, Lakṣmaṇa and Sugrīva near the Suvela mountain. Now, *3.2.97a and *3.2.98a would similarly allow *tatraja-* and *tatoja-*. For *tatra-s*, *tatas-s* respectively designate an adhikaraṇa and an apādāna. **A** 3.2.97 and 3.2.98, on the other hand, would not allow these derivates, since *tatra-s* and *tatas-s* terminate in a first-triplet ending, not in endings of the seventh and fifth triplets. It is reasonable to conclude that if Pāṇini had had to account for derivates *tatraja-*, *tatoja-*, he would have formulated *3.2.97a and *3.2.98a. Since he formulated **A** 3.2.97 and **A** 3.2.98, it is equally reasonable to say that the Sanskrit he describes had *tajja-* but not *tatraja-*, *tatoja-*. I cannot prove this definitively, but it is certainly no less plausible than Joshi and Roodbergen's suggestion — based purely on terminology — that **A** 3.2.97 and **A** 3.2.98 might be later additions to an original grammar.

Joshi and Roodbergen should be expected to consider alternatives such as the one I have given. They should also reasonably be expected not simply to suggest that Pāṇini might not have known the future type *kartā*. The derivation of forms of this type involves introducing the L-affix *luṭ*. Suppose that Pāṇini had in fact not allowed for such derivates. Then, the L-affixes *lṛṭ*, *leṭ*, *loṭ* of the series *laṭ*, *liṭ*, [*luṭ*], *lṛṭ*, *leṭ*, *loṭ* would be surprising in view of the observed order *laṅ*, *liṅ*, *luṅ*, *lṛṅ*. Presumably, Joshi and Roodbergen would assume a clever interpolator fixed things up to make them appear harmonious. The same interpolator would have introduced the sūtra **A** 3.3.15: *anadyatane luṭ* and modified an earlier sūtra to give it the received form of **A** 3.1.33: *syatāsī lṛluṭoḥ*. Perhaps such speculation might be the topic of the later discussion Joshi and Roodbergen speak of when they 'note that the rule **A** 2.4.85 itself is somewhat suspect' because it occurs at the end of a pāda and has no apparent connection to preceding sūtras.

Finally, one could reasonably expect Joshi and Roodbergen to take cognizance of and mention at least in passing the impoverishment that their main thesis would entail. The original grammar as they envision it had rules introducing kṛt affixes but not rules of composition. As noted above, however, some derivates with kṛt affixes occur only in compounds. Should one assume under Joshi and Roodbergen's view that the original grammar excluded from its purview the kṛt affixation rules which result in derivates that occur only as parts of compounds? To treat Pāṇini as an eminent grammarian and at the same time have him overlook an important and obvious distinction between certain free and bound items is at best less than felicitous.

In sum, although Joshi and Roodbergen have some interesting and challenging things to say and despite Kiparsky's efforts to portray their thesis — which he calls (1991a:359) a 'ground-breaking theory' — as having great importance, the evidence supports a very different evaluation of their claims. I consider myself fully justified in concluding once more (see Cardona [1989:51]) that their enterprise reflects an exaggerated eagerness to find difficulties where there are none. I also consider a much more conservative approach to be appropriate. Now, it is well known that even earliest Pāṇinīyas knew of variants in the formulation of sūtras; see Cardona (1976a:153-154, 1997:577 [**854**]), Radicchi (1985-88:I:16), and, for a very thorough consideration of variants in sūtras, Venkitasubramonia Iyer (1983, 1985). It is also well known that some Pāṇinian usage is best considered to stem from earlier teachers. A standard instance of this is the divergence between the use of *ṭ* and *ṅ* as markers with endings (see Cardona [1976a:147-148]): *auṭ* is the form of the dual ending in the second triplet of nominal endings as introduced in **A** 4.1.2, but Pāṇini also uses the pratyāhāra *auṅ* (**A** 7.1.18: *auṅa āpaḥ*), which presupposes an ending *auṅ*, marked with *ṅ*. *ṭā* is the form of the singular ending in the third triplet of nominal endings introduced in **A** 4.1.2. In **A** 7.1.12: *ṭāṅasiṅasām inātsyāḥ*, Pāṇini also uses *ṭā*; but in **A** 7.3.120: *āṅo nāstriyām*, he refers to this ending as marked with *ṅ*. It would be less than reasonable to assume that the rule which provides for replacing *ṭā* with *ina* after a stem in *-a* was composed by Pāṇini but that the rule according to which *nā* replaces *āṅ* after a non-feminine ghi stem is a post-Pāṇinian interpolation. It is more proper to suppose that the latter reflects a pre-Pāṇinian procedure which Pāṇini has maintained. There are also variations best considered, I think, to accord with dialectal differences both in Pāṇini's time and earlier. Thus, according to prevalent usage, consonants are referred to by terms with a vowel *a*: *ka* ('k') and so on. For example, Pāṇini uses *ta* 't' (e.g. **A** 3.1.108: *hanas ta ca*), *sasya* as a genitive singular referring to *s* (**A** 8.2.24: *rāt sasya*), and *ye* as a locative singular form referring to *y*- (e.g. **A** 6.4.49: *ye vibhāṣā*). He also uses forms of consonant stems, of the type *taḥ* (gen. sg., e.g. **A** 7.1.41: *lopas ta ātmanepadeṣu*), *saḥ* (e.g. **A** 7.4.49: *saḥ sy ārdhadhātuke*), *yi* (loc. sg., e.g. **A** 6.1.79: *vānto yi pratyaye*), *si* (e.g. **A** 7.4.49). In addition, there are instances that reflect the use of *i* instead of *a*. For example, in **A** 3.4.107: *suṭ tithoḥ*, *ti*- refers to *t* and *th*- refers to *th*; the genitive *aseḥ* ('not ending in *s*': **A** 8.2.80: *adaso'ser dād u do maḥ*) contains *si* referrring to *s*. Such variation is comparable to the use of different colored vowel segments in *ṛ* and the svarabhakti segment inserted between *r* and consonants. That is, one can reasonably suppose that Pāṇini's grammar reflects work of his precedessors as well as dialect variations of his predecessors and contemporaries. Moreover, if Pāṇini could adopt terms like ***auṅ*** and ***ṅā*** into his grammar, one also cannot dismiss the possibility that he took over sūtras of his predecessors and that he did not necessarily modify their formulations, which accords with a cultural norm (cf. Cardona [1989:75 note 9]). To be sure, this means that the Aṣṭādhyāyī is to be viewed as the work of a vyāsa comparable to the Vyāsa of the Mahābhārata. In and of itself, however, there is nothing strange about such a situation in the early Indian context. It means, however, that we must live with certain apparent inconsistencies and learn to differentiate between these and true conflicts within the Aṣṭādhyāyī that point to interpolation. This Joshi and Roodbergen have failed to do.[19]

2.1.2.4. *The dhātupāṭha* (III.1.3.5)

A second edition of part of the Mysore edition of the Mādhavīyadhātuvṛtti has appeared (Mahadeva Sastri and Panditaratnam K. Rangacharya [1984]).

The question whether the original dhātupāṭha associated with the Aṣṭādhyāyī included meaning entries (Cardona [1976a:161-163]) has been brought up anew by Bronkhorst (1981a), who concludes his paper saying (1981a:355):

> We have now come to think that the meaning entries were probably part of the DhP.

since its beginning. The question with which this paper must end is therefore: Is it possible that, after all, meaning played a far greater role in Pāṇini's grammar than has often been supposed?

A major piece of evidence indicating that meaning entries did not occur in the original dhātupāṭha is what Kātyāyana says in his first two vārttikas on **A** 1.3.1 (see Cardona [1976a:162]). Bronkhorst (1981a:345-350) considers this and other evidence from the Mahābhāṣya and attempts to show that the evidence does not require one to conclude that Patañjali knew a dhātupātha without meaning entries. Cardona (1984) once more took up the major Mahābhāṣya evidence and concluded that, on the contrary, this indicates the dhātupāṭha received by earliest Pāṇinīyas did not have meaning entries.

Bronkhorst's argumentation is based on a flawed understanding of the crucial texts at issue and on vague reasoning. Thus, he takes up 1.3.1 vtts. 1-2 (*pāṭhena dhātusaṁjñāyāṁ samānaśabdapratiṣedhaḥ, parimāṇagrahaṇaṁ ca*) and says (1981a:346):

> In view of the context, it is permissible to think that *pāṭhena* means *dhātupāṭhena* "owing to the Dhātupāṭha". The vārttikas can then be translated: "Owing to the Dhātupātha, [utterances] of the same sound-pattern [as verbal roots] are prevented from [assuming] the designation 'root'; and the measure [of the individual roots] is known." If this translation is correct, the two vārttikas describe the advantages of having a separate Dhp., rather than a sūtra where all roots are given in the form of a huge compound or a long list. This interpretation of the vārttikas makes only sense [sic] if Kātyāyana knew of a Dhp. *with* meaning entries. By virtue of these meaning entries it can be known that no non-roots are meant in the Dhp., and also of what length the individual roots are.
>
> I do not wish to push this interpretation of the two vārttikas. The main thing is that Patañjali may have been led to his abstract problem by a vārttika which he had not correctly understood. And if his understanding of the vārttika was correct, he took his abstract problem from Kātyāyana. Neither way does the Bhāṣya passage under study compel us to believe that Patañjali knew a Dhp. without meaning entries.

Bronkhorst's interpretation of 1.3.1 vt. 2 depends on considering that *grahaṇa* in *parimāṇagrahaṇam* means 'grasping, knowing, understanding' instead of 'mentioning, stating'. The latter is the usual interpretation adopted by Pāṇinīyas and is to be accepted (Cardona [1984]). Bronkhorst does not even mention this, much less attempt to justify his interpretation.

He also does not note that his interpretation fails to take into consideration what is said in the third and fourth vārttikas (*kriyāvacana upasarga-pratiṣedhaḥ, saṅghātenārthegateḥ*) on **A** 1.3.1. Here, Kātyāyana remarks that if the class name *dhātu* is assigned by a rule stating that this class name applies to an item which signifies an action (*kriyāvacane*), then one must state a prohibition (*pratiṣedhaḥ*) denying this name to preverbs, since a meaning is understood by means of a complex including a preverb, as in *prapacati* 'cooks excellently'. This fits neatly, as all Pāṇinīyas have accepted, into a sequence of arguments such that one begins with the position that the name *dhātu* is given to elements known as recited in a separate ancillary text and not as defined semantically. In addition, the argument made in the third and fourth vārttikas assumes such an alternative manner of assigning the class name because the first way of doing this leads to perceived difficulties.

Bronkhorst's use of evidence from later sources is equally flawed. Thus, he cites (1981a:352) a kārikā from the Upagrahasamuddeśa of the Vākyapadīya,[20] which he translates, 'Since the meaning is fixed, a marker is attached to aid memory. Moreover, [roots] which have the same meanings, do not necessarily all have the same properties.' Immediately thereafter, Bronkhorst goes on to say:

> What is under discussion is the use of markers (such as *Ñ*, *Ṅ*) which determine whether a root takes Ātmanepada or Parasmaipada endings. This choice can be made on the basis of the meaning which the root is to convey. What purpose is then served by these markers? The first half of the stanza explains that the markers merely remind us of the exact meaning of the root concerned.
>
> The second half of the stanza seems to contradict this. It speaks of roots which have the same meanings, but take different endings because they have different properties. I can think of only one satisfactory interpretation of this line. Here the word *artha* 'meaning' refers to the meaning entries in the Dhp. The second half then means that roots which have the same, or synonymous, meaning entries in the Dhp., do not on that account take the same endings, for they may have different properties.

Bronkhorst concludes his discussion of VP 3.2.12 (1981a:353) as follows:

> The above seems to show that, in Bhartṛhari's opinion, the markers attached to roots are supplementary to the meaning entries which those roots have in the Dhp. No one doubts that markers were attached to roots since Pāṇini. We may conclude that in Bhartṛhari's opinion also meaning entries accompanied roots since Pāṇini.

The Vākyapadīya verse in question concerns specifically bases marked with a svarita vowel or with *ñ*, which take ātmanepada affixes — as provided for in **A** 1.3.72: *svaritañitaḥ kartrabhiprāye kriyāphale* — if the results of the acts in question are intended for their agents. In the Mahābhāṣya on **A** 1.3.72, Patañjali begins his discussion by considering the need to include *svaritañitaḥ* in the rule. The immediate answer is: so as not to allow the introduction of ātmanepada affixes after bases such as *yā* 'go' (*yāti*), *vā* 'blow' (*vāti*), *drā* 'run' (*drāti*), *psā* 'eat' (*psāti*). This is rejected, however, and Patañjali claims *svaritañitaḥ* can be omitted. As for how this can be done while still disallowing **yāte* and so on, Patañjali reasons as follows. The abbreviated sūtra *kartrabhiprāye kriyāphale* provides for ātmanepada affixes after a base on condition that the result of an action is intended for its agent. Moreover, acts denoted by all verbs can have results intended for their agents. Accordingly, the condition stated by *kartrabhiprāye kriyāphale* must be intended to allow ātmanepada affixes after bases denoting actions whose results can be both intended and not intended for their agents. And it is such bases that are marked with svarita vowels and *ñ* as they are recited in the dhātupāṭha. The bases *yā* and so forth are not such that the acts they signify are spoken of as having results intended for their agents and also not so intended.[21] On the other hand, the act denoted by a base like *nī* (*ṇīñ*) 'lead, take somewhere' is spoken of in both ways, and one says both *nayate* and *nayati*. It is this discussion that VP 3.12.12 concerns. This is patent from the preceding kārikā,[22] where Bhartṛhari says that for some verbs the capacity (*sāmarthyam*) to signify a particular sort of action[23] is suppressed,while there are others for which this does not hold; these are marked with svarita vowels and *ñ*. What Bhartṛhari says in Vākyapadīya 3.12.12, then, is this: for those who are familiar with the usage in question, a particular meaning for particular verbs is given as established (*siddhe'rthe*); that is, some verbs are known to be used to signify actions whose results are both intended for their agents and not, so that one can consider them to include in their meanings the particular act of making provision for carrying out an act. All verbs have in common that they signify acts, so that they share a general meaning (*tulyārtheṣv api ca*), and groups of verbs — such as *yā* and *nī* — share a particular meaning. Yet they do not all have the same property (*na sarveṣv ekadharmatā*). The use of verbs like *nī* to signify acts qualified in a particular way, then, is a given; svarita vowels and *ñ* are appended to such bases merely for the purpose of calling this to mind (*smṛtyartham*). This is pointed out by Helārāja, who remarks[24] that *yā* signifies reaching a place (*prāpaṇa*) but *ñī* signifies having someone reach a place (*prāpaṇā*).[25]

It is clear, I think, that the first and second halves of VP 3.12.12 do not involve any contradiction. Nor does what Bhartṛhari say justify Bronkhorst's interpretation that *arthe* in the first part of the verse must refer to meaning entries in the dhātupāṭha. Finally, although there can hardly be any doubt that Helārāja knew a dhātupāṭha version that included meaning entries, what he says (see note 24) does not justify Bronkhorst's claiming that Helārāja agrees with him (1981a:352):

> This interpretation is also the one accepted by the commentator Helārāja (*Prakīrṇaprakāśa*, part ii, p. 122). As an illustration he contrasts *yā prāpaṇe* (Dhp. II.40) with *ṇīÑ prāpaṇe* (Dhp. I.950). These two roots differ considerably in meaning: 'go' as against 'lead'. They have nevertheless been assigned a common meaning in the Dhp. In order to remind the reader of that part of the meaning which has not been given in the Dhp., the marker *Ñ* has been added to *ṇī*.

In sum, Bronkhorst's arguments are both vague and based on hasty conclusions reached on the basis of an insufficient understanding of the sources he uses. I consider it fairly well established that, in accordance with what Kātyāyana and Patañjali say, the dhātupāṭha known to the earliest Pāṇinīyas did not include meaning entries.[26]

2.1.2.5. *The gaṇapāṭha* (III.1.3.6)

Anna Radicchi (1991) discusses the gaṇapāṭha from a historical and comparative point of view. Earlier, Dyen (1939:73) had concluded that if the gaṇas found in the Cāndra-vṛtti, the Jainendravyākaraṇa (Mahāvṛtti of Abhayanandin), the Kāśikāvṛtti, and the Śākaṭāyanavyākaraṇa agree, one might conclude that this represents an original list. Radicchi differs, considering instead (1991:66): 'It seems more reasonable to believe that all the grammarians of that period drew on a common store of *gaṇas*.' Subsequently, she observes (1991:68):

> The *gaṇapāṭha* emerging from this comparison is not a reconstructed but a historic *gaṇapāṭha*, with its various readings and additions on older lists. It is what we have called the common store, valid from the fifth to the eighth-ninth century A.D., the

basis for Candra and Abhayanandin's *gaṇas* as well as those of the critically read Kāśikā.

Radicchi had briefly discussed the gaṇapāṭha earlier (1985-1988:II.18-23, 116-123).

2.1.2.6. *Metarules* (III.1.3.7)

Two recently published dissertations have dealt with paribhāṣā collections: V. M. Bhatt (1987a) and Wujastyk (1993). Bhatt's work is a very good study of Puruṣottamadeva's Laghuparibhāṣāvṛtti. It also includes discussions concerning more general points, such as paribhāṣāsūtras stated in the Aṣṭādhyāyī, the position of Vyāḍi's work, and chapters comparing Puruṣottama's paribhāṣā collection with those of Sīradeva, Nīlakaṇṭha, Haribhāskara, and Nāgeśa. Wujastyk has supplied a critical edition of the Vyāḍīyaparibhāṣāvṛtti and shown with fair certainty, I think, that the commentary owes much to the Mahābhāṣya and is not as early as had been thought. Wujastyk's translations are accompanied by references that are informative though incomplete. I do not consider the translation itself very successful; see Cardona (forthcoming j). In a chapter devoted to the Paribhāṣāvṛtti (1991:87-107), Narendra Kumar Dash gives a table of paribhāṣās included in 18 paribhāṣā collections (1991:88-95). Amita Sharma (1995) has recently edited and commented on Puruṣottamadeva's Jñāpakasamuccaya.

In an earlier work, originally a dissertation, Bronkhorst (1986) takes up the paribhāṣā *asiddhaṁ bahiraṅgam antaraṅge* (no. 50 in Kielhorn [1868]). He translates much of Nāgeśa's text and interprets it, concentrating especially on the term *antar* of *antaraṅgam*. He considers also what commentators on Nāgeśa's text have said, especially what Vaidyanātha says in his Gadā, and reaches novel conclusions. Bronkhorst states his major thesis as follows (1986:xiii):

> In the following pages an attempt will be made to establish that the part of Nāgeśa's *Paribhāṣenduśekhara* (*PŚ*) which deals with Par. L (*asiddhaṃ bahiraṅgam antaraṅge*) has not been correctly understood from Vaidyanātha Pāyaguṇḍa — Nāgeśa's own pupil — onward. In other words, it is here claimed that an important portion (*l'apogée du Paribhāṣenduśekhara*, as Renou calls it) of the most widely studied book written by the most recent grammarian of importance has been misinterpreted.

The principal conclusion Bronkhorst reaches is that Nāgeśa had a conception of the bahiraṅgaparibhāṣā which '... may well be unique in the history of Sanskrit grammar in its simplicity' (1986:153). Bronkhorst goes on to say (1986:153):

> It is the tragedy of Nāgeśa that this beautiful construction remained unknown to almost all but himself. Some change which had inexplicably found its way into the text prevented Nāgeśa's direct student, Vaidyanātha Pāyaguṇḍa, from grasping his master's intentions. The only other person who may have been Nāgeśa's pupil, and commented upon the *PŚ*, Bhairava Miśra, does not deviate much from Vaidyanātha's interpretation.
>
> If there is a moral to be drawn from all this, it clearly is that the much cherished *guru-śiṣya-paramparā* is not always such an infallible guide in interpreting a text as is often supposed. Vaidyanātha, though Nāgeśa's direct pupil, interprets the *PŚ* as if he had never known its author.

To deal appropriately with Bronkhorst's challenging study would require considering all the examples Nāgeśa deals with along with the next paribhāṣā (pbh. 51: *nājānantarye bahiṣṭvaprakḷptiḥ*) as well as places in the Mahābhāṣya where these issues are also taken up. I cannot do this in the present survey.[27]

Nāgeśa's Paribhāṣenduśekhara has been published again with more commentaries: Śrīnārāyaṇa Miśra (1981), Girijeśa Kumāra Dīxita (1987), P. Sri Ramachandrudu (1987), Kālikā Prasāda Śukla (1991).

Volume III.2 of the Osmania edition of the Kāśikā with indexes (Ramachandrudu and V. Sundara Sarma [1985]) contains (1985:242-281) collections of paribhāṣās. As far as I can determine, these do not differ from the collections in K. V. Abhyankar (1967).

Karunasindhu Das (1986) considers paribhāṣās formulated in the Aṣṭādhyāyī and others brought into play by commentators but which Pāṇini does not explicitly state. He also treatss metarules in prātiśākhya works. The most recent study I know of in this area is by P. P. Pathak (1995).

2.1.3. *Other texts usually associated with the Aṣṭādhyāyī*

2.1.3.1. *The uṇādisūtras* (III.1.4.1a)

Volume III.1 of the Osmania edition of the Kāśikā with indexes (B. R.

Sastry and V. Sundara Sarma [1976]) includes the daśapādī text (1976:146-168), an index to this accompanied by references to the pañcapādī (1976:169-191), an index of derivates together with verbal bases, affixes, and operations (1976:192-293), and an index of affixes (1976:294-337).

2.1.3.2. *The phiṭsūtras* (III.1.4.2a)

Volume III.2 of the Osmania edition of the Kāśikā with indexes (Ramachandrudu and V. Sundara Sarma [1985]) includes an edition of the phiṭsūtras (1985:285-286), which, as far as I can see, is identical with the one in Pathak and Chitrao (1935).

2.1.3.3. *The liṅgānuśāsana* (III.1.4.3a)

Volume III.2 of the Osmania edition of the Kāśikā with indexes (Ramachandrudu and V. Sundara Sarma [1985]) includes an edition of the liṅgānuśāsana (1985:282-284), identical, as far as I can tell, with the one in Pathak and Chitrao (1935).

2.1.3.4. *The Pāṇinīyaśikṣā* (III.1.4.4a)

The metrical version of the Pāṇinīyaśikṣā has been republished again recently: Goswami Prahlad Giri (1987). The śikṣā text alone appears on pages 317-322 of Rāmaprasāda Tripāṭhī (1989). In addition, Manmohan Ghosh's edition of the śikṣā in various versions has been reprinted (Ghosh [1986]), as has Raghu Vira's study of 1931 (1981).

2.1.4. *The system of the Aṣṭādhyāyī*

2.1.4.1. *Pāṇini's derivational system* (III.1.5.1a,b)

Junnarkar's work (1977-1988) is an excellent introduction to Pāṇini's system in general.[28] R. N. Sharma (1987:165-211) presents the broad aspects of Pāṇini's derivational system and of compound derivation in particular. This is a lucid and perceptive discussion.[29] Cardona also (1997a:136-400 [**212 - 622**]) has described in general all aspects of Pāṇini's derivational system. Jag Deva Singh (1991) too takes up Pāṇini's general system,[30] and P. S. Subrahmanyam (1975, 1988, 1992) has dealt with particular aspects of this, as has Kapil Kapoor (1991-92).

Filliozat (1988) takes up Pāṇinian grammar as a whole, from a particular point of view, which the author sets forth as follows (1988:1): 'Le présent ouvrage vise à mettre en évidence les éléments de la conscience linguistique des pandits ou lettrés sanskrits de notre époque.' There is also a much more abbreviated presentation by Filliozat (1992a:37-43).[31]

Although based on secondary sources, as the author himself says, Pinault's (1989b, c, d) is a lucid presentation of Pāṇini's work, the Pāṇinian system and its background. Kiparsky (1995) treats the background of Pāṇinian grammar, its 'method of grammatical analysis', morphology/ syntax, and phonetics and phonology. The presentation is quite general and abstract, and one is struck by the absence of concrete examples illustrating what Pāṇini did. In thirteen columns of text, I find cited one example and one sūtra. The example *bhāryā rājñaḥ puruṣo devadattasya* is quoted (1995:63a) to illustrate the restriction of compound formation to padas that are semantically and syntactically connected, and the sūtra **A** 6.1.77: *iko yaṇ aci* is used (1995:65a) to show how classes of sounds denoted by terms connected with Pāṇini's akṣarasamāmnāya are associated with an operational rule.[32]

Several scholars have emphasized that Pāṇini's grammar is an explanation of usage known to him (see Cardona [1976a:327 note 148]). In a recent paper, Satya Vrat Shastri (1992) once more stresses this. Satya Vrat's examples are generally well chosen and serve to illustrate his point. The following argument (1992:63), on the other hand, is somewhat curious:

> There could not be a more convincing evidence of Pāṇini's regard for usage than his framing of the Sūtra उदीचां माङो व्यतीहारे (3.4.19). The people of the north used an expression अपमित्य (अपमाय) याचते which is palpably wrong and in no way justifiable. क्त्वा is used here in the absence of पौर्वकाल्य which grammar does not permit. Both the Vṛttikāra and the Kaumudīkāra agree in declaring that the Sūtra is to provide for the use of क्त्वा in the case of अपूर्वकाल (absence of priority of action). It is only after a Brāhmaṇa has got something by begging that he seeks to barter it for something else. Naturally, therefore, याचित्वाऽपमयते is what is reasonably expected. Pāṇini accepts अपमाय याचते out of sheer regard for usage. But for it, he would have rejected it forthwith.

There is, I think, some confusion here. All that is involved is dialectal difference. In general, *ktvā* follows a verb signifying an action performed by a single agent prior to performing another act. Northerners, on the other hand, use *apamitya yācate* to refer to someone's begging for something in exchange for something else, so that he first begs and then exchanges what he has said he would exchange for the object requested. To declare that such usage is palpably wrong fails to acknowledge the very aspect of usage that Pāṇini so correctly recognized. This is the sort of confusion one sees in discussion of so-called "un-Pāṇinian" usage in certain texts.

According to Pāṇini, terms such as *tatas* 'from that, thence', *avika* 'sheep' are derivates with affixes (*ka*, ***tral***) that follow items with which the derivates are synonymous: *tad-as* (→ *tasmāt* etc.), *avi* 'sheep'. Cardona (1976a:183) spoke of such as affixes as being introduced redundantly; see also Cardona (1997a:441-442 [**686-687**]). In this connection, Pāṇinīyas speak of *svārthika* affixes, and suffixes like *ka* in *avika* are said to be *atyantasvārthika* ('absolutely redundant'). Wezler (1980) objected to Cardona's rendition of the term *svārtha* and to his accepting the view which, in Wezler's opinion, was maintained by later Pāṇinīyas but not by Kātyāyana and Patañjali. Subsequently, Cardona (1983a:89-116) once more took up the issue and in the course of his discussion pointed out (1983a:101-102, note 222) that Wezler could maintain the alleged distinction only because he ignored a passage where Patañjali explicitly says an affix like the *ka* of *avika* does not convey anything.

S. D. Joshi and J. A. F. Roodbergen (1983) have attempted to show that Pāṇini's grammar originally dealt only with the derivation of simple padas, including those with kṛt affixes, but excluding compounds and derivates with taddhita affixes. For reasons I have given above (section 1.2.3), I consider their attempt unsuccessful.

J. A. F. Roodbergen (1991) reaches the following conclusion (1991:313):

> The word-building process proceeds in what is visually a left-to-right direction. This direction corresponds to what (in the order of application of rules) is a time sequence, earlier-later. This correspondence lies at the base of the *sati śiṣṭa* accent principle. But, stripped of its accent connotation, it can be said to be the governing principle of both the word-building process and of the organization of the *Aṣṭādhyāyī*. That is to say, Pāṇini's derivational procedure as reflected in the organization of the *Aṣṭādhyāyī* is dependent on one principle, namely that of the left-to-right processing order. Rules

dealing with left-side elements are introduced earlier than rules dealing with right-side elements.

In reaching this conclusion, Roodbergen argues that vikaraṇa affixes like ***śap*** in *bhū-a-ti* (→ ... *bhavati* 'is, becomes') — which usually have been considered to be introduced before sārvadhātuka affixes — should be considered to be introduced before L-affixes. That is, instead of a derivational sequence *bhū-l* (affix ***laṭ***) → *bhū-ti* → *bhū-a-ti* → *bho-a-ti* → *bhavati*, the sequence is: *bhū-l* → *bhū-a-l* → *bhū-a-ti* → *bho-a-ti* → *bhavati*. Under the traditional way of deriving such forms, *sārvadhātuke*, stated in **A** 3.1.67: *sārvadhātuke yak* and understood to recur in subsequent rules that introduce vikaraṇas, is considered a parasaptamī, so that the vikaraṇas are introduced when a sārvadhātuka affix follows. Roodbergen proposes (1991:311) to take *sārvadhātuke* here as a viṣayayasaptamī, so that, as he says, 'In that case, the formal presence of a finite verb ending is no longer required for introducing the *sārvadhātuka vikaraṇa*s. We could add them at the *lakāra*-stage.' In support of this, Roodbergen invokes (1991:311) the satiśiṣṭasvara principle concerning accentuation. According to this principle, the accentuation of an element that is newly introduced (*śiṣṭa* 'taught') cancels the accentuation of a previously present element. If a vikaraṇa such as ***śnu*** is introduced after a verb like *su* 'press juice out of something' when a sārvadhātuka affix denoting an agent is already present, the derivational sequence for *sunutas* (3rd du. pres. act.) is: *su-l* → *su-tas* → *su-nu-tas*. The accentual principle in question would wrongly let the vikaraṇa ***śnu*** be high-pitched instead of the ending. Under the traditional interpretation, **A** 6.1.186: *tāsyanudāttenṅidadupadeśāl lasārvadhātukam anudāttam ahnviṅoḥ* is considered to indicate that, contrary to the usual procedure, the accentuation of a vikaraṇa does not cancel the accentuation of a sārvadhātuka that replaces an L-affix. The rule provides that such a sārvadhātuka has low pitch if it follows ***tāsi***, a provision that would be useless if the satiśiṣṭasvara procedure held without exception. Under Roodbergen's alternative, this problem does not arise.

Roodbergen ends his article (1991:313-314) with a suggestion concerning the sets of rules that introduce taddhita affixes and provide for compounds:

> It is this left-to-right processing order that is violated by the position of the *taddhita* and *samāsa* sections in the present edition of the *Aṣṭādhyāyī*. The structural reason is

> that the rules belonging to these sections presuppose the existence of a fully derived *pada*. Therefore, in order to make the *Aṣṭādhyāyī* a more perfect processing machine, a *word-processor* in the literary (sic! [literal]) sense of the word, these sections should be lifted from their present position and placed after the *asiddha* section.

Roodbergen draws some interesting conclusions. His arguments are also well put. There is, nevertheless, at least one important point that, so far as I have been able to discern, Roodbergen does not consider. He appears to assume that the strict left-to-right processing order is maintained even if one has a derivation like *bhū-l* → *bhū-a-l* → *bhū-a-ti* → *bho-a-ti* → *bhavati*. For this to be appropriate, however, it is necessary that the L-affix not be a proper part of the derivate at any stage. For, if a lakāra such as ***laṭ*** is an affix (*pratyaya*), the vikaraṇa of *bhū-a-l* is indeed introduced when another affix already follows the verbal base, thus violating the strict left-to-right order. This order would require one to have a stage *bhū-a*. As far as I can see, Roodbergen does not confront this issue. Moreover, even assuming that Roodbergen means the left-to-right processing to apply after one has complexes of the type *bhū-l*, the difficulty remains if L-affixes are indeed affixes (*pratyaya*) which have to be introduced in a derivation. In addition, **A** 1.4.13: *yasmāt pratyayavidhis tadādi pratyaye' ṅgam* has to be considered. According to this sūtra, an element Y that begins with an item X after which an affix is introduced and is followed by that affix is called *aṅga*. Thus, in (((*bhū-*)*a-*)*mi*), ((*bhū-*)*a-*) is an aṅga with respect to the ending *mi*, so that the rule whereby *-a* of an aṅga is replaced by the corresponding long vowel (**A** 7.3.103: *ato dīrgho yañi*) applies in deriving *bhavāmi*. **A** 1.4.13 includes the term *tadādi* 'beginning with x'. Under the absolute left-to-right processing procedure envisioned by Roodbergen, **A** 1.4.13 could be formulated simply as *yasmāt pratyayavidhiḥ pratyaye' ṅgam*. That Pāṇini formulated the rule in his manner fits best with the traditional procedure, not with an absolute left-to-right processing procedure.

There are also some minor problems. Thus, Roodbergen's derivation of *bhavet* (1991:302) involves a stage *bhū* + ***yāsuṭ*** + ***liṅ***. Regarding this he says, 'Here the augment *yāsUṬ* is regarded as part of *lIṄ*, and *lIṄ* is replaced by *tiP*.' Roodbergen does not mention a possible problem that arises. According to **A** 1.1.55: *anekālśit sarvasya*, a replacement that consists of more than one sound substitutes for the entire substituend referred to by a genitive. As Roodbergen says, *yāsu**ṭ*** is part of the affix to which it is added; in particular, it is the initial part of the affix (**A** 1.1.46: *ādyantau ṭakitau*). The affix *ti* (*ti**p***) consists of more than one sound. Consequently, under the derivation Roodbergen envisions, this should replace all of *yāsl*, not merely the segment *l*, so that the replacement which should apply to *-yā-* in order to derive *bhavet* cannot apply. Moreover, the context in which the sūtra that provides for the augment *yāsuṭ* (**A** 3.4.103: *yāsuṭ parasmaipadeṣūdātto ṅic ca*) is stated indicates clearly that this is added to endings that replace *li**ṅ***. *liṅaḥ* of **A** 3.4.102: *liṅaḥ sīyuṭ* has to be understood to recur in subsequent rules such as **A** 3.4.105: *jhasya ran*; this sūtra thereby provides that *ran* substitutes for the ending *jha* which replaces the L-affix *li**ṅ***. *liṅaḥ* is thus to be understood as a genitive referring to the source of endings which are subject to particular operations. Letting *yāsu**ṭ*** be an augment added to a parasmaipada ending which replaces *li**ṅ*** allows the appropriate derivation of a form like *bhavet*.

For such reasons, I cannot accept Roodbergen's major conclusion or its consequence concerning the status of taddhita and composition rules.

As most recently noted by G. B. Palsule (1991a, see section 2.1.4.7a below), the sort of derivational procedure Roodbergen opts for was known to some grammarians.[33]

Building on his earlier work (1975), R. N. Sharma considers (1992:29) '... variable references, insofar as they illustrate representation of knowledge with some built-in mechanism for information retrieval'. In particular, though not exclusively, Sharma deals with references by means of the relative and correlative pronouns, illustrating by means of detailed derivations the procedures that come into play.

M. D. Pandit (1990) expands on earlier work (1962) and treats in some detail questions concerning anubandhas and anuvṛtti.

S. D. Joshi and J.A.F. Roodbergen (1992)[34] seek to demonstrate that the procedure of single remainder as provided for in **A** 1.2.64: *sarūpāṇām ekaśeṣa ekavibhaktau* and subsequent rules is not acceptable. Thus, the first two points of their summary (1992:109) are:

a. *Ekaśeṣa* as a word-derivation technique (*vṛtti*) is a failure, because it starts from the wrong assumption.

b. *Ekaśeṣa* goes against Pāṇini's prescription of number in P. 1.4.21 - 22 and against Pāṇini's word-derivation technique as known from the *kṛt-* and *tiṅ*-sections of the

Aṣṭādhyāyī.

The assumption Joshi and Roodbergen speak of is the one mentioned on page 102 of their article, namely that terms like *vṛkṣa-* 'tree' denote individuals only, so that reference to more than one individual would require the use of more than one such term. I agree that this assumption is unjustified. On the other hand, this is not necessarily the basis for the ekaśeṣa procedure. By **A** 2.2.29: *cārthe dvandvaḥ*, Pāṇini allows for combining any number of related nominal padas to form a dvandva compound. There are compounds of the type *mātāpitarau* 'mother and father' and synonymous terms like *pitarau* 'parents'. A sensible approach to account for this is to allow *pitṛ-* optionally to be a single remainder, as Pāṇini does (**A** 1.2.70: *pitā mātrā*). In addition, granting the usage known to earliest Pāṇinīyas, there are terms like *akṣāḥ*, which can refer to several different entities — an axel, a die, and a kind of seed — and which accordingly also can be treated as involving a single remainder of several homophonous terms with different meanings. Joshi and Roodbergen say (1992:103), 'Whether a plural form like *akṣāḥ* used in speech ever has the three meanings mentioned is doubtful. Exception must be made, of course, for the literary device known as *śleṣa*.' This reflects only the authors' predilection and cannot weigh against usage that Pāṇinīyas like Patañjali knew. Moreover, the fact remains that **A** 2.2.29 would indeed allow for any number of homophonous nominals to combine in a dvandva compound regardless of their meanings, so that **A** 1.2.64 would make sense as a rule precluding particular strings of terms. Of course, a great deal of what Kātyāyana and Patañjali say in their long discussion of this rule rests on particular philosophical view points and extreme positions taken. This does not demonstrate, however, that **A** 1.2.64 is either unnecessary or infelicitous. But then, Joshi and Roodbergen also wish to deny that compounding rules are part of the original Aṣṭādhyāyī (see section 2.1.2.3), so that their attitude towards ekaśeṣa is understandable if not justifiable.[35]

Karunasindhu Das (1984) has briefly discussed, with examples, the various types of zero with which Pāṇini operates, designated *lopa*, *luk*, *ślu*, and *lup*. Mithilesh Chaturvedi (1975) considers one type in particular, with special emphasis on the derivation of terms like *gargāḥ* 'the male descendants of Garga' and the use of adjectives such as *śukla* 'white'.

2.1.4.2. *The composition of the grammar : general organization, rule order, types of rules*

2.1.4.2a. *General organization* (III.1.5.2a)

Viśana Lāla Gauḍa 'Vyomaśekhara' (1985) deals with the general principles which Pāṇini follows, the kinds of rules found in the Aṣṭādhyāyī, their relations to each other, and other general topics.

The greater part of V. B. Bhagavat (1988) is devoted to a fairly detailed outline of the contents of the Aṣṭādhyāyī, adhyāya by adhyāya (1988:69-174). The author also devotes separate chapters to brief expositions of the kinds of rules in the grammar (1988:12-24) and ways of achieving brevity (1988:25-41). R. N. Sharma (1987:74-88) also gives a general description of how the Aṣṭādhyāyī is organized.

The major subject covered in Kripa Ram Tripathi (1991) is the taddhita section, but before dealing with this the author considers general aspects of how the Aṣṭādhyāyī is organized..

As noted in section 2.1.4.1, J. A. F. Roodbergen (1991) has argued that the sections of the Aṣṭādhyāyī which introduce taddhita affixes and provide for nominal compounds are to be relegated to the asiddha section of the grammar.

S. D. Joshi and S. Bhate (1984) deal with anuvṛtti in great detail; see also Joshi and Bhate (1983).

2.1.4.2b. *Rule order and the application of rules* (III.1.5.2b)

The order of rules in the Aṣṭādhyāyī and the principles which Pāṇini follows in having these rules apply so as to account for the facts of the language described presuppose a set of rules which Pāṇini considered appropriate to the task, even if he did not compose all of them himself (see 2.1.2.3). Accordingly, an investigation of principles governing how sūtras apply is intimately connected with the study of the Aṣṭādhyāyī text and possible modifications this may have undergone. S. D. Joshi has formulated how one might conduct such investigations. According to Joshi (1982a:168), there is an underlying theory of Pāṇini's which the later tradition could not trace because the Aṣṭādhyāyī with which it was concerned contained old and new layers incompatible with each other. A major task, then, is to find the oldest layer in order to learn what was Pāṇini's underlying theory. As Joshi puts it (1982a:168), 'Once we find out and sweep away these later layers of rules perhaps it will be possible for us to discover the basic theory as intended by Pāṇini which perhaps occurs in the original layer of the *Aṣṭādhyāyī*.' As I pointed out earlier (section 2.1.2.3), Joshi and Roodbergen have attempted to demonstrate that large sections of the received Aṣṭādhyāyī were not part of the original text. Joshi and scholars with whom he has worked also have tried to show that Pāṇinīyas could not capture Pāṇini's original principles and overgeneralized some procedures. Two major topics of discussion are: the status of sūtras in terms of whether certain rules are considered to be nonexistent with respect to others or not; the domains in which a bracketing principle applies.

It is well known that **A** 8.1.2: *pūrvatrāsiddham* divides the Aṣṭādhyāyī into two major sections: the last three pādas — the Tripādī — opposed to the first seven and one-fourth pādas. Unless otherwise indicated, a sūtra of the Tripādī is suspended (*asiddha*) — that is, treated as nonexistent — with respect to a sūtra of the preceding group and within the tripādī a sūtra is suspended with respect to a prior rule. Rabi Sankar Banerjee (1984:1-28) presents lucidly and succinctly what is accomplished by this suspension.

In recent times there has been some controversy concerning just what is meant by *asiddha* and *siddha*. It is worthwhile summarizing briefly the history of the controversy. Joshi and Kiparsky (1979) tried to maintain that the terms *siddha* and *asiddha* had particular values in Pāṇini's grammar. They say (1979:225):

> Let B(A(ϕ)) denote the result of applying, to a given input ϕ, rule A and rule B *in that order*; and let B, A (ϕ) denote the result of applying, to a given input ϕ, rules A and B *simultaneously*. Then:
>
> (1a) A is *siddha* w. r. t. B = For all ϕ such that B(A(ϕ)) ≠ B, A (ϕ), A is applied before B to ϕ.
>
> (1b) A is *asiddha* w. r. t. B = For all ϕ such that B(A(ϕ)) ≠ B, A (ϕ), A is not applied before B to ϕ.

They also enunciate a general principle (1979:228):

> The most general principle governing the order in which rules are to be applied is that of transparent ordering:
>
> (2) All rules are *siddha* w. r. t. all rules (*sarvatra siddham*).

Joshi and Kiparsky go on to give five examples, among them the derivation of *tudati* 'goads, wounds'. At the stage *tud-ti*, two operations could apply: by **A** 3.1.77: *tudādibhyaḥ śaḥ*, the vikaraṇa *śa* is introduced to give *tud-a-ti*; by **A** 7.3.86: *pugantalaghūpadhasya ca*, guṇa replacement applies to substitute the guṇa vowel *o* for the penultimate sound of *tud*. If the latter applies first to give *tod-ti*, the fomer can still apply, but if the former applies first to give *tud-a-ti*, the latter cannot then apply. For, *śa* is a sārvadhātuka affix treated as marked with *ṅ* (**A** 1.2.4: *sārvadhātukam apit*), so that it does not serve as a context for guṇa substitution in its stem (**A** 1.1.5: *kṅiti ca*), and the *-u-* of the stem *tud-a-* relative to the sārvadhātuka affix ***tip*** is not the penultimate sound of the stem, so that guṇa replacement cannot apply to *tud-a-*. Immediately before this example, Joshi and Kiparsky take up two other examples: *śiṣṭāt* 'may you/he command', *rudihi* 'weep, cry' (2nd sg. imper.). They then say (1979:231-232):

> Cases like Examples 3-5 are common. But the later tradition, interestingly enough, does not account for them by (2). It instead supposes a separate principle to the effect that a *nitya* 'constant' rule takes precedence over a non-*nitya* rule. Given two rules A and B which are applicable to a given form, rule A is *nitya* (and rule B non-*nitya*) when A is still applicable if B applies first, but B is no longer applicable if A applies first. Saying that *nitya* rules precede is equivalent to saying that rules are applied in bleeding order.
>
> In Kātyāyana's *vārttikas*, the *nitya* relation is very rarely utilized (e.g., on 6.4.88 [sic!]). It may be a later development necessitated by the illegitimate expansion of the *antaranga/bahiranga* relation to the word-internal domain (see below).

Kiparsky (1982) devotes a section of a chapter (1982:77-87) to the issues he and Joshi had earlier considered. Here he says the following (1982:77-78):

> Suppose that we have a process
>
> (1) A → B
>
> and processes P and Q applying in the environments A and B respectively:
>
> (2) P in env. A
>
> (3) Q in env. B
>
> Then to say that rule (1) is *asiddha* with respect to rule (2), is to say that P is applicable in the environment A even if A should become B by rule (1) — *utsargalakṣaṇabhāvārtham.* And to say that rule (1) is *asiddha* w. r. t. rule (3), is to say that Q is *not* applicable to an A even if it should become B by rule (1) —

> *ādeśalakṣaṇapratiṣedhārtham.* Or, to use terms common in linguisitics, *asiddhatva* blocks *bleeding* and *feeding* between rules. Thus, that (1) is *asiddha* w. r. t. (2) means that it does not bleed (2), i.e. (1) does not deprive (2) of A's to which (2) can apply, and that (1) is *asiddha* w. r. t. (3) means that (1) does not feed (3), i.e. (1) does not provide (3) with B's to which (3) is allowed to apply.

Subsequently (1982:79), Kiparsky formulates principle (2) noted above as '(4) *sarvatra siddham*', now referred to as 'the *siddha*-principle', concerning which he says:

> What the *siddha*-principle says is that in the general case we have *ādeśalakṣaṇabhāva* and *utsargalakṣaṇapratiṣedha.* That is, reverting to our schematic example, if we have a form A and the above rules (1-3) are in the grammar, then rule (2) will ordinarily *not* apply to that form because it will be bled by rule (1) — *utsargalakṣaṇapratiṣedha* — and (3) *will* ordinarily apply to that form because it will be fed by rule (1) — *ādeślakṣaṇabhāva.* In short, the *siddha* relations of feeding and bleeding are given free by the underlying theory of the Aṣṭādhyāyī and if we do *not* want to have them in some particular case, *then* only something must be said in the grammar itself.

Later on (1982:84-85), Kiparsky notes, 'By this point, anyone familiar with the topic will already have recognized that the principle of bleeding order (*utsargalakṣaṇapratiṣedha*) is simply equivalent to the *nitya*-principle formulated in the traditional inventory of *paribhāṣās.* To say that rules are applied in bleeding order amounts to the same thing as saying that *nitya* rules are applied first.' On the final page of his discussion concerning *siddha* and *asiddha*, Kiparsky (1982:87) then says:

> *Siddha* literally means 'effected' and so the idea of *sarvatra siddham* is that when any rule is applied, the rules pertinent to its application should have been 'effected', i.e. applied. In short, *environment-changing rules are applied first.* The environments of P, Q, R in (2, 3, 5) are A and/or B and the *siddha* principle says that you first apply the rules that affect A or B (either by creating or eliminating them) and then only apply the rules that are applicable in the context of A and B. More precisely, let A(X) denote the result of applying rule A to a form X; B(A(x) [sic!] then denotes the result of applying A and B in that order to X, and A, B (X) denotes the result of simultaneously applying A and B to X. Then we define
>
> (7) A is *siddha* w. r. t. B = for all X such that B(A(X)) is different from A, B(X), A is applied before B to X and formulate the *siddha*-principle as
>
> (8) All rules are *siddha* w. r. t. all rules.[36]

Bronkhorst (1984b) objected to Joshi and Kiparsky's principle and noted (1984b:311) that they had not fully understood the meanings of the terms they made use of. Kiparsky (1987) attempted to answer Bronkhorst's objections, then Bronkhorst (1990a) in turn replied to Kiparsky's retort.[37] Cardona too (1989:59-60) objected to Joshi and Kiparsky's procedure, and noted (1989:59)

> The claim that principle (2) says that rules are to be applied in bleeding order, however, is not so obvious. If we take the term *siddha* in its usual meaning, saying that rules such as Aṣṭādhyāyī 3.1.77 and 7.3.86 are siddha with respect to each other amounts to saying that they are in force with respect to each other, so that they can interact if the proper conditions are met, nothing more.

He also remarked (Cardona [1989:60]), 'Nor is it immediately acceptable to say that this claim is justified by virtue of Pāṇini's having declared certain sūtras to be suspended with respect to each other.' Kiparsky (1991a:342-343) replied to these objections concerning the '*siddha*-principle' by reiterating the principle and saying (1991a:343):

> The meaning of *siddha* in ordinary usage is perfectly well known. Cardona's rendering "established", "accomplished", "which has come about" (p 57, 54) is in no way at odds with my statement that '*siddha* literally means "effected"' (p. 87); all these agree with the standard dictionaries. And this is the meaning of *siddha* in terms of which I stated the *siddha*-principle in [3]. So there is no point in complaining that Joshi and I did not "justify the *siddha*-principle through a thorough investigation of what *siddha* means in ordinary usage" (p. 80).
>
> The *siddha*-principle does not merely say that rules "can interact if the proper conditions are met" (Cardona p. 59); it says that they *must*.

I consider this ingenuous. What Cardona objected to was and remains Joshi and Kiparsky inventing a '*siddha*-principle' which gives to the term *siddha* an extraordinarily strong meaning that goes well beyond rules being merely established. It is in a note (Cardona [1989:80 note 66]) that Cardona says, 'Note that neither in **Joshi-Kiparsky** 1979 nor in **Kiparsky** 1982:77-87 is any attempt made to justify the *siddha* principle through a thorough investigation of what *siddha* means in ordinary usage.' Moreover, Kiparsky gives the partial citation 'can interact if the proper conditions are met' as though Cardona had attributed this claim to him and his '*siddha*-principle' and had thereby misrepresented him. As shown above, this is part of the statement of my own view. The extensive citations given above can leave no doubt whatever that Joshi and Kiparsky do indeed give *siddha* a very precise, strong value that goes well beyond what this term means in ordinary Sanskrit.

Moreover, it should be clear from these quotations that their understanding is based on a misapplication of something Kātyāyana and others say. Consider, for example, what is said in the first vārttika on A 6.1.86: *ṣatvatukor asiddhaḥ* (see Cardona [1997a:68, 419-420 (**110**, **654**)]). Patañjali introduces this vārttika by asking the purpose for which this is stated (Kielhorn [1880-85:III.65.8]: *kimartham idam ucyate*). The response in the vārttika (6.1.86 vt. 1: *ṣatvatukor asiddhavacanam ādeśalakṣaṇa-pratiṣedhārtham utsargalakṣaṇabhāvārthaṁ ca*) is that this has the following as its purpose: to disallow something that is conditioned by a replacement (*ādeśalakṣaṇapratiṣedhārtham*); to allow to occur something that is conditioned by an original element subject to replacement (*utsarga-lakṣaṇabhāvārtham*). According to the usual Pāṇinīya understanding of the term *asiddha* — which is in harmony with the ordinary meaning of *siddha* and the verb *sidh* of which this is a participle — to say that a sūtra is asiddha with respect to another is to superimpose absence (*abhāva*) on that sūtra (see Cardona [1989:57-58]). Thus, saying that R_2 is asiddha with respect to R_1 amounts to saying that the former does not exist with respect to the latter. I have accordingly adopted the term 'suspended'. This of course has consequences. If R_2 is suspended with respect to R_1, it cannot be a source of a result to which the latter could apply. In addition, in instances where contexts would allow both tentatively to apply, since R_2 is treated as non-existent with respect to R_1, only the latter can possibly apply. These are the effects of rule suspension. Conversely, if two rules are siddha with respect to each other, this means simply that they exist with respect to each other and are free to interact when the occasion arises.

What Kiparsky has done is to consider the effect of a rule's being suspended to be the property that characterizes its being suspended: 'to say that rule (1) is *asiddha* with respect to rule (2), is to say that P is applicable in the environment A even if A should become B by rule (1) — *utsargalakṣaṇabhāvārtham.* And to say that rule (1) is *asiddha* w r. t. rule (3), is to say that Q is *not* applicable to an A even if it should become B by rule (1) — *ādeśalakṣaṇapratiṣedhārtham.*' Having done this, he considers the complements of utsargalakṣaṇabhāva and ādeśalakṣaṇapratiṣedha to characterize rules that are siddha: 'What the *siddha*-principle says is that in the general case we have *ādeśalakṣaṇabhāva* and *utsargalakṣaṇa-pratiṣedha*.' Note that the term *-artha-* is absent here. It is no longer a question of the purpose that a rule's being siddha serves. A rule is siddha if it interacts with another rule in a particular manner. It is this unjustified overextension that I objected to and to which I still object. And Kiparsky's protest does not remedy his claim.

Recall also that Joshi and Kiparsky equate what they consider the '*siddha*-principle' in one of its aspects with the Pāṇinīyas' principle that a nitya operation takes precedence over one that is anitya, so that Kiparsky can assert 'that the principle of bleeding order (*utsargalakṣaṇapratiṣedha*) is simply equivalent to the *nitya*-principle formulated in the traditional inventory of *paribhāṣās*.' In the traditional Pāṇinīya view, not only are Pāṇinian sūtras siddha or asiddha with respect to each other, operations are also nitya or anitya with respect to other operations. Obviously, if Pāṇini is supposed to have operated with the so-called '*siddha*-principle' of Joshi and Kiparsky, he cannot, in their opinion, also have operated with a nitya principle as formulated by Pāṇinīyas. Hence, it is understandable that, as noted above, Joshi and Kiparsky have to claim that the nitya principle is a post-Pāṇinian invention: 'In Kātyāyana's *vārttikas*, the *nitya* relation is very rarely utilized (e.g., on 6.4.88). It may be a later development necessitated by the illegitimate expansion of the *antaranga/bahiraṅga* relation to the word-internal domain ....' Kātyāyana does indeed refer to the nityatva in question explicitly on three occasions (1.2.6 vt. 1: ... *bhuvo vuko nityatvāt* ..., 1.3.60 vt. 4: *nityatvāl lādeśasyātmanepade aḍāgama iti ced aṭo'pi nityanimittatvād ātmanepadābhāvaḥ*, 7.1.6 vt. 4: *na vā nityatvād āṭaḥ*), though not in any vārttika on **A** 6.4.88, of which there is no separate discussion in the Bhāṣya. To say that this 'may be a later development' is vague and serves to demonstrate only that Joshi and Kiparsky cannot allow nityatva as a separate principle because of the manner in which they interpret asiddhatva and siddhatva. But this itself is based on a misunderstanding of *siddha* — as though a sūtra's being siddha meant that it had already applied — and an unjustified conclusion drawn from what Kātyāyana and others say concerning asiddhatva.

Joshi and Roodbergen (1993b) merely build on what Joshi and Kiparsky had earlier claimed.[38] On the other hand, Toru Yagi (1992) correctly distinguishes between Pāṇini's use of *asiddha* and *asiddhavat* in sūtras that provide for different types of suspension.[39]

As shown above, Kiparsky and Joshi also claim that the principle whereby an internally conditioned (*antaraṅga*) operation takes precedence over one that is externally conditioned (*bahiraṅga*) originally did not apply with regard to operations within a pada. Cardona (1989:60-64) presented arguments against this claim, and Kiparsky (1991a:343-348) attempted to answer these arguments. As I think I have demonstrated (Cardona [1997a:xiv-xxiii]), Kiparsky's attempt shows him persisting in not understanding fairly obvious matters. For example, he cannot understand that the form in **A** 6.1.9: *sanyaṅoḥ* has to be interpreted as a genitive, not a locative. Moreover, neither Joshi nor Kiparsky has given a principled reason why in Pāṇini's system the relation between internally and externally conditioned operations should be limited to operations across word boundaries. After all, Pāṇini operates with syntactic padas of the type (((*bhav-*)*a-*)*ti*) which contain well-defined stems (*aṅga*) within them, and there are operations, such as the replacement of prevocalic *o* by *av*, that apply across stem boundaries and word boundaries. Similarly, in (((*kṣi-*)*a-*)*ti*), ((*kṣi-*)*a-*) is a stem with respect to the ending ***tip***, which could, therefore, condition the replacement of the penultimate light vowel *-i-* of this stem by the corresponding guṇa vowel, a replacement that has to be prevented in order to provide for the desired form *kṣiyati*.

In a recent paper, Bhagyalata Pataskar (1991) has discussed the principle that a rule lacking a proper domain of application has to capture such a domain.

Yashodhara Kar (1994) once more takes up the set of rules headed by **A** 1.4.1 (see Cardona [1976a:189]).

2.1.4.2c. *Types of rules* (III.1.5.2c)

The work of Viśana Lāla Gauḍa 'Vyomaśekhara' (1985) contains a section dealing with the six types of rules (1985:102-120) and sections devoted to metarules and restrictive rules (1985:211-222), extension rules and headings (1985:223-230). R. N. Sharma (1987:89-120) and Cardona (1997a:4-79 [**9-127**]) deal in some detail with the various kinds of Pāṇinian rules. Laddu (1983) briefly discusses five instances of nipātanasūtras which involve accentuation and concludes (1983:232), 'The upshot of the above discussion points to our not taking accent as granted among the factors of irregularity in a *Nipātana.*'

2.1.4.3. *Metalanguage: technical terminology, metarules, stylistics*

2.1.4.3a. *Pāṇini's technical terminology*: *generalities* (III.1.5.3a)

The most wide-ranging study of Pāṇinian terminology recently carried out is by H. P. Dvivedi (1978). In the first five chapters, the author covers Pāṇini's use of the term *saṁjñā*, suggests a classification of terms into three major types, discusses Pāṇinian and pre-Pāṇinian terminology and the use of terms in both technical and non-technical values, and deals with questions concerning why Pāṇini introduces particular terms in different parts of the Aṣṭādhyāyī. In addition, one chapter (6 [167-185]) is devoted to contrasting the Aṣṭādhyāyī and the Cāndravyākaraṇa with respect to the use of technical terms, with emphasis on Candra's avoidance of much terminology, so that his grammar is referred to as *asaṁjñakaṁ vyākaraṇam* (see Cardona [1976a:333, note 196]). Dvivedi also devotes a separate chapter (7 [186-191]) to the issue of how sūtras in which technical terms are introduced interact with sūtras in which these terms are used, as formally stated in the paribhāṣās *yathoddeśaṁ saṁjñāparibhāṣam* and *kāryakālaṁ saṁjñāparibhāṣam.*

Ananthanarayana (1981) takes up anew Pāṇini's use of abbreviatory terms of the type *ac*, *hal*, lists the pratyāhāras used in the Aṣṭādhyāyī and considers the sūtras in which they are used.

R. N. Sharma (1987:121-125) deals briefly with seventy-five saṁjñāsūtras. Cardona (1997a:13-52 [**28-88**]) considers saṁjñāsūtras in general, those which establish general conventions as well as those that serve to establish classes, and the operational rules with which these are connected.

2.1.4.3b. *Pāṇini's technical terminology*: *particular terms* (III.1.5.3b)

The most important and influential monograph published recently concerning Pāṇinian terminology is by Kiparsky (1979), who attempts to establish that Pāṇini used the terms *vā*, *vibhāṣā*, and *anyatarasyām* to refer respectively to three different kinds of options: those that are preferable (*vā*), those that are marginal (*vibhāṣā*) and those that are simple options. As was pointed out to Kiparsky, this brings up problems concerning **A** 7.2.15: *yasya vibhāṣā*. According to this sūtra, if a verb is such that an ārdhadhātuka affix following it takes the initial augment *iṭ* optionally (*vibhāṣā*), that verb does not condition the addition of this augment to a niṣṭhā suffix following it. This sūtra should account for forms like *dhvasta*: The verb is marked with *u* (*dhvánsu*), and **A** 7.2.56: *udito vā* provides that ***ktvā*** following a verb marked with *u* optionally takes the initial augment *iṭ* (*dhvastvā*, *dhvaṁsitvā*). Now, **A** 7.2.56 uses *vā*, which under Kiparsky's thesis denotes a preferable option. If, then, *vibhāṣā* of **A** 7.2.15 cannot include reference to such an option, the latter will not apply with respect to verbs marked with *u*, with the result that Pāṇini's rules fail to account for known usage. Kiparsky attempted (1979:157-159) to avoid the problems of such rules by suggesting two possible interpretations of **A** 7.2.15: 'The question is whether 7.2.15 is to be read as prohibiting *iṬ* in *niṣṭhā* endings for a given root when there is another suffix where *iṬ* is (1) *at most* (*only*) a marginal option, or (2) *at least* a marginal option, i.e. possibly even a preferred option' (1979:157).[40] After a brief discussion of pertinent sūtras, he concludes (1979:158), 'In sum, there appears to be an inconsistency in the system which is not removed by either reading (1) or reading (2), or, of course, by the traditional interpretation.' He goes on further to discuss possible things to be done with the sūtras in question — including a suggestion that **A** 7.2.56 be read simply as *uditaḥ*, with *na vā* understood by anuvṛtti, and that *vā* be incorporated into the followng sūtra — and ends by saying (1979:159), 'The above is intended to be merely a suggestion for resolving the problem. If it proves to be workable, then reading (1) should be accepted. If not, then reading (2) is preferable, though it shares with the traditional interpretation an unexplained anomaly in the verbs of 7.2.57.'

In support of the textual revision he suggests, Kiparsky cites (1979:159) two pieces of evidence: (a) the participle *lubdha*- 'confused', found in Aitareyabrāhmaṇa 3.3, where *lubdham* is repeated seven times in passages of the type *yaṁ kāmayeta ... vyardhayānīti ... asya lubdhaṁ śaṁset* '(The Hotṛ) should recite in a confused manner the ... of the yajamāna whom he would deprive of ...' (e.g. *yaṁ kāmayeta prāṇenainaṁ vyardhayānīti vāyavyam asya lubdhaṁ śaṁset*); (b) the absolutive *vṛṣṭvā*, found in one passage of the Atharvaveda (Śaunakīya 8.3.2d: *kravyādò vṛṣṭvāpì dhatsvāsan*). According to Aṣṭādhyāyī **A** 7.2.54 (*lubho vimohane*) and **A** 7.2.55 (*jṝvraścyoḥ ktvi*) as traditionally understood, ***ktvā***, ***kta*** and ***ktavatu*** take the initial augment ***iṭ*** obligatorily when they follow *lubh* used in the sense 'confuse' (*vimohane*) and ***ktvā*** obligatorily takes this augment after *jṝ* 'age, wear away' and *vraśc* 'cut'. Kiparsky suggests that *na* and *vā* of **A** 7.2.39, 41 respectively be understood to recur in the following sūtras, so that **A** 7.2.54, 55 would include these terms. Accordingly, these rules would provide for what Kiparsky calls marginal options. Since *vibhāṣā* = *na vā*, then, **A** 7.2.15 applies to deny ***iṭ*** with ***kta*** and ***ktavatu*** after *vraśc* and *lubh* 'confuse'.

As shown above, in his 1979 monograph Kiparsky put this forth merely as a tentative suggestion, not his firm conclusion. In a later article however, Kiparsky remarks (1991a:336) that his earlier statement 'In sum ...' — which I have cited above — represents only his summary of the prima facie problem. He is also much more assertive. What was earlier 'intended to be merely a suggestion' is now characterized as (1991a:336) '... my actual conclusion and proposed solution.' Kiparsky now also adds a textual reference for *lubdham* (1991a:363 note 8) and some additional evidence that he considers conclusive. To avoid misrepresenting him, I cite what he says in toto (1991a:337-338):

> On the old reading, 7.2.53 *añceḥ pūjāyām* says that after *añcU* in the sense "to honor" (*pūjāyām*) the augment *iṬ* is added obligatorily to the gerund ending *Ktvā* and to the *niṣṭhā* endings (*Kta* and *KtavatU*). The other endings (sic!) after *añcU* get *iṬ* optionally (by 7.2.56 *udito vā* as explained above). After *añcU* in its other senses, the augment is also optional, except for the *niṣṭhā* endings, where 7.2.15 *yasya vibhāṣā* forbids it. The problem here is that *akna* in what seems to be its *pūjāyām* meaning (in *jānvakna* "on bended knees" etc.) is not accounted for. If, however, 7.2.53 is read with *na vā* as I propose, the rule says instead that *Ktvā* and *niṣṭhā* endings allow marginal *iṬ* after *añcU* in the meaning "honored", countermanding 7.2.15, which otherwise blocks it after *añcU* for *niṣṭhā* endings, since 7.2.56 makes *iṬ* marginal after this root.[9]

In note 9 (1991a:363), Kiparsky adds, 'The traditional reading has another shortcoming, that it does not account for the attested use of *añcita* in the non-honorific meaning "bent". This remains on the present reading as well.' Kiparsky also says (1979:159), 'In 53 *añceḥ pūjāyām*, though, the *iṬ* forms (*e.g. añcita*) are evidently the normal ones.'

Under the reading Kiparsky proposes, then, the past participle of ***añcu*** in the sense 'honored' should have two forms: *akna-* (varying with *akta-*) and *añcita-*. The former is the preferred form, since *na vā* is to be understood in **A** 7.2.53, so that this states a marginal option. The use of derivates such as *jānvakna-*, which Kiparsky translates "on bended knees", is supposed to support this. Similarly, *lubdham* and *vṛṣṭvā* are said to support Kiparsky's interpretation of **A** 7.2.54 and **A** 7.2.55.

Upon closer examination, what appears to be real philological evidence, presented in an assertive and confident manner, does not stand up. Let me begin with a discussion of ***añcu*** and its forms as accounted for under the Pāṇinīya interpretation of **A** 7.2.53, 56.

A 7.2.53: *añceḥ pūjāyām* (*ktvāniṣṭhayoḥ* 50, *iṭ* 35) provides that *iṭ* is added to ***ktvā***, ***kta*** and ***ktavatu*** after ***añcu*** used in the meaning 'honor'. By **A** 7.2.56: *udito vā* (*ktvi*), after a verb marked with *u* (*uditaḥ*), *iṭ* is optionally (*vā*) added to ***ktvā***. **A** 7.2.15: *yasya vibhāṣā* denies *iṭ* to ***kta*** and ***ktavatu*** if these occur with a verb relative to which an option is stated in subsequent rules. Accordingly, **A** 7.2.53 makes obligatory the initial augmenting for ***ktvā*** after ***añcu*** in the sense 'honor', contrary to the option augmenting allowed by **A** 7.2.56. **A** 7.2.53 also provides for the augmenting in ***kta*** and ***ktavatu*** after ***añcu*** in the same meaning, contrary to **A** 7.2.15, which would deny the augmenting. In addition, **A** 8.2.48: *añco'napādāne* provides that the *t-* of ***kta*** and ***ktavatu*** is replaced by *n-* after *añc*, provided that the verb is not construed with a term signifying an apādāna. In accordance with these provisions the following are derived: *akna-*, *akta-* (← *anc-ta-*), *aktvā-* (← *anc-tvā-*), *añcita-*, *añcitvā-*. Moreover, the evidence of Vedic usage supports the use thus provided for in the case of *akna-*, *akta-*.

Let me now take up Kiparsky's example *jānvakna*. It is clear from what he says about this form and from his translation ("on bended knees") that he understands the term to be used with reference to someone who has assumed a supplicant's stance with regard to someone or something that is being honored. He does this without giving any textual reference. Consider, however, the Vedic texts where the terms *jānvakna-*, *jānvākna-* are actually used. The passages in question concern the initiation of the yajamāna during the Jyotiṣṭoma rite, specifically the time when the yajamāna is to approach and get on an antelope skin that has been spread (or two such skins sewn together). He is to do this bending the right knee. The Āpastambaśrautasūtra (10.9.2: *atha prāṅmukho jānvakno' bhisarpati*) says that he approaches with bent knee, while facing east. The Bhāradvāja-śrautasūtra (10.5.16) says *bhasatto jānvakna ārohati* ('He gets on from behind, with bent knee'). The Baudhāyanaśrautasūtra (6.5) specifies that the yajamāna bends his right knee (*dakṣiṇaṁ jānu*): *atha dakṣiṇaṁ jānv ācyābhisarpati* ('He bends his right knee down and crawls towards it'). In the Śuklayajurveda tradition, Śatapathabrāhmaṇa 3.2.1.5 says *a̱tha jagha̱nena kṛṣṇājine̱ paścāt pra̱ṅ jānvākna u̱paviśati* ('Now he sits facing east to the rear part of the two krṣṇājina with his knee bent.'), and Kātyāyanaśrautasūtra 7.3.19 (*dakṣiṇaṁ jānv ācyāste paścād enayoḥ*) specifies that the yajamāna bends his right knee. As for why, according to the Kṛṣṇayajurveda texts, the yajamāna should bend his right knee when approaching the antelope skin, the same texts supply the image in question. According to Baudhāyanaśrautasūtra 6.5 (*atha dakṣiṇaṁ jānv ācyābhisarpatīmāṁ dhiyaṁ* ...) the act in question is accompanied by the recitation of Taittirīyasaṁhitā 1.2.2.2: *i̱māṁ dhiya̱ṃ śikṣàmāṇasya deva̱ kratu̱n dakṣàṃ varuṇa̱ saṃ śiśādhi̱ yayāti̱ viśvà duri̱tā tarèma su̱tarmàṇa̱m adhi̱ nāvàṃ ruhe̱ma.* That is, the antelope skin that one mounts is likened to a ship by which one crosses all hardships. Sāyaṇa is obviously correct when he says in his comments on this passage: *imāṁ krṣṇājinarūpāṁ nāvam adhi ruhema* 'We would mount this ship that is the black antelope skin.' The Baudhāyanaśrautasūtra (25.7) invokes the same image: *athedaṁ kṛṣṇājinam naur uktaṁ bhavati | ācya jānv etat pārśvata evābhisarpet dakṣiṇaṁ prati randhraṁ yathā nāvam* 'Now this black antelope skin is said to be a ship. After bending his knee, he should crawl sideways, towards the crook of the right knee (*dakṣiṇaṁ prati randhram* 'towards the right hole'), in the way (one approaches) a ship.' That is, the right knee is crooked and the yajamāna approaches the antelope skin in the way one gets on a ship. Clearly, the image is not that of someone "on bended knees". It is equally clear that no sense of honoring is involved, so that *akna-* as accounted for by the Pāṇinīya interpretation is appropriate.

Now, *jānvākna-* and *jānvakna-* are of the type *agnyāhita-*; as this last term is equivalent to *āhitāgni-* 'one who has set up the sacrificial fire', so are the former equivalent to *āknajānu-*, *aknajānu-*. A comparable compound *nyaknāṅguli-* occurs in Śatapathabrāhmaṇa 3.2.1.6 (*garbho vā eṣa bhavati yo dīkṣate sa chandāṁsi pra viśati tasmān nyaknāṅgulir iva bhavati nyknāṅgulaya iva garbhāḥ*), where the yajamāna being initiated is likened to a foetus: he has his fingers curled (*nyaknāṅguliḥ*), as feotuses have their fingers curled into a fist (*nyaknāṅgulayaḥ*). In a passage concerning the mythological associations of the southern vedi in the Varuṇapraghāsa offering, the Taittirīyabrāhmaṇa speaks of creatures having a straight (*prasṛta*-'stretched forth') left arm but a crooked (*nyakna-*) right arm. Prajāpati formed the southern vedi to the south/right of the northern one and thereby straightened out the right arm of creatures. TBr. 1.6.4.2: ... *tāsāṁ dakṣiṇo bāhur nyàkna āsīt savyaḥ prasṛtaḥ* | *sa etām dvitīyāṁ dakṣiṇato vedim udàhan* | *tato vai sa prajānāṁ dakṣìṇaṁ bāhuṁ prāsàrayat.* In none of these instances does *akna-* have the sense of honoring. Similarly, one has *nyaknāḥ* 'bent down, subject' in Kāṭhakasaṁhitā 29.9: *tā asmād abibhayus tā nyācyanta* | *tasmāt paśavo nyaknāḥ* ('They were afraid of him [Prajāpati]; they bent down in subservience. Therefore are animals subject.')[41] This involves animals making themselves amenable to Prajāpati's wishes, but it does not involve honoring.

Moreover, the contrast between *akna-* and *akta-* covered by Pāṇinian sūtras is seen in Vedic also. Thus in ... *ā vàvṛtrannadharāg udàktāḥ* ... (Vājasaneyisaṁhitā 10.19, Maitrāyaṇīsaṁhitā 2.6.11, Kāṭhakasaṁhitā 15.7) *udàktāḥ* 'directed up' is used with reference to the waters used for anointing and contrasts with *adharāk* 'below'. Taittirīyasaṁhitā 1.8.14.2 has *ā vàvṛtrannadharāg udìcīḥ*.

As shown, in the available Vedic texts, the past participle of ***añcu*** occurs quite a few times, and the form is *akna-*, *akta-*, used without a sense of honoring, and *jānvakna* does not mean 'on bended knees'. *añcita* in the sense 'bent, subjected' fails to occur in these early texts. In sum, the claims Kiparsky asserts about ***añcu*** and **A** 7.2.53 are not supported by available textual data. Consequently, even under Kiparsky's understanding of *vibhāṣā* and *na vā*, there is no need to have *na vā* recur in **A** 7.2.53. On the contrary, since Kiparsky's interpretation allows for *akna-* as the preferred variant in the sense 'honored', having *na vā* understood in **A** 7.2.53 is inimical to the usage attested.

The traditional Pāṇinīya interpretation of this and preceding sūtras is alone in order. According to this interpretation, *vā* 'optionally' stated in A 7.2.41: *iṭ sani vā* is understood to recur in A 7.2.42: *liṅsicor ātmanepadeṣu* and A 7.2.43: *ṛtaś ca saṁyogādeḥ*. A 7.2.44: *svaratisūtisūyatidhūñūdito vā* repeats *vā* in order to reinstate a term for option not linked with any other term, as it is in A 7.2.42-43: both rules provide that *iṭ* is optionally added to ātmanepada endings replacing ***liṅ*** and ***sic*** followed by ātmanepada endings. This term *vā* is now understood to recur in subsequent rules, including A 7.2.46: *niraḥ kuṣaḥ*, which provides for optionally augmenting with *iṭ* an ārdhadhātuka affix whose first sound is a consonant other than *y*, if this follows *kuṣ* preceded by the preverb *nir* (e.g. *niṣkoṣṭum*, *niṣkoṣitum* 'draw out'). The next sūtra (A 7.2.47: *iṇ niṣṭhāyām*) again has to do specifically with *kuṣ* preceded by *nir*: ***kta*** and ***ktavatu*** receive the augment *iṭ* after this complex (*niṣkuṣita*). The term *iṭ* is stated in A 7.2.35: *ārdhadhātukasyeḍ valādeḥ*, the major heading for the entire section of rules at issue. Repeating *iṭ* in A 7.2.47, then, has the effect of making the augmenting obligatory (*nitya*). This holds, however, only for the particular complex involving *nir* and *kuṣ*, since A 7.2.47 is bracketed with A 7.2.46. Accordingly, *vā* is understood to recur in subsequent rules. Now, *iṭ* is again stated in A 7.2.52: *vasatikṣudhor iṭ* (*ktvāniṣṭhayoḥ* 50). As in the earlier instance, this has the effect making the augment obligatory, this time for ***ktvā***, ***kta***, and ***ktavatu*** used with *vas* 'remain, dwell' (*uṣitvā-*, *uṣita-*) and *kṣudh* 'be hungry' (*kṣudhitvā-*, *kṣudhita-*). However, this sūtra is not bracketed — as is A 7.2.47 — with a preceding one having to do with a particular complex involving particular elements. Restating *iṭ* here, then, has the effect of reinstating this augment as an obligatory addition to affixes. Accordingly, A 7.2.53 and subsequent sūtras provide for obligatory augmenting. Since, on the other hand, after verbs like *śam* 'become calm' (***śámû***) ***ktvā*** only optionally has the initial augment (*śāntvā*, *śamitvā*), A 7.2.56 must now include *vā*.

As shown, the evidence concerning ***añcu*** supports this Pāṇinīya interpretation and speaks against Kiparsky's proposed readings. Now, we have to contrast the facts found in Vedic texts attesting to the use of *akna-*, *akta-* as accounted for by Pāṇinian sūtras under their traditional interpretation with the evidence Kiparsky adduces in the form of *vṛṣṭvā* and *lubdham*. Each of these is a hapax legomenon. In addition, the former occurs in an Atharvaveda passage that mirrors a Ṛgvedic verse (ṚV 10.87.2), which has *vr̥ktvī*. Moreover, the commentator on the Atharvaveda passage treats it as though the form in question were *dhr̥ṣṭvā*, and there is a variant *dr̥ṣṭvā*. As concerns *lubdham* in the Aitareyabrāhmaṇa, to be sure the form is securely attested and the context assures the interpretation. On the other hand, the Aitareyabrāhmaṇa also has, as is well known, the type *mantrayām āsa*, with *āsa* instead of *cakāra*, which alone is allowed by Pāṇini strictly interpreted (**A** 3.1.40: *kr̥ñ cānuprayujyate liṭi*). Accordingly, whatever other conclusions one may reach about the relation between the Aitareyabrāhmaṇa and Pāṇini, one cannot insist that the use of *lubdham* in this Brāhmaṇa has decisive status for interpreting a Pāṇinian rule. Thus, when compared with the evidence concerning *añcu*, the two forms *vr̥ṣṭvā* and *lubdham* cannot carry the same weight as this evidence. Consequently, *na vā* should not be understood to recur in **A** 7.2.53-55. For **A** 7.2.56 appropriately to provide that after verbs marked with *u* the augment *iṭ* is optionally added to ***k***tvā, then, this rule too must contain a term conveying an option. Under the Pāṇinīya tradition, the sūtra is *udito vā*, with *vā*. In the same tradition, after verbs covered by **A** 7.2.56 are subject to **A** 7.2.15: *yasya vibhāṣā*, the affixes ***kta*** and ***ktavatu*** do not receive the augment *iṭ* when they follow these verbs. Since Kiparsky maintains that *vibhāṣā* and *vā* refer to different types of options, however, he cannot account for the facts in this manner. Hence, his attempt to have *na vā* understood in **A** 7.2.56 also.

Let us return now to *añc**u***. I cannot find a Vedic example of *añcita-* in accordance with **A** 7.2.53. There are, however, instances of such usage in later works. Consider three examples from Kālidāsa's poetry. Kumārasambhava 1.34 (*sā rājahaṁsair iva saṁnatāṅgī gateṣu līlāñcitavikrameṣu* | *vyanīyata pratyupadeśalubdhair āditsubhir nūpurasiñjitāni*) describes the beauty of Pārvatī's gait through an utprekṣā: it is as though she had been instructed in her gait by rājahaṁsa geese anxious to acquire the beautiful sound of her nūpura in exchange for teaching her how to sway gracefully while walking. The gaits (*gateṣu*) are described as having steps graced by her playful movements (*līlāñcitavikrameṣu*). Mallinātha appropriately cites **A** 7.2.53 in his commentary. Raghuvaṁśa 2.18 (... *ubhāv alaṁ cakratur añcitābhyām tapovanāvr̥ttipatham gatābhyām*) describes how Dilīpa and the cow Nandinī both adorned the way to Vasiṣṭha's āśrama with their movements (*gatābhyām*), which are qualified as *añcitābhyām*. Mallinātha (*añcitābhyāṁ cārubhyām gatābhyāṁ gamanābhyām* ...) and Hemādri (*añcitābhyāṁ cārubhyāṁ gamanābhyām*) paraphrase with *cārubhyām* 'charming, lovely' given as the equivalent of *añcitābhyām.* The last verse of Raghuvaṁśa 5 (*atha vidhim avasāyya śāstradṛṣṭaṁ divasamukhocitam añcitākṣipakṣmā* | ... *kṣitipasamājam agāt svayaṁvarastham*) speaks of Aja going to the assembly of kings in the svayaṁvara hall after completing the morning rites that are prescribed and describes him as *añcitākṣipakṣmā*, which Mallinātha (5.76) paraphrases as *añcitāni cārūṇy akṣipakṣmāṇi yasya so' jaḥ* 'Aja, who has beautiful eyelashes'. Hemādri (5.77: *añcitāni pūjitāni praśastāni akṣṇoḥ pakṣmāṇi yasya saḥ ... añcitaśabdaḥ praśastārthaḥ. nāñceḥ pūjāyām* [**A** 6.4.30] *iti nalopābhāvaḥ*) is more explicit in that he glosses *añcitāni* with both *pūjitāni* and *praśastāni*, remarks that *añcita* has the meaning of *praśasta* 'praised, praiseworthy', and refers to Pāṇini's sūtra that accounts for the nasal of *añcita-* not being dropped. He also mentions another reading known to him: *añjitākṣipakṣmā.* Now, Pāṇini (**A** 3.2.188: *matibuddhipūjārthebhyaś ca*) provides that after verbs meaning 'wish', 'perceive', 'honor, revere' the affix ***kta*** is used when reference is made to current time, not past. Accordingly, *añcita-* in the passages cited has present reference. That is, the movements in question are lovely, hence praiseworthy, as are Aja's eyelids, and Pārvatī's movements are now graced by playful movements, so that they are praiseworthy. Given the time reference of *añcita-*, the use of this term in the meaning 'charming, lovely' is easily understandable: just as *praśasta-* means 'praiseworthy', so can *añcita-* mean 'worthy of honor', the worthiness being due to beauty.

There are, nevertheless, places where *añcita-* is used and the context does not indicate any necessary sense of honoring or charm. Thus, for example, Raghuvaṁśa 18.51 (*vyūhya sthitaḥ kiñcid ivottarārdham unnaddhacūḍo' ñcitasavyajānuḥ* | *ākarṇam ākṛṣṭasabāṇadhanvā vyarocatāstreṣu vinīyamānaḥ*) describes Sudarśana's position as he is being instructed in archery: he has his upper body spread, his top knot is erect, he has the bow with arrow stretched so that it reaches back to his ear, and he has his left knee bent (*añcitasavyajānuḥ*). Mallinātha, whose version of the text is given, simply glosses *añcita-* with *ākuñcita-* (*añcitam ākuñcitaṁ savyaṁ jānu yasya saḥ ...*). To be sure, Hemādri, who reads *vyūhāsthitaḥ kiñcid ivonnatāṁsam ...*, paraphrases using *pūjitaḥ* (18.52: ... *dhanuḥ-śāstroktaprakāreṇa añcitaḥ pūjitaḥ ākuñcitaḥ savyo jānuḥ*), but he then goes on to add *ākuñcitaḥ*. The use of *añcita-* in a comparable way is fairly wide spread in Sanskrit literature, including the Bhaṭṭikāvya. For example, Bhaṭṭikāvya 2.31 (*adhijyacāpaḥ sthirabāhumuṣṭir udañcitākṣo' ñcita-dakṣiṇoruḥ* ...) describes Lakṣmaṇa as he kills the Piśācas: the string of his bow is set, his arm and fist are firm, his eyes are cast upwards (*udañcitākṣaḥ*), and his right thigh is bent (*añcitadakṣiṇoruḥ*). Jayamaṅgala recognizes that *añcita* here does not have the sense of honoring or charm and accordingly says that this is formed from the causative. The earliest example I can find of *añcita-* comparably used is in Yāska's Nirukta, where, however, *akta-* is also used; see below.

The fact remains that in the earliest Sanskrit texts, the use of *akna-*/*akta-* as participles of ***añcu*** agrees with Pāṇini's description as interpreted by Pāṇinīyas. On the other hand, the problems associated with **A** 7.2.15 under Kiparsky's proposal are not removed even after considerable effort on Kiparsky's part to maintain his original thesis. Nor are they removed by Kiparsky's repetition of his argument in a later article (1991a). In this article, Kiparsky also fails to answer other objections. In his original monograph he assumed that *vā* meant 'preferably' and that this is a primitive term in this sense, but he justified this only with a brief reference to Speijer's work on Sanskrit syntax, where two examples are cited from the Pañcatantra and the Rāmāyaṇa. Cardona (1989:83 note 100) objected: 'One quite important thing **Kiparsky** fails to do is to justify his attribution of the meaning 'preferred option' to *vā* which he treats as a primitive, on the basis of any extensive textual investigation of early Sanskrit literature — preferably Vedic, since, in **Kiparsky's** opinion, the use of *vā* in the sense he attributes to it was lost by the time of earliest Pāṇinīyas.' In addition, Cardona (1989:82-83 note 100) pointed out that *vā* 'or' is also frequently used to introduce alternatives that are not the preferred options. In his reply, Kiparsky (1991a:338) claims, 'Cardona's insistence that the meaning of *vā* in grammar must be justified by "extensive textual investigation of early Sanskrit literature" would be cogent only on the assumption that its meaning in grammar must be exactly the same as its meaning in ordinary language.' He continues: ' But it is very well known that the meanings of Pāṇini's technical terms can differ from the ordinary meanings of these words in Sanskrit literature.'

Now, Cardona's objection was that Kiparsky assumed without sufficient justification both that *vā* in ordinary Sanskrit meant 'preferably' and that Pāṇini took it as a primitive in this sense. Indeed, in his 1979 monograph Kiparsky emphasized that his hypothesis brought the meaning he assumed for this in line with the meaning of the term in ordinary Sanskrit. He said (Kiparsky [1979:2-3]):

> It is immediately evident that our hypothesis brings the technical meanings of *vā*, *vibhāṣā*, and *anyatarasyām* closely into line with their ordinary meanings, in so far as these can be established.
>
> In combination with the particle *atha*, *vā* is commonly used to introduce a preferred alternative. Correspondingly, *na vā* stands with an inferior alternative. Typical of "shastric" style are thus: *atha vā vaktavyam* 'or rather it is to be said', 'better say it', *na vā vaktavyam* 'or rather it is not to be said', 'better not say it'.

Cardona (1989:65-66 with notes 99, 100) objected that *vā* simply means 'or', and that whether the option in question is preferable or not is known from the context of argumentation. He also pointed out that *vā* is frequently used in passages of what Kiparsky calls "shastric" style to introduce an alternative that is not necessarily the preferred one. In addition, he objected to Kiparsky claiming that the meaning he attributes to *vā* is in line with the meaning this term has elsewhere and being satisfied with a brief reference to a section of Speijer's *Sanskrit Syntax*. Without remedying his lack of philological justification, Kiparsky now merely says Pāṇini used terms with meanings different from those they have in ordinary language. This is indeed true, although not so straightforward as Kiparsky appears to make it. The point Kiparsky originally started with and laid such stress upon, however, has now subtly changed. Nor does Kiparsky say anything about Taittirīyaprātiśākhya 22.7, where it is said that *vā* has the meaning of 'option' and the term *vaibhāṣika* is used (see Cardona [1989:82 note 96]). Kiparsky also fails to answer another objection (Cardona [1989:65]), namely that his insisting that **A** 1.1.44 is a definition comparable to rules that introduce class names is not justified.

Moreover, Kiparsky's original instinct was obviously right. If indeed *vā* is taken as a primitive for the definition of *vibhāṣā* as having the meaning of *na vā*, then one should be able to point to extensive use in early Sanskrit texts of *vā* meaning 'preferably', which Kiparsky obviously has not done, either in his original work or later. This is not different from being able to cite instances in early Sanskrit for the use of coordinative *ca*, which Pāṇini uses as an undefined term. Further, Kiparsky skips over the fact that, as was pointed out (Cardona [1989:64-65]), in his original monograph itself he could establish a three-tiered distinction among *vā*, *vibhāṣā*, and *anyatarasyām* only at the cost of underplaying Pāṇini's use of additional terms and Pāṇini's use of *anyatarasyām* in places where under Kiparsky's thesis one would expect *vā* or *vibhāṣā*.

As for his complaint (Kiparsky [1991:336]) that Cardona selected only one of several hundred instances he deals with, it is clear, I think, that Cardona elected to concentrate on **A** 7.2.15: *yasya vibhāṣā* as a crucial rule entailing, under Kiparsky's thesis, a failure of the grammar to account for well known forms and to predict a great many wrong forms of verbs well attested in Sanskrit of all periods.[42] In addition, **A** 7.2.15 and related sūtras show crucially the interaction of rules involving *vibhāṣā* and other terms related to options. Clearly, this is not merely one among hundreds of like instances. From what has been shown here, it is also clear that, even by resorting to a philologically unjustified meaning for *jānvakna-* — an example upon which he relies — Kiparsky has failed to overcome an important problem, a difficulty which does not arise under the traditional interpretation, where *vibhāṣā* of **A** 7.2.15 can include reference to options provided by rules using *vā*. Moreover, as is again clear both from what has been said here and in his earlier critique, Cardona has indeed pointed out other areas in which Kiparsky's claims are weakly supported. In sum, I conclude that Kiparsky's main claim fails in view of the evidence,[43] and I consider myself fully justified in maintaining, as before (Cardona [1989:66]), that his thesis is 'neither cogently maintained nor acceptable.'[44]

Let me now return to *añc**u***. As I have noted above, Yāska uses *añcita-*. He does so twice: Nirukta 5.17 (Sarup [1927a:103]): *aṅgeti kṣipranāma | aṅkitam evāñcitaṁ bhavati*; 5.25 (Sarup [1927a:107]): *kavacaṁ ku añcitaṁ bhavati kāñcitaṁ bhavati kāye 'ñcitaṁ bhavatīti vā*. The latter concerns the etymological explanation of *kavacam* 'armor': this is so called because it is naturally — and pejoratively — bent, because it is slightly bent, or because it goes on the body. Nir. 5.17 deals with *aṅga*, which is considered a term meaning 'quickly' and linked with *aṅk* or *anc* 'move'. In addition, however, Yāska also uses *acita-* and *akta-*. In Nir. 11.25 (Sarup [1927a:197]) he uses the phrase *parāñcanair acitaḥ* 'traversed with (steps) that are turned away' with reference to the path that Saramā has taken to reach the Paṇis. Durga comments: *parāñcanair acitaḥ parāṅmukhaiḥ añcanaiḥ gamanaiḥ acito gato viprakṛṣṭo devanivāsāt* '... traversed with steps that are turned away, distant from the abode of the gods.' In Nir. 6.8 (Sarup [1927a:115]), Yāska explains the instrumental singular feminine *devācyā̀* 'turned towards the gods' as *devān praty aktayā*.

Obviously, *akta-* used in a context of movement from one place to another accords with Pāṇini's description of how this participle is used, but *añcita* formed from the simple base *añc**u*** — and not from the causative *añci* — does not conform to the usage accounted for by Pāṇini. Given what has been noted above, moreover, it would be less than wise to insist that Pāṇini's sūtras should be modified somehow to take care of this. Yāska's use of *añcita-* could represent a fairly early generalization of a seṭ form of the type *nayitṛ-* instead of *netṛ-*, already found in the Jaiminīyabrāhmaṇa (*abhinayitā* : JBr. 2.99).

Of course, more such forms are met with more frequently in later literature. Moreover, Pāṇinīyas have to account for these forms on the basis of Pāṇinian sūtras. In this connection, consider **A** 7.2.57: *se'sici kṛtacṛtacchṛdatṛdanṛtaḥ* (*vā* 56). According to this sūtra, an ārdhadhātuka affix beginning with *s-*, other than ***sic*** — as in *akartīt* (3rd sg. aor.) 'cut' (- ... *kṛt-s-t*) — optionally receives the initial augment *iṭ* after the bases *kṛt* (*kṛ́tī̆* 'cut' [3rd sg. pres. *kṛntati*], 'surround' [*kṛṇatti*]), *cṛt* 'harm, bind' (*cṛ́tī̆* [*cṛtati*]), *chṛd* 'shine, play' (***uchṛ́dìr*** [*chṛṇatti, chṛntte*]), *tṛd* 'bore through, cleave' (***utṛ́dìr*** [*tṛṇatti, tṛntte*]), *nṛt* 'dance' (*nṛ́tī̆* [*nṛtyati*]); for example, *kartsyati/ kartiṣyati* (3rd sg. fut.), *akartsyat/akartiṣyat* (3rd sg. cond.), desiderative *cikṛtsa-/ cikartiṣa-* (*cikṛtsati, cikartiṣati*). Now, as shown, some of these verbs are marked with *ī*. According to **A** 7.2.14: *śvīdito niṣṭhāyām*, the affixes ***kta*** and ***ktavatu*** are not augmented with *iṭ* after a base so marked; e.g. *kṛtta-, kṛttavat-*. However, since **A** 7.2.57 provides for an option, the same absence of the initial augment would obtain by **A** 7.2.15. Pāṇinīyas make two suggestions in connection with this. According to some, Pāṇini's marking certain verbs with *ī* despite the fact that the absence of *iṭ* in ***kta*** and ***ktavatu*** following them would be accounted for by **A** 7.2.15 serves to make known that the negation stated in this rule is not obligatory.[45] In this manner, they account for participles like *dhāvita-* in addition to *dhauta-* 'washed'. The base in question is marked with *u* (*dhā́vù*), so that by **A** 7.2.56 and **A** 7.2.15, *dhāvita-* would not be allowed if the latter rule provided an obligatory negation. According to others, on the other hand, marking verbs like *kṛ́tī* and *nṛ́tī* with *ī* serves to account for intensive participles of the type *carikṛtta-, narīnṛtta-*. To be sure, **A** 7.2.15 can apply to deny augmenting in derivates like *kṛtta-*, *nṛtta-*, where the simple bases *kṛt, nṛt* are followed by ***kta***, but the lack of augmenting that applies in such simplex participles does not hold for derived bases, as in *carkarita-* from the intensive of *kṛ* (***ḍukṛñ***) 'do, make' (*kṛta-*). Marking *kṛ́tī* and so on with *ī* serves to show that these bases do not condition *iṭ* for ***kta*** and ***ktavatu*** following them whether primitive or in derived bases formed from them.[46]

Kiparsky considers **A** 7.2.57 the strongest evidence for the position he sets forth concerning **A** 7.2.15 and related rules. Concerning his textual modifications, he says (1991a:337):

> The idea has consequences not only for 7.2.56, but also for 7.2.53, 7.2.54, 7.2.55 and 7.2.57. The first three now become optional instead of obligatory. In all four of these rules the new interpretation agrees better with attested usage than the traditional one. The most straightforward cases are 7.2.54 and 7.2.55, the weightiest evidence comes from 7.2.57.

Briefly put, his argument is that, since 7.2.57 now states a preferred option (*vā*), the verbs in question are not subject to 7.2.15, which concerns a marginal option (*vibhāṣā*). He says (1991a:337), 'To both supply these roots with diacritic *Ī* and list them in rule 7.2.57 is a pointless complication. And crucially, it is not a complication which could have arisen as well-intentioned improvement in the normal course of textual transmission, since it creates an anomaly which commentators are at a loss to explain.' Precisely what Kiparsky means by 'which commentators are at a loss to explain' is not clear. He could mean that commentators were aware of the issue but could not come to a reasonable solution. On the other hand, he does not refer to any of the pertinent commentatorial statements, so that he could also mean that commentators were unaware of the issue. Or it could be that Kiparsky himself is unaware of what the commentators have said. As shown, commentators do come to grips with the complication in question. And they do suggest reasons for the marking. Moreover, the position adopted by Kṣīrasvāmin is perfectly compatible with a change in the textual transmission in order to account for participles like *carikṛtta-*. Further, although the absence of past-participle forms of intensives of such verbs in

Saṁhitās and other early literature makes it difficult to say anything definitive, it could also be the case that this was Pāṇini's reason for marking *kṛt* and so on with *ī*. Given that Kiparsky's textual interpretation, far from agreeing better with attested usage in the case of *añcu*, actually conflicts with the earliest usage known for participles of this verb, however, I do not hesitate to express doubts about his claim concerning **A** 7.2.57.

In sum, I consider that the evidence is sufficient to show that Kiparsky's thesis concerning Pāṇini's use of *vā*, *vibhāṣā*, and *anyatarasyām* is untenable.

More recently, M. M. Deshpande (1991d) has again taken up **A** 7.2.15: *yasya vibhāṣā* in connection with Kiparsky's views and made some important comments concerning these views. In connection with the two possible interpretations Kiparsky considered for **A** 7.2.15 and which I pointed out above (see pp. 161-162), Deshpande says (1991d:164):

> Of these two, reading (1) is more strictly in accordance with Kiparsky's general interpretation of the term *vibhāṣā* but, as he himself states (p. 158), "Reading (1) does not correspond to usage in the past participles of the verbs with diacritic *U* (P. 7.2.56)." Kiparsky's reading (2), in his own words (p. 158), is "equivalent in its effect" to the traditional reading. In effect, it includes all option terms under *vibhāṣā*. Even reading (2) leaves some problems unresolved, and, more importantly, its acceptance would amount to saying that *vibhāṣā* occasionally includes *vā*. This would be damaging to Kiparsky's main thesis. He is careful not to say this openly, hence his wording "at least a marginal option." However, it is unlikely that one could read the words *at least* into the rule without any textual basis for it. Strictly, the word *vibhāṣā* stands only for *vibhāṣā* and nothing else. Then, the question of whether the notion of *vibhāṣā* is inclusive of all option terms must be kept a separate issue.

Deshpande goes on to discuss other pertinent rules related to **A** 7.2.15 and to suggest (1991d:168-169) that **A** 7.2.56: *udito vā* and **A** 7.2.44: *svaratisūtisūyatidhūñudito vā* are not subject to **A** 7.2.15. He says:

> Suppose one takes a more straightforward Kiparskyan view and argues that both of these are *vā* rules because they contain the word *vā*, and that therefore they are not subject to P. 7.2.15 (*yasya vibhāṣā*). (Please note that this is not Kiparsky's own view). This would allow the derivation of past-participle forms with *iṬ* for roots with *U, Ū*, and others. While, according to Kiparsky (p. 159), this would not fit the facts reasonably well, there is evidence to show that this interpretation is not without merit.

Deshpande's evidence (1991d:169-172) is of two kinds: attested forms of verbs marked with *u*, *ū* in Pāṇini's dhātupāṭha and evidence from Kāśakṛtsna's grammar. Space allows considering only the first type of evidence which in my opinion is also the more important. Desphande lists (1991d:169) the following participles: *luñcita* (*luñcU*), *ṣṭhīvita* (*ṣṭhivU*), *dhāvita* (*dhāvU*), *śaṁsita*, *śāsita* (*śansU*, *śāsU*), *śasita* (*śasU*), *syandita* (*syandŪ*), *vanita* (*vanU*), *kliśita* (*kliśŪ*), *mṛjita* (*mṛjŪ*), *kṣamita* (*kṣamŪ*), *asita* (*asU*), *yasita* (*yasU*), *vañcita* (*vañcU*).[47] After citing these, Deshpande goes on to say (1991d:170), 'Whitney also cites many *aniṭ* forms for some of these roots but the fact remains that the past-participles with *iṬ* for roots marked with *U* are not as rare in usage as Kiparsky claims.'

The evidence Deshpande adduces, however, is not as impressive as it might appear at first sight. To begin with, one must cut out three bases. Whitney (1885:199 [sv. *syand, syad* 'move on']) lists '*syanná* V. +' but, appropriately, does not give *syandita*. Simply to list *luñcU* is not acceptable. The base in question is listed as ***lúñcá*** in the Kṣīrataraṅgiṇī (I.118, Yudhiṣṭhira Mīmāṁsaka [1957/8:39]), the Dhātupradīpa (I.184, Chakravarti [1919:21]), and the Mādhavīyadhātuvṛtti (I.117, Dwarikadas Shastri [1964:90]), as well as in Liebich's edition (I.202, Liebich [1920a:7]). Accordingly, **A** 7.2.56 should not apply to this base, so that the only alternation in the absolutive involves the presence or absence of the penultimate nasal. Nor should **A** 7.2.15 apply here, so that the past participle should be *luñcita-*, *lucita*. *-luñcita-* does occur as the second member of a compound listed in the gaṇa *rājadantādi* (e.g. Pathak-Chitrao [1935:701] [no. 194.6], Kapil Dev Shastri [1967:87]). The Mādhavīyadhātuvṛtti mentions (Dwarikadas Shastri [1964:90]) that according to some the base is recited as ***lúñcú*** and also says this is unacceptable in view of *mṛṣṭalucita* of the gaṇapāṭha. It is, moreover, not hard to account for ***lúñcú*** as due to the position of the base immediately before ***áñcú***. Deshpande lists *kliśŪ* of the ninth class (***klíśū́*** 'distress, torment' [*kliśnāti*]), but there is also a base ***klíśa*** 'be distressed' (*kliśyate*) of the fourth class. As commentators note, Pāṇini **A** 7.2.50 (*kliśaḥ ktvāniṣṭhayoḥ*) applies with respect to both: ***ktvā***, ***kta***, and ***ktavatu*** optionally get the augment ***iṭ*** after these bases. **A** 7.2.44 provides that any ārdhadhātuka affix beginning with a consonant other than *y* is augmented optionally after a base marked with *ū*, so that *kliśitvā* would be accounted for by this rule. However, by **A** 7.2.15, the augment would be denied to ***kta*** and ***ktavatu***, thus disallowing *kliśita-*, *kliśitavat-*, so that **A**

7.2.50 is needed to allow this. On the other hand, after *kliśa* all the affixes in question would obligatorily be augmented, thus disallowing *kliṣṭvā, kliṣṭa-, kliṣṭavat-*. The remaining participial forms which Deshpande cites also require some comment. Consider, for example, the past participles of *śánsú* 'praise' and *śā́sú* 'instruct'. The past participle with unaugmented *-ta* is accounted for by **A** 7.2.56 and **A** 7.2.15: *śasta-, śiṣṭa-*. Such participial forms as *praśasta-* 'praised' (nom. sg. masc. *praśastaḥ*), *anùśiṣṭaḥ* 'instructed' are attested from earliest texts, beginning with the Ṛgveda. Whitney (1885: 169, 172 [svv. *çaṅs* 'praise', *çās, çiṣ* 'order']) lists *śaṁsita-, śāsita-* as attested from the epics on. *āśaṁsitam* 'wished for' occurs in a verse found in some manuscripts of the Rāmāyaṇa but not made part of the critical edition; see the critical edition under 2.66.22 (II.398b, *1690). The occurrence of *śāsita-* listed in the Petersburg dictionary for the Rāmāyaṇa (Gorresio's edition 7.108.27) is not part of the critical edition; see also Werba (1997:242). *āśaṁsitam* also is found in the Bhāgavatapurāṇa (10.73.18: *adyaprabhṛti vo bhūpā mayy ātmany akhileśvare | sudṛḍhā jāyate bhaktir bāḍham āśaṁsitaṁ tathā*) and the Kirātārjunīya (5.52: ... *cetasāśaṁsitaṁ sa | ... śailam abhyāsasāda*). *anuśāsita-* occurs in the Bhāgavatapurāṇa (2.5.8: *etan me pṛcchataḥ sarvaṁ sarvajña sakaleśvara | vijānīhi yathaivedam ahaṁ buddhye' nuśāsitaḥ*, 4.20.17: *sa itthaṁ lokaguruṇā viṣvaksenena viśvajit | anuśāsita ādeśaṁ śirasā jagṛhe hareḥ*), and *śāsita-* occurs in some texts (e.g. Kathāsaritsāgara 18.35: *mā gās tvam apraṇamyeti rājādeśena jalpataḥ | asmān vidhūya so' yāsīc chāsito' pi hasan baṭuḥ*). Given what has long since been established concerning the language which Pāṇini describes, however, it is not appropriate to grant equal value to usage attested from Saṁhitās, Brāhmaṇas and early sūtra texts on the one hand and texts such as the epics and Purāṇas on the other. The same comment applies with respect to the following, for which Whitney lists seṭ forms: *ṣṭhīv* 'spit' (*abhiṣṭhyūta-* [Śatapathabrāhmaṇa 2.1.1.2: *abhiṣṭhyūtam*], *ava-ṣṭhyūta-* [ŚBr. 1.2.3.1: *avaṣṭhyūtāḥ*]: *ṣṭhīvita-* 'C'), *mṛj* 'wipe, clean' (*mṛṣṭá-* from Ṛgveda on: *mṛjita* 'C' [e.g. Bhāgavata 9.10.4: *mṛjitapatharujaḥ*]), *as* 'throw' (*astá-* from Ṛgveda on [ṚV 1.32.7d: *vyàstaḥ*]: *asita*: 'R[1]']). Similarly, although *dhāvita-* is certainly known from later texts and is mentioned in the Durghaṭavṛtti on **A** 7.2.15, the early form is *dhauta-* (from Sāmaveda on: *dhautáḥ* [SV 676 (II.1.1.9.2)]), which accords with Pāṇini's description. And the participle of *yas* is *yasta-* in early literature (*prayàstā* [ṚV 3.53.22: referring to an ukhā pot that is excessively heated so that it boils over]). Even where such participles are only known from later literature, there are also instances conforming to the pattern known from Pāṇini. Thus, although *kṣamitam* (*kṣam* 'forebear, forgive') occurs in the Mahābhārata text on which Nīlakāṇṭha comments (2.45.23: *śṛṇvantu me mahīpālā yenaitat kṣamitaṁ mayā | aparādhaśataṁ kṣāmyaṁ mātur asyaiva yācane*) — but not in the text arrived at for the critical edition (see II.203b: 401*) — *kṣāntam* is frequent in this text. Again, one must be careful about lexical specialization. From earliest Vedic on, the participle of *van* 'gain, win' is *vāta-*. To be sure, one also has *vanita-*, but this is most commonly found in forms of the term *vanitā* 'woman'.

In brief, once one subjects Deshpande's list to necessary pruning and scrutiny concerning the sorts of texts in which the forms at issue actually occur, it can be seen that the past participles of the bases in question conform quite well to the pattern described by **A** 7.2.44, 56, 15 as accepted and interpreted by Pāṇinīyas. The evidence does not support an interpretation such that bases for which sūtras with *vā* apply are not subject to the negation of *iṭ* provided for in 7.2.15 because of a difference in meaning between *vā* and *vibhāṣā*. Nor, as shown, does the evidence support the textual modifications which Kiparsky suggests to rescue his claim concerning *vā* and *vibhāṣā*.[48]

Pratap Bandyopadhyay (1994) discusses anew the terms *samāsa,* class names for groups of compounds — *avyayībhāva*, *tatpuruṣa*, *bahuvrīhi*, *dvandva*, *dvigu*, *karmadhāraya* — as well as *it*, *kṛt*, and *taddhita*.

2.1.4.3.c. *Pāṇini's technical terminology* : *markers* (III.1.5.3c)

In Pāṇini's system, markers are attached to elements for several reasons (see Cardona [1976a:199, 1997a:47-52 (**80-88**)]). One of these is to distinguish homophonous elements such as the endings *jas*, *śas*, *ṅasi*, *ṅas*. Ananthanarayana (1986a) considers instances of homophonous affixes in a study the purpose of which is stated as follows (1986a:50):

> It is the purpose of this paper to show that Pāṇini realised the necessity of representing each semantic specification by a different morphological specification. He introduced certain formal distinctions to their underlying representation and then dropped these characteristics after they were phonetically realized. The paper also attempts, while

discussing a homophonous suffix in Sanskrit, to focus on the descriptive techniques of Pāṇini's analysis.

2.1.4.3d. *The grammar of Pāṇini's metalanguage* (III.1.5.3d)

Scharfe (1971a:33-43) considered a construction he referred to as 'negative apposition', exemplified in the first instance by **A** 1.1.68: *svaṁ rūpaṁ śabdasyāśabdasaṁjñā.* According to Scharfe, this represents an irregular construction in that the nominative *aśabdasaṁjñā* is supposed to be in apposition with the genitive *śabdasya.* Wezler (1977) took up this and other instances of the alleged irregular construction and demonstrated that Scharfe's thesis is not acceptable. In particular, Wezler concluded (1977:64-68, 70), **A** 1.1.68 is to be interpreted as providing that the form of a speech element is the name of that element unless the term in question is a śabdasaṁjñā.[49]

2.1.4.3e. *Stylistics* (III.1.5.3g)

Filliozat (1993) briefly goes over major features of natural language observed in the sūtras of the Aṣṭādhyāyī. Earlier, S. D. Joshi and S. Bhate (1984) studied in some detail how anuvṛtti operates in the Aṣṭādhyāyī.

2.1.4.4. *Pāṇini's system of phonology and morphophonemics*

2.1.4.4a. *Phonetics* (III.1.5.4a)

The most recent summary treatment of the topic is by M. M. Deshpande (1997b:31-47), a revised and expanded version of an earlier summary (Deshpande [1995b]). I consider this is a good piece of work. Deshpande has a firm command of the subject, presents the pertinent materials lucidly, and informs readers about differences of interpretation. Deshpande has also contributed two papers (1975c, d) concerning in particular the phonetics of certain sounds assumed in Pāṇinian sūtras, arguing that *a* was definitely a close (*saṁvṛta*) vowel and that *v* was labial. The same scholar has claimed (1976b) that a distinction was made by Pāṇinīyas and others between two types of voicing, designated by the terms *nāda* and *ghoṣa*. Cardona

(1983a:6-11, 1986a) has presented evidence to show that, on the contrary, the terms in question concern phonetics and phonology. *nāda* and *śvāsa* respectively refer to an air stream produced with close and open glottis, an air stream that constitutes the basic stuff of voiced and voiceless segments: *nāda* in vowels (*svara*) and voiced consonants (*ghoṣavat*), *śvāsa* in voiceless consonants (*aghoṣa*). As shown *ghoṣavat* and *aghoṣa* originally referred to voiced and voiceless consonants only, so that they were properly phonological terms.[50]

2.1.4.4b. *Phonology, morphophonemics* (III.1.5.4b)

M. M. Deshpande has contributed a monograph (1975a) on Pāṇini's concept of homogeneity and sets of homogeneous sounds, in which he deals also and in some detail with what Pāṇinīyas say. Deshpande (1975b) treats in particular the question why the pratyāhāra *aṇ*, with the *ṇ* of the sixth subgroup in the akṣarasamāmnāya (*laṇ*), should refer to nasalized semivowels. Bare (1976) also studied Aṣṭādhyāyī rules in connection with the feature system considered to be reflected in Pāṇini's phonological system, and K. M. Tiwary (1987) once more dealt with **A** 1.1.9-10.

The lastest work known to me concerning Pāṇini's sandhi rules is by Dighe (1997), a short and elementary but lucid and useful presentation of a representative group of sūtras that concern operations which take place — or are disallowed — when items are uttered continuously.

In a recent article, G. B. Palsule (1991-92) proposes the interesting thesis that Pāṇini held both an "official view" and a "private and intuitive view" (1991-92:164a) concerning the guṇa class. The official view is the one set forth in **A** 1.1.2: *ad eṅ guṇaḥ*, whereby *a e o* are given the class name *guṇa*. Pāṇini's private view, on the other hand, is 'that *a* is the Guṇa' (Palsule [1991-92:164a]). Palsule sets forth his hypothesis (1991-92:163b-164a) in three steps:

> i) Pāṇini was in some way aware, very probably instinctively, that there was some basic unity underlying the phonemes *e*, *o* and the combinations *ar* and *al*. He must have believed that all these four entities, in spite of their external diversity, were expressions of a fundamental unity, to denote which he gave them a common name: Guṇa.
>
> ii) This unity, to go further, Pāṇini may have thought to be consisting of the

phoneme *a*. It was patent in *ar/al*. It was also believed to be the initial element in *e/o*. Pāṇini gave the name Guṇa to this highest common factor of the four linguistic units concerned.

iii) This explains why the name Guṇa is given to *a* even though a pure *a* nowhere comes as a substitute in the Guṇa phenomenon: its use is limited to roots ending in *ṛ* and *ḷ*. In hundreds of verbal roots with the medial vowel *a* the name Guṇa is without any practical purpose. But what does it matter? Is not *a* the reality of Guṇa there?

Palsule begins his article saying (1991-92:161a) why he entertains the possibility of a private view in addition to Pāṇini's official view concerning guṇa: 'But there are certain features of his Guṇa system which cannot be satisfactorily explained without some such assumption.' He goes on to note these features. To begin with, he remarks that grouping *a e o* together has no common purpose. In addition, although *a e o* are assigned a common class name, Pāṇini does not make clear what property — 'particularly a phonetic property' (1991-92:161a) — these have in common. Palsule (p. 161a) also puts particular stress on the inclusion of *a*: 'This *a* comes as a substitute only for *ṛ* (and in a solitary case of *ḷ*) and then it is invariably followed by *r* : that is the substitute is *ar*.' Finally, giving the name *guṇa* to *a* 'in thousands of words, verbal roots, nominal stems, suffixes, terminations, preverbs, etc. is simply useless. It serves no purpose.' (1991-92:161ab) In the course of his discussion, Palsule again reverts (1991-92:162) to the issue of a property common to *a e o* and again stresses (1991-92:162a) the phonetic aspect: 'What is the property common to *a*, *e*, and *o*? I mean phonetically?' He goes on to note that prātiśākhyas and the Mahābhāṣya demonstrate an awareness that *e* and *o* are complex sounds one of whose constituents is *a*, then asks rhetorically (1991-92:163a), 'And if the grammarians like Kātyāyana and Patañjali knew this fact, why not Pāṇini?'

Palsule's discussion is learned and interesting. Moreover, I consider that there is good evidence in the Aṣṭādhyāyī itself to indicate that Pāṇini did indeed adopt the position that, like the diphthongs *ai au*, the monophthongs *e o* were to be treated theoretically as though they were composites, but that he did so on the basis of phonological patterning, not because of any phonetic reasons.[51] I do not see any cogent reason, however, for attributing to Pāṇini what Palsule calls his "private view" about the guṇa class. One should consider this and Pāṇini's vṛddhi class (**A** 1.1.1:

vṛddhir ād aic) together. The two constitute parallel groups: *a e o* and *ā ai au*, whether they are introduced as replacement, using the names *guṇa* and *vṛddhi* (*tadbhāvita*), or not (*atadbhāvita*). In addition, both *a* and *ā* replacing an *ṛ*-vowel are automatically followed by *r* (**A** 1.1.51: *ur aṇ raparaḥ*). Given that in deriving forms like *pacanti* 'they cook, are cooking' and *pace* 'I cook, am cooking (something for myself)' Pāṇini operates with a stage at which one has *paca-anti*, *paca-e* and provides that *-a-* and a following guṇa vowel are both replaced by the latter (**A** 6.1.97: *ato guṇe*), there is reason for treating *a* as a member of a class including *e* and designated *guṇa*. Of course, as Palsule rightly notes, simple *a* does not occur as a final substitute for *ṛ*-vowels. It is equally true, nevertheless, that in Pāṇini's system *a* does indeed replace *ṛ*-vowels, only it is automatically followed by *r*. A crucial question, then, is why Pāṇini did not operate with a series *e o ar* as replacements for *i u ṛ*. One part of the answer has already been given: *a* as a member of the guṇa class is not always a substitute for an *ṛ*-vowel any more than *ā* as a member of the vṛddhi class is always a substitute for such a vowel. Further, in Pāṇini's system, it is not just *a* or *ā* replacing an *ṛ*-vowel that is automatically followed by *r*. *i* and *u* which substitute for *ṛ*-vowels also are followed by *r*, as in *tirati* 'crosses' (← *tṝ-a-ti* [**A** 7.1.100: *ṝta id dhātoḥ*]), *tīrṇa-* 'crossed' (← *tīr-na-* ← *tir-na-* ← *tir-ta-* ← *tṝ-ta-*), *dvaimātura-* 'a child of two mothers' (← *dvimātṛ-a-* [**A** 4.1.115: *mātur ut saṅkhyāsambhadrapūrvāyāḥ*]). Moreover, the grammatical elements before which these substitutions apply are not such as condition guṇa replacement. Given that *ar*, *ār*, *ir*, *ur* all occur as substitutes for *ṝ̆* and that the replacements do not all occur in the same kind of grammatical contexts, the appropriate generalization is to abstract the common element *r*. Pāṇini has done this. Accordingly, he does not set up a guṇa class *ar e o* in relation to *ṝ̆ ĭ ŭ*. And his guṇa class consisting of *a- e-* and *o*-vowels is justified within his system. In brief, I consider that Pāṇini's "official view" concerning his guṇa class is the only one we need deal with and that there is no cogent reason for seeking to find a "private view" concerning this class.

S. D. Joshi (1984) discusses the boundaries which involve units Pāṇini calls *aṅga*, *bha*, and *pada*, as well as the boundary at pause (*avasāna*). He remarks (1984:186), 'The introduction by Pāṇini of the *aṅga*-boundary, of which the *bha*-boundary is a specific form, must be regarded as a major step in linguistic analysis supplied by him.'

2.1.4.4c. *The śivasūtras* (III.1.5.4c.)

Bhim Sen Shastri (1979:1-35) deals thoroughly with traditional evidence concerning whether Pāṇini composed the akṣarasamāmnāya that accompanies his sūtrapāṭha or received it from Śiva and concludes that Pāṇini was indeed the author of this ancillary. In the first part of a recent article, M. M. Deshpande (1997a:444-453) has considered again in considerable detail the evidence linking Pāṇini — and his akṣarasamāmnāya in particular — with Śiva.[52]

Scholars generally accept that Pāṇini's sound catalog bears a historical relation with comparable lists of sounds found in prātiśākhya works and works on phonetics (*śikṣā*). Two recent articles in this vein are: Upendra Pandeya (1990) and Śivakumāra Miśra (1991).[53]

While not denying such a connection, Paul Kiparsky (1991b) proposes to explain features of the order of sounds in Pāṇini's akṣarasamāmnāya which, he claims, have not been accounted for properly in prior studies. He remarks (1991b:241):

> Much of the structure of the *Śivasūtra*s has been successfully explained by this kind of reasoning from economy (Faddegon 1929, Thieme 1935, Staal 1962, Cardona 1969). But there remains a substantial residue where economy is at first sight not at stake. For example, the order of *ṛ* and *ḷ* in row 2 could be reversed without complicating the grammar because every *pratyāhāra* needed in the grammar that includes one of them can also include the other. The same is true of *e* and *o* in the next row. The systematic character of Pāṇini's grammar makes it likely that there is a rational basis for the order of these elements as well — but what?

Kiparsky's answer is simplicity, linked to the overriding principle of the grammar in general, namely consideration of what is general (*sāmānya*) and particular (*viśeṣa*). For example, he says (1991b:249), 'The ordering of *e*, *o* before *ai*, *au* is dictated by simplicity because it allows a shorter *pratyāhāra* for the class *e*, *o*, *ai*, *au*, viz. *eC* (rather than **aiṄ*).'

Kiparsky stresses simplicity at the expense of historicity. Thus, along with other scholars, Cardona assumed that Pāṇini remodelled an older catalog of sounds, adapting it to serve in referring to sets of sounds in rules as required by rules of the Aṣṭādhyāyi. Under this assumption, the order *e o ai au* is simply a continuation of what is to be found in earlier lists. Specificially referring to Cardona (1969), Kiparsky explicitly rejects this approach, saying (1991b:242), 'For example, the order of *ṛ* and *ḷ* in row 2 cannot be carried over from previous homorganic sounds in the list, for there are none. And it cannot be carried over from the *Prātiśākhya*s' sound lists, because they did not include *ḷ*.[7]' His footnote 7 (1991b:258) refers to Cardona (1969:38).

From the above, one might assume that Cardona says something which supports the claim that the prātiśākhya sound lists did not include *ḷ*. However, this is not true. What Cardona (1969:38a) says is: 'While Pāṇini excludes from the *śivasūtra*s some sounds included in the lists of other treatises, he does include one sound which, properly speaking, should not be included in the lists of the *Prātiśākhya*s.' Certainly, not all prātiśākhyas lists lacked *ḷ*, as is well known and was explicitly said in Cardona (1969:7 note 2). In fact, there is irrefutable evidence that some prātiśākhyas included *ḷ* in their lists, an inclusion which is explainable on the basis of śikṣā lists. Pāṇini also presupposes a detailed knowledge of the field of learning known as *śikṣā.* It is, therefore, nonsensical to consider the śivasūtras in total isolation from this background.

Kiparsky is aware of this, but persists in trying to avoid it. Thus, he says at one point (1991b:249), 'In this case, of course, Pāṇini must have been well aware of the phonetic classification behind the correspondence. However, the fact that it emerges from the distributional analysis is still significant. It shows that, even if Pāṇini had begun with altogether different assumptions, or with none at all, he would still have come up with a parallel arrangement of vowels and semivowels.' Some of Kiparsky's arguments are also puzzling. For example, he says (1991b: 243), 'The vowels of a given quality are invariably denoted by their short representative, even though by Pāṇini's *sāvarṇya* convention (1.1.69) the long one would have done as well.' But *aṇ* refers in the first instance to short *a i u ṛ ḷ*, since *ā ī ū ṝ* are not listed. Moreover, *e o ai au* are long. Similarly, Kiparsky's claim concerning the order *e o ai au* is puzzling in that it is difficult to see how this order instead of *ai au e o* was preferred because it allows a shorter pratyāhāra. Since all the vowels in question are long (*dīrgha*), the pratyāhāras formed are equivalent in their mora value. Finally, no one can deny that the organization of the śivasūtras should reflect

Pāṇini's general principles. I still consider proper what I said earlier (Cardona [1969:33b]): 'If the *śivasūtras* are a list of sounds fashioned by Pāṇini for use in his grammatical rules, they should reflect the method involving *sāmānya* and *utsarga* as opposed to *viśeṣa* and *apavāda*, since this is the basis upon which is built his entire set of rules.' This does not mean, however, that Pāṇini devised his sound catalog in isolation from the background of śikṣā and prātiśākhya works to which he was indebted. Kiparsky has to admit this, and says (1991b:256):

> By this I do *not* mean that Pāṇini in fact started from scratch in constructing the *Śivasūtras*. On the contrary, it is virtually certain that he was acquainted with one or more phonetically arranged listings of sounds such as those found in the *Prātiśākhyas*, and it is even quite possible that there were previous *Śivasūtra*-style arrangements that he knew. It is also quite possible that Pāṇini started with one of those earlier arrangements and reordered it. What I do claim is that such earlier works are in no way required to explain the *Śivasūtras*, and that therefore we cannot make any inferences about Pāṇini's sources for the *Śivasūtras* from their structure.

Since Pāṇini explicitly assumes knowledge of phonetic properties that he uses in defining sets of homogeneous sounds, it is indeed 'virtually certain' that he was acquainted with phonetic arrangements of sounds. Given the rich documentation of prātiśākhya texts we have and the evidence from Brāhmaṇas and Pāṇinīya discussions, along with our knowledge of Indian cultural developments, the first thing one should think of is to show how Pāṇini developed the work of his prececessors to meet the needs of his system. In addition, one should not lose sight of the fact that the order of vowels, starting with *a*, and the earlier order of stops assumed by the śivasūtras, namely starting with velars, is not simply a universal given. This reflects the early śikṣā ordering of sounds in accordance with speech production. Moreover, as has been shown in works such as Cardona (1969), the Aṣṭādhyāyī stands in sharp contrast with a grammar such as the Jainendravyākaraṇa in that Pāṇini does not strive to replace all traditional category names such as *ātmanepada*, *parasmaipada*, *prathamā*, *dvitīyā* and so on with monosyllabic terms. He is clearly not interested in economy as an overriding criterion.

Accordingly, Kiparsky's study is to be considered, I think, something of a curiosity piece, a tour de force that, while admitting Pāṇini's debt to his antecedents, wrenches the śivasūtras out of their historical background which Pāṇini acknowledges implicitly and Pāṇinīyas mention explicitly, and does this with little to show for the effort.

Recently, Kamalāprasāda Pāṇḍeya (1992-93) has again taken up the reasons discussed in the Mahābhāṣya why *h* is listed twice in Pāṇini's sound catalog.[54]

2.1.4.5. *Pāṇini's system of grammar*

2.1.4.5a. *Verbal and nominal morphology* (III.1.5.5b)

It is now generally recognized that Pāṇini does not make any strict separation of morphology from syntax. Verb forms of the type *pacati* '... cooks, ... is cooking' and nominal forms like *odanam* 'rice' are derived from basic structures which contain affixes introduced under meaning and cooccurence conditions such that participants in actions are considered in relation to the actions in which they participate. A good description of Pāṇini's procedure is given by R. N. Sharma (1987:141-164); see also R. N. Sharma (1976a, b), Cardona (1997a:136-167 [**212-255**]). Cardona also deals with the formation of both deverbative and denominative bases (1997a:186-256 [**277-369**]).[55]

Pāṇini formulates particular replacement rules to account for the use of pairs of bases such as *as* 'be' (3rd sg. pres. *asti*, 3rd sg. impfct. *āsīt*) and *bhū* (3rd sg. aor. *abhūt*, 3rd sg. pfct. *babhūva*, 3rd sg fut. *bhaviṣyati*); he lets one base occur instead of another when *ārdhadhātuka* affixes are to be used. M. M. Deshpande (1992f) has discussed such suppletion and illustrated it with numerous examples from Vedic texts, the Nirukta, and the Mahābhāṣya.

General treatments of Pāṇini's manner of deriving compounds appear in Mahavir (1978:5-46), V. V. Bhandare (1986:44-269), R. N. Sharma (1987:187-211) and Cardona (1997a:205-229 [**301-329**]). K. M. Tiwary's 1968 dissertation has now been published (1984). An Italian translation, with annotations, of Pāṇini's composition rules constitutes the major part of the second volume (pp. 24-123) of a recent work by Anna Radicchi (1985-88). The first volume of Radicchi's work gives a historical and philological background for this translation and includes discussions of the general theoretical approach to nominal composition as reflected in sūtras of the Aṣṭādhyāyī and in Mahābhāṣya arguments (chapter 2 [26-39]: 'Elementi della teoria dei samāsa in Pāṇini', chapter 3 [40-53]: 'Integrazioni mahābhāṣyāne alla teoria dei samāsa di Pāṇini'). In the second part of his last large work, Charu Deva Shastri (1990:95-208) deals in his lucid and charming manner with the composition rules of the Aṣṭādhyāyī arranged according to different kinds of compounds. In the first volume of his work on Vedic compounds, M. D. Pandit (1989) treats Pāṇinian rules concerning compounds in two sections: III: 'Pāṇini's treatment of compounds' (1989:37-56) and IV: 'Inflexion, gender and number of compounds' (1989:57-64). S. T. K. S. Rangacaryulu (1989]) takes up briefly the question of meaning unification (*ekārthībhāva*) in forming compounds and the related issues of whether such formations involve components' giving up their individual meanings.

Three recent papers concerning compounding in the Pāṇinian system touch on questions regarding what are called *asamarthasamāsa*: Gillon (1993), Vergiani (1993), Scharf (1995 b).[56]

Peri Sarveswara Sharma (1985a) considers the use of *pratyakṣa* as an avyaya and as an adjectival compound and how one can account for the second usage.[57]

In the paper summarized in Vijayānanda Patel (1997), the author takes up the type of compounds for which the argument is made that certain terms enter into composition with a derivate that ends in a kṛt affix before the kṛdanta takes nominal endings (see Cardona [1997a:207 (**302**)]). Related issues are also discussed, including whether ṣaṣṭhī-tatpuruṣa are blocked by upapada compounds.

Saroja Bhate has devoted a series of studies (1987a, b, 1989) to rules that serve to form taddhita derivates. Her monograph of 1989 deals with the general organization and structure of these rules and the meanings of the derivates.[58] Chapters III-V of Kripa Ram Tripathi (1991) deal with semantic aspects of how taddhita rules are arranged, the general suffix *aṇ*, and a structural analysis of some taddhita rules.

Filliozat (1975) emphasizes that both compounds and derivates with taddhita affixes are related to strings.[59]

2.1.4.5b. *Syntax* (III.1.5.5c)

2.1.4.5b.1. *General*

M. M Deshpande has contributed a number of studies dealing with Pāṇinian syntax: 1980a, 1981a, 1985a, 1987a, b, 1991b,c, e, f, g, 1992b. I continue to consider (cf. Cardona [1989:67]) that Deshpande's studies demonstrate a solid command not only of what Pāṇinīyas have said but also of Vedic texts which he uses in many of his arguments and that they present ideas which are challenging and well worth considering. One topic to which Deshpande has returned on several occasions and about which he has some novel things to say is the treatment by Pāṇini and Pāṇinīyas of what western grammar calls *infinitives*. For example, in his most recent paper concerning derivates with ***tumun***, Deshpande remarks (1991f:47):

> This is the point where one needs to go beyond the traditional commentators and see if there is another viable interpretation of P 2.3.15 (tumarthāc ca bhāvavacanāt). I would like to suggest that the expression *tumartha* in this rule is inclusive of the meaning *kriyāyāṁ kriyārthāyām* but not limited to it. It is inclusive of all rules which prescribe the suffix *-tum*, and all the variety of meanings of the suffix *-tum*.

In the same article, Deshpande (1991f:46) maintains the thesis he had defended earlier, namely that Pāṇinīyas are not justified in considering that -***tumun*** is introduced to signify abstract action (*bhāva*), and he notes the following concerning what the Kāśikā says about *tumarthe* in **A** 3.4.9:

> The Kāśikāvṛtti does not significantly add to our knowledge of the expression *tumarthe*, and following Patañjali's opinion, it simply says that *tumarthe* in this rule refers to action (bhāva) and that all these affixes occur in the sense of action. I have pointed out previously that such an interpretation is grossly inadequate and must be rejected. In their explicit discussion of these Vedic forms, the commentators generally fail to explain the infinitival value of these Vedic forms, though some paraphrase them with *-tum*-infinitives.[60]

Deshpande differs not only with the views of Pāṇinīyas of old but also with views proposed by some modern Pāṇinian scholars. For example, in the first lecture of Deshpande (1985a), he takes exception — correctly, in my opinion — with the way in which S. D. Joshi (1982b) sought to explain particular constructions containing verb forms with ātmanepada affixes and the Pāṇinian sūtras that account for such constructions.[61]

Cardona (1976c) considered whether the facts of Sanskrit require one to operate with a category of subject and concluded that such a category is not warranted here; instead, a category of agent — in the sense of Pāṇini's kartṛ category — fits best with the system.

Questions revolving around the use of nominal endings whose occurrence is conditioned by cooccurring terms called *upapada* in Pāṇini's system have been discussed by Cardona (1980a) and Bal Shastri (1986a, b).[62] The latter has also discussed (1988b, c) sentences of the type *putreṇa sahāgataḥ* '... came with his son', *putreṇa saha sthūlaḥ* '... is stout along with his son', the instrumental forms of which are accounted for by **A** 2.3.19 (*sahayukte' pradhāne*).

The literature concerning various definitions suggested for a vākya is fairly extensive (see Cardona [1976:223 with notes 296-298]), and contributions on this topic have continued to be written, including K. Kunjunni Raja (1976), Devaswarupa Miśra (1978:155-159), and Laddu (1980b). The most recent contributions known to me are by M. M Deshpande (1987b, 1991e). Deshpande concludes that Pāṇini, Kātyāyana, and Patañjali differed with respect to three features: whether there could be pure nominal sentences, whether a finite verb was necessary or merely possible in a sentence, and whether one could have more than one finite verb in a sentence. His discussion is well documented, but I have doubts concerning some major aspects of the issues.

One point which I do think merits keeping in mind more than one might gather from what Deshpande says is the context in which Kātyāyana brings up some of his suggestions. Kātyāyana certainly says, in 2.3.1 vt. 11 (... *astir bhavantīparaḥ prathamapuruṣo' prayujyamāno' py asti*), that a third person present form of 'be' is to be considered to occur — that is, one is to understand it — even if no such form is overtly used. This is obviously brought up in connection with sentences of the type *vṛkṣaḥ plakṣaḥ* 'A plakṣa (is) a tree.' Patañjali gives this example immediately preceding the vārttika (Kielhorn [1880-85:I.443.4]). Moreover, Patañjali's example is appropriate to the context. In the previous vārttika (2.3.1 vt. 10: *anabhihitavacanam anarthakaṁ prathamāvidhānasyānavakāśatvāt*) it is proposed that stating **A** 2.3.1: *anabhihite* has no purpose, since the provision of the first triplet of endings has no independent scope. That is, the heading A 2.3.1 is supposed to preclude introducing a second-triplet ending after a nominal such as *kaṭa-* in deriving an utterance like *kriyate kaṭaḥ* 'A mat is being made'; instead, a first-triplet ending is introduced by A 2.3.46: *prātipadikārthaliṅgaparimāṇavacanamātre prathamā.* If A 2.3.46 could not apply to provide such a nominative ending, however, it would be without any scope of application. By virtue of this lack of scope, then, it will apply and thus not be vacuous. As a reply to this, the suggestion is made in the Bhāṣya that the first triplet of endings does have an independent scope of application, namely where there is no verb, hence no kāraka, as in *vṛkṣaḥ plakṣaḥ* (Kielhorn [1880-85:I.443.3-4]: *sāvakāśā prathamā* । *ko'vakāśaḥ* । *akārakam* : *vṛkṣaḥ plakṣa iti*). It is to this that 2.3.1 vt. 11 responds. That is, there is no utterance that does not involve a kāraka, and even in an equational sentence like *vṛkṣaḥ plakṣaḥ*, one has to understand that there is a kāraka, with respect to being.

The references to 2.3.1 vt. 11 in vārttikas 4 (*uktaṁ vā*) and 7 (*uktaṁ pūrveṇa*) on A 2.3.46 have the following context. The objection is raised that if a first-triplet ending is introduced on condition that only the meaning of a base, a gender, measure, and number is to be signified, then provision has to be made for instances where there are coreferential padas, since then there is an additional meaning (2.3.46 vt. 1: *prātipadikārthaliṅgaparimāṇavacanamātre prathamālakṣaṇe padasāmānādhikaraṇya upasaṁkhyānam adhikatvāt*). For example, the ending in *vīraḥ puruṣaḥ* 'The man is brave' cannot be accounted for by A 2.3.46, because there is something additional. The base meaning of *puruṣa-* 'man' has something added to it: the property of being brave now resides in the man about whom one is speaking.[63] This objection is met in the second vārttika (2.3.46 vt. 2: *na vā vākyārthatvāt*). One does not have to say this, because the additional meaning in question is a meaning of the utterance, not of the nominal base.

An alternative way of introducing first-triplet endings is then taken up to account for examples like *vīraḥ puruṣah*. A rule will be formulated letting a first-triplet ending occur on condition that meanings that are to be signified — by verb endings and so on — are already signified (Kielhorn [1880-85:I.462.6]: *athavābhihite prathamety etal lakṣaṇaṁ kariṣyate*). To this the objection is raised that one must now provide for a first-triplet ending in instances where a meaning to be signified by verb endings and so on is not already signified: 2.3.46 vt. 3: *abhihitalakṣaṇāyām anabhihite prathamāvidhiḥ.* Patañjali (Kielhorn [1880-85:I.462.8]) supplies *vṛkṣaḥ plakṣaḥ* as an example. In 2.3.46 vt. 4, this objection is met by means of a reference to what had been said in 2.3.1 vt. 11. That is, although *vṛkṣaḥ plakṣaḥ* has no overt verb form, *asti* is understood (Kielhorn [1880-85:I.462.11]: *astīti gamyate*), so that the meaning to be signified by a verb ending — here an agent signified by the ending *ti* — is already signified, albeit only implicitly.

A second objection is raised to the alternative rule: a first-triplet ending obtains thereby when a particular meaning is both signified and not signified already (2.3.46 vt. 5: *abhihitānabhihite prathamābhāvaḥ*). Patañjali supplies the examples *prāsāda āste* '... is sitting on the terrace', *śayane āste* '... is sitting on the bed'.[64] Although the bases *prāsāda-*, *śayana-* are not followed by an ending signifying a locus, these bases contain kṛt affixes that signify such a kāraka.

A third way of introducing first-triplet endings is now taken up. A rule will be formulated letting such an ending occur if it is coreferential with a verb ending (Kielhorn [1880-85:I.462.14-15]: *evaṁ tarhi tiṅsamānādhikaraṇe prathamety etal lakṣaṇaṁ kariṣyate*). Thus, a first triplet ending introduced after *prāsāda-*, *śayana-* used to signify a locus in utterances with *āste* would not be coreferential with the verb ending, which signifies an agent. Hence, this ending is not allowed in such sentences. This third formulation also meets with an objection: one must now provide for a first-triplet ending in instances where a term with a verb ending is not used (2.3.46 vt. 6: *tiṅsamānādhikaraṇa iti cet tiṅo'prayoge prathamāvidhiḥ*). Again Patañjali supplies the example *vṛkṣaḥ plakṣaḥ.* And in 2.3.46 vt. 7, this objection too is met by referring back to 2.3.1 vt. 11.

That is, the entire discussion centers around sentences of the type N N: *vīraḥ puruṣaḥ, vṛkṣaḥ plakṣaḥ.* It is for such utterances that Kātyāyana and Patañjali bring in the principle that a third person present form of 'be' is to be understood. Deshpande (1991e: 39) cites the sentences *rāmaḥ gataḥ* 'Rāma went', *rāmaḥ gantuṁ samarthaḥ* 'Rāma is able to go', and *vṛkṣaḥ plakṣaḥ* — which he labels (7), (8), (12) — and says, 'The assumption of the verb *asti* makes it possible for Kātyāyana to deal with the syntax of sentences such as (7), (8), and (12) ....' Clearly, this is true for the last. It is, however, by no means a given that this is true also of (7). It is also possible — I would say more than possible — that, in accordance with Pāṇini, both Kātyāyana and Patañjali would account for utterances like *rāmo gataḥ* in the same way as *rāmo gacchati* is described. Rāma is agent with respect to the act of going; as the verb ending *ti* of the latter signifies an agent, so does the kṛt suffix of the former (**A** 3.4.72: *gatyarthākarmaka-śliṣaśīṅsthāsavasajanaruhajīryatibhyaś ca*).[65] This is not to deny that Sanskrit could have past participles and forms of *as* in a single utterance. In fact, the dividing line between such participles used verbally as in *rāmo gataḥ* and "adjectivally" remains to be looked at in detail. On the other hand, Deshpande's discussion does not give cogent reasons to consider that for Pāṇini, as for Kātyāyana, a sentence like *vṛkṣaḥ plakṣaḥ* was to be interpreted in any way other than the manner in which it was by conventions of every day usage: a present form of the verb *as* is to be understood. On this point I agree with Johannes Bronkhorst (1991a).

As has been noted (see Cardona [1976a:223-224]), one reason for which Kātyāyana proposes to define a vākya is to allow for the accentuation of a verb form like *hara* in a string such as *ayaṁ daṇḍo harānena*. In addition, there are examples like *nadyās tiṣṭhati kūle* ('... is standing on the bank of the river'), first brought up in the Bhāṣya on 2.1.1. vt. 13.[66] The assumption is that one has to state a set of rules, including those which provide that verb forms not have high-pitched vowels, under a heading *samānavākye*, so that the operations in question apply only to items with contexts in the same vākya. One thus accounts for the accentuation of *tiṣṭhati* in *n̲adyās tìṣṭhati̲ kūlè*: by **A** 8.1.28: *tiṅṅatiṅaḥ*, the finite verb form here should not have any high-pitched vowel by virtue of following a pada that does not end with a finite verb ending. Under the assumption that **A** 2.1.1: *samarthaḥ padavidhiḥ* applies universally throughout the grammar, **A** 8.1.28 as stated fails to account for the required accentuation. This sūtra will provide for the absence of high pitched vowels in finite verb forms preceded by padas with which they are syntactically and semantically related (*samartha*). In *n̲adyās tìṣṭhati̲ kūlè*, however, the act of standing is related only to the river bank (*kūla*), not to the river. If, on the other hand, **A** 8.1.28 is stated under a heading *samānavākye* and a vākya is defined as a string with one finite verb form (2.1.1 vt. 10 : *ekatiṅ vākyam*), the required results are accounted for. On this topic, see Cardona (1983a:123-128).

M. M. Deshpande (1980b:313-316, 1987c:66-71) has discussed the concept of syntactic-semantic relation (*sāmarthya*), and has an interesting proposal. He suggests (1987c:66) that:

> For Pāṇini, the notion of *sāmarthya* represents a network of semantic-syntactic relationships, some of which may be more direct than others. Assuming that under the governing condition of P. 2.1.1 (*samarthaḥ padavidhiḥ*), rules like P. 8.1.28 (*tiṅṅ atiṅaḥ*) had a successful area of application, one may conclude that for Pāṇini, all words of a sentence belonged to a common semantic network.

This is said with reference to *nadyās tiṣṭhati kūle*, which Deshpande brings up once more a bit later (1987c:68), where he says, 'In the same manner, one may say that a sentence such as *nadyāḥ tiṣṭhati kūle* "(he) stands on the bank of the river" represents an overlap of two semantic-syntactic relations ....'

One cannot simply assume, however, that **A** 2.1.1 applies throughout the grammar. If it applies only within the more restricted set of rules in the first two pādas of the second adhyāya, thus regulating nominal composition, then two things are possible: two padas are samartha if they are semantically and syntactically related; **A** 8.1.28 does not require that the finite verb form be samartha with the nominal form that precedes and conditions the lack of high-pitched vowels. This does not mean that there are not networks of relationships involved in utterances. To the contrary. It simply means that there are direct relationships and indirect ones. Moreover, there is a continuity in viewing utterances as involving both direct relations between actions and kārakas as well as indirect relations mediated by these. Bhartṛhari puts it succinctly when he speaks of a relation between instrument and object mediated by the action in which these participate: Vākyapadīya 2.405ab: *kriyāvyavetaḥ saṁbandho dṛṣṭaḥ karaṇakarmaṇoḥ.*[67] In his Vṛtti, Bartṛhari notes that kārakas that serve to bring about the same action enter into relation with each other indirectly, through the intermediary of the action; he also harks back to the example that Patañjali invoked in the Bhāṣya (see below), of steps in a ladder that are not directly related to each other but connected via the side poles.[68] Such mediated relationship is also recognized much earlier, by Kātyāyana himself, in vārttika 7 on 2.1.34-35: *yuktārthasaṁpratyayāc ca sāmarthyam.* By **A** 2.1.34: *annena vyañjanam* (*tṛtīyā* 30), a pada that terminates in a third-triplet ending and signifies something used to impart flavor to a food (*vyañjanam*) optionally combines with a related pada signifying an edible rice (*annena*) to form a tatpuruṣa compound. By **A** 2.1.35: *bhakṣyeṇa miśrīkaraṇam*, a pada that terminates in a third-triplet ending and signifies something used to mix with food (*miśrīkaraṇa*) optionally combines with a related pada signifying an edible grain (*bhakṣyeṇa*) to form a tatpuruṣa compound. For example: *dadhyodana-* (← *dadhi-ā odana-s*) 'rice flavored with yoghurt', *guḍadhāna-* (← *guḍa-ā dhāna-as*) 'corn mixed with raw sugar'. These rules come under the heading of **A** 2.1.1, so that the padas in question have to be semantically and syntactically related to each other. The first two vārttikas on the sūtras (2.1.34-35 vt. 1: *annena vyañjanaṁ bhakṣyeṇa miśrīkaraṇam ity asamarthasamāsaḥ*, vt. 2: *kārakāṇāṁ kriyayā sāmarthyāt*) argue that, contrary to what should obtain by this heading, the compounds provided have to be considered to be formed from padas that are not related to each other, because kārakas bear a relation to an action. After a discussion which cannot be summarized here, the seventh vārttika maintains that there is indeed a relation between the padas that enter into composition, since one understands that what is signified by padas like *dadhi-ā* is intended for an appropriate action. That is, **A** 2.1.34 explicitly says that the pada with the third-triplet ending signifies something that serves to flavor something else, which is referred to in the sūtra by *annam*. There is thus assumed a relation of flavoring-flavored (*saṁskārya-saṁskārakabhāvasambandha*) between the yoghurt and rice. It is not possible, however, for something like yoghurt to function as a flavoring unless it is used to wet down rice that is to be eaten, so that the action of wetting down is implied and understood without being overtly stated. Such instances involve two kārakas, each related to the same action; such kārakas are not directly related to each other but are indirectly related through the intermediary of the shared action.

The sort of relations concerned in these instances are such that two kārakas are directly related to a single action and thereby come to be related indirectly with each other. This can be shown schematically as: K-A-K. Now, let 'R' stand for the relation 'semantically related' (*sāmarthya* 'semantic relatedness'), so that 'K_1RA' and 'K_2RA' denote that one kāraka is semantically related to a given action and another kāraka is also semantically related to that action. By the following reasoning,[69] the two kārakas are thereby related to each other: if K_1RA and K_2RA then K_1RK_2.

Examples like *nadyās tiṣṭhati kūle* '... is standing on the bank of the river' or *daśarathasya putro gacchati* 'The son of Daśaratha is going' represent another type, which can be represented schematically as: (Q)K-A, where 'Q' denotes a qualifier of a kāraka. *nadyās tiṣṭhati kūle*, *daśarathasya putro gacchati* involve each time one kāraka, which alone is related to the action in question, and this kāraka is qualified as related to something else. The river of *nadyās tiṣṭhati kūle* is indeed not related to the act of standing; the agent in question is standing on the bank alone. Daśaratha spoken of in *daśarathasya putro gacchati* is not related to the act of going; only his son is going somewhere. Obviously, Kātyāyana recognized this, and it is not surprising that Pāṇini should be aware of it, so that he would not have **A** 2.1.1 apply to govern how **A** 8.1.28 is to apply. In sum, instead of seeing a dichotomy between a "flexible" and "strict" notion of sāmarthya separating Pāṇini from Kātyāyana and others, I think it is more justifiable to see a continuity between Pāṇini and Pāṇinīyas concerning sāmarthya but a difference between them regarding how **A** 2.1.1 applied.[70]

Achyutananda Dash's paper (1991) is an extremely interesting and challenging work in which a novel idea is presented with ingenuity. The issue concerns sentences like the following (Dash's example (9)[1991:139]): *harir vaikuṇṭham adhiśete* 'Hari lies in (sleeps in) Vaikuṇṭha.' By **A** 1.4.46: *adhiśīṅsthāsāṁ karma*, the substrate (*ādhāra*) relative to the act is classed as a karman, so that, by **A** 2.3.2: *karmaṇi dvitīyā*, a second-triplet ending signifying a karman is introduced after the nominal *vaikuṇṭha-*. Dash's claim (1991:142) is:

> In the present context, *adhi-* is not an *upasarga* as it does not show the characteristics of an *upasarga.* Therefore, I assume it to be a *karmapravacanīya* (*kmpv*) because it has an intrinsic semantic relation with the NP and expresses/implies the meaning 'substratum'. Since we do not see a locative case-ending with the NP *vaikuṇṭha*, the example does not violate the general principle *ananyalabhyaś śabdārthaḥ* or *uktārthānām aprayogaḥ.* The accusative case-ending with the NP *vaikuṇṭha* is also justifiable because a *kmpv* can govern *dvitīyā* by P.2.3.8.

Dash goes on to say (1991:143-144) that the karmapravacanīya here is not of the type in *anu harim surāḥ* 'the gods are after Hari' (Dash's example (11)[1991:143]). On the contrary, he says (1991:144), 'Our present example (9) is the second variety of *kmpv* (*kmpv*-2). Such *kmpv*s are also evident in traditional examples: ... (13) *kutaḥ adhyāgacchati*.'

Interesting as Dash's discussion is, I consider his principal claim unacceptable. The term *adhi* of the type *adhiśete* does indeed behave like an upasarga, with respect to accentuation. Consider the following examples:

AV 12.1.34c-f: *uttānās tvā pratīcīṁ yat pṛṣṭībhìr adhi śemàhe | mā hìṁsīs tatrà no bhūme sarvàsya pratiśīvari* 'Earth, do not harm us because, stretched out, we lie on you with our ribs as you face us, you who are the support for all to lie on.'

ṚV 8.10.6: *yad antarìkṣe patàthaḥ purubhujā yad veme rodàsī anù | yad vā svadhābhìr adhi tiṣṭhàtho ratham ata ā yàtam aśvinā* 'Aśvins, whether you are flying in the space between heaven and earth ... or along the two world-halves, or are settled in your chariot ..., come from there.'

As can be seen, *adhi* has no udātta vowel before the accented verb forms with which it is construed. This is the norm for a gati (**A** 8.1.71: *tiṅi codāttavati*). Items of the set beginning with *pra* are classed as upasarga if they are linked with verbs (**A** 1.4.59: *upsargāḥ kiryāyoge*), and the same items are then simultaneously assigned to the gati class (**A** 1.4.60: *gatiś ca*), in part for accentual operations; see Cardona (1997a:28-30 [**55**]). A term like *ádhi* in *kutaḥ adhyāgacchati* is classed as a karmapravacanīya because it does not exhibit such accentual dependence. Instead of behaving like a regular gati, which is anudātta before another gati (**A** 8.1.70: *gatir gatau*), this keeps its udātta accentuation.[71]

2.1.4.5b.2. *Kārakas and kāraka rules*

The way in which kārakas are assigned to the kāraka classes called *apādāna, sampradāna, karaṇa, adhikaraṇa, karman, kartṛ*, and *hetu* in the Aṣṭādhyāyī, the status of kārakas, and the relations between kāraka categories and linguistic expressions are topics which continue to draw the attention of many scholars.

R. N. Sharma (1987:141-164) treats Pāṇini's kāraka classification rules and associated affixation rules in general. The first part (pp. 1-81) of Charu Deva Shastri (1990) deals with kārakas and their expression and includes also a consideration of affixation that depends on the cooccurrence of a nominal with a term other than a verb, that is, the use of what are called *upapadavibhakti*. In addition, a supplement (1990:81-93) contains a good selection illustrating usage in a wide variety of literary sources. P. S. Subrahmanyam (1976) not only deals with kāraka classification rules — which are translated in an appendix (1976:215-220) — but also compares some of the usages for which Pāṇini accounts with usages in Dravidian languages.

Some recent general articles on kārakas are: Devasthali (1980), M. M. Deshpande (1990a), Achyutananda Dash (1990, 1992), and Achyutananda Dash and Brendon S. Gillon (1990). Deshpande considers the kāraka categories and the case endings used to express them in connection with ontology and semantics, intentionality, and rule order. The other papers are at once less comprehensive and somewhat more far ranging in that they consider Pāṇini's system in less detail than does Deshpande but also bring in views of other schools (see 2.1.4.7a).[72] A recent book by the late B. K. Matilal (1990a) contains a chapter (5: 'The *kāraka* theory' [40-48]) devoted to a general discussion of kārakas.

Another interesting article of a general nature is M. M. Deshpande (1991b), in which the author argues that, although Pāṇini's grammar is not prototype-based in the way envisioned by certain modern linguists, the concept of prototype has some value in understanding what Pāṇini does. Thus, Deshpande says (1991b:468a), 'However, the notion of prototype is important in understanding Pāṇinian syntax, in that the process of defining the *kāraka* terms begins with some sort of *cultural prototypes* and ends up with non-prototypical formal categories.' What Deshpande has in mind can be illustrated by what he says (1991b:471b) concerning **A** 1.4.54: *svatantraḥ kartā* :

> To my mind, the masculine gender in this rule is a reflection of the fact that in Sanskritic culture, the notion of *kartṛ* 'maker, creator' is a predominantly male notion, and at the very least an animate notion. Thus, one could say that the 'unassimilated element' of masculine gender in *svatantraḥ kartā* suggests to us that, for Pāṇini, an agent was prototypically an animate entity, though this animacy has to be superseded at the formal level, to account for the larger domain of grammatical agents.[73]

In Pāṇini's system, a sentence such as *devadattāya rocate modakaḥ* 'Devadatta likes modaka (a sweet)' involves two kārakas — the person named Devadatta, who is pleased, and a sweet (*modaka*), which does the pleasing — respectively assigned to the sampradāna and kartṛ classes. This construction in the Pāṇinian system is the topic of a paper by Cardona

(1990e), who argues that datives like *devadattāya* in this construction should not be treated as agentive, since Sanskrit also has a causative *rocayate* used in an agentive construction. M. M. Deshpande (1990b) deals with Pāṇini's sampradāna class and concentrates on constructions with *ruc*. H. H. Hock also briefly considers (1990:120, 124) constructions with *ruc*. In an article devoted primarily to demonstrating that Sanskrit had a possessive agent construction, Hock (1991b) again deals in passing with dative experiencer constructions (1991b:57-58). In addition, the sampradāna category to which kārakas are assigned by **A** 1.4.32: *karmaṇā yam abhipraiti sa sampradānam* and following rules is the subject of an article by Keshav Kumar Ray (1988), in which the author also considers views of commentators.

Double-object constructions in connection with the Pāṇinian system have been studied in papers by H. H. Hock (1985), M. M. Deshpande (1991c, 1992b), and Lal Shankar Gayāvāla (1997).[74]

K. Meenakshi (1991a), takes up briefly (pp. 145-147) Pāṇinian rules dealing with kāraka classes in order to elucidate what is meant by *śeṣe* 'remainder' in **A** 2.3.50: *ṣaṣṭhī śeṣe*, then deals with the uses of the genitive in the Mahābhārata and the Rāmāyaṇa as an investigation of '... the extent to which the use of the genitive in the Epic Sanskrit of the Mahābhārata ... and Rāmāyaṇa ... agrees with the precepts of Pāṇini's grammar (Meenakshi [1991a:145]).'

2.1.4.5c. *Semantics* (III.1.5.5d)

It has been well known for some time (see Cardona [1976a:183, 215, 224]) that meanings serve as conditions for the introduction of affixes in Pāṇini's derivation system, and that Pāṇini's kāraka classes are associated with semantics.[75] Accordingly, many of the studies already mentioned deal with semantics in one way or the other.

Two recent articles on semantics in India briefly treat semantics within the Pāṇinian tradition: Staal (1995) and Houben (1997). Houben covers once more the basic aspects of how Pāṇini lets meanings serve as conditions for the introduction of affixes and also takes up important passages from the Mahābhāṣya that deal with semantic issues.[76] I consider Staal's treatment less knowledgable or informative. For example, concerning meaning entries in the dhātupāṭha, he says (Staal [1995:67a]), 'Following the eleventh-century grammarian Kayaṭa [sic!], others have argued that the meaning entries were added later, but there is no reason to accept this view (Bronkhorst 1981).'[77] Staal thus uncritically accepts Bronkhorst's contention that the original dhātupāṭha included meaning entries, although this view can hardly be considered established if one considers the evidence with care; see section 2.1.2.4. Understandably, though no less regrettably, in a discussion of kāraka classes, Staal (1995:67b-68a) refers only to the article he wrote with Kiparsky (1969), as though some of the principal conclusions reached in this paper had not been subject to serious objection (see Cardona [1976a:221-222]) and more insightful work had not been done since this study (see Cardona [1976a:215-221] and above, section 2.1.4.5b.2).[78]

Another recent article devoted specifically to this topic is Bronkhorst (1992b). After noting that in the Pāṇinian derivational system meanings serve to condition the introduction of speech elements (1992b:455), Bronkhorst briefly describes (1992b:455-456) how two verb forms are derived: *dāsyāmi* 'I will give' and *aśrauṣam* 'I (have) heard'. He then remarks (1992b: 456) that in this article it is not possible for him to study Pāṇini's treatment of meaning in more detail. Bronkhorst goes on to stress the affinities between Pāṇini's procedures and earlier 'Brahmanical' texts, saying (1992b:457) that the Brahmanical etymologists considered constituent parts of words as the real meaning bearers and that Pāṇini did the same thing. Subsequently (1992b:457), he adds the observation that in Pāṇini's grammar the ultimate meaning bearers are not always identical with the constitutent parts of words as uttered, and illustrates this point by noting that *aśrauṣam* has *am* as a replacement for *mi* and that *avādīt* '... (has) said' shows a loss of the aorist marker *s* which appears in *avādiṣuḥ* (3rd pl.). On the next page (1992b:458), Bronkhorst devotes a short paragraph to the view of Bhartṛhari and others that the meanings attributed by grammarians and others to elements smaller than words and utterances are mere fictions, ending with the remark that in the present paper these and other opinions are of no interest. Bronkhorst then turns to a Western parallel and the remainder of the article is devoted to Bopp, parallels between him and Pāṇini, and the influence Pāṇini had on Bopp.

From my brief summary, I think it is clear that Bronkhorst's paper does not contribute much to our knowledge of Pāṇini's views on meaning.

I also think that there is something fundamentally amiss in the author's repeatedly stressing Pāṇinian analysis and quest for ultimate units. It is by now well known that Pāṇini assumes the results of an analysis, carried out using procedures that are described by Pāṇinīyas.[79] The Aṣṭādhyāyī presents a synthetic system, whereby affixes are introduced, under meaning and cooccurrence conditions, to verbal and nominal bases, forming syntactic words (*pada*) that bear particular semantic and syntactic relations with each other.[80]

2.1.4.6. *Studies of particular rules*

2.1.4.6a. *Vedic rules* (III.1.5.6a)

The most wide ranging recent paper concerning Vedic rules and usage relative to the Aṣṭādhyāyī, Bronkhorst (1991d), is an important and interesting paper, covering quite a few areas. I think the author strikes the right note of caution concerning judgements about the status of Vedic texts and conclusions reached regarding particular usages in these texts and the usages described in the Aṣṭādhyāyī. Another important paper by the same author (Bronkhorst [1981c]) deals with some Pāṇinian sūtras that treat of exclusively Vedic matters but is mainly concerned with more general issues, the relations among Pāṇini, the Ṛgveda and the Ṛgvedaprātiśākhya; see section 2.3.1. One of the most recent papers I know of in this area is also by Bronkhorst (1996c). This article concentrates on **A** 7.4.38: *devasumnayor yajuṣi kāṭhake*. Bronkhorst's main claim is that, contrary to the traditional interpretation, **A** 7.4.37: *aśvāghasyāt* should be interpreted as *aśvāghasya at*, so that it provides for replacing the *-a* of *aśva-*, *agha-* by *-a* (instead of *-ā*) before ***kyac***. Accordingly, *at* is understood to recur in **A** 7.4.38, so that this sūtra provides for *devaya-* instead of *devāya-*. The evidence Bronkhorst adduces (1996c:60) for this is that Kāṭhakasaṁhitā manuscripts do not always have *devāya-*: 'The first illustration does occur in a sacrificial formula in prose (*yajus*), thrice over, but not always with the desired long *ā*. *KS* 3.5 and 25.6 have *devayate*, in the only Ms at the disposal of its editor Leopold VON SCHROEDER.'

In another very recent study, K. Parameswara Aithal (1996) deals not only with **A** 7.4.38 (1996:5-6) but also with a good number of additional sūtras that concern Vedic, especially rules in which the term *ṛc* is used. Aithal is circumspect and considers (1996:6) that with respect to problems such as that posed by **A** 7.4.38 one may well have to be satisfied with the principle that all rules are ultimately optional for Vedic.

Jayamanta Mishra (1994) emphasises that, by stating rules of the form *bahulaṁ chandasi*, Pāṇini recognized that Vedic usage was not amenable to the same precise description as the speech of his time and place.

Several recent studies deal with Pāṇinian rules and the Vedic verbal system. G. B. Palsule (1991b) does an excellent job of contrasting the system of modal forms in the Sanskrit of Pāṇini's time with the earlier Vedic state of affairs. Palsule's focus is, as it should be, on the fact that in the language of Pāṇini's time imperative and optative forms are connected with present-imperfect stems — those with vikaraṇas ***śap*** and so on — while in Vedic aorist and perfect stems could also have such modal forms; e.g. second singular imperative *pāhi* 'drink', corresponding to the root aorist, and *piba* 'drink' corresponding to the present. Palsule begins (1991b:55-58) by describing the way Pāṇini derives forms of the type *bhavatu* (3rd sg. imper. ← *bhū-lo**ṭ***) 'let ... be', *bhavet* (3rd sg. opt. ← *bhū-li**ṅ***), *bhavāti* (3rd sg. subj. ← *bhū-le**ṭ***). He goes on (1991b:58-60) to consider the so-called benedictive or precative and forms like *tāriṣat*, which modern grammarians treat as sigmatic aorist subjunctives but Pāṇini does not. Palsule then comes to his main issue (1991b:60-61):

> Leaving aside these two exceptions, how does Pāṇini account for Vedic modal forms based on other than Present stems? We saw that the normal rules don't account for such forms. Does Pāṇini then altogether ignore them? The answer is that he does not altogether ignore them. He has provided for them, but in only a very broad way. Since he does not recognize Imper. etc. based on Aor. or Perf. stems, his main defence seems to be that in such forms the stem is not Aor. or Perf. but a special or irregular (*chāndasa*) Present itself. Thus, what we call Perf. forms will be *loṭ* etc. in the Pāṇinian system according to the 3rd (*hu*) class. This will account for reduplication and the absence of *śap* etc. The forms which we look upon as based on root-Aor. stems will be looked upon as *loṭ*, etc. according to the 2nd (*ad-*) class. Of course Pāṇini himself does not say anything expressly, but the explanations given by commentators, both of the *Aṣṭādhyāyī* and of the Veda, give a fair idea of the procedure which was probably intended by Pāṇini himself.

Speaking from the viewpoint of historical-comparative linguistics, one can rightly say that the verbal base reflected in Skt. *pā* 'drink' was originally perfective and therefore formed a derived present; it is also possible to argue that originally non-indicative modal forms of this verb were formed only to the root stem. On the other hand, from earliest Vedic on there is no discernible aspectual difference between *pāhi* and *piba*, both second-singular imperative. Indeed, the one formation where Vedic exhibits a clear aspectual contrast is the negative imperative with *mā*: a prohibitive imperative of the type *mā vadhīḥ* 'don't kill', with an aorist injunctive, is opposed to an imperative meaning 'stop ...' (e.g. *mā dīvyaḥ* 'stop gambling'), with a present injunctive. This opposition was described definitively by Karl Hoffmann (1967); see also Cardona (1972). In early Vedic already, the verbal system was essentially temporally oriented, without aspectual contrasts connected directly with verbal morphology: *pibati* '... drinks, ... is drinking': *apāt* '... drank, has drunk'. It is difficult, however, to envision a comparable temporal contrast involving imperatives like *piba*, *pāhi*. In a derivational system like Pāṇini's, where one starts with meanings and these serve as conditions for introducing affixes, a consequence of this is that *pibati* and *apāt* can be treated as totally distinct derivates with different semantics but *piba* and *pāhi* have to be treated as alternative forms with the same signification. Thus, Pāṇini derives *pibati* from *pā-l*, with the L-affix ***laṭ***, introduced on condition that the action is spoken of as current (**A** 3.2.123: *vartamāne laṭ*), but *apāt* from *pā-l*, with the L-affix ***luṅ***, introduced on condition that the action is referred to past time (**A** 3.2.110: *luṅ* [*bhūte* 84]). The abstract affix *cli* is introduced after a verbal base accompanied by endings that replace ***luṅ*** (**A** 3.1.43: *cli luṅi*), and this is subject to replacement by ***sic*** and other affixes. After *pā* and several other verbs that form what western grammarians call root aorist active forms, however, ***sic*** is deleted before parasmaipada endings (**A** 2.4.77: *gātisthāghupābhūbhyaḥ sicaḥ parasmaipadeṣu* [*luk* 58]). On the other hand, *piba* and *pāhi* are both derived from *pā-l*, with ***loṭ*** introduced on condition that a command to an agent is to be signified (**A** 3.3.162: *loṭ ca* [*vidhi* ... 161]). The regular form in the language of Pāṇini's time is *piba*, derived as follows: *pā-l* → *pā-si* → *pā-hi* → *pā-a-hi* → ... *pib-a-hi* → *piba*. To account for Vedic *pāhi* as opposed to *piba*, Pāṇini lets *luk* replace ***śap*** of *pā-a-hi* (**A** 2.4.73: *bahulaṁ chandasi* [*śapaḥ* 72, *luk* 58]). The zero designated *luk* is such that the operations that would apply in the presence of an affix to the stem of that affix do not apply in its absence, so that *pā-* in *pā-hi* is not replaced by *piba.* Mutatis mutandis, other Vedic modal forms of aorist and perfect stems are comparably accounted for, as Palsule notes (1991b:61). Palsule also remarks (1991b:62), 'Pāṇini's treatment of Vedic modal forms is not as exhaustive, or even as sufficient, as in other topics', then gives what he considers the principal reason for this: 'The main reason for this deficiency is that the formation of any common tense stem, as a primary step, on which various moods could be formed, is not recognized in the Pāṇinian system.' Since Pāṇini describes the language of his time and formulates special rules to account for earlier Vedic usage that differs from this and since his derivational system starts with semantics, I respectfully beg to differ. That Pāṇini does not start out with separate present and aorist stems like *piba* and *pā* and enumerate forms of the indicative, imperative, and so on for each stem is not a fault; it is a function of his derivational system, which does not begin with form classes. To be sure, one may argue, as Palsule does (1991b:63), 'But, it must be submitted, in grammar, form is at least as important as, if not more important than meaning and this similarity of form, say between *abhūt* or *bhūt* with *bhūyāt* should have been sufficient for him to reach a finer distinction.' On the other hand, Pāṇini does indeed relate all such forms, within a single verbal base *bhū*. He just does not proceed in the manner that a western linguist might. This in itself does not, I think, constitute a deficiency.

Anjanī Kumārī (1990-91) takes up briefly Pāṇini's treatment of Vedic subjunctive forms, derived with endings replacing the L-affix *leṭ*.

Two recent interesting papers by M. M. Deshpande (1991f, g) deal with uses of infinitives as described by Pāṇini in comparison with Vedic usage. K. Meenakshi (1991b) also deals with this topic.

Manjul Manyank (1991) takes up evidence to demonstrate that Pāṇini was well acquainted with the Atharvaveda.

A 7.2.31-33: *hru hvarateś chandasi*, *aparihvṛtāś ca*, *some hvaritaḥ* provide for particular substitutions in the base *hvṛ* 'become crooked, go crooked' in participial forms that occur in Vedic usage: *hru-* in *hruta-* (past ptcple.), *hvṛta-* in *aparihvṛtās*, and *hvarita-* used with reference to Soma. Hoffmann (1980) dealt in detail with the Vedic passages involving forms for which these rules account. As in an earlier article (see Cardona [1976a:226]), here too Hoffmann considered the possibility that Pāṇini refers to a mantra of the Mānavaśrautasūtra. He also speculated that Pāṇini refers to the domain of usage for the form in question as *chandasi* because of the ritual use of the mantra in which *hvarita-* occurs.

Cardona (1991b) presents evidence to maintain anew that Pāṇini definitely knew Śākalya's padapāṭha to the Ṛgveda and to support the position that Pāṇini not only knew the text of the Ṛgveda but that he also accepted certain particular interpretations of commentaries that must have been available to him. Cardona (1993b) has also given evidence to demonstrate that Kielhorn was justified in accepting that the bhāṣika accentual system, attested best in the Śatapathabrāhmaṇa, represents a real change in the language.[81] In addition, Cardona has shown how, starting with the replacement of svarita syllables by udātta syllables — a change vouched for by Pāṇini — one can account for the details described in the Bhāṣikasūtra.[82]

Balasubrahmanyam (1975, 1976, 1979, 1981a, b, c, 1983b) has continued to study Pāṇinian accentual rules and Vedic evidence, particularly in connection with kṛdanta derivates.[83] Balasubrahmanyam (1984) nicely shows how Pāṇini's description helps decide in favor of a textual reading supported by the padapāṭha and traditional recitation, despite the reading found in most manuscripts. In his summary, Balasubrahmanyam concludes (1984:27), 'Since the suffixation and accentuation of the Vedic derivatives can be satisfactorily explained in the light of P.'s rules, *subhagaṁ-káraṇī* is the genuine *Saṁhitā* reading at *AV* **6**, 139, 1-b.' He goes on to remark that, through a careful application of Pāṇini's rules and principles of textual criticism, he has been able to demonstrate the validity of this reading and that '... a special *niche* must be allotted to P.'s rules in scrutinising problems concerning Vedic morphology including accentuation ....'

Palsule (1982) deals with two rules traditionally not considered to apply only for Vedic usage, considers Vedic evidence, and concludes that at least **A** 8.3.10 was indeed originally intended to account for Vedic usage alone.

Although they are not devoted to Pāṇini's grammar specifically, Michael Witzel's monograph (1989) and its complement (1990) make frequent references to Pāṇinian rules in connection with usages ascribed to different areas.[84]

2.1.4.6b. *Other rules* (III.1.5.6b)

Rāmaprasāda Tripāṭhī (1987) is a collection of discussions about a large number of sūtras, concentrated on two types of rules: restrictions (*niyamasūtra*) and exceptions (*apavādasūtra*). The book also includes, in a section of the introduction (1987:16-25), an excellent discussion of the characteristics that determine a rule's being an exception to another rule.

Bhīma Siṁha (1996) takes up a selection of rules (e.g. **A** 1.1.23, 25; 3.3.40, 6.3.9) to illustrate commentators' discussions concerning brevity: whether the formulations in question could have been briefer and the reasons commentators have for discussing this.

Recently Ram Karan Sharma (1992) has very briefly touched on rules providing for replacement by zero. M. D. Pandit (1990) dealt more extensively with the topic.

Cardona (1976e) considers sūtras such as **A** 1.4.25: *bhītrārthānāṁ bhayahetuḥ*, which Pāṇinīyas have considered not strictly necessary and only intended to expatiate (*prapañcārtha*) on what is otherwise provided for by other rules. He concludes that this involves a trade off: the set of rules is reduced and the categories in question — in this instance the kāraka category named *apādāna* — are simplified, but the semantics of verbs like *bhī* ('be afraid') are made more complicated, in a manner which is not necessarily justified by usage.

Puṣpā Dīkṣita (1997) takes up the organization of sūtras which introduce L-affixes and related rules, suggesting a reorganization in how these should be taught. Ram Karan Sharma (1995) considers in particular three sūtras dealing with time references and the derivation of verb forms (**A** 3.2.84, 123, 3.3.3)

Śivakānta Jhā (1993) is a traditional and solid presentation of Pāṇini's derivations of terms with feminine affixes.

A. C. Sarangi (1976) studies sūtras in which Pāṇini provides for the derivation of terms signifying entities characterized by their nature or habit (*śīla*), with particular emphasis on the question why a set of kṛt affixes, introduced by rules under the heading of **A** 3.2.134: *ā kves tacchīlataddharmatatsādhukāriṣu*, not only provides for derivates signifying agents that perform acts habitually but also requires that the acts be referred to current time.

Hideyo Ogawa (1987) divides the use of the restrictive particle *eva* into six types and discusses these with illustrations.

Scharf (1995b) considers sūtras in which Pāṇini uses negative compounds of the type *anupasarge*, with particular attention to **A** 3.1.100 (*gadamadacarayamaś cānupasarge*) and what is said in the Kāśikā and its commentaries on *anupasarge* in this sūtra. Scharf argues that the interpretation wherein *anupasarge* is taken to be a bahuvrīhi compound, with a seventh-triplet ending in the value of a fifth-triplet ending, is unjustified. Instead, he accepts that *anupasarge* is an asamarthasamāsa designating the absence of a preverb. What Nāgeśa says concerning *anupasarge* merits having been mentioned. Nāgeśa remarks that paraphrasing *anupasarge* in a manner which implies a bahuvrīhi compound and an ablative instead of a locative is meant only to convey the implicit sense (*phalitārtha* 'meaning which results'), not the literal meaning of the term. For example, in his Siddhāntakaumudī (Giridhara Śarmā Caturveda and Parameśvaranānanda Śarmā Bhāskara [1958-61:IV.45]) on **A** 3.2.3 (*āto' nupsarge kaḥ*), Bhaṭṭoji paraphrases the sūtra using the phrase *ādantād dhātor anupasargāt* ('after a verbal base that ends in *ā* and does not have a preverb'). In his Laghuśabdenduśekhara, Nāgeśa remarks that *anupasarge* means 'when there is the absence of a preverb' and then notes that Bhaṭṭoji's paraphrase with *anupasargāt* only conveys what results from this literal meaning.[85] Similarly, although the Bṛhacchabdenduśekhara on the Siddhāntakaumudī's paraphrase of **A** 3.1.100 mentions the use of a locative instead of an ablative, it does so only after first noting that *anupasarge* denotes the absence of a preverb, which, by proximity, is connected with the verbs given.[86] Moreover, Nāgeśa remarks that *anupasarge* is an avyayībhāva compound. That is, it is a compound formed by **A** 2.1.6 (see Cardona [1997a:209 (**304**)]), and the locative ending is optionally retained as provided for in **A** 2.4.84 (Cardona [1997a:212 (**307**)]).

V. V. Bhandare (1996) presents a very general treatment of dvandva compounds and their number and gender features.

The rule **A** 6.1.77: *iko yaṇ aci* provides for vowels denoted by ***ik*** to be replaced by semivowels (*yaṇ*) before vowels (*ac*). The abbreviatory terms ***ik***, ***yaṇ*** and ***ac***, formed in accordance with **A** 1.1.71: *ādir antyena sahetā*, denote respectively the sounds of the sets *i u ṛ ḷ*, *y v r l* and *a i u ṛ ḷ e o ai au*. By **A** 1.1.69: *aṇudit savaraṇasya cāpratyayaḥ* each of these sounds in turn is a class name that denotes a set of sounds homogeneous with itself. In addition, **A** 1.3.10: *yathāsaṁkhyam anudeśaḥ samānām* and **A** 1.1.50: *sthāne'ntaramaḥ* come into consideration. The former provides that elements stated subsequently in a rule are related in the order of occurrence to those stated earlier, if the two sets of elements are the same in number. According to **A** 1.1.50, if a choice of replacements is possible for a single substituend, that one occurs which is closest to the original. The question arises whether **A** 1.3.10 or **A** 1.1.50 should apply in interpreting **A** 6.1.77. Under the first alternative, the sounds *i u ṛ ḷ* and *y v r l* are first related in order, and these vowels and semivowels thus related then refer to classes of sounds. Under the second alternative, these vowels and semivowels are first considered to refer to classes of sounds, so that **A** 1.3.10 cannot come into play because the number of elements in one group is different from that of the other. Hence, **A** 1.1.50 comes in to determine the proper replacements for individual vowels. Hueckstedt (1995) deals thoroughly with these alternative interpretations as found in the commentatorial literature.[87] He considers not only Pāṇinīyas but also prātiśākhyas (1995:35-53), non-Pāṇinian grammars (1995:67-78), and the views of modern scholars (1995:129-136).

Jayadev M. Shukla (1983) took up Pāṇinian rules concerning the replacement of *n* by retroflex *ṇ*. The same topic is discussed again in some detail by Hari Narayana Tiwari (1988), who has also taken up (1989) Pāṇini's use of the marker *m* in both affixes and augments.

Ayodhya Chandra Dass has devoted a short paper (1988) to Pāṇini's treatment of accentual features. Thieme (1985a) considers a set of rules (in particular **A** 6.2.75-81) that, contrary to the general rule, provide for the first vowel of the prior member of a tatpuruṣa compound to be high-pitched if there follows a second constituent derived with particular affixes; e.g. *chátradhāra-* 'one who has been placed in the position of bearing the umbrella'. Thieme notes (1985a:241) that this type results from a relatively recent innovation, involving accent retraction, and argues that the accentuation reflects influence of vocative forms on the derivates in question.

S. D. Joshi (1976b) takes up **A** 1.4.49-51 along with the discussions by commentators and concludes (1976b:70-71) that the last of these sūtras may not have been part of the original Aṣṭādhyāyī. Joshi has also argued (1989a) that **A** 1.1.58 is a later insertion, remarking (1989a:228), 'As a matter of fact, we can dispense with the whole rule P. 1.1.58.'

M. M. Deshpande (1981c) again takes up **A** 7.3.73: *lug vā duhadihaliha-guhām ātmanepade dantye* and argues against Kiparsky's suggestion (1979:166-167) that Pāṇini used *dantye* instead of *tau* in order to include an ending with initial *r*-: *aduhranta*, *aduhran* (3rd pl.). I think Deshpande is correct, since *adhuhran* is an imperfect, not an aorist form. Deshpande's own study ends on an indecisive note: although he cannot accept the Pāṇinīya interpretation according to which Pāṇini used *dantye* to include the dual ending *vahi*, he himself is unable to suggest any definite solution.

Scharfe (1981) considers **A** 1.4.96: *padārthasambhāvanānvavasarga-garhāsamuccayeṣu* and claims that Pāṇinīyas have wrongly interpreted this sūtra.

Hejib and Sharma (1981) consider the historical background for the process whereby *-ā-* and a following *ṛ* are both replaced by *-ar-* (e.g. *maharṣi*), as accounted for by **A** 6.1.87 (*ād guṇaḥ*).

V. M. Bhatt (1985) gives a detailed analysis of **A** 2.1.1: *samarthaḥ padavidhiḥ*, considering the meanings of the terms in the sūtra and the purpose for this rule, with references to Kātyāyana, other Pāṇinīyas and scholars of other schools as well as modern commentators, especially S. D. Joshi (1968a).

Bhīma Siṁha (1988) takes up **A** 1.1.5: *kṅiti ca*. In the course of his discussion, the author justifies the traditional interpretation according to which this rule disallows guṇa and vṛddhi substitutions which would otherwise be conditioned by affixes if these affixes are marked with *k*, *g* or *ṅ*; on this point, see also Cardona (1997a:xiii-xiv). In addition, Bhīma Siṁha discusses Pāṇini's use of the marker *ṅ* with L-affixes. Earlier, Bhimasiṁha Vedālaṅkāra (1984) dealt in great detail with **A** 1.1.4.

V. M. Bhatt (1988) discusses anew the use of the term *hetu* in two sūtras, **A** 2.3.23 and **A** 2.3.25.

A. M. Ghatage (1991-92) reaches the conclusion that the meaning of *sāmīpye* in **A** 8.1.7: *uparyadhyadhasaḥ sāmīpye* is 'the quality of being in close proximity in the activity in the direction of above (with अधि and परि) and below (with अधः) and can be rendered by such English expression as 'higher and higher' and 'lower and lower', but without the component of comparison which is present in the English expression.'

S. M. Katre (1991) considers the headings that provide for operations in close juncture (*saṁhitāyām*) and the reasons for having such separate groups of rules.

K. Kunjunni Raja (1991) deals briefly with the sūtra according to which word-final anusvāra is optionally replaced by a sound homogeneous with a following semivowel or stop.

S. Sankaranarayana (1992) treats **A** 1.4.30: *janikartuḥ prakṛtiḥ* in detail and considers not only what Pāṇinīyas — in particular Jinendrabuddhi — have to say about this sūtra, but also what Navyanaiyāyikas have said. He concludes (1992:156-157) that Pāṇini's rule shows Sāṅkhya influence, that *prakṛti* here signifies 'a thing that is both the maker and the material of its effect', and that the sūtra says, 'the efficient-cum-material cause of what is being born is ablative.'

Girish K. Jha (1992) takes up **A** 6.1.101 to show that, contrary to what Bhaṭṭoji proposes, the sūtra as formulated is proper.

Gurusankar Mukherji's study (1992) of **A** 1.2.64: *sarūpāṇam ekaśeṣa ekavibhaktau* is far ranging and, in my opinion, diffuse, though I refrain from any discussion here; see Cardona (1997a:260 [**373-374**]).

A. N. Pandey (1997) discusses **A** 3.4.21. The author's main point is that what is meant by *samānakartṛka* has not been accurately understood.

2.1.4.7. *Comparisons of Pāṇini's system with other systems*

2.1.4.7a. *Comparisons with other Indian systems* (III.1.5.7a)

Prafulla Chandra Dash's work (1986) is the fullest recent treatment of Pāṇini's grammar compared with the Cāndravyākaraṇa. I consider Dash's second chapter ('Scheme and treatment of the two grammars' [26-69]) particularly worthy of note. Indu Davesar (1985) has carried out a comparative study of sūtras in the Aṣṭādhyāyī and the Jainendravyākaraṇa.

G. B. Palsule (1991a) deals briefly with evidence in the Mahābhāṣya and in Bhartṛhari's Mahābhāṣyaṭīkā (Dīpikā) reflecting the view that in deriving verb forms with vikaraṇas — the type *bhav-a-ti* — the vikaraṇa was introduced first to signify an agent, object or action, then personal endings followed the vikaraṇa.

Saroja Bhate (1981) contrasts Pāṇini's and Yāska's approaches, noting that the latter places less emphasis on grammatical regularity. Bronkhorst

(1981b), on the other hand, sees Pāṇini and Yāska sharing two major presuppositions: that meanings of nominal words are combinations of meanings of constituents and that constituent meanings are not assigned by convention.

Cardona (1975a) considers the ways in which Pāṇinīyas, Mīmāṁsakas and Naiyāyikas paraphrase sentences and how they relate these paraphrases to the meanings they attribute to bases and affixes. Pradip Kumar Mazumdar (1977:62-82) also takes up in an insightful way the critiques to which Pāṇinīyas like Kauṇḍabhaṭṭa and Nāgeśa subjected the views of Mīmāṁsakas and Naiyāyikas. Vidhātā Miśra (1988-89) gives a brief summary of major views held by Pāṇinian grammarians, Mīmāṁsakas and Naiyāyikas concerning what verbal bases signify. Revathy Sukumar (1997) too deals with a topic as treated by Pāṇinīyas, Mīmāṁsakas and Naiyāyikas.

M. M. Deshpande (1981a) considers constructions of the type *rāmo grāmaṁ gatvā jalam pibati* 'Rama drinks water after going to the village' as they are dealt with not only by Kātyāyana, Patañjali and Bhartṛhari but also by a famous Bhāṭṭa Mīmāṁsaka, Khaṇḍadeva. In an earlier paper, Deshpande (1978b) considers aspects of properties which allow sentences to be appropriate, from the points of view of Naiyāyikas and grammarians. On the Naiyāyikas' concepts of pada and vākya, see recently V. N. Jha (1980), who (1986:54-69, 1991) has also dealt with differences between Pāṇinian grammarians and Naiyāyikas with respect to compounds and their semantics.

V. P. Bhatta (1990) takes up views of Patañjali, Nāgeśa and Gadādhara concerning whether accusative endings used with terms denoting distance and time are to be treated as kāraka-vibhakti. Grammarians' and Naiyāyikas' views concerning karaṇa are taken up by Adyityanath Bhattacharya (1988). Other recent papers dealing with issues that contrast views of Pāṇinian grammarians and Naiyāyikas are Jayashree Gune (1980), V. N. Jha (1991) and B. K. Matilal (1991). Pāṇinian grammarians and Naiyāyikas also differ concerning whether some particles (*nipāta*) should be considered signifiers (*vācaka*) of certain meanings and other particles merely cosignifiers (*dyotaka*) of meanings attributed to items with which they are used or whether all particles should be treated as cosignifiers only. Pratap Bandyopadhyay (1981) and Viśvanātha Miśra (1993) deal with these issues.

Śaṅkara frequently speaks of anvaya and vyatireka, which some modern scholars characterized vaguely as a kind of meditation procedure. Cardona (1981a) has argued, principally on the basis of the Upadeśasāhasrī, that in early Advaita, reasoning by anvaya and vyatireka was used to establish that something is the cause of something else, as in grammar and other spheres.

Cardona (1996b) contrasts the treatment of sequences like *di̱ve dìve* 'day after day, each and every day' in Pāṇini's grammar and in padapāṭhas. Padakāras like Śākalya treated these as compounds, but Pāṇini accounts for them through doubling of a syntactic element.[88] Cardona argues that Pāṇini could not treat *di̱ve dìve* and so on as compounds because he operated with the procedure whereby a single element of two or more homophonous elements which could be combined alone remains (*ekaśeṣa*) if one is to use a single ending. Śākalyas's treating this type as a compound reflects that he did not operate with the ekaśeṣa procedure.[89]

Vijayapāla (1983) considers the Aṣṭādhyāyī and Kātyāyana's prātiśākhya to the white Yajurveda. Karunasindhu Das (1986) includes a chapter (II, pp. 6-21) dealing with paribhāṣās in major prātiśākhya works compared with Pāṇinian paribhāṣās. A recent work dealing with Pāṇini and prātiśākhyas is by Pradyot Kumar Datta (1994). Some of the materials Datta considers afford better opportunities for pertinent comparisons than others. For example, the discussions of sandhi (1994:48-58) and paribhāṣās (1994:59-66) have good bases for comparisons, but the section on verb forms (1994:75-83), with its emphasis on L-affixes, offers less opportunity for meaningful comparisons. Extensive comparisons between the Aṣṭādhyāyī and prātiśākhyas also appear in annotations in M. M. Deshpande (1997b).

Ananthanarayana (1986b) and K. Meenakshi (1984) compare Pāṇini and Tolkappiyar.[90] Rajam Ramamurti (1983) more specifically considers how Pāṇinian classifications and associated terminology borrowed into two post-Tolkappiyam grammars of Tamil undergo changes and affect the description.

In his meticulous study of Aggavaṁsa's chapter dealing with kārakas (*kārakakappa*), Kahrs (1992a) includes frequent references to and discussions of pertinent sūtras of the Aṣṭādhyāyī and commentaries thereon.

2.1.4.7b. *Comparisons with modern systems and techniques* (III.1.5.7b)

Ananthanarayana (1976:63-82) considers several parallels between Pāṇini and modern linguists and remarks (1976:82), 'To sum up, we may say that Pa:ṇini has foreshadowed many of the developments that we claim for modern linguistics.' Ananthanarayana treats parallels in the formulation of phonological rules, compound formation, and the formation of derivates with taddhita affixes.[91]

M. M. Deshpande (1994-95, see also 1997d) examines anew the phonetic features with which Pāṇini operates, along with their background in śikṣā, and considers these in comparison with modern phonology.

Achyutananda Dash (1991) draws parallels between what Pāṇini does and procedures in relational grammar. As I have noted earlier (see section 2.1.4.5b.1), I do not consider his basic claim about the status of *adhi* to be justified.

Vrashabh Prasad Jain (1989-90) considers Pāṇini's kāraka classes and modern case grammar. As has been pointed out previously (see Cardona [1976a:233]), there are some parallels, but the differences are just as important.[92]

Achyutananda Dash (1992) deals summarily with verbal cognition (*śābdabodha*) as envisioned by theoreticians of Navyanyāya, Navya-vyākaraṇa, and Mīmāṁsā, with its links to syntax and semantics. Dash proceeds then (1992:49-50) to compare these ideas with a knowledge representation scheme. He also incidentally gives (1992:52-55) a brief critique of Bhavānanda's proposal on the dependency of the *kārakas* (1992:53).

M. M. Deshpande (1992e) attempts to draw some parallels between Pāṇini's grammar, its goal and procedures, and some ideals of modern grammatical theories and computer science. As Deshpande himself acknowledges, the parallels remain of a very general nature, and there are also major differences.

It is always interesting to seek out intellectual ancestors of modern scholars. In my opinion, Rogers' study (1987) of Bloomfield and Pāṇini is generally well informed and worthwhile.[93]

2.1.4.8. *The language described by Pāṇini* (III.1.5.8a)

An important recent study on Pāṇini's language is M. M. Deshpande (1992c), in which the author discusses such issues as various domains of usage, whether Pāṇini's Sanskrit was a first or second language, who spoke Sanskrit to whom, and whether Pāṇini's bhāṣā was a koiné. Deshpande takes up related issues in chapters of his recent collection (1993a) and in earlier articles (1979a,b, 1991h); see also Hock and Pandharipande (1976, 1978). In general, I think Deshpande's discussions are well balanced and carry the right emphasis.[94] There can be no doubt, for example, that, at least by the time of Patañjali, Sanskrit as described in the Aṣṭādhyāyī was not used as the ordinary general medium of communication in every day circumstances and that Prakrit vernaculars also were in use. It is this situation which explains, Cardona has suggested (1990a), how the use of correct Sanskrit as described in Pāṇini's grammar came to have such a strong moral value, serving to gain merit for one who used proper Sanskrit speech forms and also had a knowledge of the grammar describing these.

On the other hand, I do not think one can doubt that Pāṇini describes a living language which at his time and in his area was used for ordinary discourse, albeit in a diglossic situation, and that this language continued to be used currently in certain kinds of discourse at the times of Kātyāyana and Patañjali. Thus, in Cardona (forthcoming i) I take up rules like **A** 3.2.75: *anyebhyo'pi dṛśyante*, in which Pāṇini states that certain affixes also occur after other items than those provided for, that certain affixes are introduced also when cooccurring items other than those given are used with verbs, or that vowel lengthening applies to items other than those given as subject to this substitution. These are what I would call 'escape rules'. I view such rules as additional evidence that Pāṇini describes a living language used by speakers carrying out changes such that Pāṇini could not specify the precise domains in which certain operations apply. I also note that this is related to another kind of rule dealing with indeterminacy: rules which provide that something applies variously (*bahulam*). This type of rule deals with indeterminate variation in a specifiable domain.

S. D. Joshi views the situation differently. In a recent study (1989b), he deals with several famous passages from the Mahābhāṣya that concern the use of incorrect speech forms and concludes as follows (1989b:274):

> The conclusion is that Sanskrit has stopped being a generally spoken language before 600 or 700 B.C. It is preserved as a literary language and as the second language for a relatively small group. The Prākrit vernaculars are spoken in private talk since long days.

Even couched in cautious terms as it is, this conclusion seems excessive to me. Although the evidence leaves no doubt at all that Prākrits were indeed used as vernaculars in ordinary communication from very early on, I also cannot doubt that Pāṇini describes details of usage — such as the elongation and high pitch of the last vowel of an utterance when answering a salutation (**A** 8.2.83: *pratyabhivāde'sūdre*) or when calling some one from afar (**A** 8.2.84: *dūrāddhūte ca*) — which pertain to a language that served as an active medium of communication. This point was made some time ago; see Keith (1920a:8-17) and, more recently, Laddu (1974:4-5), Sarangi (1985:5-6). In addition, as I noted above, there are rules in the Aṣṭādhyāyī which are best understood as accounting for usages in a language which was in flux.

Deshpande has emphasized the 'northwest perspective' (Deshpande [1985c:59]) of Pāṇini, whom he views as a 'frontier grammarian' (Deshpande [1983a:39, 1983b]). I have one minor doubt concerning what he says. Deshpande states (1978a:63), 'The two broad divisions of the Sanskrit speaking region mentioned by Pāṇini are *udīcya* 'northern' and *prācya* 'eastern', with the river Sutlaj (Skt. ŚARĀVATĪ) in Punjab as the dividing line between these two domains.' He cites (Deshpande [1978a:63 note 3]) the verse which the Kāśikā on **A** 1.1.75 gives and here again identifies the Śarāvatī to which the Kāśikā refers as the modern Satlaj. Later (1985c:59), Deshpande again identifies the Śarāvatī with the Satlaj and says (1985c:59 note 2), 'Since the *Kāśikāvṛtti* refers to Śarāvatī, it most likely must not be the mythical river Sarasvatī. V. S. Agrawal 1953:38 says that "it may probably be identified with the Dṛṣadvatī or Chitāṅg flowing through Ambala district." It seems likely that it is the same as the Satlaj.' Deshpande does not, however, give any reasons for his identification; nor does he mention the Śutudrī, which is generally considered identical with the modern Satlaj.

Bronkhorst (1982b:282) has again emphasized that the language Pāṇini describes approximates the language reflected in brāhmaṇas like the Aitareyabrāhmaṇa; see Cardona (1976a:238). More recently, in a lecture ("Remembering the past: late Vedic preterite forms and Pāṇini's language") presented at the sixteenth East Coast Indo-European Conference on June 13th 1997, Cardona has demonstrated that the use of aorist, imperfect, and perfect forms in the Śāṅkhāyanaśrautasūtra's telling of the Śunaḥśepha legend matches Pāṇini's usage perfectly and the use of these forms in the Aitareyabrāhmaṇa's telling of the same legend matches this almost perfectly, thus buttressing the view of Pāṇini's language maintained by Liebich and Bhandarkar.

The usual conception of what *bhāṣā* (loc. sg. *bhāṣāyām*) refers to in the Aṣṭādhyāyī is a spoken language opposed to more archaic usage, which is attested in earlier Vedic texts and to which Pāṇini makes general reference using the locative singular *chandasi*. In his work on Vedic citations in the Mahābhāṣya, Rau (1985:103-105) makes an interesting suggestion concerning the opposition *bhāṣāyām* : *chandasi*. According to Rau, these do not refer to two mutually exclusive opposites. Instead, they concern extremes of a continuum: *chandasi* refers to what is unambiguously an archaism, *bhāṣāyām* to usage that is unambiguously innovating. What falls between these — and for which there is no single name — is the language described by Pāṇini.[95]

2.2. THE MAHĀBHĀṢYA

2.2.1. *Editions and translations of the Mahābhāṣya and its commentaries*

2.2.1.1. *Editions* (III.2.2.1)

No new edition of the Mahābhāṣya based on any fresh manuscript studies has appeared.[96] Daunting as the task surely would be, it would be a wonderful thing to have a new edition based on Kielhorn's work and additional evidence from new manuscripts and testimonia, especially from South India, as Aklujkar has pointed out (1993a:31-32). In the section of his index to Vedic citations in the Mahābhāṣya where he gives the conclusions one can reach on the basis of the data to which he devotes his index, Rau makes the important point (1985:101-102) that evident errors in the textual transmission of some citations lead to concluding that Kielhorn had asserted too much when he said no evidence had been adduced to show that the text of the Mahābhāṣya as known from the manuscript materials available to him was not the original text of this work.[97] The issue of the archetype of the Mahābhāṣya in relation to Kielhorn's edition as well as Bhartṛhari's work, the Kāśikā and the Pradīpa has again been studied by Bronkhorst (1987b:14-42).

An example of textual difficulty is studied by V. B. Bhagavat (1991). The text under consideration occurs in the Bhāṣya on **A** 1.1.70: *taparas tatkālasya* and has to do with an example given to illustrate how a speech unit (*śabdaḥ*) is sphoṭa and physical sound (*dhvaniḥ*) is an accessory property of a speech unit; that is, the true speech unit is sphoṭa and the physical sound one hears serves to make manifest the sphoṭa. This is compared to the striking of a drum. What is meant by the example is obvious. When a drum is struck, there is a sound, and that sound can be heard at a distance of twenty, thirty, or forty paces. The sound remains what it is, and the relative distance at which it is heard is a function of the physical reverberation. On the other hand, there are syntactic problems which were obvious to commentators. The text in Kielhorn's edition (1880-85:I.181.19-22) is: *evaṁ tarhi sphoṭaḥ śabdo dhvaniḥ śabdaguṇaḥ | katham | bheryāghātavat | tad yathā bheryāghātaḥ | bherīm āhatya kaścid viṁśati padāni gacchati kaścit triṁśat kaścic catvāriṁśat | sphoṭaś ca tāvān eva bhavati dhvanikṛtā vṛddhiḥ.* As can be seen, *viṁśati* and *padāni* are printed as separate words. This is true also in Guruprasāda Śāstrī's edition (Bal Shastri [1988a: 531a]) and the Rohatak edition (Vedavrata [1962-63:I.539-540]). In the Nirnaya-Sagar Press edition (Bhārgavaśāstrī Joshi [1951:564a]), on the other hand, one has *viṁsatipadāni*, a compound, printed *viṁśati-padāni* because the term is distributed between two lines. In his annotations to the revision of Kielhorn's edition, K. V. Abhyankar remarks (I.567-568):

> The word विंशति, printed separately from पदानि, as done by Dr. Kielhorn, cannot be defended. The words विंशति and पदानि should be printed together as a compound word, or विंशतिं should be read for विंशति. Thus, although विंशतिपदानि can be explained, त्रिंशत् and चत्वारिंशत् cannot be defended. The wording should have been कश्चित् त्रिंशतं कश्चिच्चत्वारिंशतम् । Perhaps त्रिंशत् and चत्वारिंशत् and विंशति also, could be looked upon as words used in the neuter gender.

This is the topic with which Bhagavat deals. He considers the two readings noted and a third reading, *viṁśatiṁ padāni,* found in one manuscript. Strictly speaking, only this last reading is justifiable, since *viṁśati-* is feminine and a compound *viṁśatipada-* is not supported by Pāṇinian composition rules. Yet the manuscript evidence speaks for the reading adopted by Kielhorn. Bhagavat considers this to be the result of a corruption by a scribe who, on the basis of the neuter qualificand *padāni*, assumed that one should have a neuter qualifier *viṁśati*, assuming also that number words from *viṁśati-* on were necessarily singular but not necessarily feminine. And this reading was later adopted by editors.[98]

V. P. Limaye (1978:727-730) suggested that the reading *ākumāraṁ yaśaḥ pāṇineḥ* ('Pāṇini's fame reaches up to and includes young boys') in the Bhāṣya on **A** 1.4.89 might be emended to *ākumāri yaśaḥ pāṇineḥ*, referrring to a place — Cape Camorin — to which Pāṇini's fame extended. Wezler (1992) has shown that the emendation is uncalled for and unjustified.

Wezler also took up (1982) a short passage from the Mahābhāṣya, refuting an earlier treatment by Scharfe (1961:155).

Cardona (1998) investigates the syntax of *kiṁ tarhi* and demonstrates, on the basis of how *kas tarhi* and other comparable forms are used, that in a large number of passages where editors write *kiṁ tarhi* as a separate utterance — a question — this is instead an adversative complex introducing an assertion contrary to something said before. *kiṁ tarhi* thus used plays the same role as *kiṁ tu*, which is absent in Kielhorn's edition of the Mahābhāṣya. The total absence of a sentence-initial adversative term would be puzzling in view of the argumentative style of the text.

Vārttika 2 on **A** 6.3.3 as usually accepted reads *puṁsānujo januṣāndho vikṛtākṣa iti ca.* Since the sūtra in question provides for retention of a third-triplet ending in a prior member of a compound, *vikṛtākṣa* at first sight does not appear to fit. In fact, the Kāśikā on **A** 6.3.3 says *puṁsānujo januṣāndha iti vaktavyam*, and the Siddhāntakaumudī (960, Giridhara Śarmā Caturveda and Parameśvarānanda Śarmā Bhāskara [1958-61:II.231]) has *puṁsānujo januṣāndha iti ca.* Nāgeśa (Uddyota [Vedavrata (1962-63:IV. 585)]) notes two possible ways of accounting for the vārttika as it stands. First, *vikṛtākṣaḥ* is not an independent compound to be added under the sūtra; it is, instead, part of a phrase including the explicatory term *vikṛtākṣaḥ*. According to others, however, *vikṛtā* is an instrumental form of *vikṛt* (*vikṛtā* 'with deformation'), an action noun derived with the affix ***kvip***, so that *vikṛtākṣaḥ* is an additional compound meaning 'one who has an eye that is characterized by deformation'. Bhīmasiṁha Vedalaṅkara (1988b) argues that *vikṛtākṣaḥ* is the result of interpolation.[99]

I think it proper to note the republication of two editions. The Varanasi edition with Guru Prasāda Śāstrī's notes has been re-edited by Bal Shastri (1987, 1988a). The incomplete Nirnaya-Sagar Press edition (Bhārgavaśāstrī Joshi [1942, 1945, 1951], Śivadatta Kudāla [1912], Raghunātha Śarmā-Śivadatta Kudāla [1935, 1937]) has been reprinted (Delhi: Chaukhamba Sanskrit Pratishthan: 1987-88) and the seventh and eighth adhyāyas added (Dadhiram Sharma [1988]). The second volume is a reprint of the first edition instead of the second edition (Raghunātha (Kāśīnātha) Śāstrī and Śivadatta D. Kudāla [1935]), and the last volume, comprising the last two adhyāyas, is a copy of Guru Prasāda Śāstrī's edition without the footnotes.

The extant parts of Bhartṛhari's Mahābhāṣyadīpikā have been edited and translated into English with annotations by several scholars: V. P. Limaye, G. B. Palsule and V. B. Bhagavat (1985); G. B. Palsule (1985a, 1988); V. B. Bhagavat and Saroja Bhate (1986, 1990); Bronkhorst (1987a); G. V. Devasthali and G. B. Palsule (1989); G. B. Palsule and V. B. Bhagavat (1991). The Bhandarkar Oriental Research Institute has also published anonymously a facsimile of the sole manuscript available of this work (1980). In addition, Palsule (1993b) has presented in exemplary fashion some of the issues involved in editing the Dīpikā, to which a recent study is devoted (Savitā Pāthaka [1997]).

M. S. Narasimhacharya's monumental work of editing commentaries to the Mahābhaṣya and Kaiyaṭa's Pradīpa[100] was completed with the publication of the *Mahābhāṣyapradīpaprakāśa* of Pravartakopādhyāya (M. S. Narasimhacharya [1986]). The same editor has contributed a beautiful introduction highlighting particular aspects of each commentary.

2.2.1.2. *Translations* (III.2.2.2)

From 1968 on, for over twenty years, sections of the Mahābhāṣya were translated with annotations by S. D. Joshi and J. F. Roodbergen. The most recent part of this translation known to me is Joshi and Roodbergen (1989). Bibliographic details concerning the other sections translated by these scholars appear in Cardona (1976a, 1989:72) and in the bibliography of S. D. Joshi's writings compiled by M. M. Deshpande (Festschrift S. D. Joshi:323-331). In the preface to Joshi and Roodbergen (1989) the authors mention that the manuscript of the second part of their translation of the sthānivadbhāvāhnika was ready for publication in 1989, but I have not seen this. They also say that they will not translate any more of the Mahābhāṣya, having turned their attention to a translation of the Aṣṭādhyāyī.

Another ongoing project is the translation by Pierre-Sylvain Filliozat (1975-1986) of the Mahābhāṣya together with the Pradīpa and Uddyota; the latest installment I have seen is Filliozat (1986).

Hindi translations of sections of the Mahābhāṣya have continued to appear. Noteworthy are Yudhiṣṭhira Mīmāṁsaka (1972, 1974, 1979), Veda Prakāśa (1979), and Śivanārāyaṇa Śāstrī (1991).

Benson's book (1990) differs from the works mentioned above in that it deals with a single theme. This study includes translations and analyses of the greater part of what is said in the Mahābhāṣya concerning **A** 1.4.13 (*yasmāt pratyayavidhis tadādi pratyaye'ṅgam*), 6.4.1 (*aṅgasya*), 1.1.60 (*adarśanaṁ lopaḥ*), 1.1.62 (*pratyayalope pratyayalakṣaṇam*), 1.1.63 (*na lumatāṅgasya*), 4.1.36 (*pūtakrator ai ca*) and, in a short appendix (1990:232-239), the Bhāṣya on 4.2.72 (*matoś ca bahvajaṅgāt*), 8.2.27 (*hrasvād aṅgāt*), 8.3.78 (*iṇaḥ ṣīdhvaṁluṅliṭāṁ dho'ṅgāt*).

The initial parts of the Mahābhāṣya, in particular the Paspaśā, contain much discussion of a general nature concerning language and grammar. It is therefore understandable that there are quite a few translations of these. One such translation, which was done by Surendranatha Dasgupta many years ago but not published in his lifetime, has recently been edited by Sibajiban Bhattacharyya (Dasgupta [1991]).

Toru Yagi is devoting a series of articles to translating the Mahābhāṣya on 6.4.22-57 together with the Pradīpa and the Uddyota. The first five installments (1986, 1988, 1989a, b, 1991) cover **A** 6.4.22, the sixth installment (1994) **A** 6.4.23, and a subsequent paper (1995) deals with 6.4.24 vt. 1.

In a series of articles, Hideyo Ogawa (1988, 1989, 1992, 1993, 1994) is translating and annotating the Mahābhāṣya on **A** 1.3.1 with the Pradīpa and Uddyota. The texts are translated into and annotated in Japanese, with an English synopsis at the end of each installment. The articles thusfar published cover the texts through the section where it is explained that an action (*kriyā*) is something that can absolutely not be perceived directly and must be inferred.

2.2.2. *On the history of the Mahābhāṣya text* (III.2.4)

The history of the Mahābhāṣya, especially as portrayed in the concluding verse of the second kāṇḍa of the Vākyapadīya, continues to engage the attention of scholars, and there is a series of recent studies dealing with aspects of this topic: Cardona (1978b), Aklujkar (1981, 1982, 1991a), Laddu (1982, 1985b), Bronkhorst (1983:392-399, 1987b:14-42), Peri Sarveswara Sharma (1985/87).[101]

2.2.3. *General studies of the Mahābhāṣya* (III.2.5-III.2.6)

Two recent works deal with Kātyāyana's vārttikas in general: Satīśa Candra Jhā (1985) and Madhusudan Mishra (1996). Jhā concentrates to a great extent on the changes in the language after Pāṇini and how Kātyāyana dealt with these changes. Mishra deals with general topics concerning vārttikas,[102] but the major part of this work (chapter IV: Upasaṁkhyāna vārttikas [58-179]) concerns those vārttikas in which additions are proposed, generally using the term *upasaṅkhyāna*. Kamla Bharadvaj (1996) takes up ślokavārttikas in the Mahābhāṣya.

Laddu (1990) argues that vārttikas 3-5 on **A** 3.3.108 (*varṇāt kāraḥ*, *rād iphaḥ*, *matvarthāc chaḥ*) do not stem from Kātyāyana.

The first part of Filliozat (1991) gives a brief introduction to the Mahābhāṣya, deals with the characteristics of a śiṣṭa and ideal vaiyākaraṇa, then gives summary information on the commentaries and super-commentaries to the Mahābhāṣya.

Devaswarupa Miśra (1978) is a collection of twenty-three short essays in which the author discusses a wide range of topics brought up in the Mahābhāṣya. The discussions are characterized by a deep knowledge of the texts and the author's style is limpid.

Filliozat (1978) has studied the Ratnaprakāśa on **A** 1.1.56 to illustrate Śivarāmendra Sarasvatī's originality.

Baldeva Upadhyaya (1985b) has again taken up examples that use Devadatta to illustrate aspects of usage.[103] The same author (Upadhyaya [1985a]) has drawn attention to usage in Bhojpuri that is comparable to the use of *kṛ* meaning 'shampoo, clean', as illustrated in the Mahābhāṣya.[104]

For over a century, modern scholars have been concerned with determining what precisely are the initial vārttikas cited in the Mahābhāṣya. A brief summary of the bases for arguments will help to clarify what scholars have claimed. In Kielhorn's standard edition, the Mahābhāṣya begins (Kielhorn [1880-85:I:1.1]) with *atha śabdānuśāsanam* and immediately continues[105] with Patañjali's explanation of what the term *atha* means as used here. In the same edition, the first vārttika is *siddhe śabdārthasambandhe lokato'rthaprayukte śabdaprayoge śāstreṇa dharmaniyamo yathā laukikavaidikeṣu*, which Patañjali breaks up into three sections (Kielhorn [1880-85:I.6.16, 8.3, 8.7]) for discussion: *siddhe śabdārthasambandhe*, *lokato'rthaprayukte śabdaprayoge śāstreṇa dharmaniyamaḥ*, and *yathā laukikavaidikeṣu*. Among Pāṇinīyas it is recognized that *atha śabdānuśāsanam* is Patañjali's introduction to the grammar and that the first vārttika is as given above. Thus, Kaiyaṭa says that by saying *atha śabdānuśāsanam* Patañjali states the immediate purpose of the grammar.[106] Śivarāmendra Sarasvatī notes that Patañjali introduces the vārttika noted as the first vārttika, then goes on to explain that *siddhe śabdārthasambandhe* ... is a single vārttika, and concerning the same passage Nāgeśa remarks that the preceding text is Patañjali's.[107]

R. G. Bhandarkar (1876)[108], however, argued that *imāni prayojanāny adhyeyaṁ vyākaraṇam* (Kielhorn [1880-85:I.5.11]) too was a vārttika. The basis for Bhandarkar's conclusion was that in the Mahābhāṣya text known to him, this passage was preceded by *tebhya evaṁ vipratipannabuddhibhyo 'dhyetṛbhyo suhṛd bhūtvācārya idaṁ śāstram anvācaṣṭe.* He says (1933:137), 'The expression आचार्यः सुहृद्भूत्वान्वाचष्टे occurs in several places in the Mahābhāṣya, in all of which we have to understand Kātyāyana by the term आचार्य.' In addition, Bhandarkar (1933:139-140) considered that *atha śabdānuśāsanam* should be treated as a vārttika:

> And it appears to me that the opening words of the Mahābhāṣya: अथ शब्दानुशासनम् । are Kātyāyana's words, and form a Vārtika, notwithstanding what Kaiyaṭa says about them. For they are explained by Patañjali, just as all Vārtikas are; and to suppose that this alone of similar aphorisms was composed by him, and commented on with all the formality of a scholiast, is, I think, unreasonable. There appears no reason why in this particular case Patañjali should have resorted to this plan. If he wanted to say that he now began the Śabdānuśasanaśāstra, he might have done so more directly than by composing an aphorism and commenting on it.

Bhandarkar's premise about the expression *tad ācāryaḥ suhṛd bhūtvānvācaṣṭe* is faulty. As Bronkhorst has noted (1987b:7-8), in the Bhāṣya on **A** 1.2.32, this expression is used with reference to what Pāṇini does. In addition, textual support for Bhandarkar's conclusion regarding *imāni prayojanāny adhyeyaṁ vyākaraṇam* was eliminated with Kielhorn's critical edition, which reads (1880-85:I.5.10-11) *tebhya evaṁ vipratipanna-buddhibhyo 'dhyetṛbhya ācārya idaṁ śāstram anvācaṣṭe.* Kielhorn's apparatus criticus shows that what he considered his best manuscript, G, lacks the portion *'dhyetṛbhyo suhṛd bhūtvā.* One manuscript, g, has ऽध्येतृभ्यो सुहृद्भूत्वाचार्य and one other, C, has सुहृद्भूत्वा in the margin. It is widespread practice in paper manuscripts for a mark to be put at the place where a text portion given in a margin is to be inserted or for the number of the line where the insertion is to be made to be given along with the marginal addition. If, now, the latter procedure were followed, a marginal addition सुहृद्भूत्वा could then be placed in the text before आचार्य instead of the expected place. This is all the more understandable in that the usual phrase that occurs repeatedly (see R. G. Bhandarkar [1933:137], Bronkhorst [1987b:7 note 4]) is *tad ācāryaḥ suhṛd bhūtvānvācaṣṭe.* Hence, I think that Bronkhorst's attempt (1987b:7) to show that the absence of the words *suhṛd bhūtvā* in most of Kielhorn's manuscripts '... does not necessarily mean that they are a later addition' lacks support. Against the assumption that *suhṛd bhūtvā* was added on the basis of other places where *ācāryaḥ ... anvācaṣṭe* contained these terms, Bronkhorst says (1987b:7), 'If a scribe was knowledgeable enough to remember the usual co-occurrence of *ācāryaḥ anvācaṣṭe* and *suhṛd bhūtvā*, he should also remember that *suhṛd bhūtvā* comes always after *ācāryaḥ* and before *anvācaṣṭe.*' Bronkhorst also suggests (1987b:7), without supporting arguments, that *suhṛd bhūtvā* might have been expunged: 'The later tradition believed that there could be no vārttika on these early pages of the Mahābhāṣya, and this fact may have induced too observant scribes to drop the words that would prove the opposite.'

Joshi and Roodbergen (1986:३) give *atha śabdānuśāsanam* as the first vārttika, and they add parenthetically before this: (विषयप्रस्ताववार्त्तिकम्). In their translation (Joshi-Roodbergen [1986]:5), they also have '*1. (Vārttika : Introduction of the topic).*' Further, in note (2) to their translation, Joshi and Roodbergen say (1986:7):

> The words *atha śabdānuśāsanam* must be a *Vt.*, because they are commented upon by Patañjali. But tradition holds that they cannot be a *Vt.*, because Patañjali himself,

while commenting upon *siddhe śabdārthasaṁbandhe* (*Mbh.* I., p. 6, line 16), says that here the word *siddhe* is used for the sake of auspiciousness (*Mbh.* I., p. 6, line 28). Since *siddhe* is taken to be an auspicious word, this implies that it must stand at the beginning of a work. Therefore, according to Patañjali, *siddhe śabdārthasaṁbandhe* is the first *Vt*.

Joshi and Roodbergen thus agree with Bhandarkar with respect to what they consider to be the initial vārttika, but they differ concerning the status of *imāni prayojanāny adhyeyaṁ vyākaraṇam*, which they consider (1986:१६, 68) part of a Bhāṣya section.[109] On the other hand, Joshi and Roodbergen do consider (1986:६, 26) *rakṣohāgamalaghvasandehāḥ prayojanam* to be the second vārttika. In support of their position, they say (1986:26 note 72), 'But it must be a *Vt*., because it is commented upon (and introduced) by the *Bhāṣyakāra*.'[110]

Bronkhorst (1987b:1-13) recently has again taken up this issue, summarizing and building upon an idea of R. G. Bhandarkar. Contrary to his precedessor, Bronkhorst does not maintain that *imāni prayojanāny adhyeyaṃ vyākaraṇam* should be treated as a vārttika. Instead, he argues (1987b:9) this must be considered a paraphrase of a preceding vārttika. In support of this position, Bronkhorst refers to sections of the Bhāṣya on **A** 1.4.3 and 2.4.32. Let us consider the simpler example, concerning which Bronkhorst says:

> P. 2.4.32 vt. 2 reads: *anvādeśaś ca kathitānukathanamātram*. It is paraphrased: *anvādeśaś ca kathitānukathitamātraṃ draṣṭavyam*. This paraphrase occurs again in the next line (p. 481, l. 3-4): *tad ācāryaḥ suhṛd bhūtvānvācaṣṭe'nvādeśaś ca kathitānukathanamātraṃ draṣṭavyam iti*.

As to what precisely is paraphrased by *imāni prayojanāny adhyeyaṃ vyākaraṇam*, Bronkhorst says (1987b:9), 'Quite clearly, the section of the Mahābhāṣya that deals with the uses of grammar, i.e. p. 1, l.14 - p. 5, l. 4 in Kielhorn's edition.' In sum, according to Bronkhorst (1987b:12), the first vārttikas cited in the Mahābhāṣya are: 1. *atha śabdānuśāsanam*, 2. *rakṣohāgamalaghvasandehāḥ prayojanam*, 3. *te'surāh* etc., 4. *siddhe śabdārthasambandhe* etc.

Now, it is beyond question that *imāni prayojanāny adhyeyaṃ vyākaraṇam iti* sums up the section of the paspaśā dealing with the reasons why grammar has to be studied. It is something else, however, to claim that this is a paraphrase of vārttikas that precede. To begin with, it is most certainly not a true paraphrase of anything stated before. Nor are the two examples which Bronkhorst invokes as parallels truly parallel. Consider again the Bhāṣya on **A** 2.4.32: *idamo'nvādeśe'ś anudāttas tṛtīyādau*. The sūtra provides for replacing the proximate pronominal *idam* with *aś* before endings of triplets beginning with the third — instrumental, dative, ablative, genitive, and locative endings — when the pronominal is used anaphorically. In his first vārttika, Kātyāyana stipulates that one should specify — by explicitly saying *samānādhikaraṇasya* — that a pronominal used in subsequently referring (*anvādeśe*) to something should be coreferential with a previously used term (2.4.32 vt. 1: *anvādeśe samānādhikaraṇa-grahaṇam*). The reason for this, Kātyāyana goes on to say in the second part of the same vārttika (*devadattaṁ bhojayemaṁ cety aprasaṅgārtham*), is that replacement by an anaphoric pronoun should not possibly be allowed in examples where there is not coreference: one should say *devadattaṁ bhojaya imaṁ ca* 'Feed Devadatta and this person too', with *imam* and not the anaphoric *enam*.[111] In his second vārttika (2.4.32 vt. 2: *anvādeśaś ca kathitānukathanamātram*), Kātyāyana further remarks that, in addition, anvādeśa is merely speaking subsequently of what has been spoken of earlier. Patañjali conveys what Kātyāyana intends by repeating the vārttika with the addition of *draṣṭavyam* : *anvādeśaś ca kathitānukathitamātraṃ draṣṭavyam* (Kielhorn [1880-85:I.481.2]). He thus shows that Kātyāyana says anvādeśa should be viewed as merely speaking subsequently of what has been spoken earlier. Patañjali then goes on to say why Kātyāyana felt compelled to specify this: one might consider something contrary (*dveṣyam* 'inimical') to his intention, namely that what he said earlier applied only if there is subsequent reference using the pronoun *idam* to something referred to earlier by this very pronoun; consequently, the teacher Kātyāyana explains, assuming the role of a friend, that anvādeśa is to be viewed as merely speaking subsequently of what has been spoken earlier.[112] I think it is clear that *imāni prayojanāny adhyeyaṃ vyākaraṇam iti* is not comparable to this. Even if one insists that what precedes is a pair of vārttikas, this does not repeat either of them. Accordingly, I cannot accept Bronkhorst's conclusions.

In the most recent discussion of the question under consideration, Wezler (1994a:173-175 notes 2-3) objects, I think cogently, to the claims of Joshi, Roodbergen, and Bronkhorst. Wezler also suggests (1994a:173-174 note

2) something concerning *atha śabdānuśāsanam* which, he says, '... is as simple as plausible: Patañjali starts his criticial examination and explanation of Pāṇini's rules and of Kātyāyana vārttikas on them by repeating or quoting ... the very first words by which the study of grammar had much earlier been announced as a subject of instruction to those students whom Patañjali himself (really or fictitiously) turns to now that they have gained a good grounding, i.e. know the Aṣṭādhyāyī and the vārttikas by heart and know much of what is said in the two works.' Now, I can agree immediately that *atha śabdānusāsanam* announces the grammar. On the other hand, I think it is also proper to consider in this context what Patañjali himself says a bit later.[113] After describing the reasons for studying grammar, he notes a contrast with what was true in an earlier time and what is true at his time. Previously, students were introduced to grammar — including śikṣā — immediately after their upanayana and then they went on to study their Veda. Nowadays, on the other hand, students first study their Veda. They are thus no longer children when they come to study grammar and may question the purpose of this study: they know Vedic words from their study of the Veda and everyday words from everyday usage. For students who may be of such a perverse mind, the teacher states the reasons why grammar should be studied. If Patañjali tells us this situation obtained in his ṭime, I see no reason not to take him at his word. In accordance with what commentators say, then, the introduction using *atha śabdānuśāsanam* constitutes a statement of the immediate purpose for studying grammar, and the Bhāṣya subsequently gives additional reasons (see Cardona [1997a:545-546 (**829**)]). From what Patañjali says, moreover, it is reasonable to conclude that there was one major group of reasons upon which grammarians agreed, those handed down in the formula *rakṣohāgama-laghvasandehāḥ prayojanam*, and additional reasons, which Patañjali then proceeds to give and discuss.

All this fits with considering that everything preceding *siddhe śabdārthasambandhe* ... is a long introduction by the bhāṣyakāra prior to the first vārttika of Kātyāyana. Still another possible position has to be considered, namely that *atha śabdānuśāsanam* could actually be the introductory statement of Pāṇini's work. Under this view, *atha śabdānuśāsanam* and the bhāṣya *athety ayam adhikārāthaḥ prayujyate | śabdānuśāsanaṁ śāstram adhikṛtaṁ veditavyam* (Kielhorn [1880-85:I:1.1-

2]) are parallel to Yogasūtra 1.1: *atha yogānuśāsanam* and the bhāṣya thereon: *athety ayam adhikārārthaḥ | yogānuśāsanaṁ śāstram adhikṛtaṁ veditavyam.*

The question whether *atha śabdānuśāsanam* is to be considered the beginning of Pāṇini's work or of the Mahābhāṣya has been discussed recently by Devaswarupa Miśra (1978:9-15), who argues that this is part of Patañjali's work, and Bhim Sen Shastri (1984:19-24), who argues against Devaswarupa Miśra and maintains that this is the introduction to the Aṣṭādhyāyī. Yudhiṣṭhira Mīmāṁsaka (1984:I.226-228) also maintained that *atha śabdānuśāsanam* is Pāṇini's first sūtra. The arguments these scholars have proposed involve manuscripts and testimony of commentators on the one hand and, on the other hand, the structure of texts which are known to begin with *atha* ....

Manuscript evidence is not strong, since none of the manuscripts of the Aṣṭādhyāyī sūtrapāṭha is sufficiently old to warrant basing on it firm conclusions concerning this dispute.[114]

The evidence of commentators cuts both ways: some attribute *atha śabdānuśāsanam* to Pāṇini, others to Patañjali. In his commentary on Puruṣottamadeva's Bhāṣāvṛtti, the fifteenth-century commentator Sṛṣṭidhara says that Pāṇini, wishing to explain the name and purpose of his grammar, states *atha śabdānuśāsanam* while beginning his work.[115] Commenting on Manusmṛti 1.1, Medhātithi also speaks of Pāṇini beginning his set of sūtras with *atha śabdānuśāsanam*.[116] On the other hand, Pāṇinīyas generally consider this to be part of the Mahābhāṣya. I have already alluded to Kaiyaṭa. Similarly, Haradatta explicitly says that the Kāśikā cites *atha śabdānuśāsanam* from the Mahābhāṣya, where Patañjali recites this in stating the direct reason for studying grammar.[117]

After its introductory verses, the Kāśikāvṛtti begins with *atha śabdānuśāsanam | keṣāṁ śabdānām | laukikānāṁ vaidikānāṁ ca.* Since the Kāśikā so commonly uses the Mahābhāṣya as a source, this can be understood as an imitation of the Mahābhāṣya, where, after explaining what the term *atha* means, Patañjali goes on to say *keṣāṁ śabdānām | laukikānāṁ vaidikānāṁ ca.* There is no cogent reason for arguing that, because the Kāśikā cites *atha śabdānuśāsanam*, this must be attributed to the Aṣṭādhyāyī. In accordance with the fact that it leaves out sūtras dealing with Vedic usage, after its introductory verse, the Bhāṣāvṛtti begins:

atha śabdānuśāsanam | *laukikānām*. Here again, there is no cogent reason for claiming that Puruṣottamadeva here cites a Pāṇinian sūtra. Nor can one justifiably say that the Kāśikā and the Bhāṣāvṛtti actually comment on this putative sūtra.[118]

A major argument based on the structure of śāstric works is that, as other such works begin with *atha* ..., so should one expect the Aṣṭādhyāyī to begin with *atha śabdānuśāsanam*.[119] Devaswarupa Miśra (1978:12), however, points out that this is not a sufficient reason. He notes that other works which begin in this manner go on immediately to define what the object of instruction is. Thus, Yogasūtra 1.2 (*yogaś cittavṛttinirodhaḥ*) states that yoga is the suppression of the mind's activity. Similarly, Jaiminsūtra 1.1 (*athāto dharmajijñāsā*) is followed immediately by a sūtra (JS 1.2: *codanālakṣaṇo 'rtho dharmaḥ*) which states what dharma is. The same is not true of *atha śabdānuśāsanam* : this is not followed immediately by a sūtra stating what śabda is. Bhim Sen Shastri (1984:23) maintains, however, that Devaswarupa Miśra's reason is without substance because there are also instances where a śāstra begins with *atha* but does not then go on to define what the object of instruction is. For example, the Nidānasūtra begins in the usual manner (see note 119) but the text does not go on immediately to define what chandas is. I do not think this completely invalidates Devaswarupa Miśra's argument, since the treatises which begin with statements most similar to *atha śabdānuśāsanam* — that is, those in which *atha* or *athātaḥ* is directly followed merely by a term referring to the topic at hand — do indeed follow this procedure.

A negative argument given by those who maintain that *atha śabdānuśāsanam* is the beginning of the Aṣṭādhyāyī is that this statement cannot be part of the Mahābhāṣya because Patañjali explains that the term *atha* is used (*prayujyate*) here in a particular sense, thereby showing that he is speaking of a term used by someone else.[120] On the other hand, if one accepts, with the tradition, that a characteristic of a bhāṣya is that it explains its own terms, this argument does not hold. Devaswarupa Miśra (1978:9) makes this point. He also brings in (1978:9) a long standing argument, which involves the wording of **A** 1.1.1: *vṛddhir ād aic* as contrasted with **A** 1.1.2: *ad eṅ guṇaḥ*. Pāṇini puts *vṛddhi* first for the sake of auspiciousness, because works that begin with auspicious terms become widespread, have powerful and long-lived students. Pāṇini procedes as he does, in sum, so that his students should be endowed with prosperity.

With this, I think we reach a compromise position which may well reflect what Patañjali intended. It is appropriate to distinguish between the Aṣṭādhyāyī proper — the corpus of eight chapters of sūtras (sūtrapāṭha) — and the larger total śabdānuśāsana, which includes also distinct ancillaries: the akṣarasamāmnāya and the dhātupāṭha. Assume, then, that the larger complete work was originally introduced with *atha śabdānuśāsanam*, followed immediately by the akṣarasamāmnāya and then the sūtrapāṭha, in the manner discussed in the Mahābhāṣya. As later handed down, *atha śabdānuśāsanam* is cited by Patañjali as part of his Mahābhāṣya. This now introduces the grammatical study by implicitly stating the immediate purpose of the grammar.[121] In brief, I think that, with a minor modification, the interpretation which Wezler has given for *atha śabdānuśāsanam* is the appropriate one. This is an introduction to Pāṇini's full grammatical treatise. As such, it is cited at the beginning of the Mahābhāṣya, where it is incorporated into Patañjali's work as part of his overall discussion of Pāṇini's grammar. Accordingly, Patañjali explains how *atha* is used here and goes on to discuss what a śabda is.

2.2.4. *Historical change and Pāṇinīyas* (III.2.5.3)

Two major monographs on evidence from Kātyāyana's and Patañjali's statements for historical change in usage between Pāṇini's time and later were produced by Laddu (1974, see Cardona [1976a:378b]) and Sarangi (1985),who did his work with Laddu. Laddu covers discussions concerning 143 sūtras from the third adhyāya, dealing with kṛt affixes. As I said on another occasion (Cardona [1977c]), this is an important and well executed piece of scholarship. Laddu finds evidence of language change between the times of Pāṇini and Patañjali and judges the evidence with care. Sarangi's work complements Laddu's and covers discussions on sūtras that introduce kṛt affixes under conditions of time reference.

M. M. Deshpande (1978a:90-109) again takes up the issue and goes over some of the earlier arguments proposed by scholars such as Devasthali and Rosane Rocher. Although he refrains from entering into the controversy (1978a:92) about whether historical change is to be considered a reason for Kātyāyana's formulating vārttikas, Deshpande reiterates that there were known dialectal variations in the times of Kātyāyana and Patañjali. He also takes up issues associated with this, in particular the status of model speakers referred to as *śiṣṭa* and the gradual restriction of the use of Sanskrit over time. See also Deshpande (1979a, b, 1985b).

2.2.5. *Techniques of interpretation* (III.2.6.2)

A major work which is complete but which has not yet been published is worth mentioning: *Vārttikapratyākhyānam* by Raghunātha Śarmā, in which this learned scholar refutes arguments presented in vārttikas. The work is in manuscript and supposed to be prepared for publication by Raghunātha's son, Narendra Nātha Pāṇḍeya.

In a well documented work, Bhīma Siṁha Vedālaṅkāra (1987) covers the Mahābhāṣya passages where sūtras are rejected on various grounds. The rules dealt with are considered according to their types: saṁjñāsūtra, paribhāṣāsūtra, vidhisūtra, niyamasūtra, atideśasūtra, adhikārasūtra, Vedic rules, and nipātanasūtra. In his introduction, Bhīma Siṁha discusses perceptively the ways in which Kātyāyana and Patañjali go about rejecting sūtras and lists (1987:27) the various grounds upon which rejections are based.

Patañjali frequently invokes principles that are known to anyone from everyday life. Even the central principle that an exception (*apavāda*) blocks the application of a related general rule (*utsarga*) is said to be known in this manner, and Patañjali notes that neither does the lord command nor do authors of dharmasūtra state in their works that general rules should be blocked by their exceptions.[122] Rāmakiśora Śukla (1992) discusses passages where such principles are invoked in the Mahābhāṣya and other Pāṇinian works.[123]

A. M. Ghatage (1984) takes up the Mahābhāṣya passages where the principle is invoked that terms whose meanings are expressed by other means are not redundantly used (*uktārthānām aprayogaḥ*), concluding (1984:151) that, '... Patañjali's use of this maxim stems from a good grasp of the nature of language in general and of Sanskrit in particular.'

2.2.6. *Discussions of philosophical import* (III.2.6.3)

Bronkhorst (1987b:43-71) devotes the major part of a lecture to discussing questions about nature of sound and word and what the Mahābhāṣya has to say on this topic. After noting that several scholars had pointed out that the Mahābhāṣya presented philosophical ideas concerning the nature of the word, Bronkhorst says (1987b:71):

> The present lecture has tried to specify these ideas, and to trace them back even further. It has led to the remarkable conclusion that linguistic philosophy in India may be heavily indebted to Buddhism, from which it may have derived some of its ideas.[124]

Several recent studies are devoted to the topic of *ākṛti* 'generic property, form' as opposed to *dravya* 'substance, thing' or *vyakti* 'individual'. The most extensive of these is Scharf (1996). Scharf has also contributed two recent papers on the subject (1992, 1993). In addition, Ganeri (1995) has a section ('Patañjali on philosophical semantics' [403-410]) devoted to this topic.

Cardona (1991d) gives evidence to show that already some time before Patañjali there had been set forth systematically tenets and arguments concerning time and its subdivisions.[125]

2.2.7. *Other studies of the Mahābhāṣya* (III.2.7)

The Mahābhāṣya on **A** 3.3.18 (*bhāve*) centers about an issue which Kātyāyana brings up in his only vārttika on this sūtra. In this vārttika (3.3.18 vt. 1: *bhāve sarvaliṅgo nirdeśaḥ*), the objection is posed that the sūtra should be worded so as to refer to all genders. The sūtra as formulated uses a locative singular form (*bhāve*) of a masculine base (*bhāva*), which would thus appear to be the only way allowed for referring to an action in the abstract. In accordance with usage, however, one should be able to refer to action associated with all genders: not just *bhāve* but also *bhūtau* (fem. *bhūti*) and *bhavane* (nt. *bhavana*). Patañjali considers two ways of accounting for the usage without reformulating the sūtra. The first solution that Patañjali suggests is that the masculine singular *bhāve* is used out of necessity. To speak of an action, one has to use some ending following a term with some gender. That the masculine singular is thus used does not mean that it is intended to exclude other genders. As an alternative, Patañjali goes on to say that the sūtra states what is common to all actions in that *kṛ* ('do, make'), *bhū* ('be, become') and *as* ('be, exist') signify what is common to all verbs, as opposed to verb bases like *pac* 'cook, bake', which signify particular actions. Nevertheless, the action which *pac* signifies incorporates also the common property that inheres in all actions, namely being an action (*bhāva*). Any action, such as cooking, has two aspects, depending on what it is opposed to. With respect to action in general, viewed in the abstract, it is a particular; with respect to the component activities that make up cooking, on the other hand, it is a general composite action. The following thus come under consideration with respect to any action such as cooking: a specific action viewed in progress, as something that is brought to accomplishment and is signified by the base in forms such as *pacati*, *apākṣīt, apacat, pakṣyati*; a specific action viewed in the abstract and signified by derivates like *pāka* (masc.), *pakti* (fem.), *pacana* (nt.); an overarching property, common to all activities, signified by the abstract noun *bhāva*. To illustrate the situation such that a single entity can thus incorporate different properties in relation to different things, Patañjali invokes the parallel of a single person who is at once a maternal uncle and a teacher. This man's student comes up to his teacher's sister's son — for whom the person in question is a maternal uncle — and says to him *upādhyāyaṁ bhavān abhivādayatām* 'Greet my teacher'. The boy thus addressed then greets his maternal uncle. On the other hand, the nephew goes up to his uncle's student and says *mātulaṁ bhavān abhivādayatām* 'Greet my maternal uncle'. The student thus addressed then greets his teacher. Patañjali concludes by noting: what is referred to by *bhāve* is what is in the meaning of the base *bhū* that pertains to the meaning of a base like *pac*. That is, reference is made to an action in general, which pertains to all particular actions. Moreover, there is a precise parallel between the example of the person who is at once a teacher and a maternal uncle and what this is meant to illuminate. When a student says to his teacher's sister's son *upādhyāyaṁ bhavān abhivādayatām* and the nephew then greets his maternal uncle, the person whom the student says should be greeted has not been referred to as a maternal uncle; nevertheless, he is in fact the maternal uncle of his sister's son and by virtue of the fact that the nephew does the greeting, it is indeed as maternal uncle that he is the object of this act. Similarly, *bhāve* refers to that which is common to all actions in general, so that it does not directly refer to a particular action such as cooking. Nevertheless, a particular action is implied by the class property of action in the abstract (*bhāva*). Such a particular abstract action, moreover, is associated with different genders and numbers, and it is in the guise of such a particular that a base like *pac* receives an affix whose occurrence is determined by a general activity. Accordingly, the genders and numbers associated with *pāka* (nom. du. *pākau*), *pakti* (nom. du. *paktī*), and *pacana* (nom. du. *pacane*) are subsumed when **A** 3.3.18 states the condition *bhāve.*[126] Wezler (1986a) has taken up this discussion in detail, improving on Scharfe's earlier treatment and on what Bandini had said about the passage.[127]

Wezler has also discussed (1986b) in considerable detail and with far-ranging parallels, the import of the examples given in the Bhāṣya under 1.4.52 vt. 7 (*bhakṣer ahiṁsārthasya*).

The second part of Filliozat (1991) deals with one part of the Bhāṣya, which begins with *atha gaur ity atra kaḥ śabdaḥ*. As is known, Patañjali here deals with the question of what precisely one is to consider a speech unit (*śabda*) such as *go*. The reasons Filliozat takes up the Bhāṣya with all the commentaries and subcommentaries are given in the author's summary (Filliozat [1991:84-85]), where he rightly emphasizes that they are useful and even necessary for understanding the Mahābhāṣya.

R. C. Panda (1982) also takes up the Bhāṣya passage at the beginning of the Paspaśā (Kielhorn [1880-85:I.1.6-13]) concerning what constitutes a speech unit (*śabda*) such as *go*, where two views are set forth: that the unit *go* is that which, when uttered, serves to produce an understanding of a meaning, an animal with a dewlap and so forth; that *śabda* is a term whose meaning is well known: it signifies a sound. Panda concludes (1982:138), 'Thus, it is suggested here that both the statements probably aim at only one concept of *śabda*, i.e. a meaningful sound-group, and not two different ones.' The same Bhāṣya discussion has more recently been studied by Wezler (1994a), who includes discussions of the term *pratītapadārthaka* both in this context and elsewhere. Wezler criticizes the earlier translation and discussion by S. D. Joshi and Roodbergen (1986).[128]

Laddu (1980a) has studied the passages in which Kātyāyana and Patañjali use the term *vākya* and concluded (1980a:207) that for both of them a vākya is a '... semantically coherent statement or expression which may or may not contain a Verb or Modifiers of action.'

Sudyumna Arya (1985) takes up five terms as accounted for by Kātyāyana (*mādhyandina, paścārdha, tilataila, gogoṣṭha, pitāmaha*) as a sample to demonstrate (1985:26) that Kātyāyana's analysis is less scientific than Pāṇini's.

K. Kunjunni Raja (1987) considers the phrase *yarvāṇastarvāṇaḥ* used in connection with sages who pronounced *-r-* and *ṇ* instead of *-d-* and *n* in particular contexts, but avoided such pronunciation in ritual usage. He argues that this cannot be a dual term referring to two sages. I agree, and in my opinion (Cardona [1990a:7 with note 24]), the phrase is used to refer to a group of people characterized by a peculiarity of pronunciation, just as Śakāra is so called in the Mṛcchakaṭika on account of his speech.[129]

K. A. Krishnamacharya (1985) discusses differences in usage between Pāṇini and Patañjali in connection with four sūtras (6.4.11, 3.1.22, 3.1.45, 1.1.29).

A. M. Ghatage (1990) very briefly considers the arguments in the Bhāṣya concerning why **A** 8.1.1: *sarvasya dve* includes the genitive *sarvasya*.

A 5.1.38: *tasya nimittaṁ saṁyogotpātau* provides for introducing certain taddhita affixes after a pada of the type N-6, terminating in a sixth-triplet ending, to form a derivate denoting something that is a cause of what the nominal in such a pada signifies, if the cause in question is a relation or omen. For example, *śatya* and *śatika,* with the suffixes *yat* and *ṭhan*,[130] can be used with reference to a connection which is the cause of one's obtaining a hundred of something or to an omen which is the cause of one's knowing that one will obtain this. There are two vārttikas on this sūtra.[131] The first calls for allowing, in the section which provides for affixes under the condition 'cause relative to X' (*tasyanimittaprakaraṇe*), the suffix *ṭhak* after padas of the type N-6 with *vāta* 'wind', *pitta* 'bile' and *śleṣman* 'phlegm' as values of N to form derivates that denote exciting or calming.[132] In addition, the same affix is to occur after N-6 with *sannipāta* 'combination' to form a derivate signifying the confusion of the humors.[133] Patañjali (Kielhorn [1880-85:II.351.12, 14]) supplies the examples *vātikam*, *paittikam*, *ślaiṣmikam*, and *sānnipātikam*; he also states that *vātikam* is equivalent to *vātasya śamanam* 'calming the wind' or *vātasya kopanam* 'exciting the wind' and notes that *paittikam* and *ślaiṣmikam* have parallel meanings. Under the assumption that *vātika* and the other terms, as accounted for by Kātyāyana, refer to things which excite or calm the wind and so on, Rahul Peter Das (1992:27-29) has brought in evidence from medical texts to show that Kātyāyana's usage differs from the usage in these works and that he reflects the use of *vātika* and related terms in every day life, not specifically in medicine.

Ruegg (1994:308-310) takes up briefly passages where Patañjali speaks of Pāṇini as *pramāṇabhūta ācāryaḥ* (cf. Cardona [1997a:554 (**835**)]).

Cardona (1995) considers passages in the Mahābhāṣya where the third singular *asti* precedes an utterance and does not show agreement in person and number with other terms. He concludes that *asti* is used as a presentential term to assert that what follows is true, and points out parallels to such usage in Aśoka's inscriptions.

Rau (1985a) is a valuable contribution, completing to a great extent the early efforts of Kielhorn to trace all of the numerous Vedic citations in the Mahābhāṣya. It complements the work of V. P. Limaye (1974), whose contributions Rau acknowledges frequently. Rau's work also includes textual emendations to the Mahābhāṣya text (1985a:98-101) and Vedic texts cited (1985a:102), as well as a brief excursus on the extent of the Vedic literature known to the Mahābhāṣya (1985a:102-103) and a suggestion concerning *chandasi* and *bhāṣāyām* (see section 2.1.4.8). Additional Vedic citations are given in Rau (1985b) and additions and corrections to this index appear in a supplement of Rau's index to Vedic citations in the Kāśikā (Rau [1993a:113-114]).

2.3. CHRONOLOGY AND REALIA

2.3.1. *Pāṇini and the prātiśākhyas* (III.3.2.2)

Bronkhorst (1981c) has arrived at some far-reaching conclusions concerning Pāṇini, the Ṛgvedaprātiśākhya and the Ṛgveda. His principal claims are: Pāṇini worked with a version of the Ṛgveda which was earlier than the versions accounted for in the Ṛgvedaprātiśākhya; Pāṇini's rules that apply to basic sequences *-as a-* agree with an original Ṛgveda; Śākalya mentioned by Pāṇini antedated the final redaction of the Ṛgveda; the Ṛgvedaprātiśākhya postdates Pāṇini. Since these are sweeping claims, I think it worthwhile to consider some of Bronkhorst's arguments in order to see how he reaches his conclusions.

Bronkhorst places much emphasis on what Pāṇini has to say about sequences with original *-as a-*. He considers the sūtras **A** 8.3.17-19 (*bhobhagoaghoapūrvasya yo'śi*, *vyor laghuprayanataraḥ śākaṭāyanasya*, *lopaḥ śākalyasya*). According to the first of these rules, *-R* is replaced by *-y* if it is preceded by an *a*-vowel and there follows a voiced segment. The second sūtra states that according to Śākaṭāyana a lightly articulated glide occurs instead of *-y* and *-v*, and the third rule states that *-y* and *-v* are dropped according to Śākalya. Since by **A** 8.3.22 (*hali sarveṣām*) all authorities agree that *-y* and *-v* are deleted before a consonant, the replacements provided for in **A** 8.3.18-19 apply only before vowels.[134] Concerning these sūtras, Bronkhorst says (1981c:85):

> When these rules are applied to a word ending in *-as* that is followed by *a-*, this sandhi evolves: *-as* + *a-* > *-a-rU* + *a-* (8.2.66) > *-ay* + *a-* (8.3.17) or *-aỹ* + *a-* (8.3.17 & 18) or *-a* + *a-* (8.3.17 & 19). None of these forms is ever found in our *Ṛgveda*, which invariably has *-o-* or *-o* + *a-*. The metre requires two distinct syllables in the vast majority of cases and that the first syllable be metrically short ... Oldenberg ... has argued that the original reading was *-a* + *a-*. We note that this is the opinion of Śākalya expressed in P. 8.3.19. Oldenberg ... further shows that *-ay* for *-as* occurs in Vedic literature, and does not exclude the possibility that *-ay* + *a-* for *-as* + *a-* was the original form in the *Ṛgveda*. This would correspond to the opinions of Śākaṭāyana (P 8.3.18) and Pāṇini (if P. 8.3.17 gives indeed Pāṇini's opinion).[135]

Later (1981c:88), Bronkhorst says, 'Pāṇini seems to consider the sandhi form *-ay* + *a-* for *-as* + *a-* correct, which agrees with the original *Ṛgveda*, but not with the *Ṛgveda* known to us.' He also (1981c:86-87) deals with the relations among the rules at issue and their position in the Aṣṭādhyāyī, in connection with the outcome he envisions as showing agreement between Pāṇini and the original Ṛgveda. After noting (1981c:86) that *-as a-* 'would yield *-o-* according to the orthodox interpretation of Pāṇini's grammar' and that the Aṣṭādhyāyī text itself has *-o-* for *-as a-*, Bronkhorst remarks, 'The question is if *only* this form was accepted. Some circumstances indicate that such is not the case.' He then stresses the fact that **A** 8.2.66 (*sasajuṣo ruḥ*), whereby *-R* (***ru***) replaces pada-final *-s*, is in the Tripādī section of the Aṣṭādhyāyī, hence should be treated as non-existent with respect to **A** 6.1.113 and **A** 6.1.87 (*ād guṇaḥ*). According to these last rules, *u* replaces *-R* which is preceded and followed by short *a* and the sequence *aü* is replaced by the single vowel *-o-*.[136] Bronkhorst poses the question: 'Why was P. 6.1.113 not located in the Tripādī, somewhere after P. 8.2.66 and before P. 8.3.17?' He considers (1981c:86) two possible answers to this question, as follows:

> I think there are two answers to this question, which are simultaneously valid. The first is that P. 6.1.113 has to "feed" P. 6.1.87 in the derivation of *-o-* out of *-as + a-* (see above). This answer alone is not fully satisfying, for if the linear ordering of the Tripādī was to be broken, then why not *after* the application of P. 6.1.113? The second answer is that if P. 6.1.113 were located in the Tripādī, it would make the derivation of *-ay + a-/ -ay̆+ a-/ -a + a-* out of *-as + a-* impossible. That this second answer leads to a result which agrees so well with the original *Ṛgveda*, only confirms that it is most probably correct.

Bronkhorst then notes, 'The above shows that Śākalya was not the final redactor of the *Ṛgveda* ....' Subsequently, he says (1981c:88), 'Pāṇini seems to consider the sandhi form *-ay + a-* for *-as + a-* correct, which agrees with the original *Ṛgveda*, but not with the *Ṛgveda* known to us.' Later still, Bronkhorst (1981c:89) again stresses this point:

> P. 8.3.17, which justifies the sandhi form *-ay + a-* for *-as + a-*, occurs in the company of P. 8.3.18 and 19, which mention Śākaṭāyana and Śākalya respectively (see p. 85, above). These two authorities are mentioned in the *Ṛgveda-prātiśākhya*, and their opinions may be considered to apply also to the *Ṛgveda*, if not primarily to that work. It is therefore safe to say the same of P. 8.3.17.

To buttress the major conclusions reached earlier, Bronkhorst then (1981c:90-91) proceeds to 'enumerate a few more circumstances which seem to fit our conclusion that Pāṇini preceded the *Ṛgveda-prātiśākhya* and made use of an earlier version of the *Ṛgveda*' (1981c:90). He adduces two points as evidence: the occurrence of retroflex *-ḷ-* instead of intervocalic *-ḍ-* in the Ṛgveda as finally handed down and statements in the Ṛgvedaprātiśākhya concerning the pronunciation of svarita vowels. Bronkhorst stresses the fact that Pāṇini does not provide for *-ḷ-*. 'One way of explaining the absence of *ḻ* in the *Aṣṭādhyāyī*,' he remarks (1981c:90), 'is that Pāṇini lived before this sound made its appearance in the Veda, and therefore before the *Ṛgveda-prātiśākhya*.' In connection with the description of svarita vowels in the Aṣṭādhyāyī and the Ṛgvedaprātiśākhya,[137] Bronkhorst says (1981c:91), 'The description of the *Ṛgveda-prātiśākhya* makes the impression of being more sophisticated than the description of the *Aṣṭādhyāyī*. This may be due to the fact that the the former is of later date than the latter.'[138]

Expressions such as 'Pāṇini seems to consider the sandhi form *-ay + a-* for *-as + a-* correct' and 'This may be due to the fact that the the former is of later date than the latter' are vague, especially when one contrasts them with unequivocal assertions like, 'The above shows that Śākalya was not the final redactor of the *Ṛgveda*.' Some of Bronkhorst's arguments, moreover, amount to speculation. Thus, his statement that the Ṛgvedaprātiśākhya's description of svarita syllables gives the impression of being more sophisticated that Pāṇini's is a vague and unsubstantiated expression of opinion, with no compelling value. When Bronkhorst says that Pāṇini's not accounting for retroflex *-ḷ-* in place of intervocalic *-ḍ-* can be accounted for by assuming this sound had not yet made an appearance in the Veda at the time of Pāṇini, he once more speculates in a manner appropriate to his thesis but does not consider another possibility.

There is definite evidence to uphold the view that Pāṇini knew of and acknowledged as authoritative Śākalya's padapāṭha to the Ṛgveda; see Cardona (1991b). In this padapāṭha, Śākalya recites forms such as *īḷe* (< *īḍe*) with intervocalic *-ḷ-* instead of *-ḍ-* but *īḍyaḥ* with *ḍ* before a consonant. The received saṁhitāpāṭha agrees. Moreover, as has long been recognized, the saṁhitāpāṭha which has come down to us has preconsonantal *ḍy* and *ḍv* even in places where, through metrical considerations, one can restore *iy* and *uv* for *y* and *v*. Thus, to cite well known examples, ṚV 1.1.2ab (*a̱gniḥ pūrvèbhi̱r ṛṣìbhi̱r īḍyo̱ nūtànair u̱ta*) has *īḍyo̱* where the metre calls for eight syllables in the pāda, so that one is justified in restoring a form with *-iyo* for the original text, and ṚV 1.118.9d (*sàhasra̱sāvṁ vṛṣàṇavṁ vī̱ḍvàṅgam*) has *vī̱ḍvàṅgam* where the metre allows one to restore a form with *-uv-*. The padapāṭha for these passages has *īḍyàḥ* and *vī̱lu-àṅgam*, with *ḍ* and *ḷ* respectively. This is in order, since no part of the first term is separated from any other by a pada break but the second has a pada break between constitutents of the compound, so that the *-ḍ-* of *vī̱ḍu* comes to stand between vowels and is consequently replaced by *-ḷ-* as provided for in the Ṛgvedaprātiśākhya. Assuming that Pāṇini acknowledged Śākalya's padapāṭha and also knew of the Ṛgvedaprātiśākhya, the fact that he does not have a special rule providing for intervocalic *-ḍ-* and *-ḍh-* to be replaced by *-ḷ-* and *-ḷh-* is understandable, just as it is understandable that he does not have special rules accounting for forms like *dakṣi* instead of *dhakṣi*.[139] As for the restoration of *-iy-* and *-uv-* on metrical grounds, two points are known beyond dispute: the Ṛgvedaprātiśākhya recognizes hypometric lines and at the same time also states conditions under which *-y-* and *-v-* can be replaced by *-iy-* and *-uv-* to restore ideal metrical pādas. These facts are explicable on the assumption that the text as recited had hypometrical lines and that these could be theoretically restored to ideal lines, not in order to be recited in this manner, but to allow generalized statements concerning syllables subject to metrical lengthening. This is discussed by Cardona (forthcoming h). Barring evidence to the contrary, this is all compatible with the position that the Ṛgveda text as recited and known to Śākalya the author of the padapāṭha for this text, to Śaunaka the author of the Ṛgvedaprātiśākhya, and to Pāṇini had *-o-* for *-aḥ* before *a-*, with abhinihita sandhi (*-o-*) in certain instances, hiatus (*-o a-*) in others.

Contrary evidence would be of the sort Bronkhorst has claimed to exist. His claim concerning the outcome of *-as a-* by Pāṇinian rules, however, is unacceptable on the grounds that it rests on a faulty application of these rules. Minor issues left aside, there are two major points which Bronkhorst does not notice. First, as has been explicitly noted by Pāṇinīyas,[140] **A** 6.1.113 is an exception to and therefore should block the application of **A** 8.3.17. This being the case, then, Pāṇini's rules do not allow for *-ay* and so on before *a-*. In addition, as again Pāṇinīyas recognize,[141] there is an acknowledged principle according to which the result of an operation provided for by a rule of the Tripādī is considered to exist with respect to an operation by an earlier rule if it is the basis for this rule, which would thus be otherwise vacuous. For example, **A** 6.1.113-114 provide for replacing with *-u* an *-R* which is flanked by short *a*. If, by **A** 8.2.1 (*pūrvatrāsiddham*), **A** 8.2.66 (*sasajuṣo ruḥ*) were suspended (*asiddham*) with respect to **A** 6.1.113-114, these rules would have no basis on which to apply. Accordingly, suspension does not hold here. This is not the only instance where this procedure is followed; see Cardona (1997a:346 [**538**]) To be sure, Pāṇini does not explicitly state the principle in question. But then he also does not explicitly state the principle that an exception blocks a general rule.

Accordingly, it is appropriate to conclude that Bronkhorst's claims concerning the relative chronology of Pāṇini and the Ṛgvedaprātiśākhya and about the Ṛgveda text known to Pāṇini remain unsubstantiated.

2.3.2. *Realia* (III.3.3)

Avanindra Kumar (1981) has studied sets of terms from the Aṣṭādhyāyī having to do with various aspects of life and culture.

Ingalls (1991) considers again 3.1.28 vt. 8 and suggests that in a passage from the Taittirīyasaṁhitā (2.5.2.4-5), *ghnanti* and *pyāyayanti* are used to speak of people relating the slaying of Vṛtra and his increasing, in the manner that *ghātayati* was used to relate the slaying of Kaṁsa (see Cardona [1976a:277])

3. LATER COMMENTARIES

3.1. INTRODUCTION (IV.1)

The most ancient commentaries which have come down to us deal with sūtras in the order of Pāṇini's Aṣṭādhyāyī. The Rūpāvatāra is the earliest extant fully reordered commentary. Nevertheless, it would not be surprising that there should have been some prior work in which at least some groups of rules concerning particular formations were brought together and not organized in the order of sūtras found in the Aṣṭādhyāyī. Building on an earlier suggestion of V. S. Agrawala, Laddu (1987) has suggested that the Aṣṭādhyāyī itself supplies evidence for works of this kind antedating Pāṇini. In particular, Laddu (1987:595) points to **A** 4.3.72: *dvyajṛdbrāhmaṇarkprathamādhvarapuraścaraṇanāmākhyātāṭ ṭhak.* He considers the single vārttika on this rule and reaches the conclusion (1987:596) that at Kātyāyana's time there did exist treatises — Laddu prefers to call them commentaries — on declension and conjugation together (*nāmākhyātika*), on conjugation alone (*ākhyātika*), and probably also on declension alone (*nāmika*). Laddu appropriately refrains from concluding that treatises fully comparable to works like the Rūpāvatāra, in which the entire subject matter of the Aṣṭādhyāyī was treated in a reordered manner, existed prior to Kātyāyana.

3.2. RUNNING COMMENTARIES

3.2.1. *The Kāśikāvṛtti and its commentaries* (IV.2.1)

The Kāśikā remains a popularly used commentary, as one can see from the editions that continue to be printed. Thus, Śrīnārāyaṇa Miśra (1996) is the seventh edition of the Chowkhamba edition. Jaya Shankar Lal Tripathi and Sudhakar Malaviya (1984-94) contains the Kāśikā together with the Nyāsa and the Padamañjarī, accompanied by a Hindi exposition. Anandaprakash Medharthy's work (1993) is useful and valuable. The vārttikas found in the Kāśikā are listed by adhyāya and pāda (1993:15-72), then these and the sūtras with which they are associated are explained, along with examples.

None of the Kāśikā editions which have been published to date has a claim to being truly critical. Work on such an edition, based on over 100 manuscripts, is now being carried out in Lausanne, by Yves Ramseier and colleagues.[142]

The Nyāsa and the Padamañjarī have been reprinted and published by Osmania University under the editorship of P. Sri Ramachandrudu and V. Sundara Sarma (1981, 1985-86). M. S. Bhat (1985-86) points out that this edition of the Padamañjarī still includes many errors, a sample of which he discusses.

Two volumes of indexes complementing the Osmania edition of the Kāśikā (Aryendra Sharma, Khanderao Deshpande and D. G. Padhye [1969-70]) have been published by B. R. Sastry and V. Sundara Sarma (1976), P. Sri Ramachandrudu and V. Sundara Sarma (1985). The first part contains indexes of sūtras and vārttikas,[143] the second part an index of examples cited in the Kāśikā.

As a complement to his index of Vedic citations in the Mahābhāṣya, Wilhelm Rau compiled, in collaboration with Peri Sarveswara Sharma, an index to Vedic citations in the Kāśikā (Rau [1993a]). This includes appendixes giving textual emendations to the Kāśikā (1993a:110-112) and to three Vedic texts cited (1993a:112).

Since the publication of Raghuvir Vedalankar (1977), there has not appeared, to my knowledge, any full-fledged study of the Kāśikā.[144] Radicchi (1985-88:I:80-107) devotes a chapter to the Kāśikā, its dating, textual matters, its relation to Pāṇini and the Mahābhāṣya, as well as to other vṛttis, and its manner of paraphrasing sūtras.

The relations between the Kāśikā and grammars other than the Aṣṭādhyāyī have been the object of considerable discussion by scholars in the last twenty years. As is well known, Kielhorn (1886) compared some statements in the Kāśikā with Candragomin's grammar and concluded that the authors of the Kāśikā knew the Cāndravyākaraṇa. In view of some recent arguments, it is in order to cite Kielhorn (1886:184 [Rau (1969:245)]):

> These instances, to which I might add many others even from the incomplete copy of Chandra's grammar which is accessible to us in Europe, will sufficiently prove, that the authors of the *Kâśikâ-Vṛtti* knew the grammar and used it in the compilation of their own work. They will also show that Chandra has not, like some of the later grammarians, merely copied from the *Ashṭâdhyâyî*, the *Vârttikas*, and the *Mahâbhâshya*;

but that he also has either tried to improve on those works himself, or has in addition to them used other works, which do not seem to exist any longer.[145]

Raghuvir Vedalankar (1977) devotes a chapter of his work (chapter 8 [241-275]) to the influence of other grammars on the Kāśikā. He begins (1977:241) by citing the first introductory verse of the Kāśikā, wherein reference is made to sources for this work, including vṛtti and bhāṣya, discusses briefly what works the Kāśikākāra is referring to, then (1977:244-247) takes up the Kātantra and the Kāśikā,[146] and goes on to devote the major part of this chapter (1977:247-275) to the Cāndravyākaraṇa and the Kāśikā. Raghuvir Vedalankar's discussion is further subdivided into sections, as follows: the two works in general (1997:247-248), the authorship of the Vṛtti on the Cāndravyākaraṇa (1977:248-250),[147] six pieces of evidence showing that the Kāśikā made use of the Cāndravyākaraṇavṛtti (1977:250-252), eighteen pieces of evidence showing influence of the Cāndravyākaraṇa and its vṛtti on the Kāśikā's explanations of sūtras (1977:252-260),[148] twenty-nine pieces of evidence demonstrating influence of the Cāndravyākaraṇa on vārttikas as cited in the Kāśikā and on iṣṭis stated in this text (1977:261-269), influence of the Cāndravyākaraṇa on ślokavārttikas cited in the Kāśikā (1977:269-271) and on the gaṇapāṭha in this work (1977:271-272). Finally, he takes up (1977:272-275) seven instances where the Kāśikā definitely differs from the Cāndravyākaraṇavṛtti. Note that although Raghuvir Vedalankar definitely considers that the Cāndravyākaraṇa and its vṛtti both influenced the Kāśikā's interpretations of sūtras, he equally emphatically argues (1977:110-116) that the Kāśikākāras did not introduce modifications into the text of the Aṣṭādhyāyī sūtras under the influence of the Cāndravyākaraṇa. Instead, he maintains that the differences were created by earlier different vṛtti authors.[149]

Oberlies (1989) contains a short section (1989:4-10 [section 1.2.2: 'Verhältnis von Cāndravyākaraṇa und Kāśikā']) dealing with the relation between the Kāśikā and the Cāndravyākaraṇa. I agree with Oberlies (1989:7) that, after Vedalankar's investigation into the question, there can be little doubt that the Kāśikā knew both the Cāndravyākaraṇa and its vṛtti. That there were vṛtti works prior to the Kāśikā but later than the Mahābhāṣya can hardly be doubted, as one cannot deny that the Kāśikā itself recognizes its indebtedness to them. Nor would it be out of place that Candragomin too should have known such works.[150] Nevertheless, as Oberlies points out (1996:272), when trying to determine the possible sources to which a work like the Kāśikā is indebted, it is good method to base conclusions first on the sources which are available, before speculating about possible grammarians. More recently, Oberlies (1996) has added additional evidence and brought into consideration as a source also the Mahāvṛtti to the Jainendravyākaraṇa.[151]

Dharmendra Kumar (1996) translates into Hindi and explains the vārttikas cited in the Kāśikā. He also lists (1996:157-158) vārttikas found in the Kāśikā which do not have a source in Kātyāyana's text as cited in the Mahābhāṣya and (1996:159-163) instances where the Kāśikā's wording differs from that given by Patañjali.

Radhamadhab Dash (1993) briefly discusses a series of terms from the Kāsikā relative to ploughing, times associated with agricultural activities (e.g. *lūnayavam* 'when the barley has been harvested'), and animals.

Dipak Bhattacharya (1995) argues on the basis of the Kāśikā's citation of passages with *māmakī* from the Paippalāda Atharvaveda that the authors of this work were from Kashmir.

Roodbergen (1990) has discussed the verses that occur at the beginning of the Kāśikā, the Nyāsa, and the Padamañjarī, with a literary evaluation.

Since Bhim Sen Shastri's work (1979), there has not been published, to my knowledge, any extended study of the Nyāsa. Bhim Sen's book is an excellent study. After a general chapter concerning commentaries on the Kāśikā, the author deals in great detail with later commentators' indebtedness to the Nyāsa (1979:97-218), refutations of Jinendrabuddhi's interpretations by later grammarians (1979:221-300), and textual emendations that can be made in the Kāśikā and other commentaries on the basis of the Nyāsa (1979:303-356), as well as errors and corrupt readings in the Nyāsa itself (1979:359-414).

Tirtha Raj Tripathi (1981) is a thorough study of the Padamañjarī and its author, including a survey of evidence concerning Haradatta's epoch and place of birth along with a summary of his works, his status in the field of Pāṇinian grammar, influence on him of predecessors, his style and his contribution to the Kāśikā. Tripathi also devotes two chapters (8-9 [165-238]) to a comparison of the Padamañjarī and the Nyāsa. The most recent study I know of devoted to the Padamañjarī is by Peri Sarveswara Sharma (1985b).

3.2.2. *Other running commentaries*

3.2.2.1. *The Bhāṣāvṛtti* (IV.2.2.1)

In a study which takes up all of Puruṣottamadeva's works, Narendra Kumar Dash devotes a short chapter (1991:75-86) to the Bhāṣāvṛtti.

3.2.2.2. *The Śabdakaustubha* (IV.2.2.3)

The Chowkhamba edition of the Śabdakaustubha (see Cardona [1976a:283]) has been reprinted (Chowkhamba, 1991).

Kudo (1996, 1997) has begun a detailed translation of the Śabdakaustubha's discussion of the kāraka classification rules, including references to earlier Pāṇinīyas such as Bhartṛhari.

3.2.2.3. *The Durghaṭavṛtti* (IV.2.2.5)

T. Gaṇapati Śāstrī's edition of the Durghaṭavṛtti (1909) was recently republished (Saini [1985]). In addition, the text has been published with the brief but very lucid and useful comments of Śrīnārāyaṇa Miśra (1985) and translated into Hindi by Ūṣā Siṁhala (1989).

3.3 REORDERED COMMENTARIES (IV.3)

3.3.1. *Works prior to the Siddhāntakaumūdī* (IV.3.1)

The text of the Prakriyākaumudī with Śrīkṛṣṇa's Prakāśa commentary has been edited by Muralīdhara Miśra (1977-80).

A recent work by Suresh Chandra Sharma (1994) is devoted to a full study of the Rūpamālā. This includes a summary of the Rūpamālā section by section (1994:28-45) and evaluations of the work and its author, as well as a summary of the development of grammatical works that treat Pāṇinian rules according to derivational order.

More recently, K. S. Lalithambal (1995) has studied Dharmakīrti's Rūpāvatāra in some detail. Especially noteworthy, in my opinion, is her chapter (1995:99-116) dealing with particular readings of sūtras and vārttikas in the Rūpāvatāra.

3.3.2. *The Siddhāntakaumudī, its commentaries and abridgements* (IV.3.2.)

The popularity of the Siddhāntakaumudī guarantees that this text is constantly being republished, and it would not serve any purpose to list editions. On the other hand, I think it worthwhile to note the reissuing of two editions of the Laghuśabdenduśekhara with commentaries: Bal Shastri (1991/92), Gopāla Śāstrī Nene (1987). The Gītā Press edition of the Laghusiddhāntakaumudī has also recently been reissued (Nārāyaṇadatta Tripāṭhī and Rāmanārāyaṇa Datta Śāstrī Pāṇḍeya [saṁ. 2052]).[152]

V. M. Bhatt (1987b, 1987c) has contributed two recent translations into Gujarati of sections of the Siddhāntakaumudī, with annotations and introductions. His work on the kāraka classification rules is the more substantial, and I think it is generally a good piece of work. One could wish, nevertheless, that he had not thoughtlessly adopted (1987c: Introduction: 61) the scheme proposed wherein Pāṇini is supposed to have operated with four levels, since this has no basis in the Aṣṭādhyāyī (see Cardona [1976a:222]).

Isvara Sarma (1994) has studied Pāṇini's Vedic rules as treated in the Siddhāntakaumudī.

A. N. Pandey (1992) takes up sūtras like **A** 2.3.4: *antarāntareṇayukte* and concludes that Bhaṭṭoji and others were confused but the Kāśikā is accurate as concerns rules which involve an item being linked with another and rules which involve the use (*prayoga*) of certain elements with others.

Bronkhorst (1986:188-191) has again taken up the issue of whether the Laghuśabdaratna was composed by Nāgeśa (see Cardona [1976a:287]). He agrees with those who hold that Nāgeśa is the author of this work.[153]

4. TREATISES ON SEMANTICS AND PHILOSOPHY OF GRAMMAR

4.1. INTRODUCTION (VI.1)

V. B. Bhagavat (1985) surveys views concerning speech forms and their meanings, the relations that can hold between the two, and issues such as the status of sphoṭa and whether speech forms are perennial or not, with references to Pāṇinian works, Nirukta, Mīmāṁsā and others. Bhagavati Prasad Pandya (1988-89) discusses different points of view adopted by grammarians, Mīmāṁsakas, and Naiyāyikas concerning verbal cognition. Three other works in which are considered general semantic issues as dealt with by various schools of thought are those of Jagadīśa Caturvedī (1980), Naradeva Śāstrī (1987), and Śrīkṛṣṇaśarmā (1991). Rajendra Prasad Sharma (1993) deals in particular with arguments concerning external referents and meanings considered as mental entities. The late B. K. Matilal pondered on and wrote frequently on aspects of grammar, logic, and epistemology. In this context I think it appropriate to note in particular a part of his work of 1985 (chapter 5 [372-430]) and 1990a (see section 1.4.5.2b).

4.2. BHARTṚHARI (VI.2)

4.2.1. *Introduction*

In recent times, Bhartṛhari has attracted a great deal of attention, and the number of books and papers devoted to his ideas is quite large. Yves Ramseier's bibliography (1993) covers editions of the Vākyapadīya and the Mahābhāṣyadīpikā as well as translations and studies up to 1993. With few exceptions, I shall limit myself here to coverage of items I think call for some additional comment and works that had not appeared by the time Ramseier compiled his published bibliography.

Baldeva Upadhyaya (1985:123-128) considers again evidence for determining Bhartṛhari's place of origin. The Vākyapadīya is commented on by scholars from Kashmir — Helārāja and Puṇyarāja — and the earliest reference to the Vākyapadīya is by Jayāditya, also from Kashmir. In addition, Somānanda and Utpalācārya allude to Bhartṛhari. From these facts, Upadhyaya considers it appropriate to infer that Bhartṛhari's place of origin was Kashmir. He also concludes (1985:128) that Bhartṛhari belongs in the mid-fifth century A. D.

In his discussion concerning the Vākyapadīya, Upadhyaya (1985:122-123) takes up briefly the name *Vākyapadīya*. Contrary to the view prevalent among modern scholars (see Cardona [1976a:296 with note 501]), he considers unjustified the opinion that this name referred to the first two kāṇḍas and excluded the third kāṇḍa. Although Upadhyaya does not refute the evidence adduced by earlier scholars, in my opinion, he makes a point that merits serious consideration. There is no cogent reason for maintaining that the term *Vākyapadīya* can only refer to two kāṇḍas by virtue of this work's composition. To begin with, the first kāṇḍa is not the padakāṇḍa, so that, if *Vākyapadīya* had to designate a work composed of only two books, these would have to be the second and third chapters: the vākyakāṇḍa and padakāṇḍa (alias *prakīrṇakāṇḍa*). Yet, when *Vākyapadīya* is not used with reference to the entire work, it is the third or prakīrṇakāṇḍa which is excluded.

Moreover, there is nothing in the name *Vākyapadīya* itself that would require this to designate a work of only two books. In traditional terms, this is described, in accordance with **A** 4.3.87 (*adhikṛtya kṛte granthe*), as a derivate with the taddhita suffix *cha*, formed from the compound *vākyapada-*, used to name a work composed with reference to utterances and constituent padas (*vākyapade adhikṛtya kṛto granthaḥ*). The Vākyapadīya meets these conditions. It is also appropriate to consider the first kāṇḍa a long general introduction, in which the essential features of Bhartṛhari's principal thesis are set forth as couched in a tradition of grammarians. The first twenty-three kārikās of the first kāṇḍa, in turn, constitute a long introduction, followed by three kārikās in which the topics to be treated in the entire work are summarized.[154] In addition, this structure fits with that of Bhartṛhari's main source, the Mahābhāṣya, which contains a long introductory section — the Paspaśā — preceding the discussions about Pāṇini'a akṣarasamānāya and sūtrapāṭha. It is, nevertheless, undeniable that *Vākyapadīya* did come to be used with reference to the first two kāṇḍas, as opposed to the third book, viewed truly as a prakīrṇakāṇḍa.

In sum, I think one should accept that Bhartṛhari's treatise was from the outset designated in two ways: *Trikāṇḍī*, referring to the work in terms of its structure of three kāṇḍas, and *Vākyapadīya*, which refers to the same opus in terms of its main topics.

4.2.2. *The Vākyapadīya* : *editions and translations* (VI.2.1)

Wilhelm Rau's edition (1977a) is now accepted as the standard critical edition of the Vākyapadīya kārikā text. Rau (1984:347, 349) adds one manuscript to the descendants of **r** in his stemma and supplies some corrections and additions to his edition.[155]

Jayadev M. Shukla (1984) gives the Vākyapadīya text — following Rau's edition, with asterisks marking citations in the Vṛtti — accompanied by a Gujarati translation and brief notes based on the Vṛtti and the commentaries of Puṇyarāja, Helārāja and Raghunātha Śarmā. In my opinion, the translation is quite good and the notes very useful, as is Shukla's summary of the Vākyapadīya's contents (1984: Introduction 20-46).

Two recent editions of the first kāṇḍa with translations and commentaries merit special mention: Satyanarayana Shastri Khanduri (1987) and Shiv Shankar Avasthi (1990). The first has an extensive commentary that includes useful diagrams and charts. The second includes not only the Vṛtti but also elaborate expositions of what is said therein, with numerous references to other passages of the Vākyapadīya and to other works. In addition, the edition of Sūryanārāyaṇa Śukla and Rāmagovinda Śukla (1961) has been republished with an appendix by Rudraprasāda Avasthī (1984).

K. A. Subramania Iyer's edition of the second kāṇḍa (1983) is noteworthy both because the text with the Vṛtti and with Puṇyarāja's ṭīkā are printed separately and, more importantly, because parts of the Vṛtti not before made available in print have now been included.

Ashok Aklujkar has prepared a critical edition of the Vākyapadīya and the Vṛtti together with word indexes for the kārikās and the Vṛtti. Through the kindness of the author, I have gone through his edition of the first two kāṇḍas and parts of the third kāṇḍa as well as the indexes and can say with confidence that the scholarly community should look forward to the appearance of this edition. Aklujkar describes (1993a:13-16) what his edition will consist of and explains his procedures. He reaffirms the important point (1993a:13) that, '... it can be proven that the kārikā manuscript ... tradition ... to which Rau devoted his highly disciplined scholarship originated out of the kārikāvṛtti ms. tradition.'[156]

Raghunātha Śarmā (1980a, 1991) discusses variant readings through the Jātisamuddeśa. The second volume was seen through the press by Raghunātha Śarmā's son Narendra Nātha Pāṇḍeya, who will see the remainder of the work into print. As is to be expected, Raghunātha's discussions are not those one should anticipate from a philological consideration based strictly on manuscript materials, but they are of considerable interest for an understanding of the text.

Rau (1988) has published a complete index of words in the kārikā text as it appears in his critical edition.[157] As noted above, Aklujkar has also prepared a word-index for the Vṛtti to the first two kāṇḍas.

4.2.3. *Authorship of the Vṛtti* (VI.2.2)

The question whether the Vṛtti on the Vākyapadīya should be considered to have been composed by Bhartṛhari himself has continued to engage scholars. Among those who have argued that the Vṛtti and the Vākyapadīya are the works of different authors is Bronkhorst. In one article (1991b:17-18), Bronkhorst deals with the Vṛtti on VP 1.99 to maintain his view. In a more extensive article devoted to this topic (1988), Bronkhorst considers briefly the traditional view of the Vākyapadīya and the Vṛtti (1988:107-108), then goes on (1988:109-121) to deal with evidence in support of the view that the two works stem from different authors, concluding (1988:121):

> La situation en ce qui concerne la Vṛtti du Vākyapadīya est évidemment comme suit. Il existe des arguments de poids pour prouver que ce commentaire a un auteur différent de celui du texte commenté; des arguments contraires n'existent pas, ou mieux: ne sont pas convaincants. La seule conclusion possible est que Vṛtti et Vākyapadīya ont des auteurs différents.[158]

In a more recent article, Bronkhorst discusses (1991c:212-216) the treatment of sūtras and bhāṣyas as unified texts in several traditions. He concludes (1991c:216), 'These four examples — the Yoga Śāstra, the Tattvārthādhigama Bhāṣya, the Madhyāntavibhāga Śāstra and the Artha Śāstra — must suffice to show that there was a tendency in the period which we consider to unite sūtras and Bhāṣya into one indivisible whole, which retained no traces of the original separateness, and authorship, of the enclosed sūtras.' In addition, Bronkhorst considers (1991c:216-218) what he calls (1991c:216) 'the Vārttika style', noting that vārttika and bhāṣya were treated as integral.[159] He then (1991c:219-220) brings these two points to bear on the issue of whether or not the Vākyapadīya kārikās and Vṛtti are the work of a single author. His argumentation here is basically negative: in view of what he has shown concerning related texts, the evidence usually considered to demonstrate that the kārikās of the Vākyapadīya and the Vṛtti are by a single author[160] loses its force. As positive evidence, Bronkhorst cites some that he had adduced earlier (1988). He ends (1991c:220) saying, 'The conclusion is inescapable that the author of the Vṛtti is different from the author of the verses.'

Aklujkar (1993b) has recently reverted to this topic, dealing with the evidence adduced by Bronkhorst. Aklujkar's rebuttals are well argued and based on close textual study and intimate knowledge of their contents. I agree with him that the arguments set forth by Bronkhorst to conclude that the Vṛtti and the Vākyapadīya are works of different authors are not well wrought and that some are based on poor methodology. For example, Bronkhorst (1988:113-114) discusses part of the Vṛtti on VP 1.6.[161] He cites the verse along with Biardeau's translation, then says (1988:113):

> C'est la deuxième ligne qui nous intéresse. Sa signification n'est pas tout à fait claire. Veut-elle dire que les mêmes mots ont parfois un sens différent dans les branches du Veda? Il semble plus probable que c'est l'identité du sens des mots dans les différentes branches qui est indiqué ici.
>
> Quoi qu'il en soit, le sens attribué à cette ligne dans la Vṛtti s'éloigne des deux interpretations que nous venons d'examiner.

Bronkhorst goes on to cite and translate that part of the Vṛtti which directly concerns the term *yataśaktitvam* of the kārikā,[162] then ends his discussion of this passage saying (1988:114):

> On voit que selon l'interprétation de la Vṛtti la strophe parle de la différence de forme des mots dans les différentes branches du Veda. Selon cette interprétation il s'agit dans cette strophe, non pas de la fixité du pouvoir expressif, mais plutôt de la non-fixité de la forme des mots. Cette interprétation ne peut guère être correcte.

As shown, Bronkhorst begins by admitting that the meaning of the second half of the verse in question is not absolutely clear to him, goes on to suggest two interpretations he considers possible, then remarks that, be this as it may, the Vṛtti's interpretation is dissimilar to the two interpretations noted.[163] It is on the basis of such vague argumentation that he then concludes that the Vṛtti's interpretation can hardly be correct. I think Aklujkar (1993b:48) is right when he objects, saying, 'Besides, an interpretation like Bronkhorst's will at least not be any less specific (and, to that extent, any less arbitrary) than the interpretation found in the V.' Bronkhorst also would have done well to pay some attention to what Vṛṣabdha's Paddati — cited by Aklujkar (1993b:48 note 5) — has to say. The chief cause for Bronkhorst's unwillingness to agree with the Vṛtti is the meaning to be given to the phrase *śabdānāṁ yataśaktitvam*, more precisely what *yata-* of *yataśaktitvam* signifies. Now, the power which a speech unit has is to convey the meaning with which it is connected. If a speech unit is characterized by the property of having a restricted power (*yataśaktitvam*), then, it is not at all strange that this consists in the term's exercising its power of expression in a particular manner, that is, only when the term has a particular form or accent. To insist that *yataśaktitvam* must refer to fixity of expressive power in the sense Bronkhorst gives to this is no more justified than his vague reasoning.

Another piece of evidence Bronkhorst adduced to conclude that the Vṛttikāra and the kārikākṛt are different is the Vṛtti on VP 1.46, to which Houben (forthcoming a, a') has now devoted an article with a postscript. This is an important passage. For the point at issue is whether the Vṛtti is concerned with a difference in readings. If the author of the Vṛtti on this text can be shown to speak of two variant readings in the kārikā, this is strong evidence that the two works stem from different authors. Moreover, the arguments presented by Bronkhorst and Houben illustrate an approach which, to put it bluntly, involves vagueness and a lack of strict consideration of syntactic possibilities. Consequently, I think it appropriate to consider these arguments in some detail.

In the text established by Rau (1977a), VP 1.46 reads *ātmabhedaṁ tayoḥ ke cid astīty āhuḥ purāṇagāḥ | buddhibhedād abhinnasya bhedam eke pracakṣate.* In other editions (e.g. K. A. Subramania Iyer [1966a] verse 1.45), the first half of the kārikā is *ātmabhedas tayoḥ ke cid astīty āhuḥ purāṇagāḥ* . The verse deals with two views concerning two kinds of speech elements (*śabdau*) in connection with signifying terms, which are thereby sources of meaning cognition (*upādānaśabdeṣu*): one speech element conveys meaning and is thus used in a meaning (*arthe prayujyate*), and one is the source (*nimittam* 'cause') of the former. Some carriers of old tradition say (*āhuḥ*) that there is a true difference in identity (*ātmabheda* 'self difference') between these; some (*eke*), on the other hand, say there is a difference (*bhedam*) only due to a difference in conceptualization (*buddhibhedāt*), not a true difference, so that there is a single undivided (*abhinnasya*) entity of which these persons state a difference. The kārikā states the same opposition of views under either of the two readings noted, but this does not mean that both readings convey the very same information. Thus, the version with *ātmabhedas tayoḥ* contrasts two views with respect to what certain persons predicate of the elements in question: reordered, 1.1.46a states *kecit purāṇagāḥ ātmabhedas tayor astīty āhuḥ* 'Some carriers of old tradition say, "There is a self-difference between these two".' 1.1.46b reordered states *eke buddhibhedād abhinnasya bhedam pracakṣate* 'Some say that, due to a difference in perception, there is a difference that pertains to an undivided one.' Under the version with *ātmabhedaṁ tayoḥ*, on the other hand, the syntax of the first pāda requires this text to say that some predicate of a self-difference that it pertains to the two entities at issue; see below. Since this and the previous kārikā concern two linguistic elements as a topic of dispute, 1.1.46ab: *ātmabhedas tayoḥ kecid astīty āhuḥ purāṇagāḥ* is contextually preferable and harmonizes better with pādas c-d. One could argue, on the other hand, that *ātmabhedas tayoḥ* is a lectio facilior — the usual way of expressing oneself in Sanskrit — so that the reading adopted by Rau is to be preferred.

As scholars have recognized, however, it cannot be a question merely of deciding on the basis of kārikā manuscripts and lectiones difficiliores; the content of the Vṛtti and of Vṛṣabhadeva's Paddhati has to be taken into consideration. Now, the archetype of the kārikā manuscripts already had lacunae and errors (Rau [1977a:24]), and it already incorporated verses which the Vṛtti identifies as citations. Indeed, kārikā 1.45 of Rau's edition — concerning which he says (1977a:41) that it disturbs the connection between the preceding and the following kārikās — is preceded by *evaṁ hy āha* in the Vṛtti (K. A. Subramania Iyer [1966a:102.5]). Moreover, a subgroup of kārikā manuscripts — albeit the lowest in Rau's stemma — which comprises two of the manuscripts to which Rau gives greatest weight (1977a:30) has the reading *ātmabhedas tayoḥ kecid* in 1.46a, as does one northern manuscript. In addition, the kārikā-vṛtti manuscripts have, so far as is known, only this reading, and Vṛṣabhadeva cites *ātmabhedaḥ* in his commentary. If the kārikā manuscript tradition derives from that of the kārikā-vṛtti manuscripts, then, there is immediate reason at least to consider that the reading adopted by Rau is a development — which has to be explained — from an earlier version with *ātmabhedas tayoḥ kecid.* Under these circumstances, the question whether the Vṛtti on VP 1.46 can be shown to deal with two possible forms in the first pāda of this verse assumes importance.

Bronkhorst (1988:115-116) considers the first part of the Vṛtti on VP 1.46[164] along with Biardeau's translation, then goes on to say the following (1988:116):

> Cette traduction présuppose la forme ātmabhedas dans le vers. La phrase en sanskrit ne présuppose pas nécessairement cela. Elle montre seulement que l'auteur de la Vṛtti pensait à deux formes, ātmabhedam et ātmabhedas, la première dans le cas où ātmabheda est l'objet du verbe 'dire', la deuxième si la proposition ātmabhedas tayoh asti est imitée. Mais pourquoi l'auteur de la Vṛtti a-t-il pensé à deux formes? Deux réponses semblent possibles: (i) Il a trouvé les deux formes dans ses manuscrits. (ii) Il n'en a trouvé qu'une, mais il l'a jugée moins 'naturelle' que l'autre; en conséquence il a expliqué la forme invraisemblable. Les deux réponses ne sont possibles que si l'auteur de la Vṛtti n'était pas l'auteur des strophes. Dans le premier cas, l'auteur de la Vṛtti connaissait un variante; dans le deuxième, il jugeait la lecture qu'il trouvait difficile, mais il ne pouvait pas, ou n'osait pas la corriger.

Arguing against Bronkhorst, Aklujkar (1993b:49) considers that the Vṛtti is intended to clarify the construction, which was obscured by metrical requirements: '... the author could have thought of advising the reader that *kecit purāṇagāḥ tayoḥ ātma-bhedam āhuḥ* was not the intended construction, for failing to offer which he should be faulted, that is, viewed as having written ungrammatical Sanskrit.' Aklujkar then goes on to consider also the possibility that the statement found in the Vṛtti originally was a marginal note.

In a contribution which deals with general considerations of authorship and takes up VP 1.46a in particular, Houben (forthcoming a) defends the thesis that the author of the Vṛtti considers two different forms — *ātmabhedam* and *ātmabhedaḥ* — in this pāda.[165] He also observes that Aklujkar's second suggestion is ad hoc and argues against Aklujkar's first explanation, particularly (forthcoming a:section 4.1) against his assumption that the reading *ātmabhedaṁ* would yield incorrect Sanskrit.

To begin his detailed treatment of VP 1.46ab Houben (forthcoming a:section 2.1) cites this half of the verse with the reading adopted in Rau's edition, notes the variants in Rau's apparatus criticus, and says:

> Both readings amount to the same and may be translated as: "Some followers of the tradition say that there is an essential difference between the two (viz. the two kinds of 'basic' words)." If one wants to make a distinction, the version with *ātmabhedaṁ* could be translated as "Some followers of the tradition acknowledge an essential difference between the two, saying 'there [really] is [this difference]'."

Houben then (forthcoming a:section 2.2) takes up the initial part of the Vṛtti on 1.46, which I have cited above. One must conclude that he assumes this concerns only the first half of the verse, since he says, 'With regard to this line, the Vṛtti remarks ...', and the line in question is the half-verse cited in section 2.1. With regard to what the Vṛtti passage cited has to say, Houben says the following :

> But the purport of this remark remains unclear unless we accept that the author of the Vṛtti was either (a) referring to two different readings, or (b) that he himself proposed one of the two readings as an alternative for the reading which he found in his sources. Under (b), one may interpret the Vṛtti-passage as a laconic defence of the second possible reading referred to: *ātmabhedas* (first ending) in the kārikā.

After taking up Biardeau's and K. A. Subramania Iyer's translations of the Vṛtti passage at issue, Houben goes on (forthcoming a:section 2.2) to say:

> It is to be noted that the reading which is defended according to this hypothesis, *ātmabhedas*, is exactly the reading which is *not* supported by the mss of Rau which belong to the earliest branches in his stemma (here the mss B C F m and o; they all read, according to Rau, *ātmabhedaṁ*). Since all available mss of the Vākyapadīya-kārikas probably derive from the Vṛtti ..., the divergence noted here might imply that the Vṛtti author defended a different reading from the one he apparently maintained (according to the testimony of 'early-branch' kārikā-mss) and acknowledged as being original, in the kārikā.

In a footnote (note 20) at the end of section 2.2, Houben says, 'In the Vṛtti-mss, however, the reading with *ātmabhedaṁ* seems to have been given up in favor of *ātmabhedas*.' Houben further notes that two additional Vṛtti manuscripts he consulted also have *ātmabhedas*.

Houben's discussion is comparable to Bronkhorst's earlier treatment of the issue in that both authors emphasize only the first half of the kārikā at issue and both envision the author of the Vṛtti considering two possible forms of *ātmabheda* in 1.46a. While Bronkhorst stressed the importance of the Vṛtti manuscripts (see my note 156), on the other hand, Houben proceeds in a slightly different manner. To judge from his words, he rules out any possibility that the reading *ātmabhedas* could have been the original one in the kārikā as known to the author of the Vṛtti — and to Vṛṣabhadeva — and that this could have been changed to *ātmabhedam* as found in kārikā manuscripts. Nevertheless, this cannot be ruled out. Houben's wording — 'might imply' — is non-committal, yet he also remarks — with equally non-committal language — that 'the reading with *ātmabhedaṁ* seems to have been given up'. In view of the indecision in these statements, it is better to proceed to consider what Houben says about the syntax of the kārikā in question.

In section 4.2 of his paper (forthcoming a), Houben deals with the syntax of the verse under the reading with *ātmabhedaṁ*, cites the Paddhati's statement[166] beginning with *āhuḥ iti*, and says, 'Apparently, according to Vṛṣabha *astīti* in the kārikā with *ātmabhedaṁ* has virtually acquired the status of an adverb.' As a parallel in support of his interpretation of *astīti* having 'virtually acquired the status of an adverb', Houben cites the first half of VP 1.87.[167] He begins his discussion of this kārikā with a statement according to which one should accept that *astīti* has not just virtually but actually acquired adverbial status: 'There is another VP-kārika, viz. 1.87, where there is hardly any choice but to accept that *astīti* has acquired the status of an adverb.'[168] After citing and translating the kārika, Houben says:

> Just as *ātmabhedaṁ* in 1.46 cannot be directly connected with *asti* but must be an object of the verb, similarly here *asataḥ ... śabdān* cannot be directly connected with *asti*, but must be the object of the verb. The Vṛtti on the latter kārikā paraphrases the construction as *śabdān astitvenābhimanyante* (VP I:152.1), from which one may infer that *śabdān* is the object of the verb, and that *astīti* has been interpreted adverbially as *astitvena*.

He concludes (forthcoming a:section 4.4) that 'Vṛṣabha unmistakably accepts that the Vṛtti on 1.46 is referring to two different forms which are both defensible.' Since his discussion centers upon the first half of VP 1.46, one must assume that Houben means two different forms defensible within this half-verse. This is compatible also with what Houben goes on to say in the same section:

> The only conclusion *we* can draw from this reference, if we reject the afore-mentioned possibility (d) of a mediocre kārikā-author lacking self-confidence, is that there was some gap, small or big, between the author of the kārikā and the author of the Vṛtti on it, either in terms of a period of time which allowed different versions to arise, or at least in terms of a difference in linguistic and stylistic intuition: what seemed perfectly all right according to the one was unnatural and slightly puzzling to the other.

At the end of this section, Houben remarks that '... Vṛṣabhadeva seems not to have been aware of this implication of the Vṛtti passage',[169] since elsewhere he unambiguously refers to the author of the Vṛtti (*vivaraṇe* 'in his explanation') as identical to the kārikā author.

Houben concludes his paper (section 5) as follows:

> Since all past events inevitably require some amount of interpretation, there can be no absolute historical truths. Nevertheless, some historical explanations are more likely than others. One important argument which was since the beginning accepted as evidence for the 'single authorship' thesis turns out to be highly disputable. We rather have a strong indication for 'separate authorship'. It is true that we have just a single case of the available Vṛtti considering different forms or readings in a kārikā. But a small piece of evidence may sometimes betray the truth behind thick layers of confusion, as in the case of the spy who happily forgot to ignore his real name when he was told he would be set free after months of trials to unmask him.
>
> It is also true that we still have to take into consideration the other arguments used in the authorship discussion. If considered in isolation, however, the evidence discussed here clearly supports 'separate authorship', and it can be adapted to the 'single authorship' thesis only at the cost of depicting Bhartṛhari as a mediocre kārikā-author lacking self-confidence, or of accepting other unattractive *ad hoc* explanations.

As is evident from the citations given above, Houben is willing to envision, as did Bronkhorst, that the Vṛttikāra might indeed be referring to two readings in his sources,[170] even while admitting that his evidence is only the passage at issue. I think this point bears emphasizing. For there is reason to consider that if he were truly considering two readings in VP 1.46a, the Vṛttikāra would have been more explicit. Now, it is accepted that the Vṛtti on the Vākyapadīya and the Mahābhāṣyadīpikā are by the same author. It is also known that the Mahābhāṣyadīpikā speaks of differences in the Mahābhāṣya text and refers to them as such. Thus, reflecting two ways of interpreting *kuśaloviśeṣaiḥ,* it speaks of a text (*granthaḥ*) accepted by others.[171] If the author of the Mahābhāṣyadīpikā does this in his comments on the Mahābhāṣya, why does not the same author do the same in the Vṛtti on VP 1.46a? The straightforward answer is: because this passage did not involve a variant reading known to the Vṛttikāra. Unless we want to get involved in contortions to avoid the obvious, therefore, it is best to eliminate from consideration the alternative, which Bronkhorst puts first and which Houben also is willing to countenance and puts first (see my note 170): that the Vṛtti on VP 1.46 might be speaking of two different readings *ātmabhedas* and *ātmabhedaṁ* known to him from his sources. One is left, then, with the other alternative envisioned by those who defend the thesis that the Vākyapadīya and the Vṛtti were composed by different persons: the Vṛttikāra had, for some reason, to consider the possibility of two forms with respect to VP 1.46a although he knew only one reading.

What Houben does not specify in his article, so far as I can see, is the reason why the Vṛttikāra should have felt obliged to say what he does if this has to do only with VP 1.46ab and the only text known to him had *ātmabhedam.* As noted earlier, Bronkhorst does suggest a possible reason: that *ātmabhedaṁ tayoḥ kecid astīty āhuḥ* is somehow "unnatural", so that he has to explain it. Upon closer examination, however, this suggestion is seen to be flawed. On the assumption that the text available to the Vṛttikāra was as in Rau's edition and that his statement *ātmabhedasya bruvikarmatve dvitīyā* has to do only with the first pāda, the author is then explaining that *ātmabhedam* here exemplifies the syntactic pattern in which a second-triplet nominal ending follows a nominal if this is used to signify the object of saying.[172] At the same time, we are asked to accept, the author also considered this an "unnatural" construction — because of *astīti*. Yet the same author who felt it necessary to explain a form in a construction he considered "unnatural" says nothing explicit about the relative naturalness of one or the other construction or about the use of *astīti* together with *ātmabhedam.* It is difficult to see, then, how Bronkhorst's suggestion is any better than the one Aklujkar made.

We are thus invited to accept the Vṛtti on VP 1.46 as a single piece of evidence demonstrating different authorship solely on the basis of the assumption that the Vṛtti's *ātmabhedasya bruvikarmatve dvitīyā vākya-svarūpānukaraṇe tu prathamā* must have to do only with the first half of the verse and that this kārikā had a reading *ātmabhedaṁ tayoḥ* in the text commented on by the Vṛttikāra. We are also asked to accept that a perceptive commentator like Vṛṣabhadeva remained blind to a consequence of what was said in the Vṛtti.

I think such conclusions are not warranted by the evidence. Consider first the beginning of the Vṛtti on VP 1.46[173] and the Paddhati passage cited earlier (see note 166). The Vṛtti begins by saying that *ātmabheda* is followed by a nominal ending of either the second or the first triplet, depending on whether self-difference (*ātmabheda*) is the object of saying or an utterance of the ancients is cited. Vṛṣabhadeva begins by noting that Bhartṛhari says that first- and second-triplet endings are both correct after *ātmabheda*. In view of what he says later on, Vṛṣabha's *yadātmabheda eva bravītikriyayā vyāpyate* must be understood to explain the remainder of the Vṛtti sentence whose first word, *ātmabhedasya*, he has just cited. Vṛṣabhadeva deals with the first of two possibilities mentioned in the Vṛtti concerning how one can formulate the issue. When only self difference is covered by the act of saying, so that this alone is the object encompassed by this act, then a second-triplet ending is used, as in *ātmabhedam*.[174] Vṛṣabha next cites *āhuḥ* from the kārikā, asks what the ancients say, and supplies the answer: a self difference (*ātmabhedam*). This does not end the matter, however, for he goes on to note how this is stated: in the form '... is' (*astīty anena rūpeṇa*). The straightforward manner to understand this is that Vṛṣabha says the kārikā is quoting a statement of the ancients which contains *ātmabhedo'sti*. This alone is compatible with what Vṛṣabha goes on to say immediately thereafter:[175] if one cites the utterance of predecessors, stating that they say such and such, then *ātmabheda* takes a first-triplet ending.

Now, I could agree to an adverbial *asti* in Sanskrit, just as I consider there is good evidence that *asti* 'is' occurs as a presentential element,[176] but it is a very different matter to claim that *astīti* is an adverb, even if one can cite the equivalence of *kim* and *kimiti*. Nor does the Vṛtti's saying ... *asataḥ śabdān astitvenābhimanyante* '... consider nonexistent linguistic units as existent' require one to infer that *astīti* in VP 1.87ab is an adverb. The Vṛtti uses a common construction, with an instrumental form used to designate a characteristic marking something as having reached a certain state (**A** 2.3.21: *itthambhūtalakṣaṇe*): the property of being (*astitva*) characterizes something which some know as marked by this property. In addition, the singular *asti* is justified in this kārikā. Bhartṛhari uses the singular *asti* in *astīti* 'It exists' because he is speaking here of elements which are said to contribute to the final manifestation of true speech units, be these sounds, words or utterances. Raghunātha Śarmā (1963:159) is on the mark, I think, when he says in his Ambākartrī: *sphoṭasya nirbhāgatvena asatas tu yān asamastān śabdān 'asti antarāle' samastaḥ pūrvapūrva-dhvanyabhivyaktaḥ sphoṭaikadeśaḥ' iti manyate pratipattā* 'A listener considers those partial linguistic units which, because a sphoṭa is without parts, are nonexistent, (thinking), "There is in the interval a partial incomplete sphoṭa revealed by each preceding sound".' In sum, *astīti* of both VP 1.46 and 1.87 can and should be interpreted in the obvious manner: this consists of the verb form *asti* that is part of a quoted utterance and the citation particle *iti*.

I think the parallel Houben invokes between *ātmabhedaṁ tayoḥ ke cid astīty āhuḥ purāṇagāḥ* and VP 1.87ab *asataś cāntarāle yāñ chabdān astīti manyante* calls for additional comment. The construction illustrated by VP 1.87ab has an ancient pedigree. This already occurs in the Ṛgveda, as in:

ṚV 2.12.5ab: *yaṁ smā pṛcchanti kuha setì ghoram utem āhur naiṣo astīty ènam* '(Indra) about whom one would ask, "Where is he?", the fierce one about whom is said, "He does not exist".'

Another construction, commonly used in later Sanskrit, also occurs this early, as in:

ṚV 8.100.3c: *nendrò astīti nemà u tva āha* 'Some one or the other says, "Indra does not exist".'

The construction illustrated by ṚV 2.12.5ab and VP 1.87ab can be represented schematically as:

(a) $V_1 N_{1ag.} N_{2obj.}$: $(V_2 N_{3ag.} \ldots)$ iti

where V_1 is a verb with the meaning 'say', 'ask' or similar, V_2 is a verb of existence and N — a nominal or nominal phrase — refers to complements of these verbs: $N_{1ag.}$, $N_{3ag.}$: agent of V_1 and V_2, $N_{2obj.}$: object of V_1. In addition, $N_{2obj.}$ and $N_{3ag.}$ are regularly coreferential, so that the latter can be omitted, and $(V_2 N_{3ag.} \ldots)$ can contain additional complements, and can be negated. The construction illustrated by ṚV 8.100.3c may be represented as:

(b) $V_1N_{1ag.}$: $(V_2N_{2ag.} ...)$ iti

and the construction illustrated in VP 1.46cd ... *abhinnasya bhedam eke pracakṣate* may be represented as:

(c) $V_1N_{1ag.}$: $N_{2obj.}N_{3comp.}$

where $N_{3comp.}$ stands for a complement to $N_{2obj.}$, and V_1 is not as restricted as for (a). In all instances, $N_{1ag.}$ can be absent, since verb endings designate unspecified agents, and verbs of being can be omitted in non-negative phrases. Reordering and simplifying the examples to illustrate these schemata:

(a) *pṛcchanti yam* : ([*asti*] *saḥ kuha*) *iti*
āhuḥ enam : (*na asti eṣaḥ*) *iti*
manyate asataḥ śabdān : (*asti*) *iti*

(b) *āha nemaḥ u tvaḥ* : (*na asti indraḥ*) *iti*

(c) *pracakṣate kecit* : *bhedam abhinnasya*.

VP 1.46ab *ātmabhedas tayoḥ kecid astīty āhuḥ purāṇagāḥ* should be interpreted as of type (b):

āhuḥ kecit purāṇagāḥ : (*asti ātmabhedaḥ tayoḥ*) *iti*

Another possible parsing, less preferable in the context, would be *āhuḥ kecit purāṇagāḥ tayoḥ* : (*asti ātmabhedaḥ*) *iti* ('Some say of these two: "There is a self difference"').

Now, if *ātmabhedaṁ tayoḥ ke cid astīty āhuḥ purāṇagāḥ* is the reading in VP 1.46ab and this is considered an instance of type (a), it then has to be parsed in one of two ways: *āhuḥ kecit purāṇagāḥ ātmabhedam* : ([*saḥ*] *tayoḥ asti*) *iti* ('Some followers of tradition state a self difference: "(It) exists for these two"') or *āhuḥ kecit purāṇagāḥ ātmabhedam tayoḥ* : (*asti*) *iti* ('Some followers of tradition state about a self difference with respect to these two: "(It) exists"'). Given what the Vṛtti says, in the view of its author this is not what the author of the kārikā intended, since he takes pains to point out that either *ātmabheda* is linked to the verb or there is a citation of an entire utterance. *buddhibhedād abhinnasya bhedam eke pracakṣate* unequivocally states that some predicate difference of a single unsplit entity because of a difference in understanding. Emphasizing the contrast makes sense if *ātmabheda* is part of the sentence quoted. The reading with *ātmabhedam* in construction (a) thus differs vitally in emphasis, since now one is saying something about a self difference. It is this point, I think, that Aklujkar makes in his statement quoted above. In addition, as should be clear from the above, what Vṛṣabha says in the Paddhati on 1.46 does not require that he be dealing with a reading *ātmabhedaṁ tayoḥ*. On the contrary, the Paddhati on VP 1.46 begins (K. A. Subramania Iyer [1966a:103.9]): *ātmabheda iti* | *svabhāvānyatvam*. Clearly, Vṛṣabhadeva's text had the nominative *ātmabhedas*.

Finally, I think one might consider a possibility which Bronkhorst, Aklujkar, and Houben have not taken into account.[177] As shown, VP 1.46 presents two views. It also contains two verb forms: *āhuḥ*, *pracakṣate* '... say'. Now, *brū,* its alternative base *āh*,[178] and *cakṣ* all are verbs meaning 'say'. Indeed, the Pāṇinian dhātupāṭha texts transmitted by commentators gloss *cakṣ* and *brū* identically: *cakṣiṅ vyaktāyāṁ vāci*, *brūñ vyaktāyāṁ vāci* (Kṣīrataraṅginī II.9, 37 [Yudhiṣṭhira Mīmāṁsaka (1957/8: 168, 175)], Dhātupradīpa II.7, 35 [Srish Chandra Chakravarti (1919: 77, 80)], Mādhavīyadhātuvṛtti II.9, 46 [Dwarikadas Shastri (1964:324, 349)]). In addition, *ātmabhedaḥ* and *abhinnasya bhedam* are syntactically equivalent compound and analytic expressions. Accordingly, VP 1.46ab: *ātmabhedas tayoḥ kecid astīty āhuḥ* ... and 1.46cd: ... *abhinnasya bhedam eke pracakṣate* are parallel expressions using two alternative syntactic patterns: first a sentence is quoted which contains the nominative *ātmabhedaḥ*, then an accusative in construction with a verb of saying is used. On the assumption that *ātmabhedas tayoḥ* was indeed the reading for the Vṛtti also and that *bruvikarmatva* means 'being the object of an act of saying', it is appropriate to consider that *ātmabhedasya bruvikarmatve dvitīyā vākyasva-rūpānukaraṇe tu prathamā* concerns the syntactic possibilities illustrated in both parts of the kārikā, using *ātmabheda* as the instance of a term possibly followed by an accusative ending.

As noted, the interpretation given assumes that the term *bruvikarmatve* signifies the property of being an object of saying. Now, it is true that under Kātyāyana's formulation taken in isolation,[179] the suffixes ***ik*** and ***śtip*** form derivates used to refer to verbal bases (*dhātunirdeśe*). Note, however, that in his commentary on the Mahābhāṣya Nāgeśa immediately says that the suffixes are also used to form derivates used with reference to the meanings of verbal bases (*dhātvarthanirdeśe*).[180] Moreover, as Nāgeśa notes, such usage is exemplified by what Kātyāyana himself says. Thus, according to 4.4.1 vtt. 2-3 (*āhau prabhūtādibhyaḥ, pṛcchatau susnātādibhyaḥ*), the taddhita suffix *ṭhak* follows padas to form derivates meaning 'says ...', 'asks ....' The first type of derivate is formed from padas with bases of a group beginning with *prabhūta* 'plenty, abundant', the second from padas with bases of a group beginning with *susnāta* 'good bathing'; e.g. *prābhūtika* refers to someone who says 'plenty', *sausnātika* to someone who inquires whether one has had a good bath. As commentators note, *āhi* (loc. sg. *āhau*) and *pṛcchati* (loc. sg. *pṛcchatau*), with ***ik*** and ***śtip***, refer not to the verbal bases *āh* and *pracch* but to their meanings. Similarly, Bhartṛhari speaks of acts like eating (*bhujyādiḥ ... kriyā*)[181] in a context which can leave no doubt whatever that *bhuji* refers to the act of eating and not the base *bhuj*. First, *bhujyādiḥ* is construed with *kriyā*. Secondly, the reference is to examples such as *brāhmaṇā bhojyantām* 'Let the Brāhmaṇas be fed', where the act of eating is distributed, so that each one of a group of Brāhmaṇas partakes of food. Again, the Vṛtti on VP 1.51 says concerning the form of a linguisitic unit that, although it immediately appears when a term is uttered, there is an incompatibility between this form and acts such as eating, so that in the everyday world a unit's form is not used as an object and so on in these actions.[182] Here the term *bhujyādikriyā* is used. This is obviously a bahuvrīhi. Further, *ādi* is best considered to be used here with reference to a kind. In addition, it is difficult to claim that *bhuji* as used here refers to the verbal base *bhuj*. On the contrary, the context requires one to understand it as referring to eating. Given the general context in which the term is used, moreover, one is justified in saying that the act of eating is not spoken of in particular as denoted by *bhuj*, just as this is not true if one says *bhojanādikriyā*. In accordance with the above, I see nothing strange in considering that *bruvikarmatva* in the Vṛtti on VP 1.46 refers to an object of saying.[183]

One objection I can foresee being made to the interpretation noted is that the second half of the verse states the view of those who consider that there is a single entity which is split conceptually, so that *bhedam* is not equivalent to *ātmabhedam* if one holds that *ātmabheda* means 'essential difference'. In support of this, one can cite Vṛṣabha, who glosses *ātmabheda* with *svabhāvānyatva*. The Vṛtti's *ātmabhedasya bruvikarmatve* would then not concern pāda d. This is, however, only an apparent problem. *ātmabheda* means 'self difference', that is, difference in identity, which can be essential or imposed; which of the two is involved is known from context. The persons spoken of in VP 1.46ab maintain that there really are two distinct entities, so that here *ātmabheda* refers to an essential difference. *bheda* of pāda d, on the other hand, refers to a difference that is imposed conceptually, but this too is a difference in identity (*ātmabheda*). Note that, concerning the view spoken of in VP 1.46cd, the Vṛtti states that under another view there is the assumption of difference for a single entity and that the Vṛttikāra here says (see note 164) *ekasyaivātmanaḥ ... nānātvakalpanā* 'the fictitious assumption of difference for a single self'. It is undeniable that *ātmanaḥ ... nānātvakalpnā* is compatible with *ātmano bhedam*. Note also that Vṛṣabhadeva's Paddhati (K. A. Subramania Iyer [1966a:103.10-11]) explains the second half of the kārikā in a manner that is in harmony with this: *buddhibhedāt* : *na ca svagato bhedo'sti śaktidvayayogāt tu sa eva bhedena pratyavabhāsata ity apare* 'Others say: there is also no difference that inheres in the entity itself; but, because it is connected with two capacities, that selfsame one appears as different.' Accordingly, the Vṛtti's *ātmabhedasya bruvikarmatve* ... can concern both instances of *ātmabheda-*.[184]

Another objection one might be tempted to raise[185] is that the interpretation given for the Vṛtti on VP 1.46 wrongly presupposes, contrary to the usual practice of the Vṛttikāra, that, instead of beginning with the first part of a kārikā, he is here beginning with the last part. Such an objection, however, is without foundation. Under the interpretation suggested here, the Vṛtti's *ātmabhedasya bruvikarmatve dvitīyā vākya-svarūpānukaraṇe tu prathamā* does not concern pāda d alone; it concerns the syntax of the entire kārikā. Moreover, as I have pointed out (see note 164), the Vṛttikāra then proceeds specifically to contrast the two views dealt with, starting with the view spoken of in the first half of the verse. He does not subject the kārikā to piecemeal interpretation.

Finally, one could object that Vṛṣabha's Paddhati shows that the Vṛttikāra was indeed considering two distinct forms in VP 1.46a. Houben makes this claim, and his statement includes the clause, 'although according to Vṛṣabha the Vṛtti does precisely this'.[186] This is at least imprecise. What the Paddhati says (see note 166) is that the Vṛtti states the correctness of both a second- and first-triplet ending after the term *ātmabheda*. This must indeed have to do with the Vṛtti's first sentence *ātmabhedasya bruvikarmatve dvitīyā vākyasvarūpānukaraṇe tu prathamā* (see note 164). It does not, however, require that Vṛṣabha consider the Vṛtti to speak of a reading *ātmabhedam* in VP 1.46a. It requires only that, according to the Paddhati, the Vṛtti speaks of two possible constructions, such that *ātmabheda-* is followed by one of two endings. As to why the Vṛtti should do so, the points discussed above show that this is not because the Vṛttikāra sees anything unnatural in any reading known to him but because the two possible constructions are indeed exemplified in the Vākyapadīya kārikā upon which he is commenting. Finally, it would be surprising that Vṛṣabha should consider the Vṛtti to speak of two readings, with *ātmabhedam* as well as *ātmabhedas*, since the Paddhati on VP 1.46 begins precisely with *ātmabheda iti*, showing that for Vṛṣabha VP 1.46a was *ātmabhedas tayoḥ kecit*.[187]

I think I have made it clear that under the interpretation I have suggested for VP 1.46 and its commentary, the Vṛtti does not have to be pondering — for some unknown reason — a different way of saying just what is said in the first half of the kārikā, much less considering two different readings in this pāda.

There remains, of course, the issue of how to account for the reading *ātmabhedaṁ tayoḥ* favored by good kārikā manuscripts. One could speculate that this reading originates in an anticipation of *bhedam* in the next part of the kārikā.[188] This assumption fits with the fact that Vṛṣabhadeva knew the reading *ātmabhedas tayoḥ* and also with the discussion in the Vṛtti. To be sure, this is speculative. Nevertheless, I think the evidence dealt with justifies me in not considering VP 1.46 evidence for the position that the author of the Vṛtti is different from Bhartṛhari.

4.2.4. *Studies on the doctrines set forth in the Vākyapadīya* (VI.2.4)

Since K. A. Subramania Iyer's study (1969) of Bhartṛhari's thought, there has not appeared any single work covering in detail Bhartṛhari's ideas and the relations between these and views held by other thinkers. Such a work is nevertheless a desideratum, since, for all its great value, Subramania Iyer's book deals with quite a few issues in less than desirable detail. Ashok Aklujkar is preparing a general work (forthcoming d), a preliminary version of which — lacking the footnotes — has been circulated.

Aklujkar (1990) gives a good summary of the contents of the Vākyapadīya.[189] The same author (forthcoming h) not only summarizes the Vākyapadīya but also deals with Bhartṛhari in general. Other recent general surveys of Bhartṛhari are Gaurinath Śāstrī (1991) and M. M. Deshpande (1992d).[190] R. C. Dwivedi (1993) discusses briefly but with rich documentation the indebtedness of Kashmir Śaivism to Bhartṛhari, with special emphasis on the controversy involving parā vāk and śabdabrahman, as well as pratibhā.[191]

A recent general discussion concerning a basic concept of Bhartṛhari, sphoṭa, is found in Rāmanārāyaṇa Miśra (1991). Chapters 7-9 of B. K. Matilal (1990a:77-105) deal with Bhartṛhari's concept of sphoṭa, its background and its critics. General discussions concerning sphoṭa appear also in Gaurinath Sāstrī (1981), K. A. Subramania Iyer (1982:12-50), K. Subrahmanyam (1989), Patnaik (1991), Filliozat (1984, 1992b), P. Srirama Murti (1992). The most recent paper I know of devoted to this topic is by G. B. Palsule (1994), again a general treatment of Bhartṛhari's overall system; see also Palsule (1993a).[192] Other papers covering Bhartṛhari's views on semantics in broad strokes are Zimmerman (1989)[193] and H. S Ananthanarayana (1991-92).[194]

Honda (1993) studies the various views Bhartṛhari presents in the kriyāsamuddeśa of the third kāṇḍa concerning what constitutes an action. Srimannarayana Murti (1981) takes up Bhartṛhari's discussion concerning time (see also Srimannarayana Murti [1982]), and Cardona (1991d) more recently has discussed kārikās from the kālasamuddeśa.[195]

Naradeva Śāstrī (1988) concentrates on the various definitions of a vākya considered in the second kāṇḍa of the Vākyapadīya, and Ramji Pandeya (1990) briefly takes up the allied topic of pratibhā.[196]

Pradip Kumar Mazumdar (1977:118-144) discusses the concept of an indivisible utterance and the arguments advanced, principally by Bhartṛhari, against those who maintained that an utterance is composed of constituent padas, so that a sentential meaning is derived from word meanings. The complexities of the various positions presented and discussed in the Vākyapadīya with respect to what constitutes a sentence and its meaning have more recently been taken up by Houben (1995b),[197] who remarks (1995b:57), 'What is rather strange if on the basis of Puṇyarāja and later interpreters one expects to find in the second book of the *VP* a polemical exposition in which Bhartṛhari defends the 'indivisible sentence' view and refutes the 'individual word' view, is that none of the arguments is presented as an argument which should absolutely convince the other party. Rather on the contrary.' Deciding what argument should absolutely convince an opponent is a matter of judgement. Nevertheless, Bhartṛhari does present arguments which are meant to demonstrate that an opponent is driven to contradicting a basic tenet of his system. Thus, in VP 2.16 (*aśabdo yadi vākyārthaḥ padārtho'pi tathā bhavet | evaṁ sati ca sambandhaḥ śabdasyārthena hīyeta*)[198] he argues that if, as a Bhāṭṭa Mīmāṁsaka does, what is considered a sentence meaning is not directly associated with a speech unit, then one is driven to conclude that what is considered the meaning of individual words also has the same status, with the consequence that the relation between a speech unit and a meaning — which a Mīmāṁsaka holds to be fixed without any human convention intervening — would be given up. This is discussed in Cardona (forthcoming k: section 3.5).

Bhartṛhari is indeed characterized by what Houben calls 'perspectivism' — in that he sets forth the views espoused and defended by various thinkers.[199] It is also true that he does not organize his work in the manner of such later Pāṇinīyas as Kauṇḍabhaṭṭa and Nāgeśa, in terms of pūrvapakṣas to be refuted explicitly and siddhāntas to be established and defended. In both these aspects, the Vākyapadīya is more like the Mahābhāṣya. Yet Bhartṛhari does indeed indicate — not brutally but still not obscurely — what his final views are, and he does indicate problems with the views of others. Perhaps he understood better than modern scholars how hard it is to convince absolutely holders of opposing views.

Two large works, by Vīrendra Sharma (1977) and Jan Houben (1995a) deal with the Sambandhasamuddeśa and both discuss Bhartṛhari's ideas and their background.[200] In his treatment of the text Sharma sticks very close to the commentatorial traditions, so that, for example, his understanding of kārikās in the Sambandhasamuddeśa closely follows what Helārāja says, although Sharma does not present a running translation of the kārikās or their commentary. Houben translates Helārāja's commentary as well as the kārikās and supplies extensive comments and references, so that his work goes well beyond that of K. A. Subramania Iyer (1971a). He also is quite willing to disagree not only with Helārāja but also with the author of the Vṛtti on pertinent verses of the first kāṇḍa (e.g. 1995a:239). Obviously, Houben's study is the more easily accessible to most western scholars. It is also a work of wide-ranging breadth. There are many points — including major ones — about which I disagree with the author (see Cardona [forthcoming k]), but I consider this a valuable piece of scholarship.

Kanta Rani Bhatia's book (1992) has the fairly limited purpose of presenting the ideas of the second kāṇḍa through the intermediary of Puṇyarāja's commentary, and the author does this well. Her book is organized according to topics dealt with in the Vākyakāṇḍa.[201]

Of a very different nature is the book by Tandra Patnaik (1994). This work does not limit itself to the usual ground. The author considers Bhartṛhari's ideas also in relation to such modern thinkers as Austin, Grice, Searle, and Wittgenstein. The influence of B. K. Matilal is evident and acknowledged (Patnaik [1994:x]). Despite details on which one may differ with the author, her presentation is lucid and valuable. Aklujkar's study of prāmāṇya (1988-89) is also very valuable and comparable to Patnaik's work with respect to its approach, in that Aklujkar goes beyond the strictly Indian context and considers conceptual schemes of philosophers such as Quine.

One of the topics which Patnaik has of course to consider is Bhartṛhari's ideas about language in relation to Buddhist thinkers such as Diṅnāga (1994:126-137). While Patnaik touches on the subject in a very broad manner, Radhika Herzberger devotes most of her work (1986) to a close exposition — based on passages from the Vākyapadīya and the Pramāṇasamuccaya, translations for which are given and justified — of some basic views held by Bhartṛhari and Diṅnāga.[202]

Bronkhorst (1989, 1994a) has again considered Bhartṛhari's acquaintaince with ritual and Mīmāṁsā. He comes to interesting conclusions (1989:114 = 1994a:385):

> Bhartṛhari was acquainted with Mīmāṁsā, but did not use it where we would expect him to use it. In the context of ritual details he rather draws upon another tradition, most probably on the traditional manuals current in his Vedic school, that of the Maitrāyaṇīyas. And where he makes references to Mīmāṁsā, it is never to Śabara's Bhāṣya, but rather to a Mīmāṁsā work in verse, or containing verse, which has not survived, but may have been Bhavadāsa's Vṛtti. He may have known the Pūrva Mīmāṁsā Sūtra, or a part of it, but this is not certain.

The most recent published papers available to me concerning general aspects of Bhartṛhari's thinking and argumentation are by Yves Ramseier

(1994) and Jan E. M. Houben (1995c, cf. 1995a:214-228). The latter takes up anew a group of verses from the sambandhasamuddeśa (Vākyapadīya 3.3.20-28) that deal with a paradox. One of these kārikās (VP 3.3.25: *sarvaṁ mithyā bravīmīti naitad vākyaṁ vivakṣyate* ...) explicitly concerns the statement *sarvaṁ mithyā bravīmi* 'All I say is lies.' Houben considers first VP 3.3.1-4, then skips to the above-mentioned group. His conclusion begins (1995c:394), 'With this passage 20-28 has come to a close. Bhartṛhari's solution was intended to silence the (real or imaginative) objector who points out the paradoxical problem with regard to the statement that '[something is] unsignifiable'.'[203] Houben also suggests (1995c:395) that VP 3.3.20-28 '... amounts, in fact, to a strong defence for the Mādhyamika position as held e.g. in Nāgārjuna's Vigraha-Vyāvartanī.' It is of interest to note that Helārāja introduces VP 3.3.20 saying (K. A. Subramania Iyer [1963a:137.9]: *atrāvācyatve samavāyasyokte naiyāyiko vākchalam udbhāvayati*) that a Naiyāyika now brings up a quibble, once it has been stated that inherence is not signifiable as such. In fact, VP 3.3.12 (*padārthīkṛta evānyaiḥ ... sambandhaḥ ...*) speaks of others making a relation into an ontological category signifiable by a term (*padārtha*), and the next kārikā (VP 3.3.13: *samavāyāt sva ādhāraḥ svā ca jātiḥ pratīyate ...*) explicitly refers to inherence (*samavāya*) and says it is due to this relation that a substrate or a generic property is understood. This pair of verses is best understood as portraying the Vaiśeṣika-Naiyāyika stand that inherence is a separate permanent relation. It is curious that Houben skips the intervening kārikās and jumps from VP 3.3.4 directly to the set 3.3.20-28.[204]

Unebe (1994) deals with one of the possible relations Bhartṛhari views as connecting speech forms and meanings, a natural aptness (*yogyatā*), and considers also views of Mīmāṁsakas, Naiyāyikas and Vaiśeṣikas.

4.3. LATER SEMANTIC TREATISES

4.3.1. *Editions, translations and studies* (VI.3.2)

Pandit Manudeva Bhaṭṭāchārya (1985) has edited and published the Vaiyākaraṇabhūṣaṇa with his Sanskrit commentary and useful appendixes. The same work has been republished in an edition by Vidya Niwas Misra (1987).[205] Four recent editions of the Vaiyākaraṇabhūṣaṇasāra have appeared, three with Hindi translations and comments (Prabhākara Miśra [1982], Brahma Dutta Dwivedī [1985]), Adyāprasāda Miśra [1988]), the other with an English translation (Karunasindhu Das [1990]).

S. D. Joshi (1990a) summarizes the contents of Kauṇḍabhaṭṭa's two works. Joshi earlier (1980b, 1981) had discussed Kauṇḍabhaṭṭa's exposition of sphoṭa and discussion of compounds. Ogawa (1990) is a translation with extensive notes of the Vaiyākaraṇabhūṣaṇasāra on the first two kārikās of the Vaiyākaraṇasiddhāntakārikā, in Japanese, with an English outline (1990:117-119). S. D. Joshi (1960) has now been published (1993, 1995, 1997). In addition, a revised version of M. M. Deshpande (1972b) has appeared (1992a), and Jayashree Gune's dissertation (1974) also has been published (1978). Radheshyam Sharma (1984-85) briefly takes up what properties are considered to characterize a karman, mainly from the point of view of Kauṇḍa Bhaṭṭa.[206]

As I noted on an earlier occasion (Cardona [1989:49]), two editions of the Vaiyākaraṇasiddhāntamañjūṣā have now been published: Kālikā Prasāda Śukla (1977), Kapil Dev Shastri (1985). The latter is enhanced by valuable appendixes comparing passages from the Vaiyākaraṇasiddhāntamañjūṣā, the Vaiyākaraṇabhūṣaṇa, and the Laghumañjūṣā.

The Laghumañjūṣā edition of 1925 has been reprinted (Varanasi: Chowkhamba, 1989).[207] In addition, the Laghumañjūṣā with the Kuñjikā and Kalā commentaries and a detailed Hindi explanation by Rāmaprasāda Tripāṭhī is in course of publication; its first part has appeared (1990). Peri Suryanarayana Shastri (1987, 1988) has composed an original Sanskrit commentary on parts of the Laghumañjūṣā.

The Paramalaghumañjūṣā has recently been published with translations and commentaries in Hindi (Kapil Dev Shastri [1975]),[208] Jaya Shankar Lal Tripathi [1985]) and Marathi (V. B. Bhagavat [1984]). K. Kunjunni Raja (1990b, c) summarizes the contents of the Paramalaghumañjūṣā, based on Kalika Prasad Sukla's edition,[209] and of the Sphoṭavāda. Cardona (1991c) has pointed out that a section of the Paramalaghumañjūṣā is indebted strongly to Bhavānanda's Kārakacakra.

Rāmamanohara Miśra (1983) deals in some detail with the topics covered in the Vaiyākaraṇabhūṣaṇasāra and the Paramalaghumañjūṣā, which entails his considering also views of Mīmāṁsakas and Naiyāyikas. Shankarji Jha's recent work (1995) presents the basic views discussed in various treatises concerning all the major topics which works such as the Vaiyākaraṇabhūṣaṇa and the Vaiyākaraṇasiddhāntalaghumañjūṣā treat.[210]

Ramakrishnamacharya (1985) has studied a verse section from Bhaṭṭoji's Vaiyākaraṇasiddhāntakārikā concerning padasphoṭa.

Nāgeśa shows the influence of tāntric thought. For example, his description in the Laghumañjūṣā of four levels of speech in connection with speech production clearly shows such influence. Rājanātha Tripāṭhī (1988) has studied the impact of tantra on Nāgeśa.

5. PĀṆINIAN STUDIES AND COGNITIVE STUDIES AND TECHNOLOGY

Recent years have witnessed a rapid rise in cognitive studies and technology and this has had an effect on Pāṇinian studies. Some recent papers reflect the growing interaction between work on Pāṇinian grammar and computer science and artificial intelligence. Thus, Bhate and Kak (1993:93) say their article is intended to highlight several formal features in Pāṇini's grammar which have parallels in computer science.[211] Le Mée's programatic paper (1988-89) is particularly intriguing in that his stated purpose is (1988-89:114), '... to indicate some possible avenues where a fruitful collaboration between traditional grammarians and engineers could take place and contribute to solve some of the problems of modern technology.' The most recent monograph I know of in this general area is by Bharati, Chaitanya and Sangal (1995).

Scholars are now also taking seriously the possibility of writing computer programs replicating Pāṇini's derivational system. The work of two scholars in this area merits special mention: P. Ramanujan of the Centre for Development of Advanced Computing, Bangalore, and Shivamurthy Swamiji (Taralabalu Kendra, Bangalore). In my opinion, Ramanujan's work in developing programs replicating Pāṇinian prakriyā and analysis of strings in terms of Pāṇinian rules has particular merit and quality.

Data bases are also being developed for materials pertinent to these studies. For example, two former students of mine — Peter Scharf and Elliot Stern — and I carried out a four-year project, in which Bruce Perry also participated as a consultant, the result of which is a set of data files[212] that comprise the Aṣṭādhyāyī, the Mahābhāṣya, Kātyāyana's vārttikas, the Kāśikāvṛtti, the Ṛgvedaprātiśākhya, Taittirīyaprātiśākhya, Vājasaneyi-prātiśākhya, the Āpiśalaśikṣā and Pāṇinīyaśikṣā (in various versions), the padapāṭha to the Ṛgveda, and the Nirukta. As time allows, I am completing concordances to be included in fields within these files. When the work is completed, the data will be made available to interested scholars. In connection with this work, programs have also been developed for applying Pāṇinian sandhi rules to text entered without observing these rules, for converting from Romanization to various Devanāgarī fonts, and for sorting, in both Devanāgarī and Romanization.

Finally, scholars are now using 'ftp' [file transfer protocol] sites and web sites to make materials available to their colleagues, who can transfer them electronically. Also, archives of files usable on computers are maintained in various institutions. In addition, the Indology discussion group based in Liverpool serves as a forum in which one finds — though not as commonly as one could wish for — serious discussion of scholarly points concerning Sanskrit grammar and, on occasion, matters Pāṇinian.

6. LITERARY WORKS ILLUSTRATING GRAMMATICAL RULES (VII)

Śaśi Bālā (1994) is the only recent study of the Bhaṭṭikāvya known to me. After an introductory chapter, Śaśi Bālā devotes chapters to the sound system, sandhi, compounds, nominal forms, verb forms, derivates with kṛt and taddhita affixes, and the utterance. In this last chapter, Bhaṭṭi's section on kārakas is treated. Most noteworthy, in my estimation, is the sixth chapter (101-171), in which the author deals extensively with Bhaṭṭi's use of verb forms, including particular usages that have prompted disapproval from other Pāṇinīyas.

K. Kunjunni Raja (1979) and T. Venkatacharya, (1980) have edited two works which deal with usages in literary works that are objects of dispute concerning their correctness in terms of Pāṇinian rules.

I think it is also worth mentioning publications of non-Pāṇinian works in this area. Jambūvijaya (1983-87) has reedited Hemacandra's Dvyāśraya-mahākāvya, with a commentary by Abhayatilaka. In addition, Forthomme (1993) has recently reedited and translated Nārāyaṇabhaṭṭa's Dhātukāvya (see Cardona [1976a:370 note 553]). The text of the poem and its French translation are preceded by a study concerning the state of the text, its sources, metrics, and structure.

7. A SUMMARY OF TRENDS (VIII)

Towards the end of my earlier survey (Cardona [1976a:309-310]), I noted an ever increasing interest in works on semantics and philosophy of grammar, especially in Bhartṛhari's Vākyapadīya. This trend has continued, as is evident from the number of articles and monographs devoted to the Vākyapadīya and the work on editing the text of the kārikās and the Vṛtti. The recent international conference on Bhartṛhari is another manifestation of this interest. At the same time, even the sample of work covered in Cardona (1989) and in the present survey suffices to show that scholarship in many areas of Pāṇinian studies is also still quite lively and liable to give rise to sharp differences. There are enough scholars, in the West and Far East as well as in India, seeking to understand the history of Indian grammatical work in all its complexities and working closely on textual matters so as to assure both that ideas will continue to flow and that conclusions finally reached and accepted — possibly after vigorous exchanges and controversies— are based on a firm command of texts and their traditions.

One major new development which could not be foreseen immediately twenty years ago is the expanding use of technology in connection with Indology and particularly the application of computer science methods to Pāṇini.

NOTES AND INDEXES

NOTES

[1]Sures Chandra Banerji's more recent work (1996) hardly fits the category. The two main chapters of this book, covering authors and works, consist of lists of names, arranged alphabetically, with some comments. The select bibliography (209-220) is skimpy and lacks much information one expects to find in a bibliography.

[2]For details, see Cardona (1997a:145-158 [**230-244**]).

[3]Kielhorn (1880-85:II.69.15-18): *sṛjiyujyoḥ sakarmakayoḥ kartā bahulaṁ karmavad bhavatīti vaktavyam* । *śyaṁs tu bhavati* । *sṛjeḥ śraddhopapanne kartari karmavadbhāvo vācyaś ciṇātmanepadārthaḥ* । *sṛjyate mālām asarji mālām* । *yujes tu nyāyye karmakartari yako' bhāvāya* । *yujyate brahmacārī yogam.*

[4]Pradīpa (Vedavrata [1962-63:III.175]): *yujyata iti* । *yogo brahmacāriṇaṁ yunakti* । *sambadhnātīty arthaḥ* । *tato brahmacāriṇaḥ kartṛtvavivakṣāyāṁ yujyate brahmacārī yogam iti bhavati.*

[5]I think the passages I have cited above from Bronkhorst's article also illustrate that he is willing to draw major conclusions from less than cogent arguments and to then base further arguments on these conclusions, but I cannot take these up here. Suffice it to say that I agree with Aklujkar (1993b:46-47 note 2) in finding Bronkhorst's 'second-level argumentation' unsatisfactory.

[6]Rocher (1975) was in press when my earlier survey appeared; see Cardona (1976a:141).

[7]I have not yet compared the texts for possible divergences.

[8]Note that in no way is this intended to be considered a critical edition of the text in the manner discussed recently by Aklujkar (1983a). Nor do I include all variants mentioned by commentators and reflected in various Pāṇinīya works. I will take up such variants under individual sūtras in future volumes of *Pāṇini : His Work and its Traditions.* Yudhiṣṭhira Mīmāṁsaka (1984:III:46-58, 59-61) lists readings noted by Nāgeśa and readings noted in an undated manuscript of a work by Anantarāma, according

with the Mahābhāṣya. P. Visalakshy (1989:63-82) also deals with variants.

[9]Volume 5, covering **A** 2.1.1-2.1.72, has been published but at the time I was completing this work I had not yet seen it.

[10]S. D. Joshi (1982c:123): 'To make this point clear I have chosen P. 2.2.11 and 2.4.2. But the remarks made above hold good for many more rules.'

[11]I wish this to be understood as couched in very cautious language, since I cannot enter into a discussion of just what sort of native control and at what registers such later authors may be presumed to have had.

[12]Late 19th century; see p. 11 of the introduction.

[13]There are places where I would differ from Avanindra Kumar. Thus, under 'चङ् - III.i.48' (1996:244b), the entry is, ण्यन्त धातु, श्रि, द्रु, और स्रु धातुओं से उत्तर कर्तृवाची लुङ् परे रहते च्लि के स्थान मे चङ् आदेश होता है। I think it can be demonstrated, however, that the replacement of ***cli*** by ***caṅ*** takes place after the L-affix itself has been replaced by endings. **A** 3.1.53 (*lipisicihvaś ca*), where *luṅi* is also understood to recur from 3.1.43, provides for replacing ***cli*** with ***aṅ*** after *lip* 'smear, anoint', *sic* 'pour, sprinkle, irrigate', and *hve* 'call, challenge'. The next sūtra (**A** 3.1.54: *ātmanepadeṣv anyatarasyām*) lets this substitution apply optionally after the same verbs when ātmanepada affixes follow, accounting for pairs such as *alipta*, *alipata*. This assumes that 3.1.53 would otherwise obtain obligatorily. Since *ātmanepada* refers to endings *ta* through *mahiṅ* and to participial *āna*, the substitution in question has to apply after the L-affix has been replaced by endings. There are also some omissions. Thus, under तवै (1996:295a), references are given to **A** 3.4.14 and 6.2.51 but not to 3.4.9, and 6.1.200. Let me emphasize, nevertheless, that so far as I have been able to see from a first reading of this work, it is generally quite trustworthy.

[14]Deshpande also emphasizes that some differences among grammarians can be due not to differences of usage but to various ways of accounting for the same facts. On this point see also Cardona (1987a).

[15]In the same vein, Bhate (1980a, 1987b); see Cardona (1989:75 note 3).

[16]In a more recent paper also, Joshi and Roodbergen (1994b:90) again dismiss Pāṇinian sūtras because they prefer their own interpretations of

Sanskrit words to Pāṇini's. As is known, according to **A** 3.4.73 (*dāśagoghnau sampradāne*) and **A** 3.4.74 (*bhīmādayo' pādāne*), *goghna* refers to someone for whom a cow is killed, a guest, and *bhīma* signifies an apādāna, someone of whom one is afraid. Joshi and Roodbergen disagree, saying:

> But *goghna* can be taken to mean 'one who kills a cow', as a simple *upapada* formation. Its mocking application to a guest in whose honour a cow was killed may have lead to the derivation of *goghna* in the sense of *saṃpradāna*. The word *bhīma* may as well be taken in the sense of 'one who inspires fear'. Why a derivation in the sense of *apādāna* is required is not clear. We note that the rules P. 3.4.73 occur at the end of a section, just before the mention of *uṇādi* suffixes, and just before a new section is introduced.

The attitude which Joshi and Roodbergen evince can also be seen reflected in other work. Thus, Hari Mohan Mishra (1986) devotes his short book (92 pages, including introduction and bibliography) to demonstrating that Pāṇini's grammar '... is not scientifically written' and '... cannot logically be termed either descriptive or generative.'(1986:10) One sort of evidence which Mishra invokes to demonstrate his thesis is what he calls (1986:50) 'arbitrary derivation', and one type of such derivation involves affixes which in Mishra's opinion (1986:51) '... are really independent words.' For example, he says (1986:51) of *-kalpa* in a derivate like *vidvat-kalpa-* 'a little learned', ''Kalpa' is really a primary derivative of the verb kḷp. 'Vidvat-kalpa' should be analyzed as a compound word.' Though I do not wish to dismiss him or say that his work is not challenging, I nevertheless do not think it worthwhile to consider here in detail the evidence which Mishra sets forth in this work. Saroja Bhate (1994) has recently discussed objections to Pāṇini brought up by Rajavade and shown them to be baseless.

[17]In section **3.5** of their paper, Joshi and Roodbergen (1983:76) claim that a group of taddhita affixation rules relative to Vedic (*chandasi*), **A** 4.4.110-144, is anomalous in that the rules in question are all gathered together instead of being distributed among sections of rules dealing with comparable derivates in the bhāṣā. In section 4 of a forthcoming paper, M. M. Deshpande (forthcoming a) argues against this position as taken by Joshi and Roodbergen and also by Joshi and Bhate (1984).

[18]The issue is first broached in vārttikas 4-9 on **A** 2.4.85. In vārttika 7 (*ḍiti ṭer lopāl lopaḥ*), Kātyāyana brings up the possibility that in a complex

like *kṛ-tās-tā* (← *kṛ-tās-ti*), the segment called *ṭi* — that is, the part of the complex that precedes *ḍā* and begins with its last vowel — is deleted (*kṛ-tās-tā* → *kṛ-t-ā*) because such segments are deleted before items marked with *ḍ*. The Bhāṣya on 2.4.85 vt. 7 remarks that, by virtue of *ḍā* being marked with *ḍ*, this deletion will apply even though the complex which precedes *ḍā* is not a bha stem with respect to this element (Kielhorn [1880-85:I.501.13-14]: *ḍiti ṭer lopena lopo bhaviṣyati* | *abhatvān na prāpnoti* | *ḍitkaraṇasāmarthyād bhaviṣyati*).

[19]I have considered here only materials and arguments presented by Joshi and Roodbergen in support of their thesis. Joshi and Bhate (1984) contains a chapter titled 'Associative digression, *maṇḍūkapluti* and intervention by unrelated topics' (1984:196-219) in which the same thesis is maintained on the basis of additional evidence. Joshi and Bhate remark (1984:196):

> But even the pre-Kātyāyana text of Pāṇini's rules appears to have contained interpolations or borrowings. It is hard to accept that the text of the *A*. received by Kātyāyana and Patañjali was the work of one person. It seems that the *A*. represents the whole grammatical literature collected from several sources, rather than a single unified work. Pāṇini's successors found the *A*. a convenient handbook in which they could insert their additions or modifications to supplement the text of the *sūtras*.

As can be seen, one of the arguments Joshi and Bhate appeal to is of the same kind as is used by Joshi and Roodbergen: what they consider to be the interruption of a sequence by an unrelated topic. Space limitations preclude my considering here the evidence Joshi and Bhate present. For the same reason, I cannot take up in detail Joshi and Bhate's study (1983) of how *ca* is used in the Aṣṭādhyāyī. Here too, the authors find inconsistency in the use of *ca* in the available text of Pāṇini's work and they say (1983:215):

> The *A*. does not appear to be consistent in its use of *ca*. In the present text of the *A*., the particle *ca* is used in several rules where it is not required, whereas in some other rules it is not used although it is required. If the *A*. in its present form is a work of a single person, we must conclude that sometimes Pāṇini very ingeniously uses *ca* to offer the correct division and interpretation of his rules, whereas at other times he indulges in unscientific and incorrect use. We cannot reasonably expect a methodical scholar like Pāṇini to take liberties with his own system on a relatively large scale. Therefore, our hypothesis is that the rules containing redundant *ca* have been added later on.

Joshi and Bhate also argue that traditional interpretations of certain sūtras containing *ca* are wrong. One example will illustrate their way of arguing. They assert (1983:171 note 6), 'In the *A.*, *ca* is never used as an item-connective but always as a sentence-connective.' Subsequently (1983:174-175), they consider examples such as **A** 1.2.7: *mṛḍmṛdagudhakuṣa-kliśavadavasaḥ ktvā* (*kit* 5), **A** 1.2.8: *rudavidamuṣagrahisvapipracchaḥ saṁś ca* (*ktvā* 7, *kit* 5), concerning which they say (1983:175):

> Here two processes, namely, *ktvā kit* and *san kit* cannot be co-applied in one and the same derivation. Therefore these two rules, namely,
>
> (i) *rudavidamuṣagrahisvapipracchaḥ*, and
>
> (ii) *saṁś ca* are considered to be linked by disjunction.
>
> Here the particle *ca* indicates abbreviated disjunctive interpretation between two statements:
>
> (i) *rudavidamuṣagrahisvapipracchaḥ* (*ktvā kit*)
>
> and *(ca)*,
>
> (ii) (*rudavidamuṣagrahisvapipracchaḥ*) *san* (*kit*).

Later on (1983:184-185), Joshi and Bhate take this example up once more and say of **A** 1.2.8:

> We derive this rule from the following two rules where both repeated and unrepeated items occur:
>
> (*a*) *rudavidamuṣagrahisvapipracchaḥ* (*ktvā kit*), and
>
> (*b*) (*rudavidamuṣagrahisvapipracchaḥ*) *saṁś ca* (*kit*).
>
> The repeated items are put in brackets. When we leave out the repeated items and retain the unrepeated items in (*a*) and (*b*), we get the following *sūtra* consisting of two parts:
>
> (29) (i) *rudavidamuṣagrahisvapipracchaḥ*, and
>
> (ii) *saṁś ca*.
>
> The repeated items supplied by the *anuvṛtti* device are left out in the contents of (i) and (ii). The traditional commentators could not detect the hidden pause between (i) and (ii). They thought that 1.1.8 [sic!] is a single rule where *ca* allows continuation of an incompatible item. In their opinion P. 1.1.8 [sic!] combines a unit of *san* and *ktvā* together which is to be connected with the same process *kit* and the same environment *rudavidamuṣagrahisvapipracchaḥ*.
>
> This is, however, not the correct interpretation of P. 1.1.8 [sic!]. The particle *ca* after *san* indicates that a preceding statement (i) is a different rule. This is the only

satistactory explanation, because it does not violate the rule that the sentence-connective *ca* is always placed after the first word in a sentence.

The argument holds only if *ca* must be a sentence connective. On the other hand, if one admits nominal conjunction with *ca*, there is no problem. Once this is allowed, **A** 1.2.8 as a single rule provides that ***ktvā*** and ***san*** (*ktvā saṁś ca*) are both marked with *k* (*kitau* [*bhavataḥ*]) after the verb bases given; see Cardona (1997a:337-338 [**520**]). This type of conjunction — what is traditionally called *itaretaryoga* — is known to have been used since earliest Indo-Aryan, attested as early as the Ṛgveda; e.g. ṚV 1.22.13: *mahī dyauḥ pṛthivī cà na imaym̐ yajñam mìmikṣatām | pipṛtān no bharīmabhiḥ*, where *dyauḥ* and *pṛthivī* are coordinated ('heaven and earth') and equally connected with the dual verb forms *mìmikṣatām* and *pipṛtām*. For a full study, see Klein (1985), in particular pp. 64-65 for the type illustrated here. Moreover, so far as I can discern, Joshi and Bhate do not give a justification for their assertion that such nominal coordination is absent in the Aṣṭādhyāyī. Joshi (1990b:32-34) argues in support of the thesis he and Roodbergen earlier maintained and (1990b:34-35) briefly takes up a few examples to demonstrate that commentaries have not understood the import of how Pāṇini used *vā*, *vibhāṣā*, and *anyatarasyām* (see section 2.1.4.3b). Bhate (1980a) also argues for eliminating **A** 1.1.6 (*dīdhīvevīṭām*) and **A** 7.4.52 (*ha eti*) from the original text of Pāṇini's work and goes so far as to say (1980a:11), 'It is obvious from even the superficial study of the Vedic rules that such rules appear in the *A* only as patch-up rules appended to the rules stating certain facts about classical language. Their occurrence in the *A* is, therefore, of a secondary character.'

[20]VP 3.12.12: *anubandhaś ca siddhe'rthe smṛtyartham anuṣajyate | tulyārtheṣv api cāvaśyaṁ na sarveṣv ekadharmatā.*

[21]Mahābhāṣya 1.3.72 (Kielhorn [1880-85:I.29218-23]): *svaritañita iti kimartham | yāti vāti drāti psāti | svaritañita iti śakyam akartum | kasmān na bhavati yāti vāti drāti psātīti | kartrabhipraye kriyāphala ity ucyate sarveṣāṁ ca kartrabhiprāyaṁ kriyāphalam asti | ta evaṁ vijñāsyāmaḥ : yeṣāṁ kartrabhiprāyam akartrabhiprāyaṁ ca kriyāphalam asti tebhya ātmanepadaṁ bhavatīti | na caiteṣāṁ kartrabhiprāyaṁ akartrabhiprāyaṁ ca kriyāphalam asti | tathājātīyakāḥ khalv ācāryeṇa svaritañitaḥ paṭhitā ye ubhayavanto yeṣāṁ kartrabhiprāyaṁ cākartrabhiprāyaṁ ca kriyāphalam*

asti.

[22]VP 3.12.11: *kriyāviśeṣavacane sāmarthyam uparudhyate | keṣāñcid anye tu kṛtāḥ svariteto ñitas tathā.*

[23]*kriyāviśeṣavacane.* The compound *kriyāviśeṣa* can be a ṣaṣṭhī-tatpuruṣa referring to a particular feature of an action, namely that its result is intended for the agent, or a karmadhāraya referring to a particular action implied by this feature, namely the act of making provision (*pratividhāna, saṁvidhāna*), which Bhartṛhari speaks of earlier in connection with the use of ātmanepada affixes and causatives. Helārāja (K. A. Subramania Iyer [1973:121.25-26]) interprets it in the second way: *kartrabhiprāyakriyopalakṣite saṁvidhānalakṣaṇe kriyāviśeṣe pratyāyye yātiprabhṛtīnāṁ dhātūnāṁ śaktiḥ pratihanyate.*

[24]Prakīrṇaprakāśa on VP 3.12.12 (K. A. Subramania Iyer [1973:122.9-16]): *iha kriyāmātravacanatvena samānābhidheyeṣv api dhātuṣu na sarveṣu kriyāmātrasvabhāvaḥ api tu śabdaśaktivaicitryād yathāsvaṁ viśiṣṭakriyāvacanatvam | tathā hi yā prāpaṇe ṇīñ prāpaṇa iti tulye'py arthanirdeśe yāteḥ prāptiḥ prāpaṇam arthaḥ nayates tu prāpaṇā prāpaṇam iti saṁvidhānam artho'vagamyate | evam anyeṣām api saṁvidhānārthatā svābhāvikī boddhavyā | tām eva sūcayituṁ ñakārādyanubandhaḥ smaraṇārthaṁ niveśyate | yo hi prayogād eva svabhāvaviśeṣam avadhārayitum aśaktas taṁ prati smṛtyartho'nubandhāsaṅgaḥ prayogajñaṁ tu prati nārthas tena | tathā ca prayogadarśinaṁ ca prati svaritañidgrahaṇaṁ śakyam akartum iti pratyākhyātam etad bhāṣye.* As seen, Helārāja considers it natural that certain verbs signify the causal act of making provision for an act to be carried out. This is also the view expressed in the Vṛtti on VP 1.26 (K. A. Subramania Iyer [1966a:80.2-3]), which cites the Mahābhāṣya on A 1.3.72.

[25]*prāpaṇa* can derive from *pra-āp* or the causative *pra-āpi*; for the latter, there is also a feminine action noun *prāpaṇā.*

[26]Bhāgīratha Prasāda Tripāṭhī (1980) is, strictly speaking, not a work on the dhātupāṭha per se but still is of considerable interest. The author takes up verb bases in alphabetical order, considering their various meanings, with rich citations of texts from the Vedas on. Hill and Harrison (1991) offers nothing to serious scholarship on the dhātupāṭha; see Wujastyk

(1996). Werba (1997) reached me after I had completed the text of this survey, so that I could peruse it only superficially.

[27]I also do not know of any major review to consider Bronkhorst's arguments.

[28]That the author does not always concur with the strictly Pāṇinian formulation and procedure does not detract, in my opinion, from the clarity of Junnarkar's presentation.

[29]Ananthanarayana (1976) devotes one chapter to what he calls Pāṇini's technique of description. This deals broadly with several topics: markers, abbreviational terms formed with markers, gaṇas, technical terms, paribhāṣās, and adhikāras. I have not had access to Ananthanaryana (1980), a reference to which is made by C. R. S. Sarma (1995:138-139). Amita Sharma (1984) once more takes up two approaches discussed by Pāṇinīyas: whether padas can be derived independently or as parts of utterances.

[30]I think it is not worthwhile to discuss this or other works by J. D. Singh listed in the bibliography, since, at least in my opinion, the presentation and argumentation are confused to the point of making meaningful discussion very difficult. One example will have to suffice to demonstrate my point. Singh (1985-86:150) says, 'A close scrutiny of Pāṇini's statements here indicates that his use of *lakāras* or their substitutes *tiṅ* types, is a distinction without any structural implication.' A long note (Singh [1985-86:150-151 note 2]) accompanying this statement begins as follows: 'However, structurally an anomalous situation is created by Pāṇini's statements describing occurrence of both *sīyuṭ* and *suṭ* before *ātmanepada* substitutes of *liṅ* beginning with *t* or *th*. In this context the commentators interpret lakāra and tiṅ as two d i s t i n c t grammatical entities.' [emphasis in the original] He goes on to consider that A 3.4.107 (*suṭ tithoḥ*) is an exception to A 3.4.102 (*liṅaḥ sīyuṭ*), which, as he immediately realizes, creates difficulties in accounting for the known usage which these rules should describe. Subsequently in the same note, Singh gives the Kāśikā's explanation of A 3.4.107 and rejects it. In the final paragraph of the note, he then proposes what he considers a plausible alternative, namely that ātmanepada substitutes for ***liṅ*** that contain *t* or *th* '... have two roles at two different levels of structure', namely a morphological and a phonological level.

[31]Dinabandhu Kar (1991) goes over, in a schematic fashion, major categories in Pāṇini's system and the terms associated with these: *dravyavacana, ekaśeṣa, jātivacana, bhāvavacana* vs. *kriyāvacana, guṇavacana, sarvanāman,* and adverbs. Kar (1991:237) draws a distinction between major and minor classes of parts of speech. The principal characteristic of the major class is that its members enter into syntactic relations with verbs. Kar ends (1991:237) by saying:

> Another interesting feature of both classes is that items in the major class are always inflected words, whereas items in the minor class are not inflected in Pāṇini's system of description. Thus, we see a sort of correspondence between the syntactic and semantic functions of items described by Pāṇini. This correspondence is found in a majority of cases. Therefore, it will not be an exaggeration to assert that Pāṇini, in his description of parts of speech, followed a consistent plan and accordingly used those semantic classes for an adequate description of grammatical facts.

I assume these assertions are stated more clearly and justified in Kar (1980).

[32]Concerning this sūtra, Kiparsky (1995:65a) says, 'The proper pairings *i* → *y*, *u* → *v*, *ṛ* → *r*, *ḷ* → *l* (rather than, for example, *i* → *r*) are ensured by a further general condition: among alternative possible replacements, the *closest* must be chosen.' He thus ignores the possible application of A 1.3.10: *yathāsaṅkhayam anudeśaḥ samānām*, whereby the direct referents of ***ik*** and ***yaṇ*** — *i u ṛ ḷ* and *y v r l* — would be related respectively. See also 2.1.4.6b.

[33]M. M. Deshpande (1986b:480-483) also takes up vikaraṇas, but with the aim of showing that they are pratyayas in Pāṇini's system.

[34]One aim of this paper is to refute what was said by the late B. K. Matilal (1983). Needless to say, Matilal could not answer Joshi and Roodbergen's attempted refutation.

[35]On ekaśeṣa see also Jag Deva Singh (1991-92).

[36]The most recent formulation of the principle appears in Kiparsky (1995:62), where he says:

> The *para*-principle (4a) and the *antaraṅga*-principle (4c) have probably been overgeneralized by the tradition, though both have a valid kernel. Modern scholars agree that the former is intended to apply only in the section which provides definitions

(1.4-2.3 [sic!]). More controversial is the claim (5) that the latter should be restricted to give priority to word phonology over sentence phonology,

> The *Word-integrity Principle*: rules apply first within words and then to combinations of words. (5)

and that the *nitya* and feeding principles are to be unified into the *siddha*-principle (6), which, with the *apavāda*-principle, is solely responsible for the ordering of rules within words:

> The *Siddha Principle*: when any rule is applied, the rules pertinent to its application should be 'effected' (*siddha*). (6)

Here, A is defined as 'pertinent' to the application of rule B with respect to a form F if the result of applying A and B to F in that order is different from the result of applying A and B to F simultaneously.

[37]See also S. D. Joshi (1982a) and Joshi-Roodbergen (1987).

[38]An earlier discussion by S. D. Joshi (1978:668-669) of the section of rules under the heading **A** 6.4.22: *asiddhavad atrābhāt* again illustrates Joshi's approach. He takes up the derivation of the well known examples *śādhi* and *jahi* (see Cardona [1997a:423-424 (**659**)]), then says (1978:669):

> But we see no justification for the simultaneous application of rules. The hypothesis that rules apply in sequence and in a fixed order would solve the problem. If we phrase the rule *śā dhau* instead of *śā hau* (P. 6.4.35) and make the conditioning environment *-dhi* instead of *-hi*, the linear principle of ordering would explain the form.

Joshi concludes the discussion of these examples and rules saying (1978:669):

> Instead of drawing help from the strange hypothesis of simultaneous application or that of mutual reverse ordering, we can manage with the simpler principle of linear ordering. But for that we will have to change the numbering of the rules in the text of *Aṣṭādhyāyī*.

[39]This study was preceded by others on the same rules, notably Yagi (1987-88); see also section 3.1.2. On the topic of *asiddhavat* in **A** 6.4.22 as opposed to *asiddhaḥ* in **A** 6.1.86 and *asiddham* in **A** 8.2.1, see also Cardona (1997a:419-425 [**653-661**]). In the present discussion, I have not taken up a controversy concerning particular cases where a rule blocks another. To discuss this topic adequately would require a great deal more space than is available to me even with the indulgence of the publishers.

All examples dealt with in the Mahābhāṣya and the Kāśikā, along with their treatment in later Pāṇinīya treatises, are taken up in volume II of my *Pāṇini : His Work and its Traditions.* I must beg the reader's indulgence in making an additional comment here about something Kiparsky has said (1991a:360): 'It is almost as if Cardona, instead of responding to the ideas themselves, is out to discredit their authors instead. Somehow they must be portrayed as barbarians pounding their battering rams at the gates of the Pāṇinian citadel, with himself in the role of the beleaguered defender, drenching the intruders with hot oil from the ramparts.' My discussion of Kiparsky's monograph began (Cardona [1989:64]), 'Kiparsky's study has the merit of dealing, in some detail, with the use of the concerned terms in the Aṣṭādhyāyī and of doing so with a certain rigor. Nevertheless, as the author himself has to recognize, albeit obliquely and with much reluctance, his major claim remains only that, a claim.' I then went on to discuss issues I have rehearsed here, presented evidence Kiparsky had not considered, and ended my discussion (Cardona [1989:66]) saying, 'In sum, although Kiparsky's thesis is both intelligently conceived and generally well argued, in the end I find it neither cogently maintained nor acceptable. The commentatorial tradition, which he is so willing to disparage may, in this case, be perfectly right in not having any inkling of the supposed systematic semantic distinction among the three terms for optionality.' Kiparsky's shrill and intemperate tone, is, I think, hardly warranted by the tenor of my discussion, which I believe I have maintained in the present discussion. My earlier discussion of Joshi and Roodbergen's paper concerning interpolations and inconsistencies began (Cardona [1989:50]) as follows: 'One of the major reasons claimed for considering that rules contained in the Aṣṭādhyāyī as known to Pāṇinīyas represent additions to an earlier version of the text is that the received textual version shows inconsistencies. Of course, what is claimed to be inconsistent may well appear to be so only in the limited vision of the scholar putting forth the claim.' I then took up what I took to be Joshi and Roodbergen's principal argument and argued against it. If Kiparsky, Joshi and Roodbergen feel discredited by what I said there and the arguments I have presented here, this is regrettable but in my opinion does not justify claiming that my aim was to discredit individuals personally. I have concentrated on ideas and facts, not on personal attacks, and I have had to mention names because of the bibliographic style adopted. Finally, I find it interesting that Kiparsky (1991a:361) brings up the notion of a "school" (his inverted commas), despite the fact that, aside from referring jointly to him and Joshi and to Joshi and Roodbergen when they are co-authors of works, I have said nothing about their constituting any sort of school or even loose group. Perhaps that Kiparsky is so touchy on this topic and that he, not S. D. Joshi or Roodbergen, responded to my critique of Joshi and Roodbergen's work reflects a feeling of connection.

[40] Italics in the original.

[41]In a passage relating to the same rite as concerns Kāṭhakasaṁhitā 29.9, the Śatapathabrāhmaṇa uses *anuka*-'subject, subordinate, favorable', as in ŚBr 3.9.1.8: *annam a̲nukam ātma̲naḥ kurute* '(The yajamāna) makes food subject to himself.' Sāyaṇa glosses with forms of *anukūla*- 'favorable'.

[42]For lists of bases marked with *u* and *ū* see Liebich (1920a:42-44, 49).

[43]On what Kiparsky has to say concerning **A** 7.2.57, see below.

[44]It would require even more than the fairly large amount of space I have devoted here to discussing evidence in connection with Kiparsky's view to treat the full evidence in the appropriate manner. Suffice it to say for the moment that Kiparsky himself obviously has to exert himself to fit the facts into his theory not just in the instances I have discussed here but elsewhere also. Thus, consider **A** 7.3.58: *vibhāṣā ceḥ* (*sanliṭoḥ* 57, *ku* 52), according to which the *c*- of *ci* 'heap up, gather, pluck' is optionally replaced by the corresponding velar following an abhyāsa syllable, when there follows either ***san*** or an ending that derives from ***liṭ***. According to Kiparsky's thesis, one expects to find forms like *cicīṣati* (3rd sg. pres. desid.), *cicāya* (3rd sg. pfct. act.) predominantly and forms like *cikīṣati* and *cikāya* only marginally, yet the opposite is true: forms of the latter type predominate and are the absolute norm in Vedic, although Patañjali uses *cicīṣati* several times. Concerning this, Kiparsky says (1979:161), 'It is conceivable that the post-Vedic forms with *k* lean on Vedic usage, and that the living language of Pāṇini's own time had begun to eliminate this irregularity in the paradigm of *ci*.' Subsequently (1979:186), he lists **A** 7.3.58 among the nineteen rules not favorable to his thesis but puts it

within parentheses to indicate that 'the data is scant or the interpretation is moot.'

[45]This is the view of Ātreya and Maitreya: Mādhavīyadhātuvṛtti IV.9 (Dwarikadas Shastri [1964:404]): *īditkaraṇaṁ yasya vibhāṣetyasyānityatva-jñāpanārtham* | *tena dhāvita ityādi siddhyatīti ātreyamaitreyau* | Dhātupradīpa VI.44 (Srish Chandra Chakravarti [1919:108]): *yasya vibhāṣetyaniṭtve siddhe'syedittvena tasyānityatvajñāpanād dhāvita iti siddham* | Cf. Durghaṭavṛtti 7.2.15: *katham ākheṭake tayā nītaḥ dhāvitaḥ paṭaḥ iti* | *se'sicītyādinā nṛter vikalpe yasya vibhāṣeti niṣedhe prāpte nṛtidhātor ītvenāsyānityatvajñāpanāt.*

[46]Kṣīrataraṅgiṇī IV.8 (Yudhiṣṭhira Mīmāṁsaka [1957/8:199]): *nṛtam yasya vibhāṣety aniṭtve siddhe īdittvaṁ yaṅlugargham* : *narīnṛttaḥ.* Mādhavīyadhātuvṛtti IV.9: *svāmikāśyapau tu avayave'caritārthatvād yaṅluṅnivṛttyartham iti.*

[47]The verbs are listed according to Böhtlingk's edition of the Dhātu-pāṭha; under the heading '**Forms**', Deshpande has 'Whitney's *Roots* (1885), etc.' Verb bases are shown in parentheses, as given in Deshpande's article.

[48]My own view is that **A** 1.1.44 serves to establish a convention such that a term signifying an option is construed with a verb form that is to be understood; see Cardona (1989: 66). That is, a term such as *vā* in **A** 4.1.82: *samarthānām prathamād vā* is construed with an understood form of a verb meaning 'be, occur', e.g. *asti* or *bhavati*: *asti/bhavati na vā* 'occurs or not'. The sūtra thereby allows a taddhita affix to occur or not, that is, to occur optionally, after particular padas to be specified. This is comparable to what is normal in Sanskrit, where a sentence like *gacchati na vā* means 'Is he going or not?' That **A** 1.1.44 occurs in a section of rules wherein most sūtras are saṁjñāsūtras of the usual type does not mean it too must be this kind of rule any more than the presence of **A** 1.1.72: *yena vidhis tadantasya* in the first pāda requires this to be a saṁjñāsutra of the general kind. Indeed, neither of these can be considered a classification rule. Soon after **A** 1.1.44, moreover, Pāṇini states two sūtras (**A** 1.1.46-47: *ādyantau ṭakitau*, *mid aco'ntyāt paraḥ*) that are not saṁjñāsūtras at all. As for the possible objection that Pāṇini does not need to have **A** 1.1.44 in order to interpret possibly ambiguous statements, one need only consider that **A** 1.1.66-67: *tasminniti nirdiṣṭe pūrvasya*, *tasmād ity uttarasya* serve

to provide unambiguous interpretations for locative and ablative forms in contexts where a native Sanskrit speaker would not otherwise be able to reach a single interpretation. That the precise scope of an adhikāra is not always determined from the text as we now have it, so that there is some possible ambiguity, does not mitigate against my interpretation of **A** 1.1.44 either, since this does not concern uniquely the unambiguous syntactic construction of a single term in a single sūtra. Nor does the possibility that a sūtra might be interpreted as an adhikārasūtra or a paribhāṣā mitigate in any way against the interpretation I have proposed. Later commentators — including modern scholars — may suggest interpretations of this kind, but these do not require that the rules in question originally have been systematically ambiguous. It is also not the case that the possibility of interpreting a negative compound as involving prasajyapratiṣedha or paryudāsa implies Pāṇini's having tolerated massive syntactic ambiguity in his sūtras. As is well known, although Pāṇinīyas do indeed consider the prasajyapratiṣedha interpretation, a compound like *anapuṁsakasya* is appropriately taken as involving paryudāsa. To be sure, there is at least one instance (**A** 6.1.45: *ād eca upadeśe' śiti*) where the prasjyapratiṣedha interpretation is preferred. However, again this does not involve massive syntactic ambiguity in the grammar. Finally, the possibility of interpreting **A** 4.1.82 as meaning "... or it is not the case that the suffix should be added after the first element" (Kiparsky, [1991a:340]), so that the rule would presumably not allow affixation at all, does not arise under **A** 1.1.44 as I have interpreted it. This rule lets a term signifying an option be understood to have the meaning of *na vā* as usually construed with a verb, so that **A** 4.1.82 states *samarthānām prathamād bhavati na vā*, just as one can say *gacchati na vā*. That is, what is involved is first the possible occurrence (*prasaṅga*) of an affix and then its optional negation. In brief, Kiparsky's objections to my interpretation (1991a:339-340) are not cogent. As for the possible objection that Pāṇini should have used a single term meaning 'optionally', one can as little require this of the Aṣṭādhyāyī as one can require, for example, that a single term meaning 'action' be used instead of *kriyā*, *karman*, *bhāva*, or that Pāṇini have used only terms of the type *ka* in referring to sounds instead of using also terms such as *ti*, *si*. Moreover, even though Pāṇini introduces *gotra* by a regular saṁjñāsūtra, he nevertheless uses *vṛddha* also with reference to a gotra descendant.

[49]See also Cardona (1997a:xxiv-xxvii). Wezler has also discussed (1976) Pāṇini's use of *saṁjñā*, on which see Palsule (1966) and H. P. Dvivedi (1978:9-27).

[50]Deshpande has reiterated his viewpoint (1997b:58-59), but without any new arguments, so that I still find his claim unacceptable. Cardona (1980b) has also argued that some of the formulations in the Āpiśalaśikṣā are best understood as reflecting the influence of phonology. Ladukeshvar Shatapathi Sharma (1985) deals with anusvāra both within the Pāṇinian system and in other spheres.

[51]See Cardona (1983a:13-31).

[52]Deshpande goes on to explore Buddhist connections.

[53]Upendra Pandeya is very traditional, accepting (1990:51) that the akṣarasamāmnāya was produced by Śiva. In a much more speculative vein, Thieme (1985b) reconstructs an ancient sound list: *a i u ṛ e o ai au y r l v k c ṭ t p ś ṣ s h*, 'which', he says (1985b:559), 'must have been known to the author of the first verse of the triṣaptīyam.' This is based on the assumption that *trìṣaptā́ḥ* in the Vedic text he interprets must refer to twenty-one sounds and that Pāṇini's grammar antedates all prātiśākhyas.

[54]See also Srimannarayana Murti (1991). G. H. Khare (1984) ignores the phonological status of *h* and prefers to see a pronunciation difference as the basis for listing what he considers two phonetically distinct sounds.

[55]Goparaju Rama (1995) gives derivates with kṛt affixes (including uṇādi suffixes) along with their bases, according to the alphabetical order of verb bases.

[56]Despite its title, Gillon's paper is an insightful discussion of asamarthasamāsas in general, with good examples. For a brief discussion of Scharf's paper, see section 2.1.4.6b.

[57]Peri Sarveswara Sharma has also considered (1981a) the vocative *subhru* and concluded that, although this vocative is used by poets, strictly speaking it is grammatically incorrect in that it cannot be accounted for straightforwardly by Pāṇinian rules.

[58]In a section entitled '*Taddhita* as a *Vṛtti*' (1989:3-9), Bhate has some interesting things to say concerning the structure and status of derivates

with taddhita and kṛt affixes. There are also some things that to me appear somewhat confused. For example, she distinguishes (1989:4) between inflectional and derivational morphology in Pāṇini's system and says, 'The *tad.* and *kṛt* are two types of lexical morphology. In many respects the derivational morphology which involves the *kṛt* and the *tad.* derivation is common.' This gives the impression that formations involving kṛt and taddhita affixes concern what in the west is called derivational morphology. Yet, as she goes on to say (1989:5), the introduction of a kṛt suffix such as ***kta*** of a derivate like *bhuk-ta-* 'eaten' in *odano bhuktas tena* 'He has eaten some rice' involves syntax, not derivational morphology. Let me note also that Bhate does not, so far as I can see, mention the work done by precedessors such as D. M. Joshi (1969) and Wezler (1975).

[59]Filliozat speaks in terms of propositions and (1975:)83 'transformations of propositions', emphasizing that for Indian grammarians both derivation and composition are taken as transformations of propositions into nominal units. Scharfe (1983) also deals with compounds and taddhita derivates, but, in my opinion, less well than Filliozat. Thus, Scharfe (1983:57) says:

> We get then a hierarchy of constructions. For related words there will be an open syntagma; for words with a single meaning there will be, as a general rule (*utsarga*), a compound. In special cases, however, composition may be superseded by secondary noun formation. These special cases are listed in the rules following IV.1.76 *taddhitāḥ* "[The following suffixes are called] *taddhita*". Not all compounds can be replaced by an appropriate secondary noun, and in those cases composition remains a must .... This view of open syntagma, compound and taddhita allows us a strict generation of Sanskrit expressions not available otherwise.

Immediately after this, Scharfe remarks, 'The only question that remains, is why this understanding was lost amongst the Pāṇinīya-s.'

[60]The problem here, I think, is that the notion of 'infinitival value' is left vague. It is important to note that in Indo-Aryan so-called 'infinitives' are generally forms of action nouns and are used syntactically as what western grammarians call 'datives of purpose' or with values equivalent to those of such case forms as ablatives of nominals as well as in construction with particular cooccuring items (e.g. forms of *śak* 'be able').

[61]On **A** 3.1.87 (*karmavat karmaṇā tulyakriyaḥ*) in particular, see also

Bhate (1982), Filliozat (1983), Kudo (1994); on **A** 1.3.67 (*ṇer aṇau yat karma ṇau cet sa kartānādhyāne*), see S. D. Joshi (1982b:204-209, 1983).

[62]There is a paribhāṣā according to which an affix introduced on condition that a kāraka is to be signified takes precedence over one whose occurrence is determined by the use of an upapada (*upapadavibhakteḥ kārakavibhaktir balīyasī*). Cardona (1980a) has given evidence showing that this paribhāṣā is not necessary for the proper application of Pāṇinian rules.

[63]Kielhorn (1880-85:I.461.25-462.2): *prātipadikārthaliṅgaparimāṇa-vacanamātre prathamālakṣaṇe padasāmānādhikaraṇya upasaṁkhyānaṁ kartavyam : vīraḥ puruṣaḥ | kiṁ punaḥ kāraṇaṁ na sidhyati | adhikatvāt | vyatiriktaḥ prātipadikārtha iti kṛtvā prathamā na prāpnoti | kathaṁ vyatiriktaḥ | puruṣe vīratvam..*

[64]Kielhorn (1880-85:I.462.13-14): *abhihitānabhihite prathamā prāpnoti | kva | prāsāda āste śayana āste | sadipratyayenābhihitam adhikaraṇam iti kṛtvā prathamā prāpnoti.*

[65]Note that the affix ***kta*** in *gataḥ* of the example given has a time reference, just as does the ending of *gacchati*: the former is introduced (**A** 3.2.102: *niṣṭhā*) on condition that an action is referred to past time, the latter replaces ***laṭ*** introduced (**A** 3.2.123: *vartamāne laṭ*) on condition that an action is referred to current time. In this context, consider the affix ***ṇvul*** of derivates like *pācaka-*. This affix can be introduced merely to signify an agent (**A** 3.1.133: *ṇvultṛcau*, **A** 3.4.67: *kartari kṛt*), as in *devadatta odanasya pācakaḥ* 'Devadatta is a rice cooker.' The same affix can also be introduced (**A** 3.3.10: *tumunṇvulau kriyāyāṁ kriyārthāyām*) under the same conditions as ***tumun***, that is, after a base denoting an action for the purpose of performing which another action, denoted by a cooccurring verb, is performed; in addition, the act in question is referred to the future. For example, Rāmāyaṇa 2.84.17: *ahaṁ tu taṁ naravyāghram upayātaḥ prasādakaḥ | pratinetum ayodhyāṁ ca pādau tasyābhivanditum* 'On the contrary, I (Bharata) have come to propitiate (Rāma), tiger among men, to take him back to Ayodhyā, and to touch his feet.' Note that as *abhivanditum* is construed with the accusative *pādau*, so is *prasādakaḥ* construed with the accusative *naravyāghram*. A derivate of the type *prasādaka-* equivalent to a derivate with ***tumun*** (*prasādayitum*) differs syntactically from an atemporal derivate with ***ṇvul***. The latter is construed in the manner of a

nominal, with a genitive form denoting an object (**A** 2.3.65: *kartṛkarmaṇoḥ kṛti*). The other is not construed in this manner, as Pāṇini himself explicitly recognizes in **A** 2.3.69-70: *na lokāvyayaniṣṭhākhalarthatṛnām, akenor bhaviṣyadādhamarṇyayoḥ.* Instead, to signify an object with respect to the action denoted by the verb with ***ṇvul*** or *tum**un*** a second-triplet ending follows a nominal base (**A** 2.3.2: *karmaṇi dvitīyā*). Given this difference, it is reasonable to consider that in *devadatta odanasya pācakaḥ*, where ***ṇvul*** has no specific time reference, one understands a present form of the verb 'be': *asti*. I mention this because Kiparsky (1982:11) supposes that a sentence like *devadattaḥ pācaka odanasya* in which the affix of *pācaka-* does not have any particular time reference — Deshpande (1987c:55) refers to Kiparsky and translates 'D (is) the cook (who cooks) rice' — is a complete sentence that does not require understanding *asti*. This fails to observe an important distinction. I agree with Bronkhorst (1984:310), who criticized Kiparsky's position.

[66]Kielhorn (1880-85:I.368.6-8): *yuktayukte : nadyās tiṣṭhati kūle vṛkṣasya lambate śākhā śālīnāṁ ta odanaṁ dadāmi śālīnāṁ ma odanaṁ dadāti | kiṁ punaḥ kāraṇaṁ na sidhyati | asamarthatvāt.*

[67]Cited according to Wilhelm Rau's edition of the kārikā text (Rau [1977a]).

[68]Vākyapadīya Vṛtti (K. A. Subramania Iyer edition [1983:303]): *iha kārakāṇāṁ niśreṇīparvaṇāṁ iva sākṣāt sambandho nāsti | kriyāyāṁ tv ekasyāṁ sannipatitāni tannibandhanāni kriyāvyavahitaṁ sambandham anubhavanti.* The verse number is 2.401 in this edition. Puṇyarāja, on the other hand, invokes the parallel of ribs of an umbrella: Ṭīkā (K. A Subramania Iyer [1983:162]): *iha kārakāṇy ayaḥśalākākalpāni parasparam asambaddhāny eva | teṣāṁ ca yathā kriyāvyavadhānena kriyāsamāśrayeṇa sambandho dṛśyate ....*

[69]I am grateful to my colleague Robin Clark for discussion on this point.

[70]As far as the concept of sāmarthya is concerned, then, I am in general agreement with Mahavir, who devotes a section of his theoretical chapter (1984:19-24) to arguing that *samartha* in Pāṇini refers to a direct syntactic relationship. See also Mahavir (1978:22).

[71]On karmapravacanīyas, see also Sudhi Kant Bharadvaj (1994).

[72]Joshi and Roodbergen (1994b) deal with **A** 1.4.23 in particular.

[73]Deshpande views the "prototypical" value of *kartṛ* and so on as ultimately based in the ritual. He again stresses this, with respect to *karman*, in section 14 of Deshpande (forthcoming a). **A** 1.4.54 is the subject of a recent article by M. D. Pandit (1992). S. P. Thompson's paper on kārakas (1989-90) conceives of a universal grammar in a manner that differs from that which most linguists would envision. He says (1989-90:384-385):

> We have assumed a philosophical significance to lie behind the seven *Kāraka sūtras* because *Vyākaraṇa* is an *aṅga* limb or handmaid of the *Veda* serving to protect and explain its meaning. Hence the order of the *sūtras* is taken as of great importance.
>
> *Kārake* we have suggested really means in relation to the (one) activity having its source in the *Śabda brahman*. *Dhruvam* we have suggested is deliberately used because of its significance in the *Upaniṣads* as the Eternal Unmoving. The first four *kārakas*: *apādāna*, *samapradāna*, *karaṇa*, and *adhikaraṇa* it has been suggested directly link with the Universal principle expressing relationships essential to all human communication. Finally we treat *kartṛ* and *karman* as more particular, mutually dependent and generally expressing a relative relationship of subject and object which in the last analysis would be realized as two ways of speaking of the One.

[74]Śaṭhakopatātācārya (1988) deals with object constructions which involve in particular *gam* 'go' and *tyaj* 'leave'; he considers the semantics to be assumed for the verbs and the verb endings used with them, from the viewpoints of earlier and later grammarians.

[75]It is unfortunate that S. D. Joshi (1993:11) leaves unchanged what he said over thirty years earlier: 'Pāṇini avoids problems of semantics as studiously as do the modern Western linguists. The *Aṣṭādhyāyī*, *Gaṇapāṭha*, and *Dhātupāṭha* describe the grammatical or linguistic structure of the Sanskrit language in terms of morphemes (base form and suffix) and rules of combination.' It would have been well, I think, at least to add a clarificatory note. S. M. Katre (1989:86) too underplays the role of semantics in Pāṇini's system, although he has to recognize it has some status. This topic was dealt with earlier also by Bronkhorst (1980b). Given his avowed aim of proving that in Pāṇini's system meanings played the role of input to the grammar, Bronkhorst might have considered an important piece of evidence which he omits. **A** 3.3.139 (*liṅnimitte lṛṅ*) introduces the L-affix

lṛṅ under a condition that determines that the L-affix ***liṅ*** is introduced, provided an action does not come about (see Cardona [1997a:169 (**258**)]). The wording of the sūtra shows that for Pāṇini a semantic relation served as a condition (*nimitta* 'cause, condition') for the introduction of an affix. Accordingly, a translation such as 'The second [nominal] ending (= accusative ending) [appears] when a *karman* (direct object) [is to be designated]' (Thieme [1958:25]) for **A** 2.3.2: *karmaṇi dvitīyā* is appropriate. Similarly appropriate are paraphrases such as the following (Cardona [1967b:207]): '2.3.28 (*apādane pañcamī*) introduces the fifth when *apādāna* is to be expressed; 2.3.13 (*caturthī samapradāne*) the fourth when a *sampradāna*; 2.3.18 (*kartṛkaraṇayos tṛtīyā*) when *kartṛ* or *karaṇa*; 2.3.36 (*saptamy adhikaraṇe ca*) the seventh when *adhikaraṇa*; and 2.3.2 (*karmaṇi dvitīyā*) the second when *karman* is to be expressed.' All such rules introduce affixes under meaning conditions. Moreover, 'when ... is to be signified, designated, expressed' is simply a correct translation of Sanskrit statements in which locative forms are used in a particular manner. It is because of such considerations that Cardona (1976a:186) noted that this was well known and did not require being proved anew. That Bronkhorst (1980b:148) chose to consider this unfair is perhaps unfortunate but ultimately irrelevant. In view of what I have noted, moreover, his statement (1980b:147) that earlier authors he mentions — including Thieme — '... merely posit their view regarding the role of meanings in the *Aṣṭādhyāyī*' is not well founded.

[76]Possibly because he felt obliged to supply simple translations for all terms, Houben (1997:89) translates *apādāna* with 'taking away' and *sampradāna* with 'giving'. He also heads the column in which these and other kāraka category names are given with 'syntactic/semantic label (*kāraka*)'. This is apt to be misleading. There are kārakas: direct participants in the accomplishment of acts. These are assigned to categories so that they are designated by the category names *apādāna*, *sampradāna*, *karaṇa*, *adhikaraṇa*, *karman*, *kartṛ* (and *hetu*). These category names are then used to state that such and such elements occur when such and such a kāraka as assigned to a kāraka category is to be signified. Further, *apādāna* and *sampradāna* certainly do not have the meanings Houben gives. I think the table which R. N. Sharma supplies (1987:147-149) for kāraka classification rules is superior, and that Houben would have done well to

mention Sharma's work. See also Cardona (1997a:44-45 [**77**], 137-139 [**214**]).

[77]This is part of nearly an entire column — all but 6 lines — that Staal (1995:67a) devotes to the dhātupāṭha. Since Staal obviously accepts what Bronkhorst (1981a) has said about meaning entries in Pāṇini's dhātupāṭha, it is noteworthy that later in the same column (1995:67a) he says:

> The following are examples from the fourth and seventh classes:
>
> iv.68 *yuja samādhau* 'the root *yuj-* in the meaning of concentration'
>
> vii.7 *yujir yoge* 'the root *yuj-* in the meaning of conjunction'

For, as I have noted in section 1.1, Bronkhorst (1983:357) argues that ***yuja*** of the fourth class was added to the dhātupāṭha after Patañjali.

[78]Staal also continues to demonstrate a shallow command of primary sources. Thus, concerning markers, he says (1995:68a):

> In the finally derived surface forms, the *anubandha* marker has to be removed. Patañjali explains how this is similar to ordinary usage—a crow that sits on the roof of a house, for example, may be utilized to identify the house: '"Which of these two is Devadatta's house?" "That where the crow sits." When the crow flies away and the house is no longer marked, one knows in consequence which house was indicated' (*Mahābhāṣya*, ed. Kielhorn 84.21-85.3).

To be sure, this conveys in a very general way the ultimate intent of what Patañjali says. On the other hand, Staal's use of quotation marks shows he means to present a translation of the text referred to in Kielhorn's edition (I.84.21-85.3), but this can hardly be considered a translation of the following: *anubandho 'nyatvakara iti cet tan na* I *kiṁ kāraṇam* I *lopāt* I *lupyate' trānubandhaḥ* I *lupte' trānubandhe nānyatvaṁ bhaviṣyati* I *tad yathā katarad devadattasya gṛham* I *ado yatrāsau kāka iti* I *utpatite kāke naṣṭaṁ tad gṛhaṁ bhavati* I *evam ihāpi lupte' nubandhe naṣṭaḥ pratyayo bhavati* I *yady api lupyate jānāti tv asau sānubandhasyeyaṁ saṁjñā kṛteti* I *tad yathetartrāpi* : *katarad devadattasya gṛham* I *ado yatrāsau kāka iti* I *utpatite kāke yady api naṣṭaṁ tad gṛhaṁ bhavaty antatas tam uddeśaṁ jānāti*. The discussion concerns whether one should explicitly say that the class name *niṣṭhā* — which by **A** 1.1.26: *ktaktavatū niṣṭhā* should apply to the affixes ***kta*** and ***ktavatu***, as in *kṛta-* 'done, made', *kṛtavat-* 'someone who has done ..., made ...' — does not apply to homophonous items like the *-ta* of *lota-* 'ram', *garta-* 'hole'. The first answer is that such a negation serves no purpose, since a marker serves to differentiate the items in question. In his third vārttika on **A** 1.1.26 (*anubandho' nyatvakara iti cen na lopāt*), Kātyāyana argues that this is not acceptable, because any marker there is dropped. Patañjali invokes the example of a house with a crow on it as a parallel. Once a marker is dropped, there will be no difference between the *ta* of *lota-*, *garta-* and the *ta* of *kṛta*. This is comparable to the situation where someone asks which house is Devadatta's and is told that a house yonder, on which there is a crow, is Devadatta's. Once the crow has flown off, that house is no longer known as characterized by the crow (*naṣṭaṁ tad gṛhaṁ bhavati* 'That house is gone'); similarly, once the marker is dropped, the affix is no longer differentiated (*naṣṭaḥ pratyayo bhavati* 'The affix is gone'). Patañjali goes on to counter this, again invoking the same parallel. Although the marker is deleted, one knows that this name *niṣṭhā* was assigned to the element with a marker. Similarly, once the crow used to identify Devadatta's house has flown off, although the house is no longer known as characterized by the crow, one still knows that it was originally so described.

[79]See Cardona (1997a:428-542 [**666-825**]). M. M. Deshpande (1996b:155-156) remarks on the process '... in the middle and late Vedic period ...' of breaking down larger structures into well delineated parts.

[80]In an article which I find extremely interesting, Bhate remarks (1991:61) that examples she has dealt with, 'All show how minutely Pāṇini has observed the nuances and their correspondence with the formal structure of linguistic expressions. He has linked feelings such as anger, jealousy, love, hatred, and insult with diverse linguistic elements. His treatment of a large number of word formations that are linked with the *dhvani* indicates that the emotive and attitudinal meanings can be formalized at least to a certain extent.'

[81]I take this opportunity to correct some typographical errors in Cardona (1993b): p. 26, example (4), 8.6.3.23, line 3: read: u̱dbudhyasvāgne, example (5), 9.2.3.27, line 4: read: svarya̱nto nā̱pekṣanta ā, p. 27, example (12), 1.1.2.17, line 7: read: savitu̱ḥ prasa̱veśvi̱nor. I am grateful to John Gardner and Charles Wikner for pointing these out to me. If, out of old transliteration habits, any acute accent marks have crept into the Śataspathabrāhmaṇa transliteratations without my noticing them, they should be eliminated. At

the time I wrote the article in question, I still followed the usual western transliteration for accents in the Ṛgveda, Atharvaveda and so on. I now have given that up in favor of a transliteration that is more faithful both to the original script and to the recitations represented therein.

[82]In Cardona (1976a:note 308), references are given to papers dealing with so called un-Pāṇinian usage in various texts. Cardona (forthcoming a) presents evidence to argue that viewing ārṣaprayoga as equivalent to un-Pāṇinian usage is not appropriate, that speaking of such usage found in the Rāmāyaṇa as being un-Pāṇinian would destroy the status of the ādikāvya, so that commentators must explain the usage as in conformity with Pāṇini, and that the Aṣṭādhyāyī has a series of what can be called escape rules which allow flexibility in accordance with tendencies of the language.

[83]Balasubrahmanyam (1983a) deals with the general rule governing accentuation but without bringing under consideration the satiśiṣṭasvara procedure; see Cardona (1997a:376-378 [**588**, **591**]).

[84]V. P. Limaye (1975) also is not concerned specifically with Vedic rules, but the author gathers together references in Darila's Bhāṣya to Pāṇini and Pāṇinīyas. Cardona (1991a) considers, with reference both to Vedic attestation and to Pāṇini's way of accounting for the facts in question, variants of the type *dakṣi* and *dhakṣi* ('burn' [2nd sg. imper.]), and concludes that they represented different dialects in early Vedic. Cardona's appreciation of the facts assumes Sag's and Schindler's earlier justification of Pāṇinian forms of the type *dah* (instead of *dhagh*) as "underlying" for Sanskrit, which in turn requires that forms with initial aspirates represent the result of an analogic process. Scharfe (1996) prefers to explain as much as he can by pure sound laws, though even he has to admit a residue explicable only by analogy (1996:377). Scharfe also remarks (1996:353) that the way in which Cardona arranged materials — by forms — 'has limited his vision', and he himself arranges the data gathered by Cardona according to books of the Ṛgveda, although he also admits (1996:356-357), 'It is difficult to get one's geographical bearings from the hints offered in the hymns of the Ṛgveda.' I agree, hence still prefer to arrange things as I did, and to consider, as I also did, the forms in connection with families of particular ṛṣis and recitors, which must represent dialectal traditions. Scharfe's insistance on sound rules alone also requires him to adopt a

claim (1996:367) about Bartholomae's law which is at best open to doubt — though I cannot discuss this here. He also fails to pay enough attention to the fact that the vowel length in a derivate like *dīpsa-*, which varies with *dipsa-*, can hardly be explained except by analogy to a parallel type, namely *īpsa-*, and that the same holds for *śīkṣā* as opposed to the usual *śikṣā*.

[85]Gopāla Śāstrī Nene (1987:II.768): *anupasarge satīty arthaḥ* | *tatphalitam āha* : *anupasargād iti*.

[86]Sitaram Shastri (1960:2012): *pratyāsattyā gaḍādisambandhyupasargābhāve satīty arthaḥ* | *avyayībhāvo'yam* | *vyatyayena pañcamyarthe saptamī vā*.

[87]Concerning the domain of **A** 1.3.10, see also Cardona (1981b).

[88]For a general study of the padapāṭha to the Ṛgveda, see V. N. Jha (1992). Bronkhorst (1982a) argued that the Ṛgvedapadapāṭha preserves archaic features that disappeared from the saṁhitāpāṭha, so that a reason must be found to explain why the padapāṭha remained '... outside the stream of sound development, when the Saṁhitāpāṭha could not' (Bronkhorst [1982a]:184). His answer is, 'I know of but one plausible explanation: the Padapāṭha of the *Ṛgveda* was *written down* from its beginning.' Falk (1993:250) remarks that this assumption is not necessary. I agree. Additional consideration of Bronkhorst's evidence and arguments is not called for in the present context.

[89]On Pāṇini and Śākalya see also V. N. Jha (1992:56-61). K. V. Abhyankar (1976) has again considered briefly Patañjali's statement that the padakāras are to follow grammatical rules and not vice versa. He remarks (1976:314) that, since Śaunaka and others were well versed in grammar, what Patañjali says is merely a bold assertion.

[90]Meenakshi has also prepared a monograph on this topic, which I have read through the kindness of the author. I do not know, however, whether it is to be published.

[91]Ananthanarayana (1976:73) speaks of the 'concept of nominalization' but his examples make it clear that he is dealing with taddhitānta derivates based on padas in sentences.

[92]C. R. S. Sarma (1995) again takes up case grammar in relation to Pāṇini and concludes that Pāṇini's way of treating the kartṛ category is

the more insightful.

[93]Also of interest is Wujastyk's paper (1982) concerning Bloomfield's terms for compounds, in particular those corresponding to bahuvrīhis and tatpuruṣas. I do not think the same can be said of Makkai and Christie (1981) which, as far as I can tell, shows no evidence of first-hand acquaintance with Pāṇini, although the authors rightly say that the true inheritors of Pāṇini's tradition are later Indian scholars.

[94]I say 'in general' because Deshpande and I differ with respect to some important issues, upon which I cannot elaborate here. Aklujkar (1996a) strongly disagrees with many of Deshpande's ideas and claims; in a forthcoming monograph (forthcoming f), Aklujkar will elaborate on his differences with Deshpande.

[95]In a very different vein, Satya Pal Narang (1988-89) claims that the sūtras in which Pāṇini refers to Śākalya reflect usage of Sialkot.

[96]Abhyankar's revision of Kielhorn's edition (1962-72) has been reissued. The title page of the first volume (Pune, 1985) labels this as the third edition and also, at the bottom of the title page, as a fourth edition.

[97]Bronkhorst (1987e) has written an important review of Rau's work in which he makes some interesting speculations concerning some passages cited in the Bhāṣya and considers that '... not all Vedic texts were completely fixed in the time of the Mahābhāṣya ... ' (1987e:56). Bronkhorst (1987e:56) also expresses dissatisfaction with '... an (unfortunately) still large group of Indologists who cherish the mistaken idea that scholarship can, wholly or largely, exist without what they consider 'speculation', i.e., the formulation and testing of theories.' On this issue, see also Cardona (1989:83, note 104).

[98]The passage discussed also involves other syntactic problems, which Abhyankar considered in his note and with which I cannot deal here. I nevertheless think it worth noting that, in his Laghumañjūṣā, Nāgeśa (Mādhava Śāstrī Bhāṇḍārī [1925:234]) interprets *āhatya* and *gacchati* of *bherīm āhatya kaścid viṁśati padāni gacchati kaścit triṁśat kaścic catvāriṁśat* as referring to actions with the same agent, namely the person who strikes the drum, and supplies *taṁ śabdam upalabhamānaḥ* 'perceiving that sound' to complement *āhatya* 'after striking', so that the passage

refers to one who strikes a drum and then continues to perceive its sound while moving certain distances away.

[99]He also argues that another vārttika was subject to modification by interpolation. Vārttika 3 on **A** 6.3.21: *ṣaṣṭhyā ākrośe* in its original form is *devānāmpriya iti ca.* The version found in the Siddhāntakaumudī (979, Giridhara Śarmā Caturveda and Parameśvarānanda Śarmā Bhāskara [1958-61] II.237) adds *mūrkhe* : *devānāmpriya iti ca mūrkhe*. This too is a gloss. Palsule (1984) has again taken up the term *devānāmpriya*, with which he dealt earlier (1969a), now inquiring about the origin of this compound. He considers Vedic passages in which forms of *priya-* are construed with *devānām* and concludes (1984:316) that the origin of the title *devānāṁ-priyaḥ* is not in the Veda and is to be sought elsewhere: 'The compound expression *devānāṁ-priyaḥ*, conveying a particular unified meaning, is found for the first time in Aśoka's inscription in Prakrit, not in Sanskrit.'

[100]Concerning Kaiyaṭa's date (Cardona [1976a:347 note 344]), V. Raghavan (1976) adduced evidence from Bhoja's Śṛṅgāraprakāśa to show that Kaiyaṭa lived at a time before Bhoja, that is, prior to the first half of the eleventh century. A recent work is devoted in particular to Nāgeśa and his Uddyota: Meenambal Narayan (1991).

[101]Some discussion has continued into recent times concerning Patañjali's dates (see Cardona [1976a:263-266]). For example, Laddu (1986) suggests that in the Mahābhāṣya on **A** 3.2.123: *vartamāne laṭ*, *parvatāḥ* may refer to a line of kings instead of to mountains. Assuming that '... it was not unlikely that this royal family of Parvata-s was mentioned by Patañjali ...' (1986:195), Laddu suggests lowering Patañjali's date to the middle of the first century B. C.

[102]These include Kātyāyana's time and place, definitions of *vārttika*, the purposes served by vārttikas, and their style.

[103]See Cardona (1976a:349 note 371).

[104]See Cardona (1976a:162-163).

[105]Kielhorn (1880-85:I.1.2-3): *athety ayaṁ śabdo' dhikārārthaḥ* । *śabdānuśāsanaṁ śāstram adhikṛtaṁ veditavyam.* On this passage and what commentators say concerning it, see most recently Cardona (1997a:543, 545-546 [**827**, **829**]) and on Kātyāyana's first vārttika see Cardona

(1997a:546-547 [**830**]).

[106]Pradīpa (Vedavrata [1962-63:I.2]): *bhāṣyakāro vivaraṇakāratvāt vyākaraṇasya sākṣātprayojanam āha*: *atha śabdānuśāsanam iti.* Similarly, the Sarvadarśanasaṅgraha (V. S. Abhyankar [1978:288]) speaks of *atha śabdānuśāsanam* as Patañjali's initial utterance: *tathā hi patañjaler bhagavato mahābhāṣyakārasyedam ādimaṁ vākyam atha śabdānuśāsanam iti.*

[107]M. S. Narasimhacharya (1973-83:I.76): ... *idānīṁ vyākaraṇaśāstrasya niyamārthatāpratipādakam ādyaṁ vārtikam avatārayati* ... Bhārgavaśāstrī Joshi (1951:58b), Vedavrata (1962-63:I.27): ... *itaḥ pūrvaṁ tu savārtika-śāstrānvākhyānaprayojanaviṣayapradarśanaparo bhāṣyakārasyaiva grantha iti bodhyam.*

[108]In what follows, I refer to the reprint of this article: 1933:136-147.

[109]Previously, Joshi (1976a, 1980c) had considered this a vārttika. As Bronkhorst notes (1987b:13), Joshi does not support this assumption with cogent arguments. Thus, he says (1980c:40):

> As a matter of fact, Bhandarkar's reasoning applies to two more statements at the beginning of the *Mbh*. We could thus postulate the following *Vts*:
>
> I *Atha śabdānuśāsanam* (*Mbh.* I. p. 1, line 1)
>
> II *Laukikānāṁ vaidikānāṁ ca* (*Mbh*. I. p. 1, line 2)
>
> III *Rakṣohāgamalaghvasaṁdehāḥ prayojanam* (*Mbh*. I. p. 1, line 14)

No further discussion appears necessary.

[110]In the same note, Joshi and Roodbergen refer to K. C. Chatterji as a precedent: 'Compare K. C. Chatterji (1972), p. 7. ... According to Chatterji (1272 [sic!]), p. 7, Sāyaṇa in the introduction to his *Ṛgbhāṣya* treats the statement as a *Vt*. attributing it to Vararuci.' I do not have access to the fourth edition of K. C. Chatterji's work, but the evidence alluded to appears in K. C. Chatterji (1957:६). It is true that Sāyaṇa does indeed refer to the passage in question as a vārttika of Vararuci; see the Vaidika-Saṁśodhana-Maṇḍala edition of the Ṛgveda, volume I.26, to which Bronkhorst (1987b:11) also refers. However, as Chatterji goes on to note, the Sarvadarśanasaṅgraha attributes the same passage to the bhāṣyakāra; see V. S. Abhyankar (1978:295).

[111]As provided for by **A** 2.4.34: *dvitīyāṭaussv enaḥ*; see Cardona

(1997a:305 [**460**]).

[112]Kielhorn (1880-85:I.481.2-4): *tad dveṣyaṁ vijānīyāt : idamā kathitam idamaiva yadānukathyate iti* | *tad ācāryaḥ suhṛd bhūtvānvācaṣṭe : anvādeśaś ca kathitānukathitamātraṁ draṣṭavyam iti.*

[113]Kielhorn (1880-85:I.5.5-11); see Joshi-Roodbergen (1986:67-68).

[114]Yudhiṣṭhira Mīmāṁsaka (1984:I.227) refers to a manuscript dated saṁvat 1662. See also Bhim Sen Shastri (1984:21).

[115]Srish Chandra Chakravarti (1918:Introduction 12): *vyākaraṇaśāstram ārabhamāṇo bhagavān pāṇinimuniḥ prayojananāmanī vyācikhyāsuḥ pratijānīte*: *atha śabdānuśāsanam iti*. Yudhiṣṭhira Mīmāṁsaka (1984:I.227) and Bhim Sen Shastri (1984:20) refer to this passage in support of attributing *atha śabdānuśāsanam* to Pāṇini, but Srish Chandra Chakravarti (1918: Introduction 12 note X) says, 'This assertion is wrong. "अथ शब्दानुशासनम्" are not the Sutrakara's words. They belong to the भाष्यकार.' He goes on to cite Kaiyaṭa as authority.

[116]Medhātithi, Manubhāṣya 1.1: *pauruṣeyeṣv api grantheṣu naiva sarveṣu prayojanābhidhānam ādriyate* | *tathā hi bhagavān pāṇinir anuktvaiva prayojanam atha śabdānuśāsanam iti sutrasandarbham ārabhate*. I have cited from the edition by Jayantakrishna Harikrishna Dave: *Manu-Smṛti with nine Commentaries* ... volume I (Adhyāyas 1-2) (= Bhāratīya Vidyā Series 29) (Bombay: Bharatiya Vidya Bhava, 1972). Yudhiṣṭhira Mīmāṁsaka (1984:I.228) and Bhim Sen Shastri (1984:20) refer to this passage in support of attributing *atha śabdānuśāsanam* to Pāṇini.

[117]Padamañjarī (Dwarikadas Shastri and Kalika Prasad Shuka [1965-67:I.7]): *vṛttikāras tu ... bhāṣyakāreṇa paṭhitaṁ sākṣātprayojanam āha : atheti*. As pointed out earlier (see note 106), the Sarvadarśanasaṅgraha considers this as the beginning of the Mahābhāṣya. Bhim Sen Shastri (1984:19-20) has argued that Jinendrabuddhi, on the contrary, recognizes *atha śabdānuśāsanam* as the beginning of the Aṣṭādhyāyī because, in the Nyāsa on the Kāśikā to **A** 1.1.68 (Dwarikadas Shastri and Kalika Prasad Shuka [1965-67:I.240]), he says: *śabdānuśāsanaprastāvād eva hi śabdasyeti siddhe* .... Yudhiṣṭhira Mīmāṁsaka (1984:I.228) argued in the same manner, but erroneously said the text is from the Nyāsa on Kāśikā 3.4.16. Even if the conclusion drawn is appropriate this constitutes another instance where

two commentators differ in their attribution. Moreover, I think the conclusion is not obvious. Here and in other places (e.g. Nyāsa on Kāśikā 8.1.1 [Dwarikadas Shastri and Kalika Prasad Shuka (1965-67:VI.214)]) where Jinendrabuddhi uses *śabdānuśāsanaprastāvāt* in justiftying an interpretation, he can be saying merely that the topic at hand throughout is grammar, which deals with speech forms, so that one can understand a reference to linguistic elements.

[118]Yudhiṣṭhira Mīmāṁsaka (1984:I.227) made this claim.

[119]Bhim Sen Shastri (1984:20-21) is among those who invokes this argument. He cites the beginning of Jaimini's Mīmāṁsāsūtra (*athāto dharmajijñāsā*), the Vedāntasūtra (*athāto brahmajijñāsā*), Vaiśeṣikasūtra (*athāto dharmaṁ vyākyāsyāmaḥ*), Yogasūtra (*atha yogānuśāsanam*), Nidānasūtra (*athātaś chandasāṁ nicayam vyākyāsyāmaḥ*), Carakasaṁhitā (*athāto dīrghañ jīvatīyam adhyāyaṁ vyākhyāsyāmaḥ*), Suśrutasaṁhitā (*athāto vedotpattināmādhyāyaṁ vyākhyāsyāmaḥ*), Pāraskaragṛhyasūtra (*athāto gṛhasthālīpākānāṁ karma*), Khadiragṛhyasūtra (*athāto gṛhya-karmāṇi*), and Gobhilīyagṛhyasūtra (*athāto gṛhyakarmāṇy upadekṣyāmaḥ*).

[120]This argument is given by Bhim Sen Shastri (1984:19).

[121]In his Uddyota (Vedavrata 1962-63:I.2), Nāgeśa remarks that thereby are also implied the remaining three anubandhas usually given at the beginning of a work: the object of study, the relation between this and the work, and the person who is to take up the study.

[122]Bhāṣya on 1.1.47 (Kielhorn [1880-85:I.114.24-115.2]): *naiveśvara ājñāpayati nāpi dharmasūtrakārāḥ paṭhanty apavādair utsargā bādhyantām iti kiṁ tarhi laukiko' ayaṁ dṛṣṭāntaḥ.*

[123]In connection with vivakṣā and grammatical description (see Cardona [1976a:255 with note 376]), there is a recent study by Peter M. Scharf (1995a), arguing against van Nooten (1983). See also Radicchi (1993), whose discussion is not restricted to the Vākyapadīya.

[124]Bronkhorst (1995) follows up on this theme. In addition, other scholars recently have continued to stress that grammar serves as a model for various schools of thought. Torella (1987) is wideranging in its coverage, though the author places emphasis on Kashmir Shaivism. Ruegg (1978) and Kamaleswar Bhattacharya (1980, 1980-81) concern more particularly

Buddhistic thought. Bhattacharya (1980) deals quite insightfully with a passage from the second chapter of Nāgārjuna's Madhyamakaśāstra, showing the influence of Pāṇinian grammar in the argument and phrasing. Wayman (1985:584-587) also deals with this section of Nāgārjuna's work.

[125]A thorough survey of views concerning time in a wide variety of texts and schools is found in Hārāṇacandra Bhaṭṭācārya's work, edited and reissued by Gaurinath Śāstrī (1984). Vīrendrakumāra Vidyālaṅkāra (1992-93) also discusses the concept of time in Sanskrit grammar. The most recently published work on the topic is by Ganesh Prasad Panda (1997).

[126]This point is brought out by Helārāja in his commentary on VP 3.8.63 (K. A. Subramania Iyer [1973:40.20-24]): *svagataviśeṣāpekṣayā sāmānyasvabhāvo'pi pacir bhāvaṁ prati viśeṣaḥ | bhāvaḥ punaḥ paktiṁ prati sāmānyam eva | tataś ca yathopādhyāyśabdena mātularūpatayā-nabhidīyamāno'pi mātulo vastuvṛttena tattvāt svakāryaṁ pratipadyate tathā bhāvaśabdena sāmānyavācinā sākṣād anabhidhīyamāno 'pi viśeṣaḥ sāmarthyād anumīyamānasannidhir iti sāmānyaprayuktaṁ kāryaṁ pratipadyate* 'Although cooking is a general thing with respect to the particulars which pertain to it, it is a particular with respect to abtract action in general. Hence the following: although the maternal uncle, when he is referred to by the term "teacher", is not referred to in the guise of maternal uncle, by virtue of what obtains in reality, he partakes in the act due him since he has the property of being that. In the same way, although a particular is not directly referred to by the term *bhāva*, which signifies something general, by dint of what actually is, its presence is inferred, so that this partakes in the operation conditioned by what is general.'

[127]As far as I can see, however, Wezler has not noted the passage I have cited in note 126 from Helārāja's commentary or pointed out explicitly this exact parallel between the grammatical situation and the example of the teacher of a student who is also simultaneously maternal uncle of another person.

[128]I agree with Wezler (1994a:185) that, '... *pratītapadārthakaḥ* [*śabdaḥ*] cannot but mean: "The word '*śabda*' is one the meaning of which is well known".' Cf. Cardona (1988:660 = 1997a:567 [**847c**]): 'Immediately after this, however, he goes on to remark that *śabda* is a term whose meaning is known (*pratītapadārthakaḥ*) in the world of everyday usage (*loke*) ....'

Wezler's most original contribution to the discussion of the passage in question is his suggestion (1994a:187), which I find convincing, that this involves a syllogistic reasoning.

[129]On the Mahābhāṣya passage in question see also Deshpande (1987d:83-84, 1993a:26), Cardona (1988:638-639, 1997a:550 [**833**]).

[130]**A** 5.1.21: *śatāc ca ṭhanyatāv aśate.* *śata-ām-ya* → *śata-ya* → *śatya*, *śata-ām-ṭha* → *śata-ṭha* → *śata-ika* → *śatika.*

[131]5.1.38 vtt. 1-2: *tasyanimittaprakaraṇe vātapittaśleṣmabhyaḥ śamana-kopanayor upasaṅkhyānam, sannipātāc ca.*

[132]The Bālamanoramā on Siddhāntakaumudī 1704 (= **A** 5.1.38: Giridhara Śarmā Caturveda and Parameśvarānanda Śarmā Bhāskara [1958-61:II.500]) explains that by *kopana* is meant the increase (*vṛddhi*) of the wind and so on. Vāsudeva thus takes *kopana* to be an action noun. *śamana* and *kopana* are ambiguously either action or instrument nouns.

[133]In Kumārasambhava 2.48: *tasminnupāyāḥ sarve naḥ krūre pratihatakriyāḥ* | *vīryavanty auṣadhīnīva vikāre sānnipātike*, Kālidāsa uses *sānnipātika* with reference to an illness (*vikāra*) against which strong herbal medicines are without effect. Comparably, the Carakasaṁhitā (Cikitsāsthāna 18.16: *pratataṁ kāsamānaś ca jyotīṁṣi ca paśyati* | *śleṣmāṇaṁ pittasaṁsṛṣṭaṁ niṣṭhīvati ca paittike*) uses *paittika* with reference to a variety of cough, caused by perturbed bile, such that a person coughs constantly, sees lights, and spits out phlegm mixed with bile.

[134]On these rules, see Cardona (1997a:357-358 [**557-558**]).

[135]The citation given shows lacunae because I have omitted text references which Bronkhorst supplies. I have also repeated '*-a-rU + a-*' as it appears in the article cited. On abhinihita sandhi and an intermediate stage with *-ĕy ĕ-*, *-ŏv ŏ-* containing short *e-* and *o*-colored vowels, see also Cardona (1987b).

[136]By **A** 6.1.109 (*eṅaḥ padāntād ati*) *-o-* is the single replacement for pada-final *-o* and a following short *a-*: *-as a-* → *-aR a-* → *-aü a-* → *-o a-* → *-o-*.

[137]By **A** 1.2.31 (*samāhāraḥ svaritaḥ*), a vowel with a combination of high and low pitches is called *svarita*, and according to **A** 1.2.32 (*tasyādita udāttam ardhahrasvam*) the first half mora of such a vowel is high-pitched; see Cardona (1968a, 1997a:17 [**36**]). According to Ṛgvedaprātiśākhya

3.4-6 (*tasyodāttarodāttād ardhamātrārdham eva vā, anudāttaḥ paraḥ śeṣaḥ sa udāttaśrutiḥ, na ced udāttaṁ vocyate kiñcit svaritaṁ vākṣaram param*), the first half mora or the first half of a svarita vowel is pronounced higher than a normal high-pitched vowel and the remainder which follows is a low-pitched segment which, however, has the sound of a high-pitched vowel unless there follows a high-pitched or svarita syllable. That is, the second part of a svarita is raised to the level of an udātta unless an udātta or svarita follows. Here and in earlier discussions, I have omitted details of the Ṛgvedaprātiśākhya's description of svarita and pracaya. I will deal with these in volume VI.6 of *Pāṇini : His Work and its Traditions*.

[138]In a footnote accompanying this, Bronkhorst says (1981c:94 note 18), 'Cardona (1968:459) thinks that the description of *svarita* in the *Aṣṭādhyāyī* was only meant for svarita vowels occurring in the *Aṣṭādhyāyī*. This seems unlikely.' What Cardona actually sought to demonstrate is that the reason Pāṇini had to include the one sūtra concerned exclusively with describing a phonetic detail is that he used svarita vowels metalinguistically and such vowels were subject to various different pronunciations, which he knew. This may seem unlikely to Bronkhorst, but he has not adduced evidence to support his feeling.

[139]Thieme (1985b:562a [**14**]) says, 'Pāṇini's grammar, our oldest grammatical description, knows all the sounds mentioned in the preceding paragraphs, except the domal *l*, which is a specialty of the south (and the Śaunaka recension of RV), whereas Pāṇini hails from the extreme North-West (in the Kashmir mscpt.s of the RV *ḍ* between vowels is not replaced by *ḷ*).' Once one accepts that Pāṇini knew the padapāṭha composed by Śākalya, this view becomes difficult to maintain. Note also that, as Witzel (1989:165) has pointed out, scholars earlier failed to recognize the symbol for retroflex *-ḷ-* in Śāradā script, namely symbol for *-ḍ-* with a diacritic.

[140]For example, the Kāśikā on **A** 6.1.113 says (Aryendra Sharma et al. [1969-70:II.626]) that replacement by *u* is provided where replacement by *y* according to **A** 8.3.17 would otherwise obtain: *bhobhagoaghoapūrvasya yo'śīty asmin prāpta uttvaṁ vidhīyate*.

[141]For example, the Kāśikā on **A** 6.1.113 says (Aryendra Sharma et al. [1969-70:II.626]) that since *-R* by **A** 8.2.66 is the basis for the operation stated in **A** 6.1.113, it is not non-existent by **A** 8.2.1: *pūrvatrāsiddham* :

rutvam apy āśrayāt pūrvatrāsiddham ity asiddhaṁ na bhavati.

[142]This scholar and his colleagues have also compiled an electronic text of the Kāśikā in collaboration with the University of Poona. In addition, there is an electronic version of the Osmania edition of this text, compiled by Elliott Stern and George Cardona. The latter includes references to sūtras alluded to through illustrations as well as to citations from the Vedas and other texts, which are lacking in the Lausanne-Poona electronic text.

[143]Raghuvir Vedalankar (1977) also lists vārttikas found in the Kāśikā, vārttikas given in the Kāśikā but not found in the Mahābhāṣya and vārttikas with different readings in these two works.

[144]May I be permitted incidentally to comment on an alleged omission. Oberlies (1989:7, note 31) says the following concerning Raghuvir Vedalankar's work: 'Auch in Cardonas Survey nicht verzeichnet.' My survey was published in 1976 and covered work which I could consult before early 1975. The Indian edition of 1980 is essentially a reprint, with no new additions to the bibliography. Obviously, then, a work published in 1977 could not be covered. To be sure, I mentioned some works as forthcoming, but at the time I compiled the survey I did not have information about Raghuvir Vedalankar's work.

[145]Echoing Kielhorn, to whom he refers, Thieme (1956:18 with note 42 [Budruss (1971:590)]) says of the Kāśikā, 'But we can prove that it has used, beside Patañjali, Candragomin's grammar.'

[146]On the Kāśikā's indebtedness to the Kātantra and Cāndravyākaraṇa see also Visalakshy (1981, 1989:105-123 and appendixes).

[147]Quite a bit has been written recently concerning whether the vṛtti on the Cāndravyākaraṇa was composed by Candragomin himself or by someone else, namely Dharmadāsa. In addition to Raghuvir Vedalankar, see recently Harsha Natha Miśra (1974:141-147), Prafulla Chandra Dash (1986:8-21), Oberlies (1989:2-4). Raghuvir Vedalankar and Harsha Natha Miśra argue for common authorship of both the grammar and the vṛtti, the other two scholars for different authorship. Dash in particular refutes Harsha Natha Miśra's arguments as well as those of Birwé (1968). Concerning the date of the Vṛtti, see also Rau (1996:337-338).

[148]'On the basis of these examples', he concludes (1977:260), 'it is quite clear that in many places there is influence of the Cāndravyākaraṇa on the Kāśikā's interpretation. In doing so, the Kāśikākāra has depended extensively on the Cāndrasūtra and the Cāndravṛtti.' [इन उदाहरणों के आधार पर भलीभांति स्पष्ट है कि काशिका की व्याख्या पर अनेक स्थलों में चान्द्र व्याकरण का प्रभाव है। ऐसा करने में काशिकाकार ने चान्द्र सूत्रों एवं चान्द्रवृत्ति, दोनों का पर्याप्त आश्रय लिया है।] Later (1977:348), Raghuvir Vedalankar again emphasizes that the Kāśikā has made use of the texts noted as well as the Kātantra.

[149]This does not contradict what Kielhorn said many years earlier (see above with note 145), although Raghuvir Vedalankar thinks (1977:109) that Kielhorn and Thieme among others said that the Kāśikā changed sūtras under the influence of the Cāndravyākaraṇa.

[150]In this vein, see also Radicchi (1985).

[151]Aklujkar (1991a:30), on the other hand, argues for maintaining the earlier view, that Abhayanandin is to be dated after the Kāśikā. He points out, 'Moreover, two of the *Kāśikā* phrases that could be said to have been inspired by the *Mahā-vṛtti* are not as precise as their counterparts (compare *tatra saktūn pāsyāmaḥ* and *yuktā adhyaimahi* with *tatra ... dviḥ saktūn pāsyāmaḥ* and *yuktā dvir adhyaimahi*). If the *Kāśikā* were at the borrowing end, why would it sacrifice the existing precision?'

[152]A new edition of the Vyākaraṇasiddhāntasudhānidhi (see Cardona [1976a:361 note 484]), by Satya Prakash Dubey (1995) is underway.

[153]Bronkhorst also devotes an appendix (1986:173-176) to the relative chronology of Nāgeśa's works; see Cardona (1976a:347 note 345).

[154]The Vṛtti (K. A. Subramania Iyer [1966:65.1]) notes this: *triṣv api ślokeṣu prastutasya parisamāptiḥ.* The Paddhati (K. A. Subramania Iyer [1966:64.24-25]: *prastutasyeti : vākyapadīyākhye śāstre yad anugantum iṣṭaṁ tasya*) notes that *prastutasya* in the Vṛtti refers to what the author wishes to cover in the work called *Vākyapadīya.* See also Peri Sarveswara Sharma (1987b).

[155]See also Rau (1977b, 1985c, 1991) for additional manuscript materials.

[156]See also Bronkhorst (1988:124): 'D'autre part tous les manuscrits du Vākyapadīya que nous possédons dérivent de la Vṛtti; par conséquent, des renseignements portant sur la lecture du Vākyapadīya que la Vṛtti pourrait

nous fournir sont plus valables que le témoignage de n'importe quel manuscrit, puisque les lectures du texte que l'auteur de la Vṛtti connaissait sont plus anciennes que celles des manuscrits suivants; elles sont, en effet, la base de ces derniers. (Ce dernier point, notons-le bien, n'implique point que les manuscrits qui contiennent la Vṛtti ont pour cette raison une valeur spéciale pour la lecture des strophes.)'

[157]Bhate and Kar (1993) derives from Rau's work, with correction of some errors.

[158]One piece of evidence adduced by Bronkhorst, the use of *tatrabhavat-*, is the topic of a much more extensive treatment by Houben (forthcoming d).

[159]See also Bronkhorst's earlier article (1990a), to which he refers the reader.

[160]See Cardona (1976a:297 with note 516).

[161]VP 1.6: *bhedānāṁ bahumārgatvaṁ karmaṇy ekatra cāṅgatā* | *śabdānāṁ yataśaktitvaṁ tasya śākhāsu dṛśyate.*

[162]K. A. Subramania Iyer (1966a:27.6-8): *śabdānāṁ yataśaktitvam* | *tathārthapratyāyane sāmarthyāt tathābhudayahetutvāt* | *tasya śākhāsu dṛśyata iti* | *devasumnayor yajuṣi* (**A** 7.4.38) *simasyātharvaṇe' nta udāttaḥ* (Phiṭsūtra 4.11) *ity evamādi.*

[163]The phrase 'que nous venons d'examiner' seems out of place, since Bronkhorst simply states the interpretations and neither justifies them with arguments nor considers their consequences.

[164]K. A. Subramania Iyer (1966a:103.3): *ātmabhedasya bruvikarmatve dvitīyā vākyasvarūpānukaraṇe tu prathamā* 'If self-difference is the object of saying, a second-triplet ending (follows *ātmabheda*), but if a sentence is cited, a first-triplet ending (follows it).' Vṛṣabhadeva explains (K. A. Subramania Iyer [1966a:103.15]): *vākyasya karmatva ātmabhedo na karmeti prathamā*) that under the second alternative the cited utterance is the object of saying, not self-difference, so that *ātmabheda* takes a first-triplet ending. This is comparable to something the Vākyapadīya considers in another context: in the situation spoken of in an utterance like *paśya mṛgo dhāvati* 'Look at how the deer runs', the act of running is something which is carried out (*sādhya*) by a deer and it is also a *kāraka* (*sādhana*) — the

object of seeing; in addition, the deer is not an object here, so that *mṛga* does not take a second-triplet ending: cf. VP 3.8.52: *mṛgo dhāvati paśyeti sādhyasādhanarūpatā | tathā viṣayabhedena saraṇasyopapadyate.* The Vṛtti on VP 1.46 goes on (K. A. Subramania Iyer [1966a:103.3-6]): *tatra kāryakāraṇayor anyatvapakṣe bhedaḥ | pakṣāntare tv ekasyaivātmanaḥ śaktipravibhāgarūpaparigrahakṛtād buddhyavacchedān nānātvakalpanā | śabdākṛtivyaktibhedābhedavyapāśrayo vā pūrveṣām ācāryāṇāṁ darśana-bheda iti | parastād etad vastugata eva prapañco bhaviṣyati*) to say that this difference of views among earlier teachers is explicable in two ways. First, there is a division of opinion concerning cause and effect. Under the view that these are separate entities, there is a split between them; under the other view, there is a fictitious assumption of distinctness (*nānātvakalpanā*) relative to an entity (*ātmanaḥ* 'self') which is just one (*ekasyaiva*), and this is due to this entity's being cognized through a cognition which is itself limited and thereby delimits its object (*buddhyavacchedāt*): the single entity has different capacities which it assumes, so that it is thereby cognized as different things. From another point of view, the difference of opinion among the predecessors is based on whether individual speech elements and their generic counterparts are viewed as distinct or identical. On the analysis of *paśya mṛgo dhāvati* from different points of view, see recently Mārtaṇḍaśāstrī Dīkṣita (1980) and Gopikamohan Bhattacharya (1993).

[165]I cite Houben's paper here, from the version of July 11th 1997, with the written permission of the author (letter of 18 August 1997).

[166]K. A. Subramania Iyer (1966a:103.12-14): *ātmabhedaśabdāt prathamādvitīyayoḥ sādhutvam āha ātmabhedasya iti | yadātmabheda eva bravītikriyayā vyāpyate | āhuḥ iti | kim | ātmabhedam | katham | astīty anena rūpeṇa* '(The Vṛttikāra) says that first- and second-triplet endings are correct after *ātmabheda*: *ātmabhedasya*. (The form with a second-triplet ending is correct) when the self-difference alone is covered by the act of saying. *āhuḥ*: What (do they state)? A self-difference. How (do they express this)? In the form "... is".' That is, if the ancients were expressing themselves at present, they could do so in either of two ways: *ātmabhedo' stīti brūmaḥ* or *ātmabhedaṁ brūmaḥ*.

[167] VP 1.87: *asataś cāntarāle yāñ chabdān astīti manyate | pratipattur*

aśaktiḥ sā grahaṇopāya eva saḥ 'And the speech units which, (though they are) nonexistent, (a listener) considers to occur in the interval (between a first element heard and his grasping an entire sound, word or sentence) — saying (of each partial unit), "It exists" — are only a means to comprehension; that is an inability in the listener.' Houben considers VP 1.87 also (1995b:40) in another context, discussing Bhartṛhari's view that the utterance is the true unit of communication.

[168]Despite Houben's continued note of uncertainty — 'hardly any choice' — I am assuming that he does indeed mean that VP 1.87 supports viewing *astīti* as an adverbial phrase. Otherwise, why bother to bring up the passage and to say what Houben says? Moreover, in an earlier footnote (note 17 under section 2.1), Houben says, 'As we will see below (sections 4.1-4.2), Vṛṣabhadeva's grammatical analysis of this version of the kārika assigns an adverbial role to *astīti* (as an answer to the question how?).'

[169]Houben also remarks (forthcoming a:section 2.3), 'Even while giving basically correct and defensible translations, neither Iyer nor Biardeau have [sic] realized the implications this Vṛtti-passage has for the authorship issue in which they were both so much interested.'

[170]Similarly, he says (forthcoming a:section 2.3), 'Whether we interpret the line in accordance with Iyer's or with Biardeau's translation, or, more generally, whether we interpret it in accordance with possibility (a): the Vṛtti author is confronted with two different readings; or (b): the Vṛtti author acknowledges only one reading in the kārikā and mentions the other one of his own accord; in either case (c): the author of the Vṛtti must have been different from the author of the kārikā, unless we assume (d): that the latter was a debutant, uncertain about his own capabilities and ready to interrupt his discourse on subtle philosophical issues with apologetic, technical comments on his choice of words.'

[171]Bronkhorst (1987a:10.5) *anyeṣāṁ granthaḥ kuśalo viśeṣair iti*.

[172]As is more straightforwardly illustrated in VP 1.46cd.

[173]*ātmabhedasya bruvikarmatve dvitīyā vākyasvarūpānukaraṇe tu prathamā*. See note 164.

[174]In effect, pādas c-d of the kārikā have this construction: *buddhibhedād abhinnasya bhedam eke pracakṣate.*

[175]K. A. Subramania Iyer (1966a:103.14-15): *vākyasvarūpa iti : yadātmabhedo* (*astīti* ?) *ty etena tadā vākyaṁ purāṇagoktaṁ* (*anukriyate* ?): *evam āhur iti*. I have cited the text with the emendations suggested by K. A. Subramania Iyer; see also note 129.

[176]See Cardona (1995). Note that *asti* so used is still a verb form, not a true adverb, as can be seen from the parallel use of non-indicative modal forms such as *syāt*, *bhavet* in comparable usages.

[177]The interpretation which follows is one that I assumed for a long time but never felt the need to explain until in late July 1997 Houben sent me a copy of his paper (Houben [forthcoming a]) concerning VP 1.46. I then (July 29th and 31st, 1997) communicated my interpretation to him, in a provisional form included as an addition to the present section. Houben subsequently reminded me (letter of 18 August 1997) that the interpretation I presented owes much to Raghunātha Śarmā's Ambākartrī on VP 1.46. Having studied the Vākyapadīya with Raghunātha, I do not doubt that, at least subconsciously, I have replicated much of what he said, although when I wrote this I did not copy from his commentary consciously. After sending Houben the preliminary version of this section, I reworked it in the present form, to include some details concerning the use of terms like *bruvi*. I subsequently received — in the second week of September, although Houben mailed it in late August — a postscript to Houben's paper (forthcoming a'), in which he subjects Raghunātha's commentary to criticism. From what I can see, Houben fails to justify his position. In what follows I cover the objections which Houben has raised. I wish to acknowledge an exchange of ideas, through e-mail, with Ashok Aklujkar, in which we find ourselves agreeing about the views presented by both Bronkhorst and Houben, though we have approached the issues differently.

[178]Forms such as *bravīti*, *brūtaḥ*, *bruvanti* alternate with forms of *āh* (*āha*, *āhatuḥ*, *āhuḥ*) according to **A** 3.4.84 (Cardona [1997a:274 (**397**)]).

[179]3.3.108 vt. 2: *ikśtipau dhātunirdeśe*.

[180]Vedavrata (1962-63:III.342): *dhātuvarthanirdeśe' py etau bāhulakāt | ata evekṣater nāśabdam āhau prabhūtādibhyaḥ gacchatau paradārādibhya iti prayogāḥ saṅgacchante*.

[181]E.g. VP 2.222: *yathaikaśeṣe bhujyādiḥ pratyekam avatiṣṭhate* |

kriyaivaṁ dvandvavācye' rthe pratyekaṁ pravibhajyate.

[182]Vṛtti 1.51 (K. A. Subramania Iyer [1966a:109.4-5 (on verse 1.50 in this edition)]): *sā* [*svarūpamātrā*] *tu sannihitapratyavabhāsāpi loke bhujyādikriyāsambandhavirodhān nāśrīyate.* For example, if one utters *odanam bhuṅkte* one means to say that someone is eating rice, not that he is eating the term *odanam*.

[183]Houben (forthcoming a') says, 'Although I am aware of cases where a reference to a verb is interpreted as a (metaphorical) reference to the meaning of that verb (see e.g. Helārāja on VP 3.3.40-41, 47), such an assumption goes one step further, and for this one would like to see relevant examples cited, especially in the light of the precision grammarians otherwise display in their discussions of linguistic matters.' His reference only to Helārāja, whether it was intended to do so or not, could give the impression that this is a relatively late metaphorical interpretation. As shown, Kātyāyana, who formulated the use of ***ik*** and ***śtip***, himself also uses forms of the type *āhi* with reference to acts. As concerns Bhartṛhari, *bhuji* is only one example, though the best I know, of the very general use in question. Note also that Pāṇini not only uses terms of the type *gami*, with reference to a base, but also says *janikartuḥ* in a sūtra (**A** 1.4.30: *janikartuḥ prakṛtiḥ*) which concerns a kāraka: the source of an agent of the act of coming into being is given the class name *apādāna*. There can be no question that *jani* here has to designate the act which the base *jan* signifies. Additional details need not be considered here.

[184]In connection with *ātmabheda*, Houben (forthcoming a') is again vague, while objecting to me through Raghunātha Śarmā. He says, 'As for the fourth point, three strong objections can be made to the assumption that *ātmabhedasya* in the Vṛtti sentence refers both to *ātmabhedas* in pāda a and to *bhedam* in pāda d. First, the kārikā itself seems to contrast quite clearly the *ātmabheda* 'essential difference, difference in identity' accepted by some thinkers, and a difference based on a difference in understanding or viewpoint accepted by others.' Since Houben's subsequent points either depend on this or say nothing different from what Raghunātha and I have said, I concentrate on this first point. Clearly, as we all recognize, the kārikā contrasts two views, under which there are either truly two distinct entities or only one which is conceived of as split into two. No one can

dispute this. The term *ātman*, however, simply means 'self' (and can include reference to physical bodies). The view of those referred to in VP 1.46cd can be paraphrased accurately by *eke'bhinnasya buddhibhedād āropitam ātmabhedam pracakṣate.* Houben's problem arises from his insistence that *ātmabheda* in and of itself must designate an essential difference. He has not demonstrated this, and his 'seems to contrast' is another instance of vagueness. Moreover, he does not refer to the Vṛtti passage I have alluded to, although this patently contains the phrase *ekasyaivātmanaḥ ... nānātvakalpanā*, which refers to the view given in VP 1.46cd.

[185]Houben (forthcoming a'): 'Third, although the normal sequence is to start to discuss the first pāda or line of a kārikā or elements therein, the present Vṛtti-sentence would start with a reference to pāda d, *bhedam eke pracakṣate.*'

[186]Houben (forthcoming a') objects that under Raghunātha Śarmā's and my interpretation, 'Second, the Vṛtti did not consider any alternative for pāda a (although according to Vṛṣabha the Vṛtti does precisely this), but thought only of *ātmabhedas* at that place.'

[187]Though I had anticipated the objections considered above, I had not anticipated another. It is brought up by Houben (forthcoming a'):

> Six, perhaps as an additional justification for the Vṛtti-sentence, Raghunātha Śarmā thought the Vṛtti-author might have anticipated the following objection: "Why does not the sentence as a whole, being the object of the verb 'to say', receive the second ending?"; the Vṛtti-sentence would imply the answer "The sentence is not a *prātipadika* '(primary or derived) nominal stem'."

This is stretching to read into the Ambākartrī an implication that is not at all obvious and seems intent on nitpicking. After all, it is not wrong for a paṇḍita to point out something that has engaged the attention of Pāṇinīyas over time and which can occur to him in this context, namely that a verb form or an utterance, though it's meaning play the role of a karman — as in *paśya mṛgo dhāvati* (see note 164) — does not take a second-triplet ending, since such endings occur only after nominals.

[188]Ashok Aklujkar (e-mail communication of August 14, 1997) suggests also the possibility that आत्मभेदस्तयोः was misread at some time as आत्मभेदन्तयोः.

[189]Bronkhorst (1992c:719-721) has a different opinion.

[190]Still another general survey of Bhartṛhari's works and general ideas appears in Pāṇḍuraṅga Viṭṭhala (1988), where the author also adopts a date for Bharṭṛhari (100 A.D.) that is earlier by several centuries than the earliest date usually accepted and does so on the assumption that Bhartṛhari was Vikramāditya's brother. Aklujkar (1994) presents evidence to support the position that the ṭīkākāra referred to in Skanda-Maheśvara's commentary on Yāska's Nirukta is Bhartṛhari.

[191]Virendra Sharma (1977:421-455) devotes a chapter to demonstrating a fundamental difference between Bhartṛhari's views and those of Kashmiri Śaivism.

[192]Sphoṭa is also the subject of Narendra Kumar Dash (1988), in which the author puts more emphasis on what is said in the Mahābhāṣya. See also Coward (1994), who outlines the main differences between Kumārila and Maṇḍanamiśra, the latter representing Bhartṛhari's position on sphoṭa, and E. R. Sreekrishna Sarma (1981)

[193]Zimmerman's is a general treatment — based on secondary sources — of thoughts concerning semantics in works of Pāṇinīyas from Patañjali on and also in other schools of thought such as Nyāya.

[194]Avanindra Kumar (1988-89) presents a brief but good summary of the issues concerning the relative status of terms viewed as corruptions (*apabhraṁśa*) and those that are considered correct usage (*sādhu*), both in the Vākyapadīya and Mīmāṁsā and elsewhere.

[195]See also Vīrendrakumāra Vidyālaṅkāra (1992-93) and Shankarji Jha (1997).

[196]Subodh Sharma (1990) discusses once more Bhartṛhari's view that all things evolve from Brahman, whose essence is speech, and are not distinct from it. Śabdabrahman is also the topic of the brief and general discussion in K. Sitaramanjaneyulu (1988).

[197]See also Houben (1993), who adduces data from the Dīpikā to support the view that Bhartṛhari produced this commentary before the Vākyapadīya, Patnaik (1989), and, with less pertinence directly to Bhartṛhari, Siderits (1985).

[198]Rau's edition (1977a:58) has *aśābdo*, which occurs also in the citation by Kumārila, but the Vṛtti (K. A Subramania Iyer [1983:199]) comments

evaṁ tarhy aśabdo vākyārthaḥ. I have accordingly cited the kārikā as it appears in editions such as Subramania Iyer's.

[199]K A. Subramania Iyer (1969:53): 'It is well known that Bhartṛhari often gives the views of others on the different topics which he expounds in the *Vākyapadīya*.'

[200]Śrīkānta Pāṇḍeya (1990) studies, with emphasis on the grammarians, the notion of relation and all sorts of specific relations, including those that are expressed by particular affixes and in particular syntactic contexts.

[201]The final two chapters (1992:210-288, 289-303) are devoted to appreciations of Puṇyarāja's scholarship and his performance as a commentator.

[202]Herzberger's translations of passages from the Pramāṇasamuccaya are based on the Sanskrit version of the Tibetan as rendered by Muni Jambūvijayaj (1966-88:I:Appendix:97-140). I was surprised not to find references to Herzberger's book in Patnaik's work and to see that Patnaik does not list the book in her bibliography. Other recent studies dealing with Bhartṛhari and Buddhist thinkers are: K. Kunjunni Raja (1983), Hattori (1993), and Lindtner (1993), not all of equal value.

[203]On the issue which Houben has discussed see also Herzberger and Herzberger (1981a, b). It may be noted that the paradox of the liar was also brought up in another, more formal context. Pāṇini's sūtra **A** 8.2.1: *pūrvatrāsiddham* states that a sūtra of the set of rules headed by this rule is suspended (*asiddham*) with respect to any preceding rule (*pūrvatra*). If **A** 8.2.1 applies with respect to itself, so that it too is suspended, of course then it ceases to have any effect on the succeeding section of rules, so that these rules are not suspended with respect to preceding rules. Kaiyaṭa points this out, saying this rule makes known that sūtras are suspended, excepting itself, since an item which conveys a meaning is not at the same time the meaning to be conveyed. If the sūtra did apply to itself, its very formulation would be purposeless. Kaiyaṭa then brings in the parallel *sarvaṁ mithyā bravīmi*, which, he says, makes known that all other utterances alone are false. Pradīpa (Vedavrata 1962-1963) V.354: *etac ca sūtram ātmānaṁ vihāya sūtrāntarāṇām asiddhatvaṁ pratipādayati na tv ātmanaḥ bodhakasya bodhyatvābhāvāt* | *etasya cāsiddhatve sarveṣāṁ siddhatvāt sūtrārambha evānarthakaḥ syāt* | *yathā sarvaṁ mithyā bravīmīti vākyaṁ*

vākyāntarāṇām eva mithyātvaṁ pratipādayati | etasyāpi mithyātve vākyāntarāṇāṁ mithyātvaṁ na syād ity anarthakam evaitad vākyaṁ syāt.

[204]A thorough exposition of the Vākyapadīya passages in question is also given by Virendra Sharma (1977:124-152). Oetke (1997) argues against Houben. Through Oetke's kindness, I was able to read a draft of his full paper, and I cannot agree entirely with his claims concerning the Vākyapadīya text and interpretation. Since, however, he may have changed his ideas after his discussions with A. Aklujkar and me and the paper has not been published, I refrain from any further comment.

[205]In his preface, Vidya Niwas Misra says (1987:v), 'The present edition fulfills a long-felt need to bring out again a critical edition of the well-known Sanskrit work in philosophy of grammar, *Vaiyākaraṇabhūṣaṇa* ....' The term 'again' deserves emphasis. The present work is not a new critical edition. Indeed, there is no indication anywhere in the preface (pp. v-viii) of any manuscripts consulted. This contrasts with K. P. Trivedi's edition (1915), in which the editor gave a detailed notice of the manuscripts he used (1915:11-15) and listed variant readings in particular manuscripts (pp. 734-765). I mention Trivedi's edition because of a feature in Vidya Niwas Misra's edition. The notes (1987:255-412) are copies of the notes given in Trivedi's edition (1915:609-727). Not even outdated references to texts have been changed. Thus, for example, Misra's notes refer to 'मनोरमा उत्तरार्ध p. 2 (Benares Pothī Edition)' (1987:259), to 'p. 66 (of the 5th Adhyāya), Pothi Edition Benares' (1987:266), to 'p. 41 (3rd Adhyāya), Pothi Edition of Benares' (1987:268). In Trivedi's edition, we have the very same references (1915:612, 618, 619) with trivial differences: 'Pothî' instead of 'Pothī' and 'Pothi', 'Adhyâya' instead of 'Adhyāya'. Again, in Trivedi's annotations we find (1915:724), 'The D_l Ms. has a marginal note: — "तथा चाप्रमत्तगीतः श्लोकः— ....' Vidya Niwas Misra's corresponding note has (1987:407): 'The D, Ms. has a marginal note:— "तथा चाप्रमत्तगीतः श्लोकः— ....' The only difference is that Trivedi's 'D_l' has wrongly been copied as 'D,'. Everything else is exactly the same, including a reference to a manuscript, although no manuscripts are mentioned anywhere in Vidya Niwas Misra's volume and his edition lacks the references to variant readings that appear in footnotes of Trivedi's edition.

[206]Banamali Biswal includes extensive explanatory notes (1995:197-

472). In addition, the text (1995:97-196) reflects Biswal's consultation of manuscripts.

[207]A study of part of the Ratnaprabhā commentary on this work has also been published: Sitala Prasada Jayaswal (1995).

[208]Kapil Dev Shastri commendably supplies exact text references for many of the frequent citations found in the Paramalaghumañjūṣā. Sabhāpati Śarmā Upādhyāya (1963) also supplies such references. Regrettably, other editions of these texts as well as of the Vaiyākaraṇabhūṣaṇa and Vaiyākaraṇabhūṣaṇasāra are lacking in this respect.

[209]My own critical edition of the Paramalaghumañjūṣā, with indexes and indications of citations, based on twenty-seven manuscripts, has been ready in script form for over ten years and read by several scholars. There remains only to complete a detailed introduction, but I am by no means sure when, if ever, this edition will appear. Let me note in passing that in several passages the Paramalaghumañjūṣā editions now available deviate from what is justified by the manuscripts.

[210]Peri Suryanarayana Shastri (1983) dealt briefly with the position that the principal meaning of a sentence containing a verb form is the meaning of the verbal base, and considered differences of interpretation between Nāgeśa and his predecessors. Girish K. Jha (1997) deals with varṇasphoṭa, that is, signifiers smaller than words, in particular with L-affixes and their replacements.

[211]See also Kak (1987), Bhate (1993b), Ramakrisnamacharyulu (1993), Krishnamacharyalu (1994), (Sujit, Suryanarayan and Singh (1994), Suryanarayan and Singh (1994).

[212]These were produced on Macintosh computers using the word-processing program Nisus and the data base program 4th Dimension. The work was done between 1991 and 1994 under the auspices of the National Endowment for the Humanities, to which I express my gratitude.

INDEXES

There are three indexes. The first is an index of names, the second an index of places referred to and cited in the present volume. The third index, a slight modification of the one which Ms. Katrin Baar of the University of Hamburg prepared, gives primary sources referred to in Cardona (1976a). As in the index to Cardona (1976a), references are to pages and notes. Note that, where appropriate, double references are given for commentaries on the Vākyapadīya, in accordance with the verse numberings found in the editions by Rau and K. A. Subramania Iyer.

Index of names

A

B

C

D

F

G

H

I

J

K

L

M

N

O

P

R

S

T

Y

Z

Index of primary sources

2.2

2.3

2.4

3.1

3.2

3.3

3.4

4.1

4.2

4.3

5.1

5.2

5.3

5.4

6.1

8.2

8.3

Atharvaveda

Bālamanoramā

Baudhāyanaśrautasūtra

Bhagavadgītā

Bhāgavatapurāṇa

Mahābhāṣya

sūtras

volume, page, line of Kielhorn's edition

I

II

Paribhāṣenduśekhara

Pradīpa

Prakīrṇaprakāśa

Raghuvaṁśa

Rāmāyaṇa

Ratnaprakāśa

Ṛgveda

Ṛgvedaprātiśākhya

Sāmaveda

Sarvadarśanasaṅgraha

Śatapathabrāhmaṇa

Siddhāntakaumudī

Śivasūtra

Taittirīyabrāhmaṇa

Taittirīyaprātiśākhya

Taittirīyasaṁhitā

Uddyota

Vājasaneyisaṁhitā

Vākyapadīya

Vākyapadīyaṭīkā

Vākyapadīyavṛtti

Vārttikas of Kātyāyana

Yogasūtra

INDEX OF PRIMARY SOURCES:
Pāṇini, A Survey of Research

Aṣṭādhyāyī

1.1

1.2

1.3

1.4

2.4

3.1

3.2

3.3

3.4

4.1

4.2

4.3

5.1

5.2

5.3

6.1

6.3

6.4

7.1

7.2

7.3

7.4

8.1

8.2

8.3

8.4

Bhāṣāvṛtti

Cāndravyākaraṇa

Jainendravyākaraṇa

Kāśikāvṛtti

Liṅgānuśāsana

Mahābhāṣya

sūtras

volume, page, line of Kielhorn's edition

I

II

III

Nirukta

Nyāsa

Pāṇinīyaśikṣā

Phiṭsūtra

Pradīpa

Ṛgveda

Siddhāntakaumudī

Śivasūtra

Uddyota

Uṇādisūtra

Pañcapādī

Daśapādī

Vākyapadīya

Vākyapadīyavṛtti

ADDITION AND CORRECTIONS

ADDITION

After the entire work had been completed and the final proof reading was almost complete, on May 27th 1998 I received from Ashok Aklujkar a copy of *Saccidānanda*, the Ānandāśrama Newsletter, number 2 (Pune: Ānandāśrama, December 1997), containing (pp. 3-7) an excerpt from Pt. V. B. Bhagavat's introduction to his edition of the *Sūktiratnākara* by Śeṣa Nārāyaṇa, a hitherto unpublished commentary on the Mahābhāṣya, which is forthcoming as Ānandāśrama Sanskrit Series no. 140. Inserting the pertinent information in my bibliography and section 2.2.1 would have entailed serious difficulties. Consequently, I summarize here the information Pt. Bhagavat supplies.

The edition is based on four manuscripts, none complete. To begin with, the first two āhnikas will be published.

Concerning the author, Pt. Bhagavat notes that he refers to Kaiyaṭa by name but does not mention Bhaṭṭojidīkṣita or later grammarians, so that Śeṣa Nārāyaṇa must have lived sometime between the twelfth and seventeenth centuries. According to Pt. Bhagavat, the *Sūktiratnākara* shows certain features whereby it stands apart from and excels other Mahābhāṣya commentaries. One of these features is the attention paid to details of prakriyā. Another is that Śeṣa Nārāyaṇa devotes much attention to views of Mīmāṁsā, Nyāya and other schools of thought. In addition, Pt. Bhagavat presents evidence which in his opinion demonstrates that Nāgeśa knew and used the *Sūktiratnākara*.

CORRECTIONS

I give below some corrections to Cardona (1976a) that I failed to include in the corrections given in the reprint (1997:385-386) and corrections which I have so far noticed are required in Cardona (1997a). I am certain more typographical errors will be noted, and these will be corrected in subsequent volumes of *Pāṇini : His Work and its Traditions*.

Additional corrections to *Pāṇini, A Survey of Research*

Page	Change	To
31, line 9 up	95*-145*	84*-94*
31, l. 8 up	84*-94*	61*-84*
42, l. 10	1885	1883
55	Ghatge	Ghatage
55, l. 20	*with two commentaries*	*with its two commentaries*
95	Pawte	Pawate
238, l. 17	... Bhandarkar (1864	... Bhandarkar (1868
360, n. 472	see section IV.2.3;	see section IV.2.2.3
384a, l. 8 up	Add a reference to this is my footnote 305	Add a reference to this in my footnote 305

Corrections to *Pāṇini, His Work and its Traditions, volume I: Background and Introduction*, second edition

Page	Change	To
xxxii, line 4 up:	न चाप्येवं विग्रहं	न चाप्येवं विग्रहः
xxxix, l. 4:	toether	together
xxxix, l. 6 up:	Vairāgyaśataka	Nītiśataka
li, l. 6 up:	प्प्रर्प्यतु	प्प्रार्प्यतु
3, l. 11:	singlular	singular
17, **36**, l. 6:	उच्चैरुत्तदात्तः	उच्चैरुदात्तः
55, **95**, l. 11:	*anekāl śit*	*anekālśit*
71, **115**, l. 4:	vārttika 5	vārttika 3
90, l. 13:	ones	one's
133, l. 4 up:	gaṇapātha	gaṇapāṭha
166, l. 5:	of of the	of the
213, l. 5 up:	*vāgbiḥ*	*vāgbhiḥ*
241, **345**, l. 8:	donotes	denotes
283, **314**, l. 10:	absolutedly	absolutely
286, **421**, l. 1:	a samprasāraṇa vowel	a samprasāraṇa vowel other than *ṛ*
286, **421**, l. 5:	*dīrghaḥ* 111	*dīrghaḥ aṇaḥ* 111
293, **439**, l. 6:	***ṭuṇídí***	***ṇídí***
296, l. 10:	ārdhādhātuka	ārdhadhātuka
321, **490**, l. 2 up:	*anaḍuh → anaḍuah*	*anaḍuh → anaḍunh*
321, **490**, l. 1 up:	*anaḍuh → anaḍuāh*	*anaḍuh → anaḍunh*
331, l. 4up:	*lakṣā-ṭha**k***	*lākṣā-ṭha**k***
353, l. 8:	of a derivate with	of a base with a derivate with
361, l. 3:	that is is not affix	that is not part of an affix
367, l. 2:	*murkhena*	*mūrkhena*

367, l. 7: *murkheṇa*	*mūrkheṇa*
383, **598**.4: ह्रस्वनुड्भ्याम्मतुप	ह्रस्वनुड्भ्याम्मतुप्
429, l. 7: can be be considered	can be considered
477, l. 9 up: straighforward	straightforward
509, l. 11 up: sytem	system
588, l. 13 up: सूत्रत्वमप्रामाणिकमेनोयोर्गण	सूत्रत्वमप्रामाणिकमनोयोर्गण
588, l. 4 up: गणसूत्रद्ववयमिदं	गणसूत्रद्वयमिदं
589, l. 6 up: applelations	appellations
596, lines 6, 8: *saṃjñā*	*saṁjñā*
608, १।१।६८: शब्दस्याशाब्दसञ्ज्ञा	शब्दस्याशब्दसञ्ज्ञा
611, १।४।४: नेयङ्यु°	नेयङु°
612, १।४।९६: °गर्हासुमुच्चयेषु	°गर्हासमुच्चयेषु
614, २।२।३: द्वितीयतृतीयचथुर्थ-	द्वितीयतृतीयचतुर्थ-
614, २।२।१८: कगतिप्रादायः	कगतिप्रादयः
615, २।३।१७: विँभाषा प्राणिषु	विँभाषाप्राणिषु
617, २।४।५६: अजेरव्यर्घञ्पोः	अजेर्व्यघञपोः
619, ३।१।१२१: पत्रे	पत्त्रे
624, ३।३।९६: °वृषैष°	°वृषेष°
625, ३।३।१११: पर्यायार्होणोत्पत्तिषु	पर्यायार्हर्णोत्पत्तिषु
625, ३।३।११९: °व्यजनापण°	°व्यजापण°
628, ३।४।११४: आर्धहातुकं	आर्धधातुकं
628, ४।१।३६: पूतक्रतोरैच	पूतक्रतोरै च
635, ४।३।१२२: पत्रपूर्वादञ्	पत्त्रपूर्वादञ्
635, ४।३।१२३: पत्रा°	पत्त्रा°
636, *४।३।१३३: आर्थवणिका°	आथर्वणिक°
636, ४।३।१३७: कोपाधाच्च	कोपधाच्च
641, ५।२।७: °पत्रपात्रं	°पत्त्रपात्रं
643, ५।२।११३: दन्तशिखरा°	दन्तशिखा°
644, ५।३।७८: °नाम्नष्ठन्वा	°नाम्नष्ठज्वा
645, ५।४।४: अनन्त्यन्तगतौ	अनत्यन्तगतौ
645, ५।४।५: सामविचने	सामिवचने
646, ५।४।५०: च्विविधाव°	च्विविधाव°
646, ५।४।५६: °सप्तम्योरर्बहुलम्	°सप्तम्योर्बहुलम्
647, ५।४।८८: अह्नोऽक्न	अह्नोऽह्न
650, *६।१।१५६: पारास्करप्रभृतिषु	पारस्करप्रभृतिषु
651, ६।१।१७९: षट्त्रिर्चतुर्भ्यो	षट्त्रिचतुर्भ्यो
653, ६।२।१०७: उदराश्वेषेषु	उदराश्वेषुषु
655, ६।३।३५: °कृत्वमसुचः	°कृत्वसुचः
661, ७।१।२१: आष्टाभ्य	अष्टाभ्य
660, ६।४।१७५: ऋत्व्यवास्तव्य°	ऋत्व्यवास्त्व्य°
662, ७।२।३२: अपरिह्वृत्ताश्च	अपरिह्वृताश्च
664, ७।२।१०६: °सावन्त्ययोः	°सावनन्त्ययोः
665, ७।३।५९: क्वाादेः	क्वादेः
665, ७।३।७४: शमामा°	शमाम°
666, ७।३।१०७: अम्बार्थनध्यो°	अम्बार्थनद्यो°

670, ८।२।७६: र्वोर्रु°	र्वोरु°
670, ८।२।७८: उपध्यायाञ्च	उपधायाञ्च
670, ८।२।१०४: °प्रैशेषु	°प्रैषेषु
671, ८।३।४७: अधःशरिसी	अधःशिरसी
673, ८।४।१४: णोपदेश्यस्य	णोपदेशस्य
675, 1.1.68: śabdasyaśābda...	śabdasyāśabda...
678, 1.3.72: prāyekriyāphale	prāye kriyāphale
678, 1.4.4: neyaṅyu...	neyaṅu...
679, 1.4.43: karmca	karma ca
679, 1.4.96: ...garhāsumuccayeṣu	...garhāsamuccayeṣu
681, 2.2.3: dvitīyatṛtīyacathurtha-	dvitīyatṛtīyacaturtha-
681, 2.2.18: kugatiprādāyaḥ	kugatiprādayaḥ
685, 3.1.121: patre	pattre
688, 3.2.149: chalādeḥ	ca halādeḥ
690, 3.3.96: vṛṣaiṣapaca-	vṛṣeṣapaca-
690, 3.3.111: paryāyārhaṇotpattiṣu	paryāyārharṇotpattiṣu
693, 3.4.114: ārdhahātukaṁ	ārdhadhātukaṁ
693, 4.1.20: vasyasi	vayasi
694, 4.1.106: madhubabhvor	madhubabhrvor
695, *4.1.166: vṛddhasyca	vṛddhasya ca
696, 4.2.65: ckopadhāt	ca kopadhāt
698, 4.3.92: śāṇḍikādibhyo	śaṇḍikādibhyo
699, 4.3.122: patrapūrvād	pattrapūrvad
699, 4.3.123: patrā...	pattrā...
699, *4.3.133: ārthavaṇika	ātharvaṇika
699, 4.3.137: kopādhāc	kopadhāc
704, 5.2.7: patrapātraṁ	pattrapātraṁ
705, 5.2.113: dantaśikharāt	dantaśikhāt
706, 5.3.20: dārhilau	dārhilau ca
707, 5.3.82: padalopaś c	padalopaś ca
707: 5.4.4: anantyantagatau	anatyantagatau
707, 5.4.5: sāmavicane	sāmivacane
714, 6.2.107: udarāśveṣeśu	udarāśveṣuṣu
716, 6.3.13: cvibhāṣā	ca vibhāṣā
716, 6.3.35: ā kṛtvamasucaḥ	ā kṛtvasucaḥ
716, 6.3.44: śeṣasyāntarasyām	śeṣasyānyatarasyām
719, 6.4.117: chau	ca hau
722, 7.2.32: aparihvṛttāś ca	aparihvṛtāś ca
723, 7.2.106: antyayoḥ	anantyayoḥ
724, 7.3.74: āṣṭānān	aṣṭānān
728, 8.2.78: upadhyāyāñ	upadhāyāñ
729, 8.2.104: kṣiyāśīḥpraiśeṣu	kṣiyāśīḥpraiṣeṣu
730, 8.4.14: ṇopadeśyasya	ṇopadeśasya
744a, last line: **464**	464
754a, l. 11: *ghaṭādayaḥ ṣitaḥ* 189(a,b), 193	*ghaṭādayaḥ ṣitaḥ* 189(a), 193

755a, l. 11: 31	831
755a, l. 13p. 829	830
755a, l. 14: 5.6-76	5.6-7